"America's leading source of self-h
information." ★★★★
—YAHOO!

LEGAL INFORMATION

24 hours a day

www.nolo.com

AT THE NOLO.COM SELF-HELP LAW CENTER, YOU'LL FIND

- **Nolo's comprehensive Legal Encyclopedia filled with plain-English information on a variety of legal topics**
- **Nolo's Law Dictionary—legal terms <u>without</u> the legalese**
- **Auntie Nolo—if you've got questions, Auntie's got answers**
- **The Law Store—over 200 self-help legal products including Downloadable Software, Books, Form Kits and eGuides**
- **Legal and product updates**
- **Frequently Asked Questions**
- **NoloBriefs, our free monthly email newsletter**
- **Legal Research Center, for access to state and federal statutes**
- **Our ever-popular lawyer jokes**

Quality **LAW BOOKS & SOFTWARE FOR EVERYONE**

Nolo's user-friendly products are consistently first-rate. Here's why:

- A dozen in-house legal editors, working with highly skilled authors, ensure that our products are accurate, up-to-date and easy to use
- We continually update every book and software program to keep up with changes in the law
- Our commitment to a more democratic legal system informs all of our work
- We appreciate & listen to your feedback. Please fill out and return the card at the back of this book.

Read This First

The information in this book is as up to date and accurate as we can make it. But it's important to realize that the law changes frequently, as do fees, forms and other important legal details. If you handle your own legal matters, it's up to you to be sure that all information you use—including the information in this book—is accurate. Here are some suggestions to help you do this:

First, check the edition number on the book's spine to make sure you've got the most recent edition of this book. To learn whether a later edition is available, go to Nolo's online Law Store at www.nolo.com or call Nolo's Customer Service Department at 800-728-3555.

Next, because the law can change overnight, users of even a current edition need to be sure it's fully up to date. At www.nolo.com, we post notices of major legal and practical changes that affect a book's current edition only. To check for updates, go to the Law Store portion of Nolo's website and find the page devoted to the book (use the "A to Z Product List" and click on the book's title). If you see an "Updates" link on the left side of the page, click on it. If you don't see a link, there are no posted changes—but check back regularly.

Finally, while Nolo believes that accurate and current legal information in its books can help you solve many of your legal problems on a cost-effective basis, this book is not intended to be a substitute for personalized advice from a knowledge-able lawyer. If you want the help of a trained professional, consult an attorney licensed to practice in your state.

8th edition

Money Troubles:

Legal Strategies to Cope With Your Debts

by Attorneys Deanne Loonin & Robin Leonard

NOLO

Eighth Edition	NOVEMBER 2002
Editor	KATHLEEN MICHON
Illustrations	MARI STEIN
Cover Design	TONI IHARA
Book Design	TERRI HEARSH
Proofreading	JOE SADUSKY
Index	JULIE SHAWVAN
Printing	CONSOLIDATED PRINTERS, INC.

Loonin Deanne.
   Money Troubles : legal strategies to cope with your debts / by Deanne Loonin & Robin Leonard.--8th ed.
     p. cm.
   Includes index.
   ISBN 0-87337-849-0
   1. Debtor and creditor--United States--Popular works. 2. Credit--Law and legislation--United States--Popular works. I. Leonard, Robin. II. Title.

KF1501.Z9 L46 2002
346.7307'7—dc21   2002075390

Quantity sales: For information on bulk purchases or corporate premium sales, please contact the Special Sales Department. For academic sales or textbook adoptions, ask for Academic Sales. Call 800-955-4775, Nolo, 950 Parker Street, Berkeley, CA 94710.

Acknowledgments

For the 8th edition, Deanne Loonin gratefully acknowledges the following people:

At Nolo, thanks to my editor and friend, Kathleen Michon, for her wonderful insight and patience. Ella Hirst for her incredible research assistance. All the other former and current Noloids, especially Robin Leonard and Janet Portman, for giving me the opportunity to work with them.

Thanks also to those who updated the law and took author-like responsibility for several chapters: Kathleen Michon for Chapter 16 and Steve Elias for Chapters 3 and 14.

My colleagues at The National Consumer Law Center for their expertise, support and flexibility. My clients at Bet Tzedek Legal Services where I first learned that sometimes consumer law really can change people's lives.

Lisa, for getting me into this in the first place way back when, and for always being my friend, fan and fellow "balanced" Libra. My amazing partner Elizabeth, my parents, Meryl, Neil, Hana and Jonah.

—Deanne Loonin

Robin Leonard gratefully acknowledges the following people for their support and creative contributions:

My delightful research assistants: Karen Chambers, who actually understands U.C.C. § 1-207; Lisa Guerin, who spent many hours breathing the fumes of her law school library; Annie Tillery, a researcher par excellence; David Freund, for his work on debtors' prisons; and Tricia Bernens, the funniest and most capable attorney in the state of Indiana. For help with the sixth edition, thanks to Ella Hirst.

My original editors, Steve Elias and Jake Warner, whose insights make Nolo books as great as they are. My editor for the later editions, Shae Irving, with whom it is a joy to work.

All the Noloids who shared their debt problems with me.

Barbara Kate Repa, Marcia Stewart, Mary Randolph and Albin Renauer, my cohorts in the editorial department, whose support was more important to me than they will ever realize.

Sherri Conrad, Amy J.D. Markowitz, Leslie Landau, Randy Michelson and Wendy Hannum, friends from my lawyering days, who answered a never-ending string of questions, and offered lots of advice and good cheer.

—Robin Leonard

Table of Contents

5 Prioritizing Your Debts

6 Negotiating With Your Creditor

7 Finding Money to Pay Your Debt

8 The Consequences of Ignoring Your Debts

9 When the Debt Collector Calls

10 Credit, Charge and Debit Cards

11 Consumer Loans

12 Reporting Credit Violations

13 Student Loans

14 Child Support and Alimony

15 If You Are Sued

16 Bankruptcy—The Ultimate Weapon

17 Property You Get To Keep

18 Rebuilding Your Credit

19 Credit Discrimination

20 Help Beyond the Book

Appendix

1 Glossary

2 State and Federal Exemption Charts

Index

Introduction

Being in Debt Is Not As Bad As You Think

The so-called debtor class ... are not dishonest because they are in debt.

— Grover Cleveland, 22nd & 24th President of the United States, 1837-1908

If you're in debt, you probably feel very alone. But you shouldn't. Millions of honest, hard-working people are having problems paying their debts. Take a look at these statistics describing American consumers:

- Over two million people each year seek assistance from debt counseling agencies such as Consumer Credit Counseling Service.
- Personal bankruptcy filings were nearly 1.5 million in 2001 and are expected to remain high.
- At the end of 2000, outstanding consumer installment debt totaled over $1.5 trillion, and it continues to grow.
- Most Americans carry five or six payment cards (credit, debit and retail cards combined). As of 2001, the average credit debt for households with at least one credit card was over $8,000.
- About three-quarters of all college students have at least one credit card. About 30% carry four or more. Most sign up before their sophomore year, responding to credit card issuers' offers of free concert tickets, computer software and discount air fares—just for submitting an application. Card issuers target college students knowing that most people hold on to their first card for as long as 15 years.

Even though your situation is far from unique, being in debt may seem like the end of the world. You may be afraid to answer your phone or open your mail. Your self-esteem may be shot. Your stomach, back and head probably ache. You may feel guilty, angry, depressed or all three. You may consider yourself a failure.

But there is good news. By knowing your legal rights and asserting them, you can get the bill collectors off your back and give yourself a fresh financial start. And often, it's easier than you think to fight back and affirmatively deal with your debt problems. One reason is that many creditors and bill collectors have modified their expectations and collections practices in response to mushrooming consumer debt. Debtors who assert themselves are getting more time to pay, late fees dropped, their debts settled for less than the full amount and even their credit reestablished.

Money Troubles can help you take charge. This book:

Shows you how to protect your legal rights. For example, *Money Troubles* explains in detail how to respond to a lawsuit, wage attachment, car repossession, foreclosure proceeding or property lien.

Helps you understand your debts. If you know how the law categorizes different kinds of debts, you'll know what kinds of collection efforts you can expect from different creditors, and which negotiating strategies you can try with them.

Shows you effective alternatives to bankruptcy. Bankruptcy is the right tool for many people to deal with their debt problems, but it's not for everyone. *Money Troubles* shows you the steps you can take to avoid bankruptcy when appropriate.

Gives you practical tips and information. *Money Troubles* contains over 20 sample letters and statements that you can use to:

- get the bill collectors off your back
- ask a creditor for more time to pay, or
- ask a creditor to lower the amount of a bill.

Money Troubles also includes over 300 addresses and phone numbers of places to lodge a complaint or ask for information, and charts of state laws summarizing consumer laws, debt collection laws, credit bureau regulations and more.

Helps you evaluate your individual debt situation. *Money Troubles* includes several worksheets to help you figure out how much you earn, how much you owe, how much you spend and what you own. With these worksheets, you can prioritize your debts,

determine if you are judgment-proof and decide what approach to take—do nothing, negotiate with your creditors, get outside help negotiating or possibly file for bankruptcy.

Icons Used in This Book

 A caution to slow down and consider potential problems.

 "Fast track" lets you know that you may be able to skip some material that doesn't apply to your situation.

Suggested references for additional information. ■

Secured and Unsecured Debts

Dreading that climax of all human ills,
The inflammation of one's weekly bills.

—George Gordon, Lord Byron,
English poet, 1788-1824

A debt is an obligation to pay someone money. It may be a large obligation, such as a home mortgage or monthly rent, or a small obligation, like a newspaper or magazine bill. If you don't pay, you often suffer some consequences. At the serious end of the scale, if you don't pay your mortgage or rent, your house may be foreclosed on or you may be evicted. At the minor inconvenience end, if you overlook paying a subscription, it will be canceled and you will be sent letters demanding that you pay for copies you've already received.

The purpose of this chapter is to help you figure out the kinds of debts you have. You may think of your debts in several different ways, such as:

- Debts to people you know, such as a loan from your Aunt Muriel or a bill you owe Angelo, the owner of the local grocery store—versus debts you owe to impersonal creditors, for example, a credit card company.
- Your regular monthly obligations, for instance, rent, phone bill or gas bill—versus debts you pay only when you buy something on credit.
- Debts for goods or services you are currently receiving, for example, a newspaper subscription or credit card bill—versus debts to repay money borrowed many years ago, such as a student loan.
- Debts you'd rather not pay and wonder if you really owe, such as back taxes—versus debts you don't have any reasonable grounds to object to paying, for example, your utility bill.

Groupings such as these may be relevant in helping you decide how and in what order you will pay your bills. Legally, however, these categories are irrelevant. Instead, the law puts debts into two primary groups: secured and unsecured. To understand your debts and to intelligently decide what to do about each one, you must understand the difference. This point cannot be overemphasized. The consequences of not paying a secured debt differ tremendously from not paying an unsecured debt. (These consequences are explained in Chapter 8.) If, after reading Sections A and B, you are still not sure you can tell a secured debt from an unsecured debt, reread the material.

A. Secured Debts

Secured debts are linked to specific items of property, called collateral. The collateral guarantees payment of the debt. If you don't pay, the creditor is entitled to take the property designated as the collateral. If you've ever had property, such as a car, repossessed when you failed to pay a loan, you already know how secured debts work.

These debts should be your highest priority. If you don't pay them, you will lose the collateral backing them up. Even if you don't hear from these creditors, don't assume they won't collect the debt. Because secured collectors have such a powerful weapon (they can seize the collateral if you stop making payments), they don't need to hound you the way that collectors with lower priority debts do.

There are two types of secured debts—those you agree to and those created without your consent.

1. Security Interests—Liens You Agree To

A security interest is an agreement in which you specify precisely what collateral (remember, that's a fancy word for property) can be taken by the creditor if you default. It also creates a "lien"—the creditor's legal right to take possession of the collateral in the event you don't pay. Security interests are of two kinds:

Purchase money. With a purchase money security interest, you pledge as collateral the property you buy using the loan proceeds. This is usually a home, motor vehicle, piece of furniture, large appliance or electronic equipment.

Nonpurchase money. With a nonpurchase money security interest, you simply borrow a sum of money and pledge some property you already own as collateral. Personal loans from a bank and home equity loans are typical nonpurchase money agreements.

Some common examples of security interests—both purchase money and nonpurchase money—include the following:

- Mortgages (sometimes called deeds of trust)—loans to buy or refinance a house or other real estate. The house or other real estate is collateral for the loan. If you fail to pay, the lender can foreclose.
- Home equity lines of credit or loans (sometimes called second mortgages) from banks or finance companies—such as loans to do work on your house. The house or other real estate is collateral for the loan. If you fail to pay, the lender can foreclose.
- Loans for cars, vans, trucks, boats, tractors, motorcycles, RVs—the vehicle is the collateral. If you fail to pay, the lender can repossess the vehicle.
- Car equity loans from banks or finance companies. You pledge your existing vehicle as collateral to obtain cash, usually used to pay down higher-interest debts.
- Store charges with a security agreement—for example, when you buy furniture or a major appliance using a store credit card. If you don't pay back the loan, the seller can come and take the property. Only a few department stores use security agreements. Most store purchases are unsecured (discussed below).
- Personal loans from finance companies—often your personal property, such as your furniture or electronics equipment, is pledged as collateral.

2. Nonconsensual Liens—Liens Created Without Your Consent

A creditor can, in some circumstances, get a lien on your property without your consent. These secured debts are termed nonconsensual liens. A creditor with a nonconsensual lien claims you owe her money, and to secure payment she places a lien on your property. To get paid, the creditor may be able to force the sale of the property. This is called a

foreclosure. In practice, however, few creditors holding nonconsensual liens foreclose on property because of the time and expense involved. Instead, creditors generally wait to get paid until you sell the property.

There are three major types of nonconsensual liens.

- **Judicial liens.** A judicial lien can be placed on your property only after somebody sues you and wins a money judgment against you. In most states, the judgment creditor then must record (file) the judgment with the local land records office. The recorded judgment creates a lien on your real property. In a few states, a judgment entered against you by a court automatically creates a lien on the real property you own in that county—that is, the judgment creditor doesn't have to record the judgment to get the lien. In some states, judicial liens apply to personal property as well.
- **Statutory liens.** Some liens are created automatically by law. For example, when you hire someone to work on your house, the worker or supplier of materials automatically gets a mechanic's lien (also called materialman's lien) on the house if you don't pay. So does a homeowners' association, in some states, if you don't pay your association dues.
- **Tax liens.** Federal, state and local governments have the authority to impose liens on your property if you owe delinquent taxes.

B. Unsecured Debts

Unsecured debts have no collateral. For example, when you charge clothing on your credit card, you don't sign a security agreement specifying that the clothing is collateral for your repayment. With no collateral, the creditor has nothing to take if you don't pay. This leaves the bank that issued the credit card only one option if you don't pay voluntarily: to sue you, get a judgment for the money you owe and try to collect on it. To try and collect on the judgment, the bank can go after a portion of your wages, your deposit accounts and other property that can be taken under your state's laws to satisfy money judgments. (See Chapter 15.)

Most debts that people incur are unsecured. Common ones include:

- credit and charge card cash advances
- credit and charge card purchases
- gasoline and department store charges, unless you sign a security agreement
- loans from friends and relatives
- student loans
- alimony and child support
- medical and dental bills
- accountants' and lawyers' bills
- rent
- utility bills
- church or synagogue dues
- health club dues
- union dues.

Not all unsecured debts are created equal. Collectors of some unsecured debts such as student loans and unpaid child support are allowed to use more aggressive collection tactics than the typical unsecured creditor. (See Chapter 13, *Student Loans*, and Chapter 14, *Child Support and Alimony*.) ■

CHAPTER

2

How Much Do You Owe?

There can be no freedom or beauty about a home life that depends on borrowing and debt.

— Henrik Ibsen, Norwegian poet and dramatist, 1828-1906

To successfully plan your strategies with your creditors, you need to spend time coming to terms with your total amount of debt. This may make you shudder. Some people with debt problems believe that the less they know, the less it hurts. They think, "I'm having trouble paying a lot of my bills. I can't stand the thought of knowing just how much I can't pay."

Happily, most credit counselors will tell you that people tend to overestimate their debt burdens. If your guess is that you owe $15,000, you may only owe $11,500. If you think you're over your head to the tune of $25,000, it may only be $15,000. This may bring little comfort to those of you who may find out that you owe more than you thought, but knowing the total amount of your debts will make a crucial difference in how you proceed.

To figure out your financial situation, you need to compare what you bring in each month with what you spend each month on your monthly expenses (such as food, housing and utilities) and your other debts (for example, student loan payments).

To figure out how much you earn, spend and owe, use the worksheets provided below. If you are married or have jointly incurred most of your debts with someone other than a spouse, fill out the worksheets together.

Warning Signs of Debt Trouble

If you have panic attacks when you try to figure out your total debt burden, you'll feel better if you skip this chapter and come back to it when you are better able to confront the information. Before doing that, however, ask yourself the following questions. If you answer "yes" to any one of them, you are probably in or headed for serious debt trouble.

- Are your credit cards charged to the maximum?
- Do you use one credit card to pay another?
- Are you making only minimum payments on your credit cards while continuing to incur charges?
- Do you skip paying certain bills each month?
- Have creditors closed any accounts on you?
- Have you taken out a consolidation loan? Are you considering doing so?
- Have you borrowed money or used your credit cards to pay for groceries, utilities or other necessities (for reasons other than to get perks on a credit card)?
- Have you bounced any checks?
- Are collection agencies calling and writing you?

A. How Much Do You Earn?

Start by figuring out how much you earn each month. Complete Worksheet 1, which is self-explanatory.

Worksheet 1: Monthly Income

(Combine for you and your spouse, partner or other joint debtor)

You need to compute your monthly net income. Net income is your gross income less deductions—federal, state and local taxes, FICA, union dues and money your employer takes out of your paycheck toward your retirement plan or health insurance, to pay your child support or to repay a loan.

To figure out your monthly net income, do the following calculations (unless you are paid once a month):

- If you're paid weekly, multiply your net income by 52 and divide by 12.
- If you're paid every two weeks, multiply your net income by 26 and divide by 12.
- If you're paid twice a month, multiply your net income by 2.
- If you're paid irregularly, divide your annual net income by 12.

Net Wages or Salary	You	Spouse, Partner or Joint Debtor	Total
Job 1			
Job 2			
Job 3			
Other Monthly Income			
Bonuses			
Dividends or interest			
Rent, lease or license payments			
Royalties			
Note or trust payments			
Alimony or child support			
Pension or retirement pay			
Social Security			
Disability pay			
Unemployment insurance			
Public assistance			
Help from relatives or friends			
Other			
Total Income	$	$	$

B. How Much Do You Owe?

In Worksheet 2, you figure out your debts. You will want to be as thorough and complete as possible. The completed Worksheet 2 will tell you exactly how much you should be paying each month (to be current on all your bills) and how far behind you are. Here's how to fill it out:

Column 1: Debts. In Column 1, enter the type of debt. Don't enter a debt more than once.

If you are married, you may not be certain which debts are yours and which belong to your spouse. If your marriage is intact and you're having mutual financial problems, approach your debt problems as a team. That is, enter all your debts in Column 1. If, however, you are separated or recently divorced, or are married but having financial problems of your own, see Chapter 3 for help on figuring out the debts for which you are obligated. If you live with someone else, determine whether you have any joint debts (debts that you both owe). If you generally share expenses and maintain a household with someone else, it is a good idea to combine your income and pay all of your debts with joint funds, regardless of who actually incurred the debt. Enter both partners' debts in Column 1.

Column 2: Outstanding balance. In Column 2, enter the entire outstanding balance on the debt. For example, if you borrowed $150,000 for a mortgage and still owe $125,000, enter $125,000. If you don't know how much you owe, consider contacting the creditor. If you'd prefer that the creditor not hear from you, make your best guess. On debts where you make monthly payments that include both principal and interest, enter only the principal.

Columns 3 and 4: Monthly payment and total you are behind. In Columns 3 and 4, enter the amount you currently owe on the debt. If the lender has not established set monthly payments—for example, a doctor's bill—enter the entire amount of the debt in Column 4 and leave Column 3 blank. If the debt is one for which you make regular monthly payments —such as your car loan or mortgage—enter the amount of the monthly payment in Column 3 and the full amount you are behind (monthly payment multiplied by the number of missed months) in Column 4.

For credit card, department store and similar debts, enter the monthly minimum payment in Column 3 and your entire balance in Column 4. But keep in mind that eventually you will probably want to make more than the minimum payment on your credit cards. (See Chapter 10, *Credit, Charge and Debit Cards*, for information on the danger of making only minimum payments each month.)

Column 5: Is the debt secured? In Column 5, indicate whether the debt is secured or unsecured. Remember, a secured debt is linked to a specific item of property—collateral. If you signed a security agreement pledging property as security for your payment or the creditor has filed a lien against your property, the debt is secured. Specify the collateral the creditor is entitled to grab if you default.

Add it up. When you've entered all your debts onto the Worksheet, do the following:

- Total up Columns 2, 3 and 4. Column 2 represents the total balance of all your debts, even though some of it may not be due now; Column 3 represents the amount you are obligated to pay each month; and Column 4 shows the amount you would have to come up with to get current on all your debts.

- Compare the numbers at the bottom of Worksheet 2, Column 3 (the amount you are obligated to pay each month) and Column 4 (the amount you would have to come up with to get current on all your debts) to the figure at the bottom of Worksheet 1 (your net income).

The figures on Worksheet 2 may far exceed the figure on Worksheet 1. For example, your income and monthly payments both might be near $2,000, while the amount you need to pay to get current is $4,500. Or, your income might be less than half of how much you need to pay each month. Whatever the situation is, don't despair. The rest of this book gives you tips on prioritizing your debts, negotiating with your creditors and using other techniques to ease your burden.

Worksheet 2: Your Debts

(Combine for you and your spouse, partner or other joint debtor)

1 Debts and other monthly living expenses	2 Outstanding balance	3 Monthly payment	4 Total you are behind	5 Is the debt secured? (If yes, list collateral)
Home loans—mortgages, home equity loans				
Motor vehicle loans				
Personal and other secured loans				
Department store charges with security agreements				
Judgment liens recorded against you				
Statutory liens recorded against you				
Total this page	$	$	$	

1 Debts and other monthly living expenses	2 Outstanding balance	3 Monthly payment	4 Total you are behind	5 Is the debt secured? (If yes, list collateral)
Tax debts (lien recorded)				
Student loans				
Unsecured personal loans				
Medical bills				
Lawyers' and accountants' bills				
Credit and charge card bills				
Total this page	$	$	$	

1 Debts and other monthly living expenses	2 Outstanding balance	3 Monthly payment	4 Total you are behind	5 Is the debt secured? (If yes, list collateral)
Department store (unsecured) and gasoline company bills				
Alimony and child support				
Back rent				
Tax debts (no lien recorded)				
Unpaid utility bills				
Other				
Total this page				
Total page 1				
Total page 2				
Grand Totals	$	$	$	

■

If You're Married, Divorced or Separated

It will be the duty of some, to prepare definitely for a separation.

— Josiah Quincy, American lawyer,
1772-1864

People who have never been legally married owe their debts and own their property as individuals. No fuss, no muss. Legal marriage, however, complicates both of these situations both during the marriage and after it ends. If marriage has been part of your life, this chapter helps you understand:

- what debts you owe individually
- what debts you owe jointly with your current or ex-spouse
- what property you own individually
- what property you own jointly with your current or ex-spouse, and
- when your property may be taken for which type of debt.

Although each state has its own rules on marital property ownership, there are several broad principles that provide a general idea of how your property and debts are owned. Which principles govern your situation depend on whether you live in a community property state or a common law property state. This distinction is by far the most important determinate of who owes and owns what in the course of a marriage.

The Community Property States

The following states are community property states:
Alaska (if the spouses agree in writing), Arizona, California, Idaho, Louisiana, Nevada, New Mexico, Texas, Washington and Wisconsin.

If your state is not listed above, it is a common law property state. Or, if you live in Alaska and have not agreed in writing to treat your property according to community property rules, then common law property law applies.

Skip the Sections That Don't Apply to You. If you live in a community property state, your debt and property situation will be governed by a set of special rules, which are explained in Sections A through C. You can skip Sections D through F. If you live in a noncommunity property state, your debt and property situation will be governed by common law property principles, which are explained in Sections D through F. You can skip Sections A through C.

A. Who Owes What Debts in a Community Property State?

If you live in a community property state (see "The Community Property States," above), which spouse owes which debts depends on when the debts were incurred and whether you are still married, separated or divorced.

1. Debts Incurred Before Marriage or After Divorce

All debts incurred by an individual before the marriage or after the marriage is dissolved are owed only by that individual.

> **EXAMPLE:**   Ted owes $3,000 to a computer company for a complete system he bought before he married Jill. Only Ted is responsible for that debt.

2. Debts Incurred During Marriage

Most debts incurred during the course of the marriage and before permanent separation are joint debts for which both spouses are liable. There is an exception to this rule: If the creditor had no knowledge of the marriage and was looking only to the spouse who incurred the debt for payment, only the spouse who incurred the debt is liable for the debt.

EXAMPLE: On a credit application for a kayak purchase, Roger claims to be unmarried and does not include his spouse's income or job. Roger's spouse, Catherine, would not be liable to pay for the kayak if Roger defaults.

3. Debts Incurred After Permanent Separation

For debts incurred during the marriage but after the spouses have permanently separated, the following rules apply: If the debt was incurred for the benefit of each spouse or their children, then both spouses are liable for paying it. If one spouse incurs a debt for that spouse's benefit only, only that spouse owes the debt.

EXAMPLE: After permanently separating from her husband, Paula uses her credit line at Home Depot to purchase some light fixtures for the family home. Since everyone in the family benefits from the light fixtures, Paula's husband would also be liable for repayment of the debt.

EXAMPLE: Justine, a married woman, uses her separate credit card to charge a trip to the Bahamas that she is taking with her lover. Ira, the spouse who stayed at home, would not be liable for the debt since it does not benefit him and the creditor was not looking to his assets for repayment.

B. Who Owns What Property in a Community Property State?

If you live in a community property state, which property is owed by which spouse (or by both) depends on when the debts were incurred; whether you are still married, separated or divorced; and, in some instances, the nature of the property.

1. Property Acquired Before Marriage or After Divorce

All property owned by a spouse prior to marriage or acquired after the marriage is dissolved is that spouse's separate property.

EXAMPLE: Gillian, a single woman, owns a summer cabin in Idaho, a community property state. She marries Otis in 2003. They remain married until 2009, when they separate and later divorce. Since Gillian came into the marriage with the cabin, it is her separate property.

2. Property Acquired During Marriage

All property acquired by one or both spouses during the marriage but before a permanent separation is community property unless:

- the spouse acquired it as a gift or inheritance, or
- the property consisted of income that was placed in a separate account.

EXAMPLE: Andy and Portia get married while they are still in school. Andy graduates and starts a business that generates a large income. Both the business and the income are community property, since they were acquired during the marriage.

EXAMPLE: Charlie and Saro get married. They both have well-paying jobs. They decide to keep most of their income separate but also open a joint account into which they each deposit 25% of their take-home pay. The joint account is community property, but each of their separate accounts is separate property.

EXAMPLE: Joan and David marry in a community property state. Shortly afterward, Joan learns that she has inherited $50,000 from her grandmother. This is Joan's separate property.

EXAMPLE: After Joan receives her inheritance, David's brother gives him an expensive bass fishing boat. Since this is a gift, it is David's separate property.

3. Property Acquired After Permanent Separation

All property acquired by a spouse during the marriage but after a permanent separation is separate property.

> **EXAMPLE:** Gillian buys a summer cabin in Idaho after she and Otis permanently separate. This is Gillian's separate property. If Otis and Gillian divorce and then get back together, the cabin would still be Gillian's separate property.

C. What Property Is Liable for Payment of Debts in a Community Property State?

If you live in a community property state, which property is liable for payment of which debts depends on two factors: whether the property is separate or community property, and whether the debt is an individual debt of one spouse or a joint debt belonging to both spouses.

1. Separate Property

The separate property of a spouse is liable for that spouse's individual debts. The separate property of one spouse is also liable for all joint debts. However, it is not liable for the other spouse's individual debts.

EXAMPLE: Bill and Hillary are married and live in a community property state. Each came into the marriage with a sizeable trust estate inherited from their respective grandfathers. These trust estates are the separate property of each spouse, since they were acquired prior to the marriage. Bill's trust estate is liable for his premartial debts, and Hillary's trust estate is liable for her premarital debts. But neither estate is liable for the other spouse's premarital debts.

EXAMPLE: Shortly after they are married, Bill and Hillary buy a business. The business fails and they become delinquent on the note. The holder of the note can go after both trust estates, even though they are separate property, because the debt was jointly incurred.

2. Community Property

Community property is liable for all joint debts. In addition, a spouse's share of the community property is liable for that spouse's separate debts.

> **EXAMPLE:** Gus and Susie marry in a community property state and buy a home. Since the home was bought during the marriage, it is community property. Without telling Susie, and using his separate credit history, Gus signs a promissory note for $100,000 to purchase a new Maserati, which he parks at his office. Several months later, Gus is unable to make the payments, and the holder of the note comes calling. The creditor can go after Gus's separate property and can also assert a claim against one-half the home's value—Gus's share of the community property.

> **EXAMPLE:** Assume now that Gus and Susie had permanently separated when Gus bought the Maserati. This would make no difference since Gus's share of the community property home is still liable for Gus's separate debts.

D. Who Owes What Debts in a Common Law State?

If you live in a common law property state (see "The Community Property States," above), who owes what debts depends on when the debt was incurred and, in some instances, what the debt was for.

1. Debts Incurred Before Marriage or After Divorce

All debts incurred by a spouse prior to the marriage or after the marriage has ended are that spouse's individual debts.

> **EXAMPLE:** Ted owes $8,000 on a professional video system he purchased before he married Jill. The $8,000 is Ted's separate debt, and only he is responsible for it.

2. Debts Incurred During Marriage

All debts incurred by the spouses' joint accounts during the marriage are joint debts. All debts incurred by an individual spouse during the marriage but before permanent separation are separately owed by that spouse unless:

- the creditor looked to both spouses for repayment or considered both spouses' credit information
- the debt was incurred for the family's necessities such as food, clothing and shelter, or
- the debt was incurred for medical purposes (in about half the states).

> **EXAMPLE:** On a credit application for the purchase of a kayak, Tammy claims to be unmarried and does not include her spouse's income or job. Tammy's spouse Chris would not be liable to pay for the kayak if Tammy defaults.

> **EXAMPLE:** Paula uses her personal credit card to pay for her husband Ray's emergency room

visit. In about half the states this would be a joint debt; in the other half only Paula would be held liable for the debt.

3. Debts Incurred After Permanent Separation

An individual spouse is liable for that spouse's debts incurred during the marriage but after permanent separation unless the debt was incurred for family necessities.

> **EXAMPLE:** After Dewevai and Angie permanently separate, Angie borrows $1,000 to pay their child's orthodontist. Since this is a family necessity, both Dewevai and Angie are liable for the debt.

E. Who Owns What Property in a Common Law State?

If you live in a common law state, how property is owned before, during and after marriage is governed by when the property was acquired, whether the property was paid for with joint or separate funds and how title is held.

1. Property Acquired Before Marriage or After Divorce

All property acquired by a spouse before the marriage or after divorce is that spouse's separate (individual) property.

> **EXAMPLE:** When Joan and Fred got married, Joan owned five valuable paintings, and Fred owned an expensive bass fishing boat. The paintings are Joan's separate property, and the boat is Fred's separate property.

2. Property Acquired During Marriage

In common law states, the rules for property ownership during marriage, whether or not the couple is permanently separated, are as follows:

- All property acquired by a spouse during marriage that carries a title document in that spouse's name only (such as a deed or investment account) is that spouse's individual property.

    EXAMPLE: After Maria and Russ marry, they buy a house and put the house in Russ's name only. The house is Russ's separate property.

- All nontitled property acquired by a spouse during marriage with that spouse's separate funds is that spouse's separate property.

    EXAMPLE: Cherish, who is married to Scott, uses her personal savings account to buy a computer. Cherish owns the computer as her separate property.

- All property acquired by the spouses jointly, or by an individual spouse from joint funds, is joint property (unless title is taken in the name of one spouse only).

    EXAMPLE: Cherish and Scott, a married couple, use their joint savings account to buy matching kitchen appliances. Since appliances don't come with title documents, Cherish and Scott own them jointly.

F. What Property Is Liable for Debts in a Common Law State?

If you live in a common law property state, which spousal property is liable for which debts depends on: whether the property is separately or jointly owned, whether separately owned property was incurred to pay for necessities and, in some states, whether joint property is held by "tenancy in the entirety."

1. Separate Property

A spouse's separate property is liable for that spouse's separate debts and for the couple's joint debts. It is also liable for the other spouse's separate debts if they were incurred for necessities.

> **EXAMPLE:** Ralph and Toni, a married couple, live in a home that Ralph owns in his name only. A bank sues Toni for payment of a $5,000 loan that she used to pay for a vacation to Italy. Since this is Toni's separate debt and the house is Ralph's separate property, the bank may not take the house to pay for Toni's separate debt.

> **EXAMPLE:** Instead of a vacation, Toni uses the loan to repair the roof on the home. Since the debt is for a necessity benefiting Ralph as well as Toni, Ralph's separate property, including the house, is liable for the debt.

2. Joint Property

With one major exception, a couple's jointly owned property is liable for the separate debts of each spouse as well as for their joint debts. The exception is this: In a number of common law states, a married couple can hold property jointly in the form of "tenancy by the entirety." In many of these states, the creditor of either spouse cannot reach property held as "tenancy by the entirety."

> **EXAMPLE:** Kai and Irina, a married couple, own a home in Wyoming in both their names as "tenants by the entirety." Kai runs up a large balance on his personal credit card. Even though the home is jointly owned, the credit card company has no recourse against it because of the way title is held.

> **EXAMPLE:** Same case, but the home is held in both names as joint tenants. Here, Kai's creditor could proceed against the home as jointly owned property. ■

Debts You May Not Owe

The buyer needs a hundred eyes, the seller not one.

— George Herbert, English poet,
1593-1633

This book is primarily about being in over your head with debts you know you owe. Less space is spent explaining your rights when you've been cheated by dishonest creditors, or when the merchandise you've purchased falls apart before you get a chance to use it. Those subjects are for a book on consumer rights.

Nevertheless, it's important to focus some attention on debts you feel you shouldn't have to pay. Consumers' rights and debtors' rights are closely linked. If you bring something home and it falls apart before you use it, do you have to pay for it if the seller refuses to refund your money or replace the item? If you want to cancel a door-to-door contract shortly after you signed it, can you? If you're sent unordered merchandise and a week later you get a bill, do you owe it?

➡ **Skip This Chapter If You Don't Dispute Any of Your Debts or If the Dispute Is Covered in Another Chapter.** Not everyone has bills they legitimately dispute. And, while some people will fight tooth and nail against any perceived injustice, others would rather try to work out a compromise with their creditors. If you really don't have anything to fight about—or if you aren't in a fighting mood—skip ahead to Chapter 6.

Also, certain types of "debts you may not owe" are covered in other chapters. See Chapter 3 for a discussion on debts incurred by your spouse, Chapter 10 for material on credit card debts you may not owe, Chapter 11 for information on your rights as a cosigner, Chapter 13 to learn about dealing with student loans and Chapter 15 to see if the creditor has taken too much time to pursue the debt—that is, the statute of limitations has run.

A. The Seller Breaches a Warranty

A warranty is a guarantee about the quality of goods or services you buy. Warranties are generally divided into two types: implied warranties and express warranties. An implied warranty is one that the law automatically entitles you to because it would be unjust for you to be without the protection.

An express warranty is different. You are not automatically entitled to an express warranty. It only kicks in if the merchant or manufacturer makes a statement about the quality of its goods or services. An express warranty is usually written down, but it can also be stated by the seller when he talks to you about your purchase or created by promises in advertisements.

Is a Guarantee a Warranty?

Many manufacturers or sellers give guarantees with their products, not warranties. If you receive a written (or oral) guarantee, it is the same thing as a warranty. The seller or manufacturer doesn't have to use the word "warranty" for you to get the protection.

1. Implied Warranties

There are two types of implied warranties: the "implied warranty of merchantability" and the "implied warranty of fitness."

- **Implied warranty of merchantability** is an assurance by the seller that the item will work if you use it for a reasonably expected purpose. For example, if you buy a refrigerator and your food spoils because the refrigerator won't go below 55 degrees—a refrigerator should be about 45 degrees—you can safely assume there's a violation of the implied warranty of merchantability.

  If you buy a used item, the warranty of merchantability is a promise that the product will work as expected, given its age and condition. If a used refrigerator cools down to 45 degrees without any problem, but the door sticks or the light flashes every so often, this isn't a breach of the warranty of merchantability.

Virtually every item you buy comes with an implied warranty of merchantability.

- **Implied warranty of fitness** applies when you buy a new or used item with a specific—even unusual—purpose in mind. If you relate your specific needs to the seller, the implied warranty of fitness assures you that the item will fill your need. For example, if you buy new tires for your bicycle after telling the store clerk you plan to do mostly off-road, mountain cycling, and the tires puncture every time you pass over a small rock, the tires don't conform to the warranty of fitness.

Many sellers try to avoid these implied warranties by informing you that the product is sold "as is" or that they are "disclaiming" the warranty. In many cases, these tactics violate federal or state laws that prohibit or limit "as is" sales. For example, "as is" sales are not allowed if:

- there is an express warranty (written or oral)
- there is a state law explicitly prohibiting or limiting "as is" sales, or
- the seller does not provide a conspicuous notice that the sale is "as is."

2. Express Warranties

Most express warranties state something like "the product is warranted against defects in materials or workmanship" for some specified time period. Here are some examples of more specific express warranties:

- furniture—"We guarantee all furniture against defects in construction for one year. When a structural defect is brought to our attention, we will repair or replace it at our option."
- fabric shield—"We warrant that if this fabric becomes stained during its lifetime as a result of ordinary water or oil-based spills, we will service the stained area of the fabric at no cost to you."
- trash can—"If your new trash can cracks during normal usage within five years of the date of purchase, we will arrange for a replacement of the broken part."

- stereo speakers—"We warrant that these speakers will perform within two decibels of their advertised specifications for five years from the date of purchase."
- wrist watch—"We promise to repair or replace, at our option, your watch if it fails to function within its original tolerances of timing, that is, within 1–5 minutes per day, fast or slow, within one year of the date of purchase."

Most express warranties either come directly from the manufacturer or are included in your sales contract. But an express warranty may also be created by a feature in an advertisement or on a sign in the store ("all dresses 100% silk").

Or an express warranty may be oral. Oral express warranties are hard to prove because they pit your word against the seller's. If the seller describes a feature about a product you are considering buying that makes your eyes light up, but the feature isn't in writing anywhere, ask the seller to jot it down.

If you purchase an item that comes with a written express warranty, the seller or manufacturer—depending on who issued the warranty—must stand behind the writing. Again, the writing may consist of a sign in the store, an advertisement, the contract you sign or a separate warranty statement. But don't be ready to call absolutely everything written about an item an express warranty; retailers are allowed to exaggerate a little when they advertise, as long as a reasonable person would know it's an exaggeration. For example, everyone knows that a retailer is exaggerating when it claims that "our product is the best in the world." If the product isn't actually the best in the world, you can't sue the retailer for breach of warranty.

Many manufacturers and some sellers provide express warranties, but you don't have an automatic right to receive one. If you are given an express warranty, however, it must be clear and easy to understand. In addition, if you ask the seller if the item comes with a warranty, and it does, the seller must make it available for your inspection before you buy the item.

In addition, you must be told whether the express warranty is limited or full. A full warranty:

- usually, but not always, says "full warranty" on it

- does not limit the implied warranties
- covers any person who buys the product from you during the warranty period
- gives you the right to have problems fixed for free and within a reasonable time period
- entitles you to a replacement or refund if the product is defective, usually for a year or two, and
- does not obligate you to do anything, other than notify the seller or manufacturer, to receive service.

Any other express warranty is a limited warranty.

3. Enforcing Warranties

If a warranty is breached, you may be entitled to a refund or damages. In most states, an implied warranty lasts forever. In a few states, however, the implied warranty lasts only as long as any written warranty that comes with a product. In either case, most states require that you sue the seller or manufacturer within four years of when you discovered the defect, if the seller or manufacturer won't make good under a warranty. In most situations, you are required to notify the seller of the problem before you sue.

In some situations, the period of time you have to make a claim under the warranty may be extended. For example, in most states, the period of time you have to make a claim under the warranty is extended by the amount of time the product is with the manufacturer or seller for repair.

A thorough discussion of how to pursue your rights in the event of a breach of a warranty is in *Everybody's Guide to Small Claims Court,* by Ralph Warner (Nolo).

Most of the time, if an item you buy is defective, the defect will show up immediately and you can ask the seller or manufacturer to fix or replace it. If he won't, or he tries only once and the fixed or replaced item is still defective, you have to decide on your next step.

In some cases, you can simply stop paying for the product or services. But, if you plan to do this, be careful. Not all problems or defects are serious enough to allow you to stop making payments. In order to have a good reason to stop payments the problem must be substantial and you must not have known about the problem when you bought the product. Even if you meet these criteria, withholding payments can be a risky strategy. The seller or manufacturer may not agree with your version of events and may sue you for not making payments. If you aren't sure what to do, consider consulting an attorney.

There may be other reasons why withholding payment is not a good option for you. For example, if maintaining a good relationship with the seller is important (perhaps the seller provides you with medical devices you can't live without), you might be better off working out a compromise or payment arrangement. If the seller refuses to cooperate, see if she'll agree to mediate the dispute through a

community or Better Business Bureau mediation program.

If you decide to withhold payment and if you are paying the seller directly (for example, you charged an item on a department store account), all you have to do is stop paying. If you charged the item on a credit or charge card, you can normally withhold payment by following a specific procedure. See Chapter 10, Section A.7, for the details.

If Your Product Breaks After the Warranty Expires

One common consumer story starts out "I bought this great _____ (fill in the blank) several years ago. It hardly gave me any trouble. But wouldn't you know it—the day after the warranty expired it died."

Most of us figure we're out of luck—but that's not necessarily the case. In most states, if your product gave you some trouble while it was under the warranty and you had it repaired by someone authorized by the manufacturer to make repairs, the manufacturer must extend your original warranty for the amount of time the item sat in the shop. Call the manufacturer and ask to speak to the department that handles warranties. Any agreement you reach should be followed up by a letter from you confirming your understanding—and asking that the manufacturer contact you if it disagrees.

If your product was trouble-free during the warranty period, the manufacturer may offer a free repair for a problem that arose after the warranty expired if the problem is a widespread one. Many manufacturers have secret "fix it" lists—items with defects that don't affect safety and therefore don't require a recall, but that the manufacturer will repair for free. It can't hurt to call and ask. A few states have specific laws covering automobile "secret warranties." See Section B, below.

Do You Have an Extended Warranty? Many consumers are encouraged by merchants to buy extended warranties or so called service contracts when buying autos, appliances or electronic items. Service contracts are a source of big profits for stores, which pocket up to 50% of the amount you pay. In addition, the salespdÚson collects 15% to 20% of the amount of the contract.

Rarely will you have the chance to exercise your rights under your extended warranty. Name-brand electronic equipment and appliances usually don't break down during the first few years, and if they do they're covered by the original warranty. Furthermore, most new items have a life span well beyond the length of the extended warranty.

If you try to get something repaired under an extended warranty, you may be told that the problem isn't covered. Or, that the company that sold the extended warranty went out of business, leaving you out in the cold. To avoid this kind of problem, some states require that companies selling extended warranties post a bond. You might be able to locate a service company by contacting your state department of consumer affairs (see Chapter 20) and asking how to locate bonded warranty companies.

B. Your Car Is a Lemon

The average new car costs over $20,000. For that amount of money, you expect a safe and reliable product. Unfortunately, hundreds of thousands of vehicles sold each year are lemons. Buyers find themselves in and out of the shop month after month, with problems ranging from annoying engine "pings," to frequent stalls, to safety hazards, such as poor acceleration or carbon monoxide leaks.

Every state has enacted some sort of "lemon law" to help consumers who get stuck with lemons. In most states, you can get help under the lemon law if you meet the following criteria:

1. Your new car must have a "substantial defect" within the shorter of one year or a certain mileage period. About a dozen states extend this period to two years. A substantial defect is one that impairs the car's use, value or safety,

such as brakes or turn signals which don't work. Unfortunately, minor defects, such as a loose radio and doorknobs—even several minor defects or one that remains unfixed after many attempts—don't qualify.

As with most legal definitions, the line between a "minor" and a "substantial" defect is not always clear. Some problems that might seem minor, such as defective paint jobs or horrible smells in the car, have been found to be substantial defects.

2. The defect must remain unfixed after three or four repair attempts or after the car has been in the shop a cumulative total of 30 days.

If your car meets the lemon law requirements, every state gives you the right to obtain a refund or replacement car from the manufacturer. The steps you must take to get this relief vary from state to state. In all states, you must first notify the manufacturer of the defect. If the manufacturer does not offer a satisfactory settlement, in most states, you must then submit the dispute to an "informal dispute mechanism" (IDM). IDM is similar to arbitration. For the most part, the arbitration is free and designed to take place without a lawyer. Automakers usually use one of the following arbitration programs:

- in-house programs run by the automakers
- programs set up by the Better Business Bureau's Auto Line
- programs run by the American Automobile Association (AAA) or the National Automobile Dealer's Association (NADA), or
- programs run through a state consumer protection agency.

Unfortunately, few consumers get to choose which program to use. If you have a choice, keep in mind that consumers who appear before a state consumer protection agency usually fare much better than those who use a manufacturer's in-house program or a private program run by the BBB, AAA or NADA.

Most IDM programs allow you to request an in-person hearing. You should do this if you can. Telling your story in person usually works in your favor. At the hearing, the hearing officer listens to both sides of the dispute. The officer then has ap-

proximately 60 days (sometimes less) to decide if the car is a lemon and if you are entitled to a refund or a replacement. Consumers who bring substantial documentation to the hearing tend to do better than those with little evidence to back up their claims. The types of documentation that can help include:

- brochures and ads about the vehicle—an arbitration panel is likely to make the manufacturer live up to its claims
- service records showing how often you took the vehicle into the shop—if the mechanic or supervisor takes your complaint orally, make sure he writes up a repair order, and
- any other documentation you can find, including calendars and phone records that show your various attempts to talk to the dealer or otherwise get the dealer to repair the car.

Manufacturers are typically bound by the hearing officer's decision, though consumers can usually go to court if they don't like the ruling. The hearing officer cannot award "consequential" damages such as the cost of renting a car while the lemon was in the shop.

This whole process can take a long time. Most lemon laws allow you to keep using your car while pursuing a claim. But be careful. Never use your car if doing so would be unsafe. Even if you can drive your car safely, some courts may view your case less favorably if they know that you were able to use your car while you awaited resolution of the problem.

If you think your new car is a lemon, you can learn more about your options at www.autopedia.com/html/HotLinks_Lemon.html. Autopedia also maintains a state-by-state summary of lemon laws. The nonprofit Center for Auto Safety (at www. autosafety.org) has detailed information about specific defects in various car makes and models. The National Highway Traffic and Safety Administration investigates and researches consumer complaints about car defects. Visit its website at www.nhtsa.dot.gov or call the NHTSA Auto Safety Hotline at 800-424-9393. Finally, *Return to Sender: Getting a Refund or Replacement for Your Lemon Car,* by Nancy Barron (NCLC), is a comprehensive guide to your rights and remedies under state lemon laws. It is available from the National

Consumer Law Center (www.consumerlaw.org or 617-524-9595).

Motor Vehicle "Secret Warranties"

Virtually all automobile manufacturers have secret warranty or warranty adjustment programs. Under these programs, a manufacturer makes repairs for free on vehicles with persistent problems after a warranty expires in order to avoid a recall and bad press.

Unfortunately, consumers aren't told of these secret warranties unless they come forward after the warranty has expired, complain about a problem and demand that the manufacturer repair it. And according to the Center for Auto Safety, at any given time there are a total of 500 secret warranty programs available through automobile manufacturers.

A few states, including California (Civil Code § 1795.92), Connecticut (General Statutes § 42-227), Virginia (Code § 59.1-207.35) and Wisconsin (Statutes Annotated § 218.0172), require manufacturers to tell eligible consumers when they adopt a secret warranty program, usually within 90 days of adopting the program.

You can find out about many of these programs from the Center for Auto Safety (www. autosafety.org).

Although lemon laws typically apply only to the purchases of defective new cars, you might have some recourse if your used car turns out to be a dud. Here are some ways you might get relief:

- Read the written sales documents or car stickers you received when you purchased the vehicle. They may create an express warranty that can-not be disclaimed by the seller. (See Section A, above.)
- Six states have lemon laws covering used cars. The states are Hawaii (Revised Statutes § 481J-17), Massachusetts (General Laws Annotated Ch. 90 ¶ 7N1/4), Minnesota (Statutes Anno-tated § 325F.662), New Jersey (Revised Statutes Annotated § 56:8-67-80), New York (General

Business Law § 198-b) and Rhode Island (General Laws § 31-5.4-4).
- In many states, used cars must meet certain minimum standards. Again, this means that the vehicle cannot simply be sold "as is."
- Several other states prohibit, limit or require special disclosures when any used product, including a motor vehicle, is sold "as is." Check your state statutes for used product sales.
- In many states, the new car lemon law applies to demonstrator cars.

C. You Are the Victim of Fraud

Every state and the federal government prohibit businesses from deceiving, misleading or cheating consumers or engaging in other unfair business practices. Laws banning this behavior are called unfair and deceptive acts and practices (UDAP) laws. They apply to most, but not all, private sellers. In addition to UDAP laws, there are many other state and federal laws that protect consumers. Often those laws apply to a particular type of business such as health clubs or a particular type of business practice.

Examples of practices that UDAP laws prohibit, include:

- using form contracts that hide unfair terms in pages and pages of complicated legal jargon
- using high-pressure sales tactics, and
- taking advantage of vulnerable groups such as children, people with physical or mental disabilities or seniors.

In some cases, you can use state UDAP and other laws to cancel a contract or get your money back. Raising these claims, however, can be tricky. If you've already been sued by a creditor or collection agency, you can raise UDAP violations (or violations of other consumer protection laws) as a defense to the lawsuit.

Another way to get relief under these laws is to bring your own lawsuit against the seller. If you plan to sue, you should first send a demand letter to the seller explaining the problem and asking for your money back. Many states require that you do this before you sue. Even if it's not a requirement in your state, it's a good idea. If the seller doesn't respond or give you what you want, you can sue in small claims court if the amount is relatively small. If you can't, or don't want to, sue in small claims court, you may need to hire a lawyer to help you bring a lawsuit in civil court. If you decide to go it alone, you'll need to find out more about the requirements of the UDAP law in your state. A good resource is *Unfair and Deceptive Acts and Practices* (NCLC). To order this book, contact the National Consumer Law Center at 617-542-9595 or visit its website at www.consumerlaw.org. Chapter 20, *Help Beyond the Book*, also provides basic information on how to find state laws.

Whether you decide to sue the seller or not, it's always a good idea to report the problem to the appropriate government consumer agency. If agencies receive enough complaints about a particular business or problem, they are more likely to take action. That could mean preventing the company from ripping off other people. In counties with active and well-funded consumer protection agencies, investigators may even try to provide help in your particular situation. But don't get your hopes up. Government investigations can take a long time and will rarely result in the return of your money.

Of course, if a government agent places even a single telephone call to the seller (which is more likely than a full-blown investigation), this may prompt the seller to return your money. And, be sure to send copies of all complaint letters to the seller. Often, if a seller knows you are complaining to authorities, it will be more willing to negotiate with you or may even return your money.

Some agencies to complaint to include:

- **Federal Trade Commission.** You will almost always want to contact the FTC, which oversees the federal consumer product warranty law, as well as advertisers, door-to-door sellers, mail-order companies, credit bureaus and most retailers. Contact information is in Chapter 12, Section F.
- **Consumer Product Safety Commission.** Let them know about hazardous consumer products.

Contact CPSC, Washington, DC 20207-0001; 800-638-2772, www.cpsc.gov.

- **Federal Communications Commission.** If you were defrauded by a telephone solicitor, or sucked in when a merchant aired a fraudulent advertisement on radio or television, tell the FCC. Contact FCC, 445 12th Street, SW, Washington, DC 20554; 202-418-0190; 888-225-5322; 888-835-5322 (TTY); www.fcc.gov.
- **Department of Transportation.** If you were cheated by an airline, contact DOT, Office of Consumer Affairs, 400 7th St., SW, Washington, DC 20590; 202-366-2220, www.dot.gov.
- **U.S. Postal Service.** If you were cheated by a mail-order company or any other seller who used the U.S. mail—including a magazine advertiser—contact a postal inspector. Look in the government listings of your telephone white pages for the local address. If you can't find one, notify the federal office, USPS, Inspection Services, 475 L'Enfant Plaza, SW, Washington, DC 20260, 202-268-2284, www.usps.gov.

One-Stop Fraud Complaining

The National Fraud Information Center, a project of the National Consumer's League, can also help you if you feel you've been defrauded. NFIC provides the following services:

- assistance in filing a complaint with appropriate federal agencies
- recorded information on current fraud schemes
- tips on how to avoid becoming a fraud victim
- direct ordering of consumer publications in English or Spanish.

Here's how to reach the NFIC:

Telephone	800-876-7060
Writing	NFIC
	1701 K Street, N.W.
	Suite 1200
	Washington, DC 20006
Web	www.fraud.org

You should also complain to state and local agencies. Addresses and phone numbers to make consumer complaints are in Chapter 20, Section A.1. You may also want to complain to:

Local prosecutor (such as the District Attorney or State's Attorney) in the county where you live. Call and ask if there is a consumer fraud division.

State licensing boards for licensed professionals, such as contractors, lawyers, doctors and funeral directors. Never hesitate to file a complaint about a licensed professional. If, for example, you ordered a $500 pine coffin, and when you arrived for the funeral your mother was laid out in a $3,000 walnut coffin and the funeral director refused to make a change, report the director to your state's funeral industry licensing board. To find the address and phone number, call directory assistance for your state capitol. If that doesn't work, ask the local prosecutor for the address and phone number.

In addition, you'll want to contact the customer service department or even the chief executive officer for the main office of any major company you complain about. Most of these corporate addresses are available on the Internet. Also, public libraries should have directories containing addresses and phone numbers of large companies.

When you send a letter to a government agency, be sure to attach copies (never the originals) of all receipts, contracts, warranties, service contracts, advertisements and other documents relating to your purchase. Keep a copy of your letter for your records.

Finally, contact your local newspaper, radio station or television station "action line." Especially in metropolitan areas, these folks often have an army of volunteers ready to try and right every consumer complaint.

D. You Want to Cancel a Contract

For the most part, you cannot cancel a contract after you sign it. However, there is an exception to this general rule for certain types of contracts. You can cancel those particular types of contracts (discussed below) if you act quickly—most laws require that you cancel a contract within three days of signing.

If you weren't told of your right, you may have longer than the standard three days to cancel.

1. Canceling Door-to-Door Sales Contracts

The Federal Trade Commission has a three-day cooling-off rule which lets you cancel certain contracts, in person or by mail, until midnight of the third business day after the contract was signed. (16 C.F.R. § 429.1.) Every state has enacted a similar law. You must be told of your right to cancel and be given a cancellation form when you sign the contract. The form must be in the same language as the oral presentation. Although the issue has not been settled in every state, in most cases if the seller did not give you a cancellation form or if there was a problem with the form that kept you from understanding your right to cancel the contract, you have a continuing right to cancel. If you are given proper notice at a later date, you have three days from that date to cancel the contract.

The contracts you can cancel are:
- door-to-door sales contracts for more than $25, and
- a contract for more than $25 made anywhere other than the seller's normal place of business if the seller personally solicited the sale—for instance, at a sales presentation at a friend's house, hotel or restaurant, outdoor exhibit, computer show or trade show. Public car auctions and crafts fairs are exempted from coverage, as are most sales made by mail or telephone, even if you called from home. But other laws may allow you to cancel mail or phone sales contracts (see below for an explanation of these other laws).

After canceling, the seller must refund your money within ten days. Then, the seller must either pick up the items purchased or reimburse you within 20 days (in some states 40 days) for your expense of mailing the goods back to the seller. If the seller doesn't come for the goods or make an arrangement for you to mail them back, you can keep them. If you send them back but aren't refunded for your mailing costs, you can sue the seller in small claims court.

2. Canceling Home Equity Loans

A second federal law, called the Truth in Lending Act, lets you cancel a home improvement loan, second mortgage or other loan where you pledge your home as security—except for a first mortgage or first deed of trust—until midnight of the third business day after you signed the contract. (15 U.S.C. § 1635.) You must be told of your right to cancel and be given a cancellation form when you sign the loan papers. This three-day period may be extended for up to three years in certain circumstances.

3. Contracts You Can Cancel Under State Laws

Most states have their own laws that allow consumers to cancel certain written contracts not covered by the FTC or state three-day cooling-off rule or the Truth in Lending Act. These contracts are usually for services purchased at the service provider's location, not necessarily at your home. Typical contracts you may be allowed to cancel include the following:

- timeshares
- health club memberships
- dating services
- credit repair services (federal law also provides for cancellation of these services)
- dance lessons, and
- camping memberships.

A few states allow you to cancel a contract if you negotiate in a language other than English and are not given a translation of the contract in that other language.

You usually have between three and ten days to cancel, depending on the state and the kind of contract. For specific information on canceling a contract in your state, contact your state department of consumer affairs. (See Chapter 20, Section A.1.)

⚠ **No Right to Cancel Auto Contract.** You don't have a right to cancel a contract to buy or lease a car. So many consumers think they have this right that one state, California (Civil Code §§ 2982 and 2985.8), requires car dealers to notify consumers that they do not have the right to cancel the contract.

4. How to Cancel a Contract

To cancel a contract under the FTC's cooling-off rule, the Truth in Lending Act or your state law, call the seller or lender and tell her you want to cancel the contract. If you call the seller, she can't claim she didn't know about your wish to cancel in the event your cancellation form is lost. But calling isn't enough. You must sign and date one copy of the cancellation form you were given. Send it by certified mail, return receipt requested, so you have proof of the date you mailed it, or for immediate notice, fax it. (Fax machines automatically date faxes when sent.) If you were not given a form, write your own letter or telegram and keep a copy.

5. Contract Defenses

Even if there is no cooling-off period, you still might be able to cancel a contract due to certain circumstances that existed at the time you signed the contract. These "contract defenses" can be complicated. If you think one might apply to your situation, you will probably want to consult with an attorney. Contract defenses include:

- **Incapacity.** You must have the mental capacity to make a contract in order for it to be valid. If you were not able to comprehend the contract when you signed it, you might be able to cancel it.

- **Minors.** If you were a minor when you signed the contract, you will not be bound by it. Although the age of minors varies by state law, in most states, minors are under the age of eighteen.
- **Duress.** You may be able to cancel a contract if you signed it under extreme duress or coercion.
- **Fraudulent misrepresentation.** A contract may be cancelled if the seller intentionally misrepresented critical terms of the contract and you relied on the seller's claims when you decided to sign the contract.
- **Unconscionability.** Courts sometimes allow you to cancel a contract because the terms are so horrible that they "shock the conscience" or because the bargaining process was extremely unfair.

E. Canceling Goods Ordered by Mail, Phone, Computer or Fax

If you order goods by mail, phone, computer or fax—other than photo development, magazine subscriptions, goods ordered COD or seeds or plants—you have rights under the Federal Trade Commission's Mail or Telephone Order Rule. (16 C.F.R. 435.) First, the seller must ship to you within the time promised ("allow 4–6 weeks for delivery") or, if no time was stated, within 30 days. This time is extended to 50 days if you are applying for credit to pay for your purchase.

If the seller cannot ship within those times, the seller must send you a notice with a new shipping date and offer you the option of canceling your order and getting a refund, or accepting the new date. If your financial picture has worsened since you ordered the goods, here is your opportunity to get your money back.

If you've already opted for the second deadline, but the seller can't meet this one, you must be sent a notice requesting your signature to agree to yet a third date. If you don't return the second notice,

your order must be automatically canceled and your money refunded. But don't rely on the seller automatically canceling. Let the seller know you want your money back.

The seller must issue the refund promptly—within seven days if you paid by check or money order and within one billing cycle if you charged your purchase. If your credit or charge card was never billed, but the time promised for sending has passed and you no longer want the goods, immediately telephone the company to cancel your order. (See Chapter 10, Section A.7, for your rights to cancel goods ordered and paid for by credit card.)

Complaining About Mail-Order Companies

The Direct Marketing Association is a membership organization made up of mail-order companies and other direct marketers. If you have a complaint about a particular company, contact the DMA, 1111 19th Street, NW, Suite 1100, Washington, DC 20036; 202-955-5030, www.the-dma.org. If you want to be removed from direct marketing lists, write Mail Preference Service, c/o DMA, P.O. Box 9008, Farmingdale, NY 11735 or call 212-768-7277 for more information. You can also register online for a $5 fee or download the form and mail (no charge) to: Mail Preference Service, Attn: Dept. 5259397, Directing Marketing Asociation, P.O. Box 3079, Grand Central Station, NY 10163.

Although many fraudulent operators will not respect your request to be removed from their mailing list, at least you will stop receiving junk mail from DMA members. Your name stays on file with DMA for five years after you register. To find out more about how mailing lists are compiled, send a stamped, self-addressed envelope to: Consumer Services—Opening the Door, Direct Marketing Association, 1111 19th St., NW, Suite 1100, Washington, DC 20036.

F. Canceling Goods Ordered From a Phone Solicitor

Telephone soliciting is a big business. The Department of Justice estimates that one out of six consumers is cheated by a telemarketing business every year. Sales through telemarketing exceed $400 billion a year. Telephone solicitation fraud is also a big business.

Although most telemarketing calls are from legitimate companies, according to the American Association for Retired People, approximately 14,000 fraudulent telemarketing operations call hundreds of thousands of callers each day. Telemarketing scams come in all shapes and sizes. A few of the common ones include:

- Recovery room scams where telemarketers prey on people who have already been victimized at least once before by other telemarketers. They promise, for a fee paid in advance, to get refunds for the victims or secure the prizes that were promised by previous scammers.
- 900 numbers where consumers are lured into paying for phone calls in order to receive information that they could otherwise get for free, such as how to save money on groceries to how to receive free credit cards.
- Sweepstakes and prize offers where telemarketers promise cash or other prizes that are never delivered.
- Groups that present themselves as nonprofit charities but operate only to steal your money (see "Beware of Scam Charities," below).

If a telephone solicitor calls you and you like what's being offered, ask for the name of the caller, the company, the address and the phone number. Also ask the solicitor to send you written materials. If the seller refuses or seems reluctant to do this, this is a warning sign. Don't order from the company. If the company is willing to send written materials, end the call and check up on the company with your state consumer protection agency and the Better Business Bureau in the city where the telemarketer is located. If all is clean and you still want to make the purchase, call the telemarketer back.

If you change your mind after making your purchase, you may have the right to cancel your contract. You can cancel your purchase if the goods don't arrive within the time promised or 30 days. (See Section E, above.) In addition, if you use a credit or charge card, you can withhold payment if there's a problem with the purchase. See Chapter 10, Section A.9.

You may also have the right to cancel a non-credit-card purchase under one of the conditions listed below. To find out if any of these laws have been adopted in your state, do some legal research. (See Chapter 20.) Also, try calling the state agency that regulates telephones, such as the Public Utilities Commission. Someone in the public information office should be able to help you.

Beware of Scam Charities

Many telemarketing and direct mail scammers will claim to be a charity. If you've never heard of the charity before or are otherwise suspicious, ask how much of your donation goes to the actual charity and how much goes to administrative costs. You should also contact your state consumer protection office (see Chapter 20, *Help Beyond the Book*, for a list of state consumer protection offices) and ask if the charity is registered. To find out if an organization claiming to be a national charity is a scam, contact the Better Business Bureaus Wise Giving Alliance Inc., 4200 Wilson Blvd., Suite 800, Arlington, VA 22203-1838; 703-276-0100; www.give.org.

To report a scam charity, contact the Federal Trade Commission's Consumer Response Center, Federal Trade Commission, 600 Pennsylvania Ave., NW, Washington, DC 20580; 877-FTC-HELP (voice); 202-326-2502 (TDD). Or, fill out a complaint form online at www.ftc.gov.

Cooling-off rules. Telephone solicitors in many states are covered by state cooling-off rules. (See Section E.1, above.) Typically, these rules require that after you agree to purchase the goods, the phone solicitor must send you a written contract confirming your order. This contract must state that you are not obligated to purchase the item you ordered unless you sign the contract and return it to the seller.

In addition, separate phone solicitation laws in a number of states provide that you have until midnight of the third business day following the day you signed the contract to cancel it.

Prohibited computer-generated calls. Computer-generated sales calls, sometimes referred to as calls generated by automatic dialing devices, are prohibited by in-state or out-of-state callers placing phone calls in several states. If you live in a state that prohibits computer-generated sales calls and you order something in response to such a call, not only shouldn't you pay for it, but you should report the company to your state Attorney General's office, the Federal Communications Commission and the Federal Trade Commission.

Regulated computer-generated calls. The federal Telephone Consumer Protection Act of 1991 prohibits telemarketing phone calls using automatic dialing devices or artificial or prerecorded voices if the seller doesn't have your prior consent. (47 U.S.C. § 227.) If the caller has your consent, the message, at the outset, must identify the caller. At some point in the call, the message must give the caller's phone number. And if you hang up, the call must disconnect within five seconds.

If you order something after being called but not being asked if you consent to the call, and you later decide you don't want it, don't pay and return the item if you've already received it. Report the company to the Federal Communications Commission and the Federal Trade Commission.

Stopping Telemarketing Calls

The Telephone Consumer Protection Act requires a telemarketer to keep a list of consumers who state that they do not want to be called again. And the law has some real teeth if companies ignore it—as many admittedly do. If you've told a telemarketer not to call you, but you get additional calls within 12 months, you can sue for $500 for each additional call. If the court finds that the telemarketer willfully or knowingly violated the law, the court can triple the amount. This is a great lawsuit to bring in small claims court.

Also, the Direct Marketing Association (described in "Complaining About Mail Order Companies," above) takes complaints about phone solicitors and will remove your name from telephone lists used by national telemarketers. Write Telephone Preference Service, c/o DMA, P.O. Box 9014, Farmingdale, NY 11735. You can also register online for a $5 fee (www.the-dma.org) or download the form and mail (no charge) to: Telephone Preference Service, Attn: Dept. 5159595, Direct Marketing Association, P.O. Box 3079, Grand Central Station, NY 10163.

A number of states have passed similar "no-call list" laws. Telemarketers that want to do business in these states must register and usually pay a fee. Currently, the states with a no-call database include Alabama, Alaska, Arkansas, Connecticut, Florida, Georgia, Idaho, Indiana, Kentucky, Louisiana, Missouri, New York, Oregon, Tennessee and Texas. Some of these states charge a few dollars each year if you want to stay on the list. To find out more, go to www.nncdb.com/Statelaws.htm.

The federal government has been talking about creating a national "do not call" registry to allow consumers to stop unwanted calls with just one request, probably to the Federal Trade Commission.

G. Miscellaneous Remedies

If you are billed for merchandise you didn't order, you need not pay. In addition, you may not owe the bill for:

- goods you put on layaway
- items you returned or tried to return, or
- a service paid for through an automatic deduction after you stopped the deduction.

1. You Receive Unordered Merchandise

You certainly don't owe any money if you receive an item you never ordered—it's considered a gift. If you get bills or collection letters from a seller who sent you something you never ordered, write to the seller stating your intention to treat the item as a gift. If the bills continue, insist that the seller send you proof of your order. If this doesn't stop the bills, notify the state consumer protection agency in the state where the merchant is located. (See Chapter 20, Section A.1.)

If you receive unordered merchandise as the result of an honest shipping error (for example, you were sent ten blankets instead of one), you may have a legal right to keep the goods, but ethically you probably shouldn't. Write the seller (or call, especially if the seller has an 800 phone number) and offer to return the items provided that the seller pays for the shipping.

Give the seller a specific length of time—ten days is about right—to pick up the merchandise or arrange for you to send it back at no cost to you. Ask the business for its UPS or other delivery service shipping number. Let the seller know that if it doesn't retrieve the goods by the end of the ten days, you plan to keep the items or dispose of them as you see fit.

If you sent away for something in response to an advertisement claiming a "free" gift or "trial" period, and are now being billed, be sure to read the fine print of the ad. It may say something about charging shipping and handling; even worse, you may have inadvertently joined a club or subscribed to a magazine. Write the seller, offer to return the merchandise and tell him you believe his ad was misleading.

Send copies of the letter to the agencies listed in Section C, above.

Subscriptions to Magazines You Didn't Order

Your mailbox contains a promotion for a new magazine—"Free trial issue. No obligation." You send for the trial issue and don't like the publication. A month later you get a bill.

Send the bill back, enclosing a note that you requested a free trial issue and you don't want a subscription, even if it is months after you requested the free trial issue. If that doesn't work, contact the Magazine Publishers of America, 919 Third Avenue, New York, NY 10022, 212-872-3700, or 1211 Connecticut Ave., NW, Washington, DC 20036, 202-296-7277, and ask them to help you get the magazine company to stop billing you.

---

2. Canceling Goods Paid on Layaway

If you're purchasing an item on a layaway plan—where the seller keeps the merchandise until you pay for it in full—and you decide before you've finished paying that you no longer want it, read your written layaway agreement. Find out if you have the right to stop paying and get a refund of what you've paid. If you do, the seller may be able to keep a portion of your payments as a service fee. But this should be a small fee—the cost of storing your goods—and you should get the rest back.

If the contract is silent about your right to a refund, stop paying and ask for your money back. If the seller refuses and there's no law giving you a right to a refund, you're probably out of luck.

3. Your Right to a Cash Refund

Unfortunately, no law requires a merchant to give you a refund. In fact, many merchants don't offer refunds and instead offer to exchange goods. And some sellers have neither a refund nor an exchange policy.

Some states do have refund laws. However, if you want to return an item you purchased in one of those states, be sure you understand your rights fully. Not all products are covered.

4. Canceling Automatic Deduction Payments

Automatic deductions from bank accounts can be a convenient way to pay some regular bills, saving you time, checks and postage. Nowadays, people pre-authorize monthly debits for everything from mortgages, student loans and utilities to car payments, life insurance premiums and health club memberships.

But you can find yourself dealing with some unusual problems when you let your bank pay your bills for you. If your bank doesn't make automatic mortgage payments on time, for example, it will be you who suffers the consequences: late fees and a blemish on your credit report.

In addition, you might find yourself with the reverse problem: you want the bank to stop deducting a payment from your account, but every time you open your bank statement, there it is again. What started out as a convenience has become a costly nuisance.

Stopping payments. You have the right to halt unauthorized and most pre-authorized deductions at any time. If you're having trouble stopping an automatic debit, the fastest way to get results is to contact your bank, not the business that's receiving payments.

Under federal law, you must call or write your financial institution requesting a stop at least three days before the scheduled debit. If you make an oral request, the bank may require you to confirm it in writing within 14 days of your call.

Late payments. If you've been hit with late fees because the bank was tardy, don't just pay up. Rules regulating electronic fund transfers state that when a debit is posted to a consumer's account, the bank can refuse the transaction for several reasons, including that you revoked the authorization for the deduction. You have 15 days from when the bank sends you a statement showing the deduction to

demand the return of your money. Your bank must credit your account within 60 days of when the transaction was originated.

5. Canceling Long Distance Phone Charges When You've Been "Slammed"

Sometimes a telephone company will switch your long distance phone service carrier without your knowledge or consent. This is called "phone slamming" and it is prohibited by federal law. According to the federal law, you do not have to pay a slammer for any calls you've made within the first 30 days after you've been slammed. After the first 30 days, you are only required to pay the amount that your preferred long distance company would have charged for the calls.

Slamming sometimes happens by mistake, but in many cases, the slammer deliberately tricks you into switching long distance carriers. If you've been slammed, you should:

- Call your local phone company and ask to be reconnected to your preferred long distance carrier. Explain that you did not order the service from the new company and that any "change charge" should be taken off of your bill.
- Call your preferred long distance carrier and report the unauthorized switch. Ask to be reconnected for free.
- Call the long distance carrier that slammed you and ask it to remove all charges incurred within 30 days of the slamming. Calls after that time should be recalculated according to your preferred provider's rate.
- To verify your phone service provider, call 700-555-4141 for the long distance provider and (your area code) + 700-4141 for your local toll service provider.
- If the company that slammed you refuses to cooperate, complain to the Federal Communications Commission by calling 888-225-5322, writing to FCC, Common Carrier Bureau Enforcement Division, Washington, DC 20554, or filling out a complaint form online at www.fcc.gov. ■

Prioritizing Your Debts

I'm living so far beyond my income that we may almost be said to be living apart.

— e.e. cummings, Poet, 1894-1962

By this time, you should have a good grasp on how much you make, how much you owe and how much (if anything) is left over to pay your other debts. This chapter helps you to prioritize your debts so that you can decide which debts are essential to pay and which you might need to ignore for a while. Chapter 6 gives tips on working with your creditors to negotiate reduced payments or payments over time. Chapter 8 explores the consequences of doing nothing.

If You're Considering Bankruptcy

If you think that filing for bankruptcy may be a viable option for you (because someone has suggested it or you have researched the option), read Chapter 16 before you make any payments on your debts. It makes no sense to pay debts you will eventually erase (discharge) in bankruptcy. Also, some payments made during the 90 days before filing for bankruptcy—or one year for payments to, or for the benefit of, a relative or business associate —may be canceled by the bankruptcy court.

If, after reading Chapter 16, you decide that Chapter 7 bankruptcy might work for you, put this book down and get a copy of either *How to File for Chapter 7 Bankruptcy*, by Stephen Elias, Albin Renauer, Robin Leonard and Kathleen Michon (Nolo) a detailed bankruptcy guide, or *Nolo's Law Form Kit: Personal Bankruptcy*, by Stephen Elias, Albin Renauer, Robin Leonard and Kathleen Michon (Nolo), a streamlined bankruptcy guide. Both contain all the forms and instructions necessary for filing your own Chapter 7 bankruptcy. If a Chapter 13 bankruptcy seems like the right approach, get a copy of *Chapter 13 Bankruptcy: Repay Your Debts*, by Robin Leonard (Nolo). If you're unsure but need more information, see *Bankruptcy: Is It the Right Solution to Your Debt Problems?*, by Robin Leonard (Nolo).

Whether or not a particular debt is essential will ultimately be dictated by your situation. Nevertheless, some debts are more important than others. Return to Chapter 2 and look at Worksheet 2: Your Debts. Then read the lists of common essential and nonessential debts, below. Use these lists as guides to help you figure out which of your debts are critical and which are not. Consider the consequences of not paying each debt. If they are severe, paying the debt is essential. If they aren't, payment is less essential. Also, review Chapter 1 (Secured and Unsecured Debts). Repayment of secured debts is almost always a top priority.

When you prioritize your debts, you will need to decide whether you can pay all of your debts or whether you need to stop paying some of your less essential debts, either temporarily or permanently.

If you decide to put some debts on hold, don't deviate from your plan just because creditors are breathing down your neck. If you give in to creditors that are trying to collect less essential debts, you may not have enough money to pay your essential debts. For example, if you pay a few dollars on an old hardware store bill just because its collector is the loudest or most persistent, you may face eviction or have your heat turned off in mid-March because you don't have enough money left to pay the rent or your utility bill.

A. Essential Debts

An essential debt is one which you should make a top—or near top—priority in paying. If you let an essential debt slide, you could face serious, even life-threatening, consequences. Usually the most important debts are those secured by collateral that you want to keep such as your house (see Chapter 1 for a review of secured and unsecured debt). However, an unsecured debt may also be essential.

EXAMPLE: Josh is taking an experimental heart medication for which his health insurance only pays 50%. His outstanding bill to his pharmacist is currently $350. Although this is unsecured debt, if he doesn't pay it, he won't be able to get the prescription refilled at that store. Because he has a poor credit history, he probably can't get credit elsewhere. Unless Josh can find other assistance such as subsidized prescription benefits, this is an essential debt that he should pay.

Other essential debts include:

Rent or mortgage. Payments for a place to live are obviously essential. Many people get into serious debt problems—and find themselves on the streets—because they fail to stay current on their rent. Unless you know you are going to move and have a place to live, you'll probably want to make paying your rent a top priority. If your landlord is a reasonable person, ask for a reduction—even a temporary one.

House payments are a little different. If you've lost your job and it looks long-term, your first thought should probably be to sell the place, get rid of a huge monthly debt, rent a moderately priced place and use the excess from the proceeds to pay your other essential bills. If you have trouble selling your house and its value has come down considerably, your options are detailed in Chapter 6, *Negotiating With Your Creditors,* below.

Don't Leave Yourself Homeless. Make sure you can replace the roof over your head before you give up the one you've got. If your credit history is so bad that a landlord isn't likely to rent to you on your own, be sure to line up a cosigner or even a roommate before you give up your apartment or sell your house. If neither of those are possibilities, find someone you can stay with until you can find your own place.

If you decide to stay put, payments on a home equity line of credit or second mortgage are also essential because you can lose your house if you don't pay.

Utility bills. Being without gas, electricity, heating oil, water or a telephone is dangerous.

Child support. Not paying can land you in jail unless you convince the judge that you really couldn't pay (which is an uphill struggle). But if your income has dropped sharply, you may be eligible for a reduction of your child support obligation. See Chapter 14.

Car payments. If you need your car to keep your job, make the payments. If you don't, consider selling it to avoid repossession, which will inevitably occur if you fall behind on the payments. You may be able to use the money to buy a cheaper car. If you sell the vehicle, but the sales amount falls short of what you owe your lender, you will have to make up any difference. If you don't sell the vehicle and it's repossessed, the lender will sell it at a fraction of its value and you'll usually owe the difference. (See Chapter 8, Section C.)

Other secured loans. Secured debts, you'll recall, are linked to specific items of property. You've already considered money owed on your house and car—both of these are secured debts. In addition, debts on furniture, boats, RVs and expensive electronic gear are likely to be secured. This means that the property (called collateral) guarantees payment of the debt. If you don't repay the debt, most states let the creditor take the property without first suing you and getting a court judgment. If you don't care if the property is taken or are confident that the creditor doesn't really want it—most creditors prefer the money, not the property—don't worry about missing a payment or two. If the property is something you cannot live without, however, and you think the creditor will take it, you'll need to keep that debt current. Or, try to work out a compromise with the creditor. (See Chapter 6.)

Unpaid taxes. If the IRS is about to take your paycheck, bank account, house or other property, you'll want to negotiate to set up a repayment plan immediately. If the amount you owe is less than $10,000, you've never defaulted on an agreement with the IRS and the IRS believes you can pay the overdue taxes within three years, you have the automatic right to a monthly payment schedule to pay your taxes. Even if the amount you owe exceeds $10,000, or you've defaulted on an agreement with the IRS in the past, the taxman might still be willing to negotiate a payment plan if you can convince the agency that you'll stick with it.

The best resource available to help you deal with the IRS is *Stand Up to the IRS,* by Frederick W. Daily (Nolo).

Essential or Nonessential?

Some debts may straddle the line between essential and nonessential. That is, not paying won't cause severe consequences in your personal life, but it could prove painful nonetheless. In deciding whether or not to pay these debts, consider your relationship with the creditor and whether the creditor has initiated collection efforts.

Some of these debts include:

- **Auto insurance.** In some states, you can lose your driver's license if you drive without insurance.

- **Medical insurance.** Especially if you are currently under a physician's care, you'll want to continue making payments on your medical insurance. Also, if you have medical insurance through work and lose your job, you'll probably be able to keep your insurance coverage for at least 18 months, and in some case 36 months, but you, not your former employer, will have to pay for it. If you let it lapse, you may have difficulty getting new insurance.

- **Car payments for a car that is not essential for your job.** The extreme inconvenience of not having a car may justify making these payments.

- **Items your children need.** Paying for a tutor for your child may not seem essential, but if the alternative is to have your child grow up unable to read, you probably want to keep paying for the help.

- **Court judgments.** Once a creditor has a judgment, the creditor can collect it by taking a portion of your wages or other property. If a particular judgment creditor is about to grab some of your pay, the fact that the original debt may have been nonessential is irrelevant. Making payments to this creditor in exchange for keeping all your income may be essential.

- **Student Loans.** Although student loans are unsecured, those debts may merit higher priority in certain circumstances. For example, a defaulted student loan can keep you from getting a new student loan or grant to go back to school. Also, student loan collectors have special rights that are not available to the average unsecured creditor. For example, the IRS can intercept your income tax refund to collect a defaulted student loan. And the holder of your loan is allowed to take up to 10% of your wages without first suing you (the government is trying to increase this amount to 15%). Finally, student loans are very difficult to discharge in bankruptcy.

For complete information on repaying student loans, see *Take Control of Your Student Loan Debt*, by Deanne Loonin and Robin Leonard (Nolo).

B. Nonessential Debts

A nonessential debt is one with no immediate or devastating effects if you fail to pay. Paying these debts is a desirable goal, but not a top priority.

Credit and charge cards. If you don't pay your credit card bill, the worst that will happen before the creditor sues you is that you will lose your credit privileges. If you need a credit card, for example, to charge an upcoming medical operation or to rent a car on a business trip, keep—and pay the minimum on—one card, and put that card on your priority list.

If, after prioritizing your debts, you decide that paying off your entire credit card bill is a realistic goal, making minimum payments should be a short-term remedy only. You'll have to pay more than the minimum if you want to make a dent in the debt. See Chapter 10, *Credit, Charge and Debit Cards*, for more on the dangers of making only minimum payments.

Department store and gasoline charges. As with credit and charge cards, if you fail to pay these bills, you'll probably lose your credit privileges and, if the debt is large enough, you may be sued. If the creditor took a security interest in personal property you bought using the credit card, the creditor may try to repossess the property. If you must keep the property (your refrigerator, for example), you may need to make minimum payments. Keep in mind, however, that personal property other than a motor vehicle is rarely repossessed. (See Chapter 8, Section C.)

Loans from friends and relatives. You may feel a moral obligation to pay, but these creditors—who probably seem the least like creditors of anyone—should be the most understanding with you.

Newspaper and magazine subscriptions. These debts are never essential.

Legal, medical and accounting bills. These debts are rarely essential. A medical bill may be, however, if you are still receiving necessary treatment from the provider to whom you owe money.

Other unsecured loans. Remember, an unsecured loan is not tied to any item of property. The creditor cannot take your property. If you refuse to pay, the creditor can collect from you only by suing you and obtaining a court judgment. These unsecured debts are rarely, if ever, essential to pay first. Keep in mind, however, that a court judgment turns an otherwise nonessential, unsecured debt into an essential one. Creditors can collect on a court judgment by taking a portion of your wages or other property. (See Chapter 15, Section F.)

C. Review Your Lists

Take a look at your essential and nonessential lists. At the end of each month, do you have enough to pay everything on the essential list? If you don't, read it over. Move the least essential debts on this list to the nonessential list, and keep moving debts until you can pay each month what is on the essential list. Remember—some things must go. You can't afford to pay for everything you'd like to. This doesn't mean you're a bad person. It just means you need to buckle down and tighten up your finances for a while.

Another option is to negotiate with creditors of essential debts so that you pay only a portion of those debts. This will leave you with more money to pay less essential debts. How to negotiate with creditors is discussed in the next chapter. ∎

Negotiating With Your Creditor

Let us never negotiate out of fear, but let us never fear to negotiate.

— John F. Kennedy, 35th President of the United States, 1917-1963

By now you have prioritized your debts and decided which are essential and which are less essential (see Chapter 5, *Prioritizing Your Debts*). You also have an idea as to whether you may not owe some debts (see Chapter 4, *Debts You May Not Owe*).

This chapter will help you negotiate with your creditors regarding debts that you owe but can't pay. You should definitely consider this strategy for essential debts such as your house and utilities. And, once you've stabilized your financial situation, you may also want to try to work out a deal with creditors for nonessential debts that you believe you can afford to keep up.

By negotiating with creditors, you may be able to get lower payments or other more favorable terms to help you get through rough times. Often, creditors are willing to work with you, especially if your financial woes will be temporary.

➡ **Skip This Chapter If You'd Prefer Not to Contact Your Creditors.** Staying in touch with your creditors is often a good idea—even if you can't pay anything. It doesn't always make sense, however. For example, if you just moved from Massachusetts to Arizona—to get a new start and, not incidentally, to get away from hounding creditors—and will probably file for bankruptcy before long, contacting your creditors is the last thing you should do. Also, you may not want to contact creditors about nonessential debts that you don't plan to pay.

A. Communicate With Your Creditors

The first step to working out a deal with creditors is to keep the lines of communication open. It may

surprise you, but creditors often will reduce payments, extend time to pay, drop late fees and make similar adjustments if they believe you are making an honest effort to deal with your debt problems.

As soon as it becomes clear to you that you're going to have trouble paying your bills, write to your creditors. Explain the problem—accident, job layoff, emergency expense for your child or aged family member, unexpected tax bill or whatever. Be sure to mention any development that points to an encouraging financial condition—disability benefits beginning soon, job prospects improving, child finishing school and the like. Also, let the creditor know that you've taken many steps to cut your expenses.

Your success with getting creditors to give you time to pay will depend on the types of debts you have, how far behind you are and the creditors' policies toward arrears.

If you are not yet behind on your bills, be aware that a number of creditors have a ridiculous policy that requires you to default—and in some cases, become at least 90 days past due—before they will negotiate with you. If any creditor makes this a condition of negotiating, find out from the creditor how you can keep the default out of your credit report.

In addition, increasing numbers of creditors simply will not negotiate with debtors. Despite the fact that creditors get at least something when they negotiate settlements with debtors, many ignore debtors' pleas for help, continue to call demanding payment and leave debtors with few options other than filing for bankruptcy. In fact, nearly one-third of the people who filed for bankruptcy during the 1990s stated that the final straw that sent them into bankruptcy was the unreasonableness of their creditors or the collection agencies hired by their creditors.

Even though some creditors may refuse to negotiate with you, it is still in your best interest to try. The following sections give you a general idea of what you can expect when you negotiate with your creditors about certain types of debts.

1. Rent Payments

Few landlords will reduce your monthly rent. But it never hurts to ask. If the landlord knows it will be difficult to re-rent your place, the landlord may agree to accept a partial payment now and the rest later, or temporarily lower your rent, rather than have to evict you. The landlord might even agree to let you pay a little bit each month to make up any back rent you owe.

If your landlord agrees to a rent reduction or lets you make up past due payments, send the landlord a letter confirming the arrangement by certified mail, return receipt requested. (See sample letter, below.) Be sure to keep a copy for yourself. Once the understanding is written down, the landlord will have a hard time evicting you for not paying the rent, as long as you make the payments under your new agreement.

Sample Letter to Landlord

Frank O'Neill
1556 North Lakefront
Minneapolis, MN 67890
September 22, 20xx

Dear Frank:

Thanks for being so understanding about my being laid off. This letter is to confirm the telephone conversation we had yesterday.

My lease requires that I pay rent of $750 per month. You agreed to reduce my rent to $600 per month, beginning October 1, 20xx, and lasting until I find another job, but not to exceed three months. That is, even if I haven't found a new job, my rent will go back to $750 per month on January 1, 20xx. If this is not your understanding, please contact me at once.

Thank you again for your understanding and help. As I mentioned on the phone, I hope to have another job shortly, and I am following all leads in order to secure employment.

Sincerely,

Abigail Landsberg
Abigail Landsberg

If you decide to move but have months remaining on a lease, your landlord might try to sue you for the months remaining on the lease. Legally, however, in most states the landlord has a duty to re-rent the place as fast as possible to minimize the loss. This is called mitigating damages. (If, despite his reasonable efforts, he can't re-rent it, you will be on the hook for the balance of the rent.) If you advanced one or two months rent or paid a security deposit when you moved in, the landlord will no doubt put that money toward any rent you owe.

2. Mortgage Payments

Over the years, lenders have learned that high foreclosure rates can cost them lots of money. As a

Tips on Negotiating

This isn't a book on negotiating. Although many such books are available, few are worth reading. No formula approach will teach you to be a great negotiator in six steps. Nevertheless, here are some basic guidelines:

- **Identify your bottom line.** If you owe a doctor $1,100 and are unwilling to pay more than $600 on the debt over six months time, don't agree to pay more.

- **Try to identify the creditor's bottom line.** If a bank offers to waive two months interest as long as you pay the principal on your car loan, that may mean that the bank will waive three or four months of interest. Push it.

- **Bill collectors lie a lot.** If they think you can pay $100, they will vow that $100 is the lowest amount they can accept. Don't believe them.

- **Make concessions to pay less rather than more.** If a creditor will settle for 50% of the total debt if you pay in a lump sum, but will insist on 100% if you pay over time, consider a way to get the money to pay the half and settle the matter. Perhaps a parent will help; if the amount is large enough, take it out of your eventual inheritance. If you settle the debt, or are put on a new payment schedule, insist that associated negative information in your credit bureau file be removed and that your account be re-aged, that is, reported as current as long as you make the payments on the new schedule. See Chapter 18.

- **Don't split the difference.** If you offer a low amount to settle a debt and the creditor proposes that you split the difference between her higher demand and your offer, don't agree to it. Treat her split-the-difference number as a new top and propose an amount between that and your original offer.

- **Mention bankruptcy.** If you mention that you may have no option but to file for bankruptcy if the creditor refuses to make concessions, you might find that an unreasonable creditor is willing to compromise. But think carefully before doing this. In most cases, a "mentioned bankruptcy" notation will immediately be added to your account file with that creditor. If you incur any additional debt after that date—even with a different creditor—you will have a very difficult time eliminating that debt in bankruptcy if you do eventually file. The creditor will argue that once you mentioned bankruptcy, you had no intention of repaying your bills and that therefore all debts you incurred after that date you should have to pay. And a bankruptcy judge is likely to agree.

If you don't feel comfortable negotiating—for example you hate bargaining at flea markets and would rather sell your used car to a dealer than find a buyer yourself—ask a friend or relative to negotiate on your behalf. This can often work well for you. As long as your negotiator knows and will keep to your bottom line, it will be hard for the creditor to shame or guilt her into agreeing that you will pay more. Some creditors are reluctant to negotiate with anyone other than you or your lawyer. If need be, prepare a power of attorney for your negotiator, giving that person the right to handle your debts on your behalf.

result, they are often willing to work with you to avoid foreclosure. Depending on your financial situation, this can mean agreeing to an informal payment plan to make up missed payments, giving you a short-term break on interest or payments or refinancing your loan so you can afford the payments.

a. Informal Payment Plans

If you want to keep your home and you've only missed a payment or two, most mortgage companies will let you make up the delinquency through a repayment plan. For example, if you missed two payments of $1,000 each, your lender may allow you to pay the $2,000 over six months. Other short-term fixes that your lender may agree to include, deferring or waiving late charges, temporarily reducing your interest rate or temporarily reducing or suspending payments.

b. Mortgage Workouts

If your problem looks like it will be long-term, most lenders will require more than an informal payment plan or short-term break on interest or payments. Usually, they will insist on a more formal process called a "mortgage workout." Many lenders will require this formal process even for short-term fixes. A workout is any agreement you make with the lender that changes how you pay the delinquency on your mortgage or otherwise keeps you out of foreclosure.

Here are some workout options your lender might agree to:

- Spread repayment of missed payments over a few months. For example, if your monthly payment is $1,000 and you missed two payments ($2,000), the lender might let you pay $1,500 for four months.
- Reduce or suspend your regular payments for a specified time and then add a portion of your overdue amount to your regular payments later on.
- Extend the length of your loan and add the missed payments at the end.
- For a period of time, suspend the amount of your monthly payment that goes towards the

principal, and only require payment of interest, taxes and insurance.
- Let you sell the property for less than you owe the lender and waive the rest. This is called a "short sale."

Before you contact the lender about a workout, you should prepare information about your situation, including:

- A reasonable budget for the future and an assessment of your current financial situation.
- A plan to deal with other essential debts such as utility payments and a car if you need it for work.
- A hardship letter explaining why you fell behind on your mortgage. Emphasize the most sympathetic aspects of your situation.
- Information about the property and its value.
- Information about your loan and the amount of the default.

When Your Loan Is Owned by the Federal Government

Millions of American homeowners' loans are owned by Fannie Mae or Freddie Mac, private corporations created by the federal government. Both Fannie Mae and Freddie Mac's default programs emphasize foreclosure prevention whenever feasible. Both mortgage holders offer rate reductions, term extensions and other changes for people in financial distress, especially for people experiencing involuntary money problems such as an illness, death of a spouse or job loss. One possible option would allow you to make partially reduced payments for up to 18 months.

If you can't get help from your loan servicer, contact Fannie Mae or Freddie Mac directly at:

- Fannie Mae—3900 Wisconsin Ave., NW, Washington, DC 20016, 202-752-7000 or 800-732-6643 (the Consumer Resource Center), www.fanniemae.com.
- Freddie Mac—800-FREDDIE, www.freddiemac.com.

You should also find out if your mortgage is insured by the Federal Housing Administration (FHA) or the U.S. Department of Housing and Urban Development (HUD). Borrowers with these types of mortgages have some special rights that those with "conventional" mortgages don't have.

It's a good idea to look for a nonprofit debt counselor or lawyer who has experience with mortgage workouts to help you. For information on HUD-approved counseling agencies in your area, call 888-466-3487. It's best to start the workout negotiations as early as possible

Be advised that workouts are not for everyone nor will the lender always agree to a workout. Be realistic about your situation before you approach the lender. If it is likely that you will lose your house anyway because of your dire financial situation or because you have other pressing financial problems, it doesn't make sense to keep paying your mortgage through a workout.

c.   Refinancing

If you can't afford your current mortgage payments, your lender may let you refinance the loan to reduce the amount of the monthly payments, assuming you can convince the lender that you have enough income to make the reduced payments. Typically, a lender looks at the ratio of your total monthly debt burden to your monthly net income. If the ratio is between 25% and 33%, you'll probably qualify for the refinancing. If your ratio is higher the lender may balk, unless the lender thinks it will be hard to resell your house at a profit if it foreclosed. Be realistic when refinancing. If you can't afford your new payments, the process is likely to hurt more than it helps.

If you need help figuring out how much mortgage payment you can afford—and what terms you'd need to qualify—visit Nolo's website. Calculators are found at www.nolo.com/calculator/index.html.

If you are considering refinancing your home loan, look out for the following:

- **Rapidly increasing interest.** For example, the interest begins low (such as 3%), so that you qualify for the loan, but after six months or a year, the interest rises to the prime rate. Every six months or year after that, the interest rate rises a point or two above the prime rate.
- **Points.** Real estate loans usually come with points, an amount of money equal to a percentage of your loan, you pay to your lender simply for the privilege of borrowing money. If you refinance with the same lender from whom you originally borrowed, the lender may waive the points.
- **Insurance and other extras.** Consumer loans, including refinanced loans, are often loaded with extra products that most consumers don't need. You should especially look out for credit insurance charges. (See Chapter 11, Section A).
- **Prepayment penalties.** Expensive prepayment penalties almost always go hand in hand with refinancing. Even if the new loan does not contain prepayment penalties, some states allow creditors to calculate payoff figures for the old loan that are to the creditor's, not the borrower's, advantage.

If you are getting a high cost (often called predatory) loan, take extra care. These are loans with very high interest rates that are usually, but not always, sold to consumers who have had credit problems in the past. Such loans often contain terms unfavorable to borrowers, such as large balloon payments (jumbo payments due at the end of the loan term) and negative amortization (loans where your monthly payment does not cover the interest due that period). (See Chapter 11 for more on consumer loans).

If you don't like what your lender offers, shop around. You may find another lender who will lend you money to pay off all or some of your first loan. If you've missed only a few payments, you can prevent foreclosure simply by paying what you missed and then obtaining the new loan. If the original lender has accelerated the loan—declared the entire balance due because you've missed several payments —you'll have to refinance the entire loan to prevent foreclosure.

> **EXAMPLE:** Jessica owes $113,000 on her mortgage, which has monthly payments of $850. She has missed four payments and received a letter from the lender stating that it has "accelerated" the mortgage as permitted under the loan agreement. All $113,000—not merely the $3,400 in missed payments—is due immediately. For Jessica to save her house, she will need to get a loan from a second lender to cover the full $113,000, unless the original lender agrees to reinstate her loan.

In this situation, it may be difficult for you to get a new loan. The new lender will do a credit check. If your original lender has reported your mortgage delinquency, it will show up on the credit check. You'll have to convince the new lender that you won't default on the new loan.

Be wary when shopping for a new loan. Many unscrupulous creditors make a lot of money by taking advantage of people facing foreclosure. These rip-off artists know that homeowners are often desperate to save their homes. If a deal seems too good to be true, it's probably a scam. In particular, you should avoid sale/leaseback schemes (where someone offers to buy your house and rent or lease it back to you) and high-rate loans offered to help get you out of foreclosure. Look with suspicion on lenders that offer "easy credit" and low-cost loans to anyone regardless of credit history. Often, there are hidden costs in the loan that will cause problems for you later. If you've already been victimized by one of these companies, seek legal help soon, before you end up defaulting and facing foreclosure.

d. Selling Your House

If you don't want to keep your house, or you've come to the conclusion that you can't afford it, your best option may be to sell it. If you've come to this conclusion, you can probably stop making mortgage payments.

If the lender chooses to foreclose, it may take anywhere from six months to a year and a half, and if you're willing to take any reasonable offer, you can probably sell your house much sooner.

The lender may also agree to a "short sale." This happens when the money you get from selling your house is less than the amount you owe to your lender. In a "short sale" the lender agrees to accept the proceeds from the sale and forego the remainder of the loan balance.

Some lenders require documentation of any financial or medical hardship you are experiencing before agreeing to a short sale. But by accepting a short sale, the lender can avoid a lengthy and costly foreclosure, and you're able to pay off the loan for less than you owe. These sales are common when the real estate market is depressed.

e. Deed in Lieu of Foreclosure

If you get no offers for your house or the lender won't approve a short sale, your other option is to simply walk away from your house. To do this, you transfer your ownership interest in your home to the lender—called a deed in lieu of foreclosure. Lenders don't have to accept your deed in lieu, but many will. Keep in mind that with a deed in lieu, you won't get any cash back, even if you have lots of equity in your home. And it may have negative tax consequences. (For more on tax costs, see Section F.) The deed in lieu may also appear on your credit report as a negative mark. If you opt for a deed in lieu, try to get concessions from the lender—after all, you are saving it the expense and hassle of foreclosing on your home. For example, ask the lender to eliminate negative references on your credit report or give you more time to stay in the house.

3. Utility and Telephone Bills

If you miss one month's utility bill—including a bill for heating oil or gas deliveries—you probably won't hear from the company, unless you have a poor payment history. If you ignore a few past due notices, however, the company will threaten to cut off your service. You want to communicate with the company before their threats become dire. Most utility companies will let you get two or three months behind as long as you let the company know when you'll be able to make up what you owe. If your service has been shut off, the company will most likely require that you make a security deposit—usually for about three times the average of your monthly bill—before it reconnects you. The deposit rates following disconnects are regulated in some states. You may want to call a Legal Aid or Legal Services office (see Chapter 20) to learn about your state's law.

Many utility companies offer reduced rates and payment plans to elderly and low-income people. In addition, the federal Low Income Home Energy Assistance Program (LIHEAP), which is state-run, helps low-income customers pay their utility bills. To find out if you qualify, call the utility company and ask. If you do, you'll be able to get future bills reduced—and may be able to spread out payments on past bills.

Most northern states prohibit termination of heat-related utilities during the winter months. Others states also have a limited prohibition against shutoffs for households with elderly or disabled residents and occasionally for households with infants. Usually, you must show financial hardship to qualify. But, even if you qualify for a prohibition against utility shutoff, you'll still owe the bill.

Finally, don't overlook the cost savings that come with conserving energy. Local utility companies offer utility conservation assistance programs, often at no cost. These measures can often cut your bill by as much as one-third to one-half.

To reduce your telephone bill, it often pays to change some of the terms of your telephone plan. For example, if you rarely make long distance calls, it might be cost-effective to cancel your long distance plan and make your rare long distance calls using a prepaid calling card or dial-around (10-10) service. If you decide to use a prepaid card, be sure to shop around. Some of these cards are rip-offs.

Can't Understand Your Phone Bill?

Of all utility bills, the phone bill is often the most difficult to understand. Charges may be posted by at least three separate companies: your local carrier, long distance carrier and Internet service provider. You might also have special features billed to you, such as call waiting or voice mail. On top of that, unscrupulous long distance companies sometimes try to switch customers' carriers without the customers' knowledge and consent.

If you can't understand your phone bill, ask for clarification. The Federal Communications Commission's "Truth-in-billing" guidelines (available at www.fcc.gov) is meant to counter the confusion, anxiety and concern expressed by the more than 60,000 consumers who call the FCC each year. Under the guidelines, consumers must be told who is asking them to pay for service, what services they are being asked to pay for, and where they can call to get more information about the charges appearing on their bill. For example, new service providers must be highlighted on the bill and all bills must contain full and non-misleading descriptions and a clear identification of the service provider responsible for each charge on their bill.

Carriers also must clarify when consumers may withhold payment for service, for example, to dispute a charge, without risking the loss of their basic local service. Finally, the guidelines require a label next to charges appearing on bills that relate to federal regulatory action.

---

4. Car Payments

Handling car payments depends on whether you are buying or leasing your vehicle.

a. Purchase Payments

If you suspect you'll have trouble making your car payments for several months, your best bet is to sell the car, pay off the lender and use whatever is left to either pay your other debts or buy a used car that can get you where you need to go.

If you want to hold onto your car and you miss a payment, immediately call the lender and speak to someone in the customer service or collections department. Don't delay. Cars are more quickly repossessed than any other type of property. One reason for this is that the creditor doesn't have to get a court judgment before seizing the car. (See Chapter 8, Section C.) Another reason creditors grab cars quickly is that cars lose value fast—if the creditor has to auction it off, it wants the largest possible return.

If you present a convincing explanation of why your situation is temporary, the lender will sometimes grant you an extension, meaning the delinquent payment can be paid at the end of your loan period. The lender probably won't grant an extension unless you've made at least six payments. Also, most lenders charge a fee for granting an extension, and don't grant more than one a year. Fees for extending car loans vary tremendously. Some lenders charge a flat fee, such as $25. Others charge a percentage (usually 1%) of the outstanding balance. Others charge you one month's worth of interest. Be sure to call your lender and ask.

Instead of granting an extension, the lender may rewrite the loan to reduce the monthly payments. This means, however, that you'll have to pay longer and you'll have to pay more total interest.

b. Lease Payments

Many new car owners decide to lease, rather than purchase, automobiles. The reasons are many—but most people like the low monthly payments which accompany vehicle lease contracts.

If you can't afford your lease payments, your first step is to review your lease agreement. If your total obligation under the lease is less than $25,000 and the lease term exceeds four months (virtually all car leases meet these two requirements), the federal Consumer Leasing Act (15 U.S.C. §§ 1667-1667e) requires that your lease include the following:

- The nonpayment terms under the lease, such as the kinds of insurance you must have, any extended warranty you are required to purchase, the penalty for defaulting, the maximum number of miles you can drive each year for free or how to terminate the lease early.
- Whether your lease is closed-ended or open-ended. A closed-ended lease means that you are obligated to pay only the monthly payments. At the end of the lease term, you simply return the vehicle and have no additional liability other than what was stated in the lease up front, such as excess mileage, or wear and tear. An open-ended lease usually means lower monthly payments than a closed-ended lease, but also usually includes a "balloon payment" at the end of the lease term. This payment covers the difference between the value stated in your agreement and the appraised value at the lease end.

In October 1996, amendments to the federal Consumer Leasing Act took effect, although compliance was optional until January 1998. These amendments require dealers to disclose information about the lease including:

- the amount due at the time the lease is signed
- payment schedule and total of payments
- payment calculation, and
- notice that the charge for early termination of the lease may be substantial.

The Act requires other disclosures as well. In addition, many states impose extra requirements.

If you want to cancel your lease, look carefully at the provisions in your contract describing what happens if you default and how you can terminate the lease early. Many of these provisions include claims that you'll owe a very large sum of money or complex formulas difficult to understand. For example, the lease agreement might say that if you terminate early, you'll owe the total of the remaining payments, plus several other fees minus the wholesale value of the car and some other fees.

If you want to cancel your lease, write to the dealer stating that you want to terminate the lease early (be sure to keep a copy of the letter). The dealer will contact you with the amount of money you owe. If the formula for calculating how much you owe if you terminate the lease early isn't defined in your lease or is defined in a very confusing way, you may be able to fight the dealer's claim that you owe this money. Or, you may be able to get the leasing company to drop any large penalties for terminating the lease early. However, because not all courts agree as to what constitutes "confusing" when it comes to early termination clauses, you'll probably have to consult with a lawyer if you want to pursue this option. (See Chapter 20, *Help Beyond the Book*, for information on how to find a lawyer.)

5. Secured Loan Payments

If a personal loan or store agreement is secured—for example, you pledged a refrigerator or couch as security for your repayment—the lender probably won't reduce what you owe. Instead, the lender may threaten to send a truck and take the property if you don't make reasonable payments. Some states require that the lender have a court judgment before taking your personal property other than a car. (See Chapter 8, Section C.)

But few lenders take non-vehicle personal property. The resale value of used property is low. Most items bought through security agreements are furniture, appliances and electronic equipment, which depreciate fast. The lender is not in the used furniture business and doesn't want your dining room table or stereo. Almost always the lender values the debt—even if it is hard to collect—as being worth more than the property. Also, the lender can't get into your house to get the property unless she has a court order or you let her in. Few lenders ever go to the expense of getting a court order. This means you have the upper hand in the negotiation.

The lender may extend your loan or rewrite it to reduce the monthly payments. Be prepared to disclose your complete financial situation.

6. Insurance Payments

You may consider your medical, homeowner's or auto insurance payments to be fairly essential debts. At the same time, your life or disability insurance payments probably aren't, unless you or other members of your family are very, very ill. Use this discussion to help you decide what to do about your various insurance policies.

Most policies have 30-day grace periods—that is, if your payment is due on the tenth of the month and you don't pay until the ninth of the following month, you won't lose your coverage. A few companies may let you get away with 60 days, but don't count on it. After 60 days, your policy is sure to lapse.

If you want to keep your insurance coverage, contact your insurance agent. If you don't have an agent, or the agent has left the company, call the office and ask to speak to the general manager. Describe the kind of insurance you have, tell the manager a little bit about yourself and ask to be given an agent who will be responsive to your particular needs.

Your insurance agent probably can't let you reduce your premium payments, or spread out back payments over a few months. But you can reduce the amount of your coverage and increase your deductibles, thereby reducing the overall amount you pay, including the premium payments. This can usually be done easily for auto, medical, dental, renter's, life and disability insurance. It will be harder for homeowner's insurance, because you'll probably have to get authorization from the lender, who won't want your house to be underinsured.

If you have a life insurance policy with a cash value that you really want to keep, you usually can apply that money toward your premium payments. And if the cash value is large enough, consider using the money for your debts. You can ask the company to use the cash reserves as a loan. Your policy's cash value won't decrease, but you are theoretically required to repay the money. If you don't repay it, when you die the proceeds your beneficiaries receive will be reduced by what you borrowed. Or you can simply ask that the cash reserves be used to pay the premiums. This will reduce your cash value, but you won't have to repay it.

Another way to keep life insurance coverage but to reduce the payments is to convert a whole or universal policy (relatively high premiums and a cash value buildup) into a term policy (low premiums and no cash value). You may lose a little of the existing cash value as a conversion fee, but if you believe life insurance coverage is essential, losing a few dollars may be worth it in exchange for getting a policy which will cost far less to maintain.

If your insurance policy—life or otherwise—has lapsed, and your financial picture is improving, many insurance companies will let you reinstate your policy if you pay up what you owe within 60 days of when the premium payment first became due. You may also have to pay interest on your back premiums, usually between 5% and 10%. After 60 days, the company will probably make you reapply for coverage. If your risk factors have increased since you originally took out the insurance—for example, you took out auto insurance two years ago, have since had a car accident and a moving violation and your insurance just lapsed—you may be denied coverage or offered coverage at a higher rate.

7. Medical, Legal and Other Service Bills

Before assuming that your bill is correct, review it carefully and be sure that you understand and agree with every charge. With hospital bills and lawyers' bills in particular, ask for specific itemization if the bill gives only broad categories. And if the bill is filled with indecipherable codes, make someone in the billing office explain to you what every code means.

Once you understand what each charge is, look for mistakes. The federal General Accounting Office estimates that 99% of all hospital bills contain overcharges, and one insurance company stated that the average hospital bill contains almost $1,400 of mistakes. The types of errors include inflated charges (such as $5 per aspirin tablet), charges for items never received by the patient (for example, an extra pillow) and billing you twice for the same item. Overbilling is also common in lawyers' bills.

Assuming you do owe the full amount of the bill or can't afford the corrected bill, many doctors, dentists, lawyers and accountants will accept partial payments, reduce the total bill, drop interest or late fees and delay sending bills to collection agencies if you clearly communicate how difficult your financial problems are and try to get their sympathy. Some doctors, especially, won't spend too much effort in collecting the outstanding bills of longtime patients who suddenly find themselves unable to pay.

Before deciding whether or not to pay a doctor, dentist, lawyer or accountant, assess how necessary that person's services are. Pay the bill to your dentist if your child desperately needs dental care before you pay the lawyer who you consulted once and who didn't help you resolve your problem.

If your problem is that your insurance will eventually cover all or most of your medical bill, but the medical provider is pursuing you because it hasn't yet been paid by your insurance company, you'll have to take a different approach. Gather together evidence of:

- your submission of the bill to your insurance company, and
- your insurance company's coverage for the specific medical care you (or your other family member) received.

Armed with this information, call the doctor or hospital's collections department and ask for an appointment. At the meeting, provide the collector with copies of your documentation and plead with the person to cease collection efforts against you. Let the collections representative know that your medical condition may worsen if the stress of the collection calls and letters doesn't stop. If you get nowhere with the collections representative, make an appointment to see the department supervisor. Also, if the bill is from a hospital, see if the facility has an ombudsman or patient's advocate. Such a person works to help resolve disputes between patients and the hospital. But remember—if you haven't yet paid the amount of any deductible, you still owe it. The insurance company won't pay it and the doctor or hospital will continue to come after you.

8. Child Support and Alimony Payments

No matter what your hardship, your duty to pay court-ordered child support or alimony won't go away unless you take affirmative steps to legally reduce your payment obligation. Because a court ordered you to pay, only a court can reduce the amount. Thus, when your income drops, immediately file a paper (usually called a motion or petition) with the court asking that your future child support or alimony payments be reduced, at least temporarily.

The court cannot retroactively reduce child support or alimony, however. The court can set up a payment schedule for you to get current, but if you miss payments before you ask for a reduction, it can't erase your debt. See Chapter 14 for a thorough discussion on reducing child support or alimony.

9. Income Taxes

You have several strategies for dealing with the IRS. For example, if you haven't recently been in trouble with the IRS, you will be given an installment agreement to pay your taxes if you owe under $50,000. If you are unable to afford an installment agreement, you can make an "offer in compromise." This means that you make a lump sum offer to the IRS to settle what you owe. Your offer must be at least the value of your non-necessary property. Finally, you may be able to eliminate, reduce or spread out your IRS debt by filing for bankruptcy. (Bankruptcy is covered in Chapter 16.)

For a complete discussion of your options with the IRS, see *Stand Up to the IRS*, by Frederick W. Daily (Nolo).

10. Student Loan Payments

If you are current on your student loan payments—that is, you are making agreed-upon payments—you can probably get your student loan payments postponed if you are out of work, disabled or suffering from an economic hardship. If you are current on your payments and you can afford something, but not the amount you are obligated to pay, you can probably negotiate a new repayment plan for lower payments over a longer period of time. If you are in default and want to avoid the harsh collection tactics of the government, you should be able to negotiate a repayment plan that's both reasonable and affordable, based on your financial situation. (For more information on student loans, see Chapter 13, *Student Loans.*)

11. Credit and Charge Card Payments

If you can't pay anything on your credit or charge card, and have decided that keeping the card isn't essential, don't pay. You will lose your credit privileges. You may also be sued, but that will take some time.

If you want to keep the card, most card companies insist that you make the monthly minimum payment, which is usually as low as 2%–2.5% of the outstanding balance. But if you can convince the company that your immediate financial situation is truly difficult, your payments may be cut in half and you won't be charged late fees while you're paying what

you owe. In some cases, the creditor may waive payments altogether for a few months. This courtesy is usually extended only to people who have never been late with a payment.

You should also call your credit card company and ask for a lower interest rate. A study conducted by the United States Public Interest Research Group in 2002 found that more than half of the consumers who complained to their credit card company were able to reduce their interest rate, usually by as much as one third. (To find out more, contact U.S. PIRG at www.uspirg.org.) The study found a number of connections between the cardholder's credit history and the likelihood of success. Not surprisingly, the deeper in debt you are, the less likely it is that the credit company will work with you. The most important factors affecting the success rate were:

- length of time with a particular card (longer is better)
- credit limit on that card (a higher limit is better)
- unpaid balance-to-limit ratio on that card—how "maxed out" the cardholder is (a lower balance is better)
- unpaid balance-to-limit ratio on all cards (a lower balance is better), and
- number of times the customer missed or paid late on a loan or a credit card other than the one at issue (fewer is better).

If you are unsuccessful in negotiating lower interest payments on your own or feel that you could use some help, try contacting a nonprofit debt counseling agency such as Consumer Credit Counseling Services. (See Chapter 20 for information on debt counseling agencies.)

Bear in mind that paying nothing or very little on your credit card should be a temporary solution. The longer you pay only a small amount, the quicker your balance will increase due to interest charges.

Below is a sample letter you can modify and send to your creditors to request a reduction, extension or other repayment program. It often helps to send a copy to the company president.

Sample Letter to Creditors

Collections Department
Big Bank of Bismarck
37 Charles Street
Bismarck, ND 77777

August 19, 20xx

Re: Amy and Robert Grange
    Account 411-900-LOAN

To Whom It May Concern:

On June 5, 20xx, your bank granted us a three-year $3,300 personal loan. Our agreement requires us to pay you $125 per month, and we have diligently made those payments since July 1, 20xx.

We now, however, face several emergencies. Robert had a heart attack last April and has been out of work ever since. His doctors do not believe that he'll be able to work again until this November. On top of that, Amy's company filed for bankruptcy and laid her off last week. She will receive unemployment and is looking for work. Unfortunately, though, many industries in our town have closed down, and the prospects for a 46-year-old semiskilled worker are few. Amy may be able to work in her uncle's office, but it's a 90-minute drive each way and she can't afford the time while Robert is recovering.

We cannot pay you more than $20 a month right now. We expect to resume the full $125 per month payments this November. We ask that you please accept our $20 a month until then, and just add the balance we miss to the end of our loan and extend it the few months necessary.

Thank you for your understanding and help. If we do not hear from you within 20 days, we will assume that this arrangement is acceptable.

Sincerely,

Amy Grange
Robert Grange
Amy and Robert Grange
(701) 555-8388

cc: Leonard O'Brien,
    President, Big Bank of Bismarck

B. Negotiating When the Creditor Has a Judgment Against You

If you don't pay a debt, the creditor may sue you. Once a creditor has a judgment against you, she also has an expanded arsenal of collection techniques. For example, she can put a lien on your house, empty your bank accounts or attach a portion of your wages. A nonessential debt may move into the essential category very fast once it is turned into a judgment. Chapter 15 gives you strategies for dealing with judgment creditors.

C. Try to Pay Off a Debt for Less Than the Full Amount

If you owe a creditor $750, you may be tempted to send a check for $450 and state on the check that "cashing this check constitutes payment in full." Before sending a "payment in full" or "full payment" check, however, be sure that your state permits this avenue of recourse. In most states, you can use this strategy only if you really believe that you don't owe the full amount. Even then, many states allow creditors to cash the check and still come after you for the balance.

In many states, if a creditor deposits a full payment check, even if she strikes out the "payment in full" notation or writes some kind of protest on the check such as "I don't agree" before cashing it, she can't come after you for the balance. Once she cashes it, you are free and clear. Although the rule emerged through common law, many states have specific laws barring creditors from suing you for the balance after cashing a full payment check.

Unfortunately, a number of states have modified this rule. In those states, if a creditor cashes a full payment check and explicitly reserves his right to sue you—by writing "under protest" or "without prejudice" with his endorsement—he can come after you for the balance. But he must use those words. If he writes "without recourse," communicates with you separately, notifies you verbally or writes on the check that it is accepted as partial payment, it is not enough.

One state—California—lets creditors cross out the full payment language and sue you for the balance. (Civil Code § 1526.) When the California legislature enacted the law, it also enacted a procedure to let debtors get around it, if they follow very specific steps and use certain language.

How Californians Can Get Around the Full Payment Law

1. Send a letter to the creditor stating that you intend to send a full payment check.
2. Wait 15–90 days to give the creditor time to object.
3. Send the check with a letter stating that the check constitutes payment in full.

Sample letters are below.

Sample Letter Before Sending Full Payment Check (California Only)

Hermann's Helpful Hardware
1145 North Francisco Blvd.
Chico, CA 90000

July 17, 20xx

Re: Philip Van Bugle

Account Number: PVB-92-4545

Dear Mr. Hermann:

This letter concerns the money I owe you. For the past three months, I have received bills from you stating that I owe $300 for a three-day rental of your New-Finish-Now hardwood floor finisher. As you will recall, I rented the finisher on a Friday evening intending to return it on Sunday, for a total of two days rental. When I came to your store on Sunday, it was closed and I could not return the finisher until Monday. I believe that I owe you no more than $200, and it is obvious that there is a good faith dispute over the amount of this bill.

To satisfy this debt, I will send you a check for $200 with a restrictive endorsement and if you cash that check, it will constitute an accord and satisfaction. In other words, you will receive from me a check that states "cashing this check constitutes payment in full." If you cash it, that check will take care of what I owe you.

Sincerely,

Philip Van Bugle
Philip Van Bugle

After sending the letter, wait at least 15 days, but not more than 90 days, before sending the check and a second letter. Below is a sample of the second letter to send.

Sample Letter When Sending Full Payment Check (California Only)

Hermann's Helpful Hardware
1145 North Francisco Blvd.
Chico, CA 90000

August 3, 20xx

Re: Philip Van Bugle
     Account Number: PVB-92-4545

Dear Mr. Hermann:

Enclosed is a check for $200 to cover the balance of account PVB-92-4545. This check is tendered in accordance with my letter of July 17, 20xx. If you cash this check you agree that my debt is satisfied in full.

Sincerely,

Philip Van Bugle
Philip Van Bugle

Enclose your check and write on the check—on the front along the top or bottom—the exact language you used in the second letter: "This check is tendered in accordance with my letter of _____ (date). If you cash this check you agree that my debt is satisfied in full."

D. Don't Write a Bad Check

People who are broke and desperate are often tempted to write bad checks. If you're faced with the prospect of no food or the electricity being cut off, writing a bad check can seem like a reasonable solution. It isn't. You may face all of the following: criminal prosecution, bad check processing fees (from the bank) and a lawsuit from the creditor to whom you wrote the bad check.

In every state, writing a bad check when you know you don't have the money to cover it is a crime. Aggressive district attorneys don't hesitate to prosecute, especially given that an estimated 450 million rubber checks are written each year. It is not a crime, however, if you stopped payment because of a good-faith dispute you are having with a merchant. (See Chapter 4, *Debts You May Not Owe.*)

If you are prosecuted, you may be able to avoid the ordeal of a trial if your county has a diversion program. Instead of being tried, you are given the option of attending classes—anywhere from four hours to 20 months—for bad check writers. If you choose to go, you must pay the tuition, which usually ranges from $40 to $125 per session, In addition, you must make restitution, that is, make good on the bad checks you wrote.

Even if you escape criminal prosecution, you'll be charged a bad check processing fee by your bank. Many banks charge as much as $20 or $30.

If $20 or $30 is all you have to pay, you'll be lucky. Most creditors who receive a bad check—or one where a stop payment was later ordered—can sue for damages unless you stopped payment because of a good-faith dispute you are having with a merchant. Before you can be sued for damages for writing a bad check, the creditor must have made a written demand that you make good on the bad check. If you don't pay within the time limits of the demand (usually 30 days), the creditor can sue you.

If the creditor wins the lawsuit, you are likely to be ordered to pay the following:

- face value of check
- collection and mailing costs
- interest from date of check, and
- court and attorney fees.

In addition, in most states the creditor can ask the court to award additional damages against you for writing a bad check. The maximum amount of damages allowed varies from state to state. In many states, you must pay three times the amount of the check, with a cap of $500 or $1,000. In a few states, the damages are limited to a small amount ($50 or $100). If you plead financial hardship, the court usually can reduce the damages.

Stale Checks—How Long Will a Check Be Honored?

If you wrote a creditor a check several months ago, but the creditor has not yet cashed it, can you add the balance back into your checkbook—that is, has the creditor taken too much time?

Perhaps, but not necessarily. A bank, savings and loan or credit union is not required to honor a check presented for cashing more than six months after the check was written. Most banks do, however, unless the check has an express notation on it "not valid after six months."

What does this mean for you? If you wrote a check more than six months ago and the creditor still hasn't cashed it, you can call your bank and put a stop payment on it. The debt, however, does not go away. Be prepared for the creditor to try and collect, arguing that your stop payment was not in good faith. You should respond that you gave the creditor six months, and if a bank isn't obligated to honor a check that old, you shouldn't be either.

E. Writing a Post-Dated Check Is a Bad Idea

Many aggressive bill collectors will try to pressure you into sending them a postdated check—a check dated with a future date. Sending a postdated check is always a bad idea. When you write a postdated check you are committing yourself to having the money in your checking account when the date on the check arrives. If you are already having debt problems, this is a commitment you can't realistically make.

Although it's usually legal for creditors to accept postdated checks, they don't always wait to deposit them until the date of the check. Instead of writing a postdated check, you might tell the creditor that you will personally deliver the check on the day you write it (assuming the creditor is local).

F. Beware of the IRS If You Settle a Debt

A tax law could cost you money if you settle a debt with a creditor. This rule may also lessen the contents of your wallet if a creditor writes off money you owe—that is, ceases collection efforts, declares the debt uncollectible and reports it as a tax loss to the IRS. (26 U.S.C. § 108.) Debts subject to this law include money owed after a house foreclosure, after a property repossession or on a credit card bill you don't pay. A creditor must set a uniform policy to write off all debts after a set period of time, such as one, two or three years after default.

Any bank, credit union, savings and loan or other financial institution that forgives or writes off $600 or more of the principal amount of a debt (the amount not attributable to interest or fees) must send you and the IRS a Form 1099-C at the end of the tax year. These forms are for the report of income, which means that when you file your tax return for the tax year in which your debt was settled or written off, the IRS will make sure that you report the entire amount forgiven on the Form 1099-C as income.

There are several exceptions stated in the Internal Revenue Code. For example, if the financial institution issues a Form 1099-C, you do not have to report the income on your tax return if:

- the cancellation or write-off of the debt is intended as a gift—this would be unusual
- you discharge the debt in bankruptcy, or
- you were insolvent before the creditor agreed to settle or wrote off the debt.

Insolvency means that your debts exceed the value of your assets. Therefore, to figure out whether or not you are insolvent, you will have to total up your assets and your debts, including the debt that was settled or written off.

> **EXAMPLE 1:** Your assets are worth $35,000 and your debts total $45,000. You are insolvent to the tune of $10,000. You settle a debt with a creditor who agrees to forgive $8,500. You do not have to report any of that money as income on your tax return.

> **EXAMPLE 2:** This time your assets are still worth $35,000 and your debts still total $45,000, but the creditor writes off a $14,000 debt. You don't have to report $10,000 of the income, but you will have to report $4,000 on your tax return.

If you conclude that your debts exceed the value of your assets, include IRS Form 982 with your tax return. You can download the form off the IRS's website at www.irs.ustreas.gov/forms_pubs/forms.html. Completing it is not difficult.

Part I

Question 1

Check box "b." (If you have discharged the debt in bankruptcy, check box "a.")

Question 2

Enter the amount you are *not* obligated to report as income. In example 1, you'd enter $8,500. In Example 2, you'd write $10,000.

Leave the rest of the form blank (other than your name and Social Security number at the top). A sample completed form is below. Be sure to attach to Form 982 an explanatory letter listing your assets and debts.

If your debts are enormous and your bank or other financial institution is willing to settle for less than you owe, it could cost you a lot in the end. You could also owe a bundle if your lender approves a short sale if you sell your home to avoid foreclosure or takes a deed in lieu of foreclosure. Before taking the deal, have a tax preparer calculate your tax liability. If your tax bill will be too high and you cannot prove you are insolvent, you may be better off filing for bankruptcy and discharging the entire debt, if possible.

If you plan on filing for bankruptcy and including this debt after the creditor settles or writes it off, talk to a bankruptcy lawyer—preferably one who knows tax law. Some lawyers have concluded that on the day the creditor settles or writes off a debt, a "taxable event" occurs. This means that if you file for bankruptcy after that date, you cannot wipe out the debt unless your tax debt could be wiped out in bankruptcy. Other lawyers feel that the taxable event occurs on April 15, when your taxes are due, and that you can file for bankruptcy and wipe out the debt before that date, assuming it otherwise qualifies to be eliminated in bankruptcy.

And bear in mind this fact: Even if you don't get a Form 1099-C from a creditor, the creditor may very well have submitted one to the IRS. If you don't list the income on your tax return and the IRS has the information, it will send you a tax bill, or worse, an audit notice, which could end up costing you more (in IRS interest and penalties) in the long run.

Form **982** (Rev. September 2000) Department of the Treasury Internal Revenue Service	**Reduction of Tax Attributes Due to Discharge of Indebtedness (and Section 1082 Basis Adjustment)** ▶ Attach this form to your income tax return.	OMB No. 1545-0046 Attachment Sequence No. **94**

Name shown on return	Identifying number
Melinda Ocho-Hattori	000-00-0000

Part I   **General Information** (see instructions)

1 Amount excluded is due to (check applicable box(es)):

a Discharge of indebtedness in a title 11 case. . . . . ☐

b Discharge of indebtedness to the extent insolvent (not in a title 11 case) . . . . ☒

c Discharge of qualified farm indebtedness . . . . ☐

d Discharge of qualified real property business indebtedness. . . . . ☐

2 Total amount of discharged indebtedness excluded from gross income. . . . . | **2** | $3,142.19 |

3 Do you elect to treat all real property described in section 1221(a)(1), relating to property held for sale to customers in the ordinary course of a trade or business, as if it were depreciable property?. . . . . . ☐ Yes ☐ No

Part II   **Reduction of Tax Attributes** (You must attach a description of any transactions resulting in the reduction in basis under section 1017. See Regulations section 1.1017-1 for basis reduction ordering rules, and, if applicable, required partnership consent statements.)

Enter amount excluded from gross income:

4 For a discharge of qualified real property business indebtedness, applied to reduce the basis of depreciable real property . . . . | **4** | |

5 That you elect under section 108(b)(5) to apply first to reduce the basis (under section 1017) of depreciable property. . . . . | **5** | |

6 Applied to reduce any net operating loss that occurred in the tax year of the discharge or carried over to the tax year of the discharge . . . . | **6** | |

7 Applied to reduce any general business credit carryover to or from the tax year of the discharge | **7** | |

8 Applied to reduce any minimum tax credit as of the beginning of the tax year immediately after the tax year of the discharge . . . . | **8** | |

9 Applied to reduce any net capital loss for the tax year of the discharge including any capital loss carryovers to the tax year of the discharge . . . . | **9** | |

10 Applied to reduce the basis of nondepreciable and depreciable property if not reduced on line 5. *DO NOT use in the case of discharge of qualified farm indebtedness* . . . . | **10** | |

11 For a discharge of qualified farm indebtedness, applied to reduce the basis of:

a Depreciable property used or held for use in a trade or business, or for the production of income, if not reduced on line 5. . . . . | **11a** | |

b Land used or held for use in a trade or business of farming . . . . | **11b** | |

c Other property used or held for use in a trade or business, or for the production of income. . | **11c** | |

12 Applied to reduce any passive activity loss and credit carryovers from the tax year of the discharge | **12** | |

13 Applied to reduce any foreign tax credit carryover to or from the tax year of the discharge . . | **13** | |

Part III   **Consent of Corporation to Adjustment of Basis of its Property Under Section 1082(a)(2)**

Under section 1081(b), the corporation named above has excluded $ ....from its gross income for the tax year beginning .... , and ending ....

Under that section the corporation consents to have the basis of its property adjusted in accordance with the regulations prescribed under section 1082(a)(2) in effect at the time of filing its income tax return for that year. The corporation is organized under the laws of ....

(State of incorporation)

Note: *You must attach a description of the transactions resulting in the nonrecognition of gain under section 1081.*

General Instructions

Section references are to the Internal Revenue Code unless otherwise noted.

Purpose of form. Generally, the amount by which you benefit from the discharge of indebtedness is included in your gross income. However, under certain circumstances described in section 108, you may exclude the amount of discharged indebtedness from your gross income. Unless you check the box on line 1d or make the election on line 5, the amount excluded from gross income reduces certain tax attributes either dollar for dollar or 33⅓ cents per dollar (see below).

Use **Part I** of Form 982 to indicate why any amount received from the discharge of indebtedness should be excluded from gross income.

Use **Part II** to report your reduction of tax attributes. The reduction must be made in the following order:

● Any net operating loss (NOL) for the tax year of the discharge (and any NOL carryover to that year) (dollar for dollar);

● Any general business credit carryover to or from the tax year of the discharge (33⅓ cents per dollar);

● Any minimum tax credit as of the beginning of the tax year immediately after the tax year of the discharge (33⅓ cents per dollar);

● Any net capital loss for the tax year of the discharge (and any capital loss carryover to that tax year) (dollar for dollar);

● Basis of property (dollar for dollar);

● Any passive activity loss (dollar for dollar) and credit (33⅓ cents per dollar) carryovers from the tax year of the discharge; and

● Any foreign tax credit carryover to or from the tax year of the discharge (33⅓ cents per dollar).

Use **Part III** to exclude from gross income under section 1081(b) any amounts of income attributable to the transfer of property described in that section.

Definitions. A "title 11 case" is a case under title 11 of the United States Code (relating to bankruptcy), but only if you are under the jurisdiction of the court in the case and the discharge of indebtedness is granted by the court or is under a plan approved by the court.

For Paperwork Reduction Act Notice, see back of form.   Cat. No. 17066E   Form **982** (Rev. 9-2000)

Finding Money to Pay Your Debt

How pleasant it is to have money.

—Arthur Hugh Clough, English poet,
1819-1861

Y ou may be considering several methods of raising cash to pay your debts. Before doing so, ask yourself if bankruptcy is a realistic option for you. (Chapter 16 can help you answer the question.) If it is, raising cash to pay debts you will ultimately erase in bankruptcy is a waste of your time and already stretched resources.

Below are several different methods of raising cash. Many have costs associated with them—such as penalties, interest and fees. A few may cost you more money than the cash raised is worth. So read on, but read cautiously.

A. Sell a Major Asset

One of the best ways you can raise cash and keep associated costs to a minimum is to sell a major asset, such as a house or car. This is particularly a good idea if you can no longer afford your house or car payments. You will almost always do better selling the property yourself rather than waiting to get cash back from a foreclosure or repossession sale. With the proceeds of the sale, you'll have to pay off the lender and any secured creditor to whom you pledged the asset as collateral. Then you'll have to pay off any liens placed on the property by your creditors. You can use what's left to help pay your other debts. Even if nothing is left, getting rid of large monthly payments may be what you need to afford your other bills.

⚠ Take precautions before you sell an asset.
Before you sell your home or car, be sure you have affordable alternative housing or transportation. Otherwise, you could end up in worse shape than before—without a roof over your head or a car to get to work.

B. Cut Your Expenses

Another excellent way to raise cash is to cut your expenses. It will also help you negotiate with your creditors, who will want to know why you can't pay your bills and what efforts you've taken to live more frugally. Here are some suggestions:

- Shrink food costs by clipping coupons, buying sale items, purchasing generic brands, buying in bulk and shopping at discount outlets.
- Improve your gas mileage by tuning up your car, checking the air in the tires and driving less—carpool, work at home (telecommute), ride your bicycle, take the bus or train and combine trips.
- Conserve gas, water and electricity. Turn off lights, televisions and stereos when they are not in use. Run the dishwasher and washing machine with full loads and less frequently.
- Discontinue cable or at least the premium channels. Most cable companies offer a very low-rate basic service that they don't advertise. Be sure to ask.
- Instead of buying books and CDs or renting videos, borrow them from the public library. Read magazines and newspapers there, too, instead of subscribing to them.
- Look for new ways to spend time socializing. Take walks with friends instead of meeting for lunch. Get together to devote time to charity work—cleaning up a park or delivering meals to the elderly.
- Make long distance calls only when necessary and at off peak hours. Also, compare programs offered by the various long distance carriers to make sure you are getting the best deal.
- Carry your lunch to work; eat dinner at home, not at restaurants.
- Buy secondhand clothing, furniture and appliances.
- Spend less on gifts and vacations.
- Cancel your private mortgage insurance (PMI). Lenders typically require home buyers who put less than 20% down to pay for insurance to protect the lenders in case the buyer defaults before building up equity. A lender never offers to cancel the policy after the buyer reaches

20% equity, however, and buyers often unnecessarily pay for PMI for years. A federal law applying to most mortgages obtained after July 29, 1999, requires lenders to automatically cancel PMI once the equity reaches 22%, and allows buyers with good payment histories to request cancellation of the PMI once the equity reaches 20%. (12 U.S.C. § 4901 et seq.) If the law doesn't apply to you (for example, you took out your mortgage earlier than July of 1999), you can still contact your lender and request cancellation. Most will do so once the equity reaches 20%. Some states also have laws regulating PMI.

There are a couple of good books available on how to cut spending substantially. See, for instance, *Dollar Pinching: A Consumer's Guide to Smart Spending,* by Shelly Branch (Warner Books), and *The Beardstown Ladies Guide to Smart Spending for Big Savings* (Hyperion).

C. Withdraw Money From a Tax-Deferred Account

If you have an IRA, 401(k) or other tax-deferred retirement account, you can get cash to pay off debts by withdrawing money from it before retirement. But if you do so, you'll probably have to pay a penalty and taxes. Another option is to borrow money from your 401(k) plan instead of withdrawing it. There are serious disadvantages to both options. You should only consider these if you have other substantial retirement funds or you are truly desperate. Always look to raise money from nonretirement resources first.

If you are considering withdrawing or borrowing money from your retirement account to pay off debts, get a copy of *IRAs, 401(k)s & Other Retirement Plans: Taking Your Money Out,* by Twila Slesnick & John C. Suttle (Nolo).

D. Consider a Home Equity Loan

Many banks, savings and loans, credit unions and other lenders offer home equity loans, also called second mortgages. Traditionally, lenders who make home equity loans establish how much you can borrow by starting with a percentage of the market value of your house—usually between 50% and 80%—and deducting what you still owe on it.

> **EXAMPLE:** Winnie's house is worth $200,000 and she owes $120,000 on her first mortgage. A bank has offered her a home equity loan at 75%, that is, for $30,000. The lender figures it like this: 75% of $200,000 is $150,000; $150,000 less $120,000 is $30,000.

Until the late 1990s, home equity lenders rarely would lend a borrower more than 80% of the equity in the house. But as the consumer lending market became more competitive, rising numbers of consumers found themselves in debt and lenders' desire for profits skyrocketed, home equity lenders began offering loans well in excess of the 80%—125% is typical, but some loans have reached 150% or 200%. This means that in the above example, on a 125% loan, Winnie could borrow $130,000. Here's how it's figured: 125% of $200,000 is $250,000; $250,000 less $120,000 is $130,000. Many people who borrow this kind of money cannot afford the payments, and lose their houses to the home equity lenders.

Obtaining even a traditional home equity loan has its advantages and disadvantages. As a general rule of thumb, if your debts are mostly unsecured and your house is exempt from collection, you are better off keeping current on your house payments or trying to negotiate a mortgage workout with the lender. (See Chapter 6, *Negotiating With Your Creditors,* for information on mortgage workouts.) If you do opt for a home equity loan, be sure you understand all the terms before you sign on the dotted line.

1. Advantages of Home Equity Loans

Home equity loans have a number advantages, including:

- You can obtain a closed-end loan. You borrow a fixed amount of money and repay it in equal monthly installments for a set period. Or you can obtain a line of credit—you borrow as you need the money, drawing against the amount granted when you opened the account. Be sure you understand the difference.
- The interest you pay may be fully deductible on your income tax return.

2. Disadvantages of Home Equity Loans

Home equity loans also have several disadvantages, including:

- Many home equity loans are sold by predatory lenders at very high rates. Predatory lenders target people in financial trouble or with past credit problems. Often, predatory lenders sell loans that borrowers have trouble paying off down the line.
- You are obligating yourself to make another monthly or periodic payment. If you are unable to pay, you may have to sell your house, or even worse, face the possibility of the lender foreclosing. *Before you take out a home equity loan, be sure you can make the monthly payment.*
- While interest may be deductible, it's often high—19% or more per year.
- You'll have to pay an assortment of up-front fees for such costs as an appraisal, credit report, title insurance and points. These fees can be as much as $1,000 or more. In addition, for giving you an open line of credit, many lenders charge a yearly fee of $25 to $50.

Before obtaining a home equity loan, carefully evaluate your situation. You're trying to take steps to help you pay your debts; you don't want to make your debt burden worse.

E. Consider a Car Equity Loan

A bank or other financial institution may make a secured loan against the value of your car. Because your car is considered used and therefore its value rapidly decreases, these loans can come with a steep interest rate—as high as 16% or more. It may be possible, however, to find a bank that will lend you money at a much lower rate, such as 9% or 10%. Many lenders will require you to use your home, as well as your car, as collateral. This means that if you miss your payments, you risk losing your house as well as the car. Nevertheless, if you want to borrow a small sum, and you can afford to make the payments, a car equity loan may be a better deal than a home equity loan. At least you can avoid the up-front fees such as costs, points and title insurance.

Canceling a Home Equity Loan

Under the federal Truth in Lending Act, you have the right to cancel a home equity loan or second mortgage until midnight of the third business day after you sign the contract. You must be given notice of your right to cancel and a cancellation form when you sign the contract. The details are spelled out in Chapter 4, Section D.1.

F. Use the Equity in Your Home If You Are Elderly

A variety of plans are designed to help older homeowners make use of the accumulated value (equity) in their homes without requiring them to move, give up title to the property or make payments on a loan. The most common types of plans are reverse mortgages and deferral loans for property tax and home repair.

These plans can raise a senior citizen's standard of living and help an older person maintain independence by providing cash for everyday living expenses, home maintenance or in-home care.

1. Reverse Mortgages

Reverse mortgages are loans against the equity in the home that provide cash advances to a home-owner and require no repayment until the end of the loan term or when the home is sold. The borrower can receive the cash in several ways—a lump sum, regular monthly payments, a line of credit or a combination.

In most cases, the reverse mortgage lender will look at your age, the amount of equity you have in your home and current interest rates to determine the amount it will lend to you. All reverse mortgages cost money—closing costs (title insurance, escrow fees and appraisal fees), loan origination fees, accrued interest, and in most cases, an additional charge to offset the lender's risk of you not repaying. Almost every state allows lenders to offer reverse mortgages.

There are a few types of reverse mortgages:

- **Fixed Term Reverse Mortgages.** You receive monthly advances for a specified period of time. At the end of the period, the advances stop and you must repay the loan.
- **Tenure Reverse Mortgages.** You receive monthly advances as long as you stay in your home. Once you leave (for example, sell your house), you must repay the loan.
- **Portable Reverse Mortgages.** You receive an advance in order to purchase an annuity that will pay you a fixed amount as long as you are alive, no matter where you live.
- **Lump Sum.** You receive the entire loan amount in one lump sum.

The most widely available reverse mortgage plans are the FHA's Home Equity Conversion Mortgage Program and Fannie Mae's Home Keeper Mortgage Program.

There are pros and cons to reverse mortgages. In general, a reverse mortgage works best for older people with a lot of equity in their homes. If you fit this category, you should still be sure that you understand some of the disadvantages of reverse mortgages, including:

- Once you borrow against your equity with a reverse mortgage, there's no turning back. This equity will not be available to you in the future.
- The costs of a reverse mortgage can be very high.
- The amount you get may not meet all of your financial needs.
- Some unscrupulous lenders offer products that sound like reverse mortgages, but are really conventional loans. Others sell reverse mortgages that are very high cost or have unfair terms.
- A reverse mortgage makes it difficult to give your home to your heirs after you die.
- A reverse mortgage may affect your ability to receive (or continue to receive) need-based government benefits such as Supplemental Security Income (SSI).

2. Deferral Payment Loans

Deferral payment loans are need-based loans used for a special purpose—to make property tax payments or to pay for home repairs. The cost of these loans is very low and repayment is deferred as long as you live in your home. Deferral payment loans are generally available through state or local government agencies.

There are two types of deferral payment loans:

- **Property Tax Deferral Loans.** Many states will provide vouchers to approved applicants to pay their property taxes. Contact your tax assessor to see if such a program is available in your county.

- **Home Repair Deferral Loans.** These are loans for home repairs at no or very low interest.

3. Additional Resources

If you want to find out more about reverse mortgages, deferred payment loans or other options to tap into your house's equity, be very wary of people or businesses that charge—as much as 10% of the loan amount—for information. Much material is available for free or little cost from the following organizations and agencies:

- U.S. Department of Housing and Urban Development, at 888-466-3487 or at www.hud.gov.
- AARP, 601 E Street NW, Washington, DC 20049, 800-424-3410, www.aarp.org.
- Fannie Mae, Consumer Education Group, 3900 Wisconsin Avenue NW, Washington, DC 20016, 800-732-6643, www.fanniemae.com.
- The National Center for Home Equity Conversion, 360 North Robert, Suite 403, St. Paul, MN 55101, 651-222-6775, www.reverse.org.

G. Borrow From Family or Friends

In times of financial crises, some people are lucky enough to have friends or relatives who can and will help out. Before asking your college roommate, Uncle Paul or someone similar, consider the following:

- Can the lender really afford to help you? If the person is on a fixed income and needs the money to get by, you should probably look elsewhere for a loan.
- Do you want to owe this person money? If the loan comes with emotional strings attached, be sure you can handle the situation before taking the money.
- Will the loan help you out or will it just delay the inevitable (most likely, filing for bankruptcy)? Don't borrow money to make payments on debts you will eventually discharge in bankruptcy.

- Will you have to repay the loan now or will the lender let you wait until you're back on your feet? If you have to make payments now, you're just adding another monthly payment to your already unmanageable pile of debts.
- If the loan is from your parents, can you treat it as part of your eventual inheritance? If so, you won't ever have to repay it. If your siblings get angry that you are getting some of your parents' money, be sure they understand that your inheritance will be reduced accordingly.

One word of warning: If a friend or relative lends you money at a below market interest rate or gives you cash as a gift, that person may have to pay gift taxes. Gifts of over $10,000 per person per year are subject to gift taxes. And the definition of "gift" includes a break on interest (although because the amount of the "gift" is the break on interest per year, not the amount loaned, most loans won't incur gift taxes).

H. Get Your Tax Refund Fast

Sometimes, getting a tax refund quickly will help you through a crisis, especially if the IRS owes you a lot. The IRS's Taxpayer Advocate Program is set up to give assistance to taxpayers. Each IRS district office has an Advocate. To contact a local office, check the government listing of your phone book for the Advocate office in your region, call the Washington, DC office toll-free at 877-777-4778 or visit the IRS website at www.irs.gov. It has lots of helpful information as well as tax forms.

Student Loan Debtors: Don't Count Your Dollars Before They're Hatched. If you are expecting a large tax refund—and you've defaulted on a student loan—don't count on seeing the money. Intercepting tax refunds is the method most frequently used by the government to collect outstanding student loan dollars. Yearly, the federal government pockets over $900 million by grabbing tax refunds and other federal offsets from defaulted student loan borrowers. And if you legitimately owe the money, stopping a tax refund intercept is very difficult.

For more information on student loan collections, see Chapter 13, *Student Loans*.

Don't Overlook Government and Agency Help

If lose your job, one of the first things you'll want to do is apply for unemployment. Your telephone book white pages should have the phone number for the closest office; check the government listing sections. Also, consider contacting other human service agencies to find out if you qualify for Food Stamps, Medicaid, general assistance, veterans' benefits, workers' compensation, Social Security or disability benefits.

Consider, too, private agency help. If you are a member of a fraternal organization or an ethnic or religious group, you qualify as a native son or daughter, or you fit into any number of other categories, there may be a host of nonprofit associations willing to help out. Perusing your phone book or calling friends may lead you to the right organization.

I. What to Avoid When You Need Money

Making wise financial decisions when the bills are piling up is not easy. But, even if you feel desperate, don't jump at every opportunity to get cash fast. If you make a bad choice, you'll just get yourself into deeper debt. This section discusses some of the options that you should avoid, if possible. It's not a complete list. Unfortunately, new scams and bad deals crop up every day. So, proceed cautiously, whatever you are considering.

1. Finance Companies

Some consumer finance companies lend money to consumers in the form of consolidation loans. Finance companies make secured consolidation loans, usually requiring that you pledge your house or car as collateral. These loans are just like second mortgages or secured vehicle loans, and you'll usually be charged interest between 10% and 15%. If you default on the loan, the finance company can foreclose on your home or take your car or other property.

Finance companies and similar lenders also make unsecured consolidation loans—that is, they lend you some money without requiring that you pledge any property as a guarantee that you'll pay. But the interest on these loans often reaches 25% or more. They also charge all kinds of fees or require you to purchase insurance, bringing the effective interest rate closer to 50%.

If you still want to take out a consolidation loan, you are better off borrowing from a bank or credit union than a finance company. Many finance companies engage in illegal or borderline collection practices if you default, and are not as willing as banks and credit unions to negotiate if you have trouble paying. Furthermore, loans from finance companies may be viewed negatively by potential creditors who see them in your credit file.

2. Tax Refund Anticipation Loans

Although getting a tax refund fast is often a good way to get quick cash (see Section H, above), you should avoid a tax refund anticipation loan. A tax refund anticipation loan is a loan, offered by a private company, for the period of time between the day you file your tax return and the day you get your refund from the IRS. The amount of the loan is equal to the amount of your anticipated refund less fees for the loan, electronic filing and tax preparation. For example, if you expect a tax refund of $500, the company might charge you $75 for all these fees. You will get only $425 of your $500 refund.

It is usually better to be patient and wait for your refund, rather than pay the high fee for a tax refund anticipation loan. In most cases, you can file your return electronically or by fax and get the money quickly. For more information on how to get a refund sooner and for answers to other tax questions, contact the IRS at 800-829-1040 (voice), 800-829-4059 (TDD) or visit its website at www.irs.gov.

3. Pawnshops

Visiting a pawnshop should be one of the last ways you consider raising cash. At a pawnshop, you leave your property—the most commonly pawned items are jewelry, electronic and photography equipment, musical instruments and firearms. In return, the pawnbroker lends you approximately 50% to 60% of the item's resale value; the average amount of a pawnshop loan is only $50 or so.

You are given a few months to repay the loan, and are charged interest, often at an exorbitant rate. Although you borrow money for only a few months, paying an average of 10% a month interest means that you are paying an annual interest rate of 120%. You might also be charged storage costs and insurance fees.

If you default on your loan to a pawnshop, the property you left at the shop to obtain the loan becomes the property of the pawnbroker. You are usually given some time to pay up your debt and get your property back; if you don't, the pawnbroker will most likely sell it. In about a dozen states, if the sale brings in money in excess of what you owe on the loan, storage fees and sales costs, you're entitled to the surplus. But don't count on getting anything.

4. Payday Loans

The payday loan industry is growing fast. In many states, these loans are illegal. In others, lenders may offer a similar type of loan, but call it something else. Either way, think twice before you get one of these loans.

A payday loan works like this: You give the lender a check and get back an amount of money less than the face value of the check. Some lenders also offer an "automatic debit" payment arrangement. For example, if you give the lender a check for $300, it may give you $250 in cash and keep the remaining $50 as its fee. The lender holds on to the check for a few weeks (often until your payday). At this time, you must pay the lender the face value of the check ($300), allow the lender to cash the check and keep the money or take out another loan and pay another fee. This is a very expensive way to borrow money. To find out more about the payday loan laws in your state, visit the National Consumer Law Center's website at www.consumerlaw.org.

5. Debt Consolidating Companies

Debt consolidating, debt pooling, budget planning, debt adjusting or debt prorating companies produce poor results. They siphon off your limited resources in debt consolidation charges, pay a few creditors and jeopardize much of your property. These companies are often merely a front for loan sharking. Some charge outrageously high interest; others charge ridiculously high fees.

Debt consolidating is either regulated or prohibited in most states. These laws usually don't apply to nonprofit organizations, lawyers and merchant-owned associations claiming to help debtors. ∎

The Consequences of Ignoring Your Debts

The payment of debts is necessary for social order. The nonpayment is quite equally necessary for social order. For centuries, humanity has oscillated, serenely unaware, between these two contradictory necessities.

—Simone Weil, Jewish labor organizer and mystic, 1909-1943

This chapter discusses the consequences of ignoring your creditors completely. While this is not usually a recommended strategy, it's one many people follow—at least for a while. It also may be your only option for nonessential debts that you can't pay. If you ignore your creditors long enough, they will probably take legal action to try and get either the money you owe or the secured property you pledged to guarantee repayment. You may lose some property, including your bank accounts, car, a portion of your wages—and possibly your house. But it's not always as bad as you might think. Exemption laws may keep creditors from taking important property such as your house or car. They will almost always protect other essential property such as your clothing, public benefits, most personal property, and for most debts, most of your wages (see Chapter 17, *Property You Get to Keep*). And most important, for all debts (except possibly child support) no matter how much you owe, you won't lose your liberty unless you do something foolish that infuriates a judge, such as deliberately disobeying an order or lying in a court document.

A. Eviction

⚠️ **Landlord-Tenant Rules Vary Throughout the Country.** Landlord-tenant rules are state- and sometimes city-specific, and vary tremendously from one place to the next. If paying your rent becomes a problem, seriously consider getting some help from a tenants' advocacy or other consumer group. Also, see *Every Tenants' Legal Guide* or *Renters' Rights*, both by Janet Portman and Marcia Stewart (Nolo), which suggest ways to deal with late rent and what happens in an eviction. If you think you have a defense to not paying your rent—for example, your living conditions are substandard—you can find out whether your state allows you to move out, withhold the rent or repair the problem yourself and deduct the cost from the rent.

If you don't have a legal reason for not paying your rent, your landlord can evict you. In many states an eviction can take as long as a month or two. In other states, where the courts are not so busy or the laws favor landlords, the process can be as short as a couple of weeks. In every state, however, the landlord must begin by given you a notice to pay or get out. If you do neither, he can file a lawsuit and serve it on you. You then have a set number of days to respond (five is common), and then a week or two later the court holds a hearing.

Even if you ignore the lawsuit and the landlord gets a default judgment against you, the landlord must take that judgment to the local sheriff. Many states require that the sheriff give you a week's advance notice of when the eviction is scheduled. If you're not out by the selected day, the sheriff comes and gives you the boot.

Evictions don't always take a month, however. In states—or communities—with few protections for tenants, an eviction can take place even faster. The landlord gives you just a few days notice to pay what you owe or defend in court, or you'll be on the street. And no matter where you live, if you're evicted, a landlord can sue you for the back rent you owe.

B. Foreclosure

If you miss several mortgage or home equity loan payments, the lender has the right to foreclose—force a sale of your house—to recover what you owe. But mortgage lenders don't always foreclose, even if they have the right. Foreclosing is expensive and time-consuming, and when the house is resold it often brings in only a part of what is owed.

The entire foreclosure process can take up to 18 months, depending on the state and type of loan. Here is a general overview of how it works.

After you miss a payment or two, the lender will send you a letter reminding you that your payment

is late and imposing a late fee—often 5% or 6% of the payment. If you still don't pay up, the lender will send more letters and often call, demanding payment.

If you don't pay or contact the lender to discuss your situation, after about 60–90 days the lender will send you a formal notice telling you that it has declared your loan in default. This notice, often called a Notice of Default, states that foreclosure proceedings will begin unless payment is received. These notices are required by state law.

⚠ Beware of Scammers. Once the foreclosure process starts, you are likely to be contacted by all sorts of people and companies offering help. Some will be legitimate. Others won't. Many unscrupulous people make money by taking advantage of people facing foreclosure.

After the lender sends you the notice of default, you usually have approximately 90 days to "cure" the default and reinstate the loan—pay all your missed payments, late fees and other charges. Even if not required by state law, some lenders will allow you to reinstate the loan before the foreclosure sale. You can avoid the actual foreclosure and often minimize the damage to your credit rating by selling the house during this period. Many buyer-investors purchase houses about to go into foreclosure, but they are not willing to pay—and you shouldn't expect to get—top dollar. Some will pay enough to

cover what you owe your lender, but you are likely to lose whatever equity you have in your house. And others will offer you less than what you owe. If you can convince your lender to take a "short sale" —that is, to let you sell the property for less than what you owe and write off the rest—you'll probably be able to avoid foreclosure. (Short sales are discussed in Chapter 6, Section A.2.)

⚠ A Short Sale Could Increase Your Tax Bill. Any time a lender writes off a portion of a debt you owe, the lender must report it to the IRS on a Form 1099-C or 1099-A, a report of miscellaneous income. This means you generally must include the written-off portion of the debt as income on your tax return the following tax year, unless you are insolvent or eliminate the debt in bankruptcy. See Chapter 6, Section F, for more information.

Mortgages and Deeds of Trust

Some home loans are called mortgages. Others are served by a deed of trust. Here's the difference:

Mortgage: A loan in which you put up the title to real estate as security for a loan. If you don't pay back the debt on time, the lender can foreclose on the real estate and have it sold through a court proceeding to pay off the loan.

Deed of trust: An alternative method of financing a real estate purchase The deed of trust transfers the title to the property to a trustee, often a title company, who holds it as security for a loan. If you default on the loan, the trustee can sell the property and pay the lender from the proceeds without going to court.

In most states, if you don't cure the default or sell the house during the time period allowed (usually about 90 days), the lender must "accelerate" the loan. When a lender accelerates a loan, the total amount of the loan becomes due. At this point, the only way you can keep your home in most states is to pay off the entire outstanding loan balance. This is called "redeeming" the loan. Usually, if you are in financial trouble, the only way to pay off the entire loan balance is to refinance the loan. Think carefully before doing so. You don't want to end up with another loan you can't afford. (See Chapter 6, Section A for more information on refinancing home loans.)

In many (but not all) states, in order to accelerate the loan, the lender must send you a notice of acceleration. If you get a notice of acceleration, be warned. The lender is serious about foreclosing and will probably move quickly to do so.

The next steps in the foreclosure process depend on what state you live in. If your state requires that a lender get a court order in order to foreclose (see "Mortgages and Deeds of Trust," above), you will receive a summons or other notice. The notice will explain your rights, including how much time you have to respond to the attached court papers. You have the right to challenge the legality of the foreclosure in court. If you don't respond to the papers or you lose in court, the court will issue a judgment to the lender, permitting it to hold a foreclosure sale.

Some states do not require a lender to go to court in order to foreclose. These types of foreclosures are called "nonjudicial foreclosures." In these states, the lenders usually are required to advertise the home for sale (after giving you the notice of default and other required notices). In order to challenge a nonjuidicial foreclosure, you must file a lawsuit asking the court to stop the sale of your house. In most cases, you will need an attorney's assistance to do this.

Once the lender has a court order permitting it to sell the house (if required) or has complied with all of the legal notice requirements (if it doesn't need a court order), it publishes a notice of the sale in a newspaper in the county where your house is located. The notice includes information about the loan and the time and location of the sale—in most states, the sale must take place at least three to five weeks after the notice is published.

At the foreclosure sale, anyone with a financial interest in your house will probably attend. This includes the first, second and even third mortgage (deed of trust) holders and any creditor, such as the IRS or a construction worker who has placed a lien on your house. Investors who like to purchase distressed property (real estate lingo for property that's been through foreclosure) will also be present.

The lender who foreclosed makes the first bid, usually for the amount owed, but often for less. It may seem like the lender is bidding to buy the house from itself. Both you and the lender have ownership interest in the house, however, and so by bidding, the lender is essentially buying you out. If the sale is for more than you owe your creditors who have a security interest in your house, you're entitled to the excess. But the foreclosing lender first gets to deduct the costs of foreclosing and selling, usually a few thousand dollars. Don't expect to leave a foreclosure sale with money in your pocket.

Any other lender or lienholder will get worried if the foreclosing lender's bid is the only one because that bid covers only what that lender is owed. If the sale goes through at that price, the other lenders and lienholders will get nothing from the sale. So if your property is worth more than the amount the foreclosing lender bid, another lender or lienholder may bid to protect her interest. So might a buyer who sees that the property's value exceeds the amount owed the lenders and lienholders. The house is sold to the highest bidder.

> **EXAMPLE:** Steve's house is worth $210,000, though he paid only $120,000 for it ten years ago. He has now hit hard times. He owes the original lender $74,000. A few years back he took out a home equity loan and owes that lender $35,000. He also owes the IRS $43,000 in back taxes, interest and penalties. Thus, Steve's creditors are owed a total of $152,000.
>
> The foreclosing lender starts the bidding at $74,000. The holder of the home equity loan then bids $109,000 (the amount of the original loan plus the home equity loan). The successful bid is by an investor for $165,000, $45,000 less than the house is worth, but enough to pay off the $152,000 due to Steve's creditors who have

a security interest in his house. Most of the $13,000 balance is used to cover the costs of the foreclosure sale. Because the house is worth $210,000, the investor enjoys a tidy "profit" of $45,000, assuming it can later sell the house at full value.

If no one bids above the foreclosing lender at the sale, the house reverts to the lender for the amount of its bid. In many states, the successful bidder doesn't actually get title to the house for a period of time, from several days to several months, known as the redemption period. During that period, you can "redeem" the property, that is, pay off the fore-closing lender the entire balance of what you owe that lender and get your house back. This is the likely scenario in very depressed markets. In stron-ger markets, however, investors or other buyers will probably bid.

Defenses to Foreclosure

You may be able to delay or stop the foreclosure because you have defenses to paying the mortgage or because the lender has not properly followed state foreclosure procedures. If you think you might have a defense to foreclosure, contact a lawyer immediately. Some possible defenses are:

- **Violations of the federal Truth in Lending law.** The federal Truth in Lending law requires the lender to provide certain information about your loan, before you sign the papers. If the lender failed to provide this information, you may be able to cancel the mortgage. This right to cancel only applies to loans *not* used to pur-chase your home.

- **Home improvement fraud.** If you took out a mortgage to finance improvements to your home, and the contractor ripped you off (for example, the work was shoddy or incomplete), you may be able to cancel the loan.

- **Interest rates or loan terms that violate state or federal law.** Some states limit how much in-terest can be charged on a loan. Federal law prohibits lenders from making deceptive or false representations about the loan and from charging high closing costs and fees. And for certain very expensive loans, federal law re-quires extra disclosures and prohibits some terms, like balloon payments. (See Chapter 11, Section A.1 for more on these expensive loans.) If your interest is very high or your lender didn't tell you the truth about the terms of your loan, consult a lawyer.

- **Failure to follow foreclosure procedures.** Each state requires lenders to follow specific proce-dures when foreclosing on a home. If the lender doesn't follow these rules (for example, by not giving proper notice of the foreclosure or failing to inform you of certain rights), you may be able to delay the foreclosure.

Finding defenses to foreclosure is not easy. Nor is raising these defenses in court. If you think you might have a defense to foreclosure, consult an attorney. (See Chapter 20, *Help Beyond the Book*, for information on how to find a good lawyer.)

States That Limit Deficiency Balances After Foreclosure

State	Code Section	Limits on Deficiency Balances After Foreclosure
Alaska	Alaska Stat. §§ 34-20-100, 09-45-180	If foreclosure is under deed of trust, debtor is not liable for deficiency. If foreclosure is made under mortgage, debtor is liable for deficiency.
Arizona	Ariz. Rev. Stat. §§ 33-729, 33-814	If foreclosure is by original lender on property of 2 ½ acres or less with a single one- or two-family residence, debtor is not liable for deficiency unless decrease in value is due to debtor's neglect. If foreclosure is under deed of trust on property of 2 ½ acres or less with a single one- or two-family residence, debtor is not liable for deficiency; on all other deed of trust foreclosures lender has 90 days to begin proceedings to recover deficiency.
Arkansas	Ark. Code Ann. §§ 18-49-105, 18-50-112	If foreclosure is under deed of trust, lender has 12 months to to begin proceedings to recover deficiency.
California	Cal. Civ. Proc. Code §§ 580b, 580d	If foreclosure is under deed of trust or mortgage, debtor is not liable for deficiency. If foreclosure is on any secondary loan (such as refinancing or liens), debtor is liable for deficiency.
	Cal. Health & Safety Code § 18038.7	If foreclosure is made by original lender under mortgage or deed of trust on a floating home that serves as a residence for no more than four families (including debtor), debtor is not liable for deficiency.
Connecticut	Conn. Gen. Stat. Ann §§ 49-14	If foreclosure is under mortgage, lender has 30 days to begin proceedings to recover deficiency.
Florida	Fla. Stat. Ann §§ 702.06 to 702.065	If original lender buys foreclosed property at sale, entitled only to deficiency set by court and may not sue debtor. If foreclosure is uncontested, debtor not liable for deficiency.
Georgia	Ga. Code Ann. § 44-14-161	If foreclosure is under mortgage or deed of trust, lender must obtain order of approval from superior court within 30 days of sale and must give debtor at least five days' notice of court hearing, or debtor is not liable for deficiency.
Hawaii	Haw. Rev. Stat. §§ 667-24 to 667-42	In alternate foreclosure by sale (lender must be a bank, credit union or institutional investor and must hold two open houses), debtor not liable for deficiency (applies to mortgages and loans created after 7/1/1999).
Idaho	Idaho Code § 45-1512	If foreclosure is under deed of trust, lender has three months to begin proceedings to recover deficiency.

States That Limit Deficiency Balances After Foreclosure (continued)		
State	**Code Section**	**Limits on Deficiency Balances After Foreclosure**
Illinois	735 Ill. Comp. Stat. §§ 5/15-1401 to -1402	If debtor and lender agree to voluntary foreclosure, debtor is not liable for deficiency. If foreclosure is under deed of trust, debtor is not liable for deficiency.
Indiana	Ind. Code Ann. § 32-30-10-4	If foreclosure is under mortgage, there must be an agreement either in the mortgage or in a separate contract for the exact payment due, or lender may not collect deficiency.
Iowa	Iowa Code Ann. §§ 628.26, .27; 654.20, .26	Debtor is not liable for deficiency: 1) if property is less than ten acres, and 2a) both parties agree to a redemption period of six months, or 2b) property is abandoned and the redemption period is reduced to 60 days. If property is a one- or two-family personal residence and lender chooses to foreclose without a redemption period, debtor is not liable for deficiency.
Kansas	Kan. Stat. Ann. § 40-3511	If debtor has mortgage insurance for a single-family owner-occupied residence, not liable to insurance company for any deficiency after foreclosure sale.
Maine	Me. Rev. Stat. Ann. tit. 14, §§ 6203-D to 6203-E	Debtor is not liable for deficiency unless: 1) at least 21 days before the foreclosure sale lender sends debtor a notice of the sale which includes a statement that debtor is liable for deficiency; 2) within 30 days of sale lender submits affidavit that notice was sent. Lender has two years to begin proceedings to recover deficiency.
Massachusetts	Mass. Gen. Laws Ann. Ch. 244 §§ 17A to 17B	Debtor is not liable for deficiency unless: 1) at least 21 days before the foreclosure sale lender sends debtor a notice of the sale which includes a statement that debtor is liable for deficiency; 2) within 30 days of sale lender submits affidavit that notice was sent. Lender has 2 years to begin proceedings to recover deficiency.
Minnesota	Minn. Stat. Ann. §§ 582.30; 582.032; 580.32, 580.23	Debtor not liable for deficiency in the following situations: 1) redemption period is six months; 2) redemption period is five weeks on property that is less than 10 acres, not used for agriculture and abandoned; 3) debtor and lender have agreed to voluntary foreclosure. If property is used for agriculture, lender has 90 days to begin proceedings to recover deficiency and 3 years to collect.
Mississippi	Miss. Code Ann. § 15-1-23	Lender has one year to begin proceedings to recover deficiency.

States That Limit Deficiency Balances After Foreclosure (continued)

State	Code Section	Limits on Deficiency Balances After Foreclosure
Montana	Mont. Code Ann. §§ 71-1-232, 71-1-317	If foreclosure is made by original lender under mortgage, debtor is not liable for deficiency. If foreclosure is under deed of trust, debtor is not liable for deficiency.
Nebraska	Neb. Rev. Stat. § 76-1013	If foreclosure is under deed of trust, lender has three months to begin proceedings to recover deficiency.
Nevada	Nev. Rev. Stat. §§ 40.455, 40.457	If lender foreclosed on single piece of property, lender has six months to begin proceedings to recover deficiency. If lender foreclosed on more than one piece of property, lender has two years to begin proceedings to recover deficiency.
New Jersey	N.J. Stat. Ann. §§ 2A:50-2, 2A:50-2.1	Lender has three months to begin proceedings to recover deficiency.
New Mexico	N.M. Rev. Stat. Ann. § 48-10-17	If foreclosure is under deed of trust, lender has 12 months to begin proceedings to recover deficiency. Low-income households are not liable for deficiency.
New York	N.Y. Real Prop. Acts. Law §§ 1371, 1419	Lender has 90 days to begin proceedings to recover deficiency.
North Carolina	N.C. Gen. Stat. § 45-21.38	If foreclosure is under deed of trust or mortgage, debtor is not liable for deficiency.
North Dakota	N.D. Cent. Code § 32-19-06	Lender has 90 days to begin proceedings to recover deficiency and three years to collect. Fair value of the property must be detemined by jury.
Ohio	Ohio Rev. Code Ann. § 2329.08	If foreclosure is on residence property for one or two families, lender has two years to collect deficiency.
Oklahoma	Okla. Stat. tit. 12, § 686 tit. 46, § 43(c)	If debtor notifies lender that property is a homestead 10 days before foreclosure sale, debtor is not liable for deficiency. If debtor does not send notice or if lender contests homestead status of property, lender has 90 days to begin proceedings to collect deficiency.
Oregon	Or. Rev. Stat. §§ 86.770; 88.070 to 88.075	If foreclosure is on a first mortgage on a primary or secondary personal residence, debtor is not liable for deficiency. If foreclosure is under deed of trust, debtor is not liable for deficiency.
Pennsylvania	42 Pa. Cons. Stat. Ann. §§ 5522, 8103	Lender has six months to begin proceedings to recover deficiency.

States That Limit Deficiency Balances After Foreclosure (continued)		
State	**Code Section**	**Limits on Deficiency Balances After Foreclosure**
South Carolina	S.C. Code Ann. §§ 15-39-760; 29-3-660	If foreclosure is under mortgage, bidding must remain open for 30 days after sale, unless lender agrees not to claim deficiency.
South Dakota	S.D. Codified Laws Ann. §§ 44-8-20; 21-48A-1; 21-47-16; 21-49-27	If foreclosure is by original lender, debtor is not liable for deficiency. If debtor and lender agree to voluntary foreclosure, debtor is not liable for deficiency. In other mortgage foreclosures where lender is bidding on the foreclosed property, lender must bid the amount of debt remaining or get a court appraisal of fair market value and bid that in order to get deficiency.
Texas	Tex. Prop. Code Ann. §§ 51.003 to .004	If foreclosure is under mortgage, lender has two years to begin proceedings to recover deficiency; if foreclosure is under deed of trust, lender has 90 days to begin proceedings to recover deficiency.
Utah	Utah Code Ann. § 57-1-32	If foreclosure is under deed of trust, lender has three months to begin proceedings to recover deficiency.
Washington	Wash. Rev. Code Ann. §§ 61.12.093 to .095; 61.24.100	If foreclosure is on property that is not used primarily for agriculture and has been abandoned for six months, debtor is not liable for deficiency. If foreclosure is under deed of trust, debtor is not liable for deficiency.

If you are in California and your lender is threatening or has started to foreclose, you will want to take a look at *Stop Foreclosure Now*, by Lloyd Segal (Nolo). It describes how foreclosures work, how to stop one and alternatives for getting out from under your mortgage.

Watch Out for Deficiency Balances. A deficiency balance is the difference between the amount you owe the foreclosing lender and the money the lender received at the sale. In many states, if the value doesn't cover what you owe, the lender is entitled to a deficiency for the difference. The lender usually must schedule a court hearing and present evidence of the value of the property to obtain the deficiency. Any balance owed to "junior" lienholders—creditors whose liens were filed after the foreclosing lender's lien was filed—are extinguished by the sale. Therefore, there is no deficiency owed to those creditors.

A lender with a deficiency can use the collection techniques covered in Chapter 9, and will often accept less than the full amount if you can offer a lump sum settlement. If you owe a lot of money or there's any easy target for collection (such as a large bank account or monthly wages), the lender is likely to pass your debt onto a collection agency or a lawyer (to sue you).

One possible way to avoid a deficiency balance is to deed the property back to the lender in lieu of foreclosure. (This strategy is discussed in Chapter 6, Section A.2.) If the lender agrees to accept the deed, the lender is essentially agreeing that the amount you owe equals the current value of the property, eliminating any deficiency balance. One catch, however, is that the IRS will probably consider the amount of the deficiency forgiven by the lender taxable income to you and require you to report it on your tax return. (See Chapter 6, Section F.)

Finally, if you plan to file for bankruptcy, you probably don't need to worry about a deficiency balance because you will probably be able to discharge the deficiency debt in the bankruptcy.

C. Repossessing or Taking Property

As explained in Chapter 1, a secured debt is one linked to a specific item of property—called collateral—that guarantees payment of the debt. If you don't pay a debt secured by personal property, the creditor has the right to take the property pledged as collateral for the loan. The creditor can't just walk into your house and take your couch, however; the creditor must have a court order or an invitation from someone in your household to enter your home.

There are two basic kinds of secured debts—voluntary security interests and liens. They are described in detail in Chapter 1, Section A.

1. What Constitutes a Default?

Unless your contract says otherwise, if you miss even one payment, you have defaulted on your loan and, under most security agreements, the creditor is entitled to take the goods. If you make your payments but otherwise fail to comply with an important term of the security agreement, the creditor can declare you in default and take the property. Be sure you read the security agreement's fine print terms carefully. Sometimes lenders have the right to declare a secured debt in default, even if you're all paid up. This may happen if:

- you sell the collateral
- the collateral is destroyed or stolen, or its value substantially depreciates
- you let required insurance lapse—some lenders require that you have collision and comprehensive insurance on motor vehicles, or that you buy credit life or credit disability insurance
- you become insolvent (as defined by your lender) or file for bankruptcy
- you refuse to let the creditor examine the collateral at his request, or
- the creditor "feels" that the prospect of your paying is uncertain.

2. When You Have Defaulted

Whether a creditor has to notify you before it takes your property depends on what state you live in and on the terms of your original agreement with the creditor. Unless the contract specifically says otherwise, the creditor must notify you that it has accelerated the debt (which means that all payments are now due) and that the full amount is due. This advance warning can give you time to figure out a plan. However, in many contracts, you waive the right to receive advance notice. In some cases you can challenge these waiver clauses, but you will likely need the assistance of an attorney to do so.

Fortunately for consumers, many states require creditors to notify you of a "right to cure" the default. If you want to take advantage of the "right to cure," you must do so before the debt is accelerated and before the property is repossessed. You get a certain period of time (usually a few weeks) to pay back what you owe plus any late charges. You will need to research your state law to see if you have a right to cure where you live. (See Chapter 20, *Help Beyond the Book*, for information on how to research your state law.)

A few states, including Louisiana and Wisconsin, prohibit creditors from repossessing property without first getting a court order. Some Native American tribes have also passed laws prohibiting repossessions without court orders. And in California, creditors need a court order to take certain property worth less than $1,000. If the property is used in a trade, the limit is $5,000. (Cal. Civil Code §1799.100.) This California law does not apply to motor vehicles.

But even outside of these states, a creditor is unlikely to go ahead and take your property unless you have defaulted in the past, have missed several payments or are uncooperative, or if the creditor has learned something worrisome about your finances.

You can voluntarily return the collateral to the creditor, but he doesn't have to take it. And he probably won't if it's worth far less than you owe. If you want to give the property back, first call the creditor—ask to speak to someone in the collections department—and find out if your entire debt will be canceled when the collateral is returned. If the creditor agrees to cancel the entire debt, get it in writing. Also see if the creditor will refrain from reporting the default on your credit report. If it isn't canceled, there probably isn't much point in returning the item, as you'll be liable for the difference between what the collateral sells for and what you owe. (See Section 4, below.)

a. How Motor Vehicles Are Repossessed

The first property most lenders go after is a motor vehicle, especially if the loan agreement was to finance the purchase of a new car or truck. In a number of states, however, the lender must first send you notice of the default and give you the right to make up the payments, called a right to "cure," before repossessing your car.

In addition, a repossession company can't use force to get to your vehicle—repossessions must occur without any breach of the peace. Unfortunately, breach of the peace is defined very broadly. It's legal to hotwire a car. It's legal to use a duplicate key and take a car. Most courts have said it's legal to remove a car from a carport or an open garage (meaning the door is up). In most states, it's legal to take a car from a garage where the door is closed but unlocked, but a few cautious repossessors won't do this. It's illegal to break into a locked garage, even by using a duplicate key. But a repossessor might anyway, especially in parts of the country where the repossession won't be nullified and all the lender will be required to do is fix the lock.

The repossession company can't take your car until it finds it. The lender will supply it with your home and work addresses, and any other useful information such as where you attend school. Then the repossessor starts looking. If the repossessor finds the car in your driveway or on the street in front of your house, the repossessor will wait until you're asleep or out, use a master key or hotwire it and then drive away.

If the car isn't near your house, the repossessor will search the neighborhood. Many debtors, fearful of having their car repossessed, park it about three blocks from their home. This is the distance they figure is far enough away to be hard to find, but close enough to still be convenient to use. Repossessors know this trick, however, and often find a car within ten minutes after starting to search. Knowing this, some people leave their car in a neighbor's locked garage, an approach that will frustrate the repossessor at least for a little while. If, however, a court finds that you acted in bad faith, you may lose your right to get the car back. (See Section 3, below.)

Although it might seem otherwise, the repossession company does not have unlimited power to take your car. If you or someone else (like a relative) objects at the time the repossessor tries to take your car, he or she must stop. However, this doesn't mean you get to keep your car. The repossessor can try again another day or get a court order to take the car.

b. How Other Property Is Taken or Repossessed

Few creditors use their collections personnel or hire repossessors to take back personal property other than motor vehicles because:

- the loan is often only a few thousand dollars or less
- the property may be worth far less than you owe, and
- the repossessor will have a hard time getting into your house.

A few major department stores, especially Sears, encourage debtors to return property. If the property is less than a year old, Sears will usually credit your account for 100% of what you owe. This means that if you return property, your entire balance is wiped out, even if the property is worth less than the amount you owe.

If the lender hires a repossessor to take back your property, you don't have to give the property back or let her into your house unless a sheriff shows up with a court order telling you to do so. If, however, your property is sitting in the backyard—for example, the repossessor has come to take your new gas barbecue and lawn furniture—it's generally fair game. But the repossessor can't use force to get into your house or to take your backyard furniture—for example, you can't be thrown out of a lawn chair. Some repossessors will jump a fence or even pick a lock, but most won't enter the premises unless they are invited or are in possession of a court order. Entering your house when you are away with a duplicate key to take your refrigerator or living room sofa is seldom done by repossessors because it is illegal. Only the rarest of repossessors would take this risk. As stated above, repossessions must occur without any breach of the peace.

As with car repossessions, if you or a member of your family ask the repossessor to leave your property, and she doesn't, this is a breach of the peace. So is using abusive language or violence or showing up with a gun-carrying sheriff in an effort to intimidate you. But lying or tricking you usually isn't a breach of the peace.

3. Can You Get Your Property Back?

If your car or other property is taken, some states give you a short time during which you can get it back by reinstating the contract. Reinstatement means paying the balance due plus any repossession costs.

Reinstating the contract—getting the property back and resuming the payments under the same terms of the original agreement—requires that you pay all the past due installments and late fees, as well as the costs the lender has incurred in taking and storing the property, often a few hundred dollars. This right of reinstatement is limited, however, and, depending on your state law, you probably can't get the property back if you:

- had the contract reinstated in the past
- lied on your credit application
- hid the property to avoid repossession, or
- didn't take care of the property and its value has substantially diminished.

The lender must give you a notice of your right to reinstate the contract after repossession, even if the lender thinks you have given up the right. If the lender doesn't, you may have the right to get the property back for nothing—but you will have to resume making payments on your loan. If you have been given notice and want to try to reinstate the contract, contact the lender as soon as possible to work out an agreement.

If you don't reinstate the contract within the time permitted by the agreement, the lender will send you a formal notice of its intent to sell the property.

Although only some states allow you to reinstate the contract, every state allows you to redeem the property. There are important differences between reinstatement and redeeming. Reinstatement allows you to get the property back by paying past due amounts plus repossession costs. In addition, re-instatement is usually limited to a specific period of time after the repossession. To redeem property, you must pay the entire balance of the contract (instead of just the past amounts due) plus repossession and storage costs. You can redeem property any time before it is sold.

Despite its seeming advantages, redemption is rarely feasible. If you couldn't make payments in the first place, you probably can't come up with the entire balance due under the contract. Some people take out a home equity loan to get the money. This is dangerous; you might end up losing your house instead of the personal property. Redemption might make sense if the property, such as your car, is essential to your livelihood and you can get someone to help you come up with the money to redeem it.

Personal Property in Repossessed Motor Vehicles

If the repossessor takes your motor vehicle, you're entitled to get back all your personal belongings not attached to, but inside of, the vehicle when it was repossessed. This means that you can probably get back your gym shorts but not the $500 stereo system you installed. (You are entitled to a removable radio, however.) Also, make sure you look at your loan agreement. Some say that you must make that request within 24 hours of the repossession. Although such time limits may not hold up in court, it's safest to act quickly. Promptly contact the lender after your vehicle is repossessed and ask that your property be returned. Put the request in writing and list everything you left in the car. If the lender is uncooperative—which is unlikely—consider suing in small claims court.

4. Beware of Deficiency Balances

If you don't reinstate or redeem the property within the time provided in the lender's notice of its intent to sell the property, the property will be sold. If the proceeds don't cover the total of what you owe—and they never do—you may be liable for the balance, called a deficiency. Often that balance is a lot.

If You're Planning to File for Bankruptcy. If you're planning to file for bankruptcy, you probably don't have to worry about any deficiency—it will likely be wiped out in your bankruptcy case. You can skip ahead to Section D.

The lender must send you a notice that the property will be sold and must give the date, time and location of the sale. The notice must also tell you whether you are liable for any deficiency and must provide a phone number where you can find out what is still owing. You are entitled to attend the sale and bid, and the lender is required to give you

Limitations on Liability for Deficiency Balance After Repossession

If your state is not listed here you will probably be likely for any deficiency following the sale of repossessed goods. Check with your state department of consumer affairs or consumer protection office to make sure. (See chapter 20 for a list of state offices.)

State	Code Section	After Repossessions
Alabama	Ala. Code. § 5-19-13	If sales price was $1,000 or less, debtor is not liable for deficiency.
Arizona	Ariz. Rev. Stat. § 44-5501	If sales price was $1,000 or less, debtor is not liable for deficiency.
California	Cal. Civil Code § 1812.5	If goods are bought on installment, debtor is not liable for any deficiency.
	Cal. Health & Safety Code § 18038.7	Under a sales contract for a mobile home, manufactured home, floating home, commercial coach or truck camper where seller transfers title when buyer pays purchase price in full, debtor who defaults on balance not liable for deficiency.
Colorado	Colo. Rev. Stat. § 4-9-609(d)	Lender cannot repossess mobile home or trailer used as residence unless the property is vacated or abandoned or the lender has a court judgment.
	Colo. Rev. Stat. § 5-5-103(3)	If unpaid balance is $2,100 or less, debtor is not liable for deficiency.
Connecticut	Conn. Gen. Stat. § 36a-785(f)(g)	Debtor is not liable for any deficiency except for a car or boat with a cash price over $2,000.
District of Columbia	D.C. Code Ann. § 28-3812(e)	If sales price was $2,000 or less, debtor is not liable for deficiency.
Florida	Fla. Stat. Ann. § 516.31(3)	If unpaid balance is $2,000 or less, debtor is not liable for deficiency.
Idaho	Idaho Code § 28-45-103(3)	If sales price was $1,000 or less, debtor is not liable for deficiency.
Indiana	Ind. Code Ann. § 24-4.5-5-503; Ind. Admin. Code tit. 750, r. 1-1-1	If sales price was $3,200 or less, debtor is not liable for deficiency.
Kansas	Kan. Stat. Ann. § 16a-5-103	If sales price was $1,000 or less, debtor is not liable for deficiency.
Louisiana	La. Rev. Stat. Ann. § 13:4108.2	If seller does not get a court-approved appraisal before the sale, debtor is not liable for a deficiency (unless debtor has agreed in writing to a sale without an appraisal).

	Limitations on Liability for Deficiency Balance After Repossession	
State	**Code Section**	**After Repossessions**
Maine	Me. Rev. Stat. Ann. tit. 9-A, § 5-103	If amount financed was $2,800 or less, debtor is not liable for deficiency.
Maryland	Md. Code Ann. [Com. Law] § 12-626(e)	If sales price was $2,000 or less, debtor is not liable for deficiency.
Massachusetts	Mass. Gen. Laws ch. 255, § 13J(e)	If unpaid balance is under $2,000, debtor is not liable for deficiency.
Minnesota	Minn. Stat. Ann. § 325G.22	If amount financed was $5,400 or less, debtor is not liable for deficiency.
Missouri	Mo. Rev. Stat. § 408.556	If amount financed was $500 or less, debtor is not liable for deficiency.
Nebraska	Neb. Rev Stat. § 45-1054	If unpaid balance is $3,000 or less, debtor is not liable for deficiency.
New York credit	N.Y. Pers. Prop. Law §§ 315, 422	In any retail installment sales transaction (including motor vehicles), seller must deduct from deficiency balance the buyer would have received for paying off the loan.
Ohio	Ohio Rev. Code Ann. § 1317.13	Except for a motor vehicle, manufactured home or mobile home, creditor can't repossess goods if the unpaid balance is less than 25%.
Oklahoma	Okla. Stat. tit. 14A, § 5-103	If sales price was $3,700 or less, debtor is not liable for deficiency.
Pennsylvania	69 Pa. Cons. Stat. Ann. § 627	If lender repossesses a motor vehicle, debtor has right to have court determine the reasonable value of vehicle when lender tries to recover deficiency. Whichever is higher, the reasonable value or the actual sale price, will be credited to buyer.
South Carolina	S.C. Code Ann. § 37-5-103 S.C. Code of Regs. R. 28-62	If sales price was $4,050 or less, debtor is not liable for deficiency.
Utah	Utah Code Ann. § 70C-7-101	If sales price was $3,000 or less, debtor is not liable for deficiency.
West Virginia	W. Va. Code Ann. § 46A-2-119	If unpaid balance is $1,000 or less, debtor is not liable for deficiency.
Wisconsin	Wis. Stat. §425.209	If unpaid balance is $1,000 or less, debtor is not liable for deficiency.
Wyoming	Wyo. Stat. Ann. § 40-14-503	If sales price was $1,000 or less, debtor is not liable for deficiency.

this information. There are two kinds of sale: a public sale, which is open to anyone; or a private sale, where the lender tells certain people who it feels might be interested. A private sale can only be held if the item "is of a type customarily sold in a recognized market" or "is the subject of widely distributed standard price quotations." Cars are frequently sold at private sales to which used car dealers and others who regularly buy repossessed cars are invited. If the notice doesn't give you the date and location of the sale, call the lender and find out.

The law requires that the lender conduct every aspect of the disposition of the vehicle in a "commercially reasonable" manner, but no one knows quite what that means. In fact, repossession sales are often attended only by used car dealers, who have a motive to keep the bids very low. This is one reason why most property sold at repossession sales bring in far less than what is owed the lender. For instance, a car valued at $12,000 might sell for $5,000, and a refrigerator worth $800 might sell for $250. And even though you could have sold the item for twice as much, the sale usually will be considered "commercially reasonable." If you attend, you can bid (if you have the cash), but the dealers are apt to outbid you.

After the item is sold, the sale price is subtracted from what you owe the lender. Then, the cost of repossessing, storing and selling the property is added to the difference. Very often, you are liable for that balance—the deficiency balance.

Here's one suggestion of a way to avoid any deficiency balance. If your property, especially a motor vehicle, is about to be repossessed, ask for a contract reinstatement just to get the vehicle back so you can sell it yourself. Even if you get $7,000 for a $9,000 car, it's better than the lender repossessing it and selling it for $3,000. You can use the $7,000 to pay off your lender and will owe only $2,000 more, far less than the $6,000 you'd owe if the lender sold it through repossession.

Are You Always Liable for a Deficiency?

In half the states (see chart, above), you won't be liable for a deficiency balance if the amount you originally paid is less than a few thousand dollars. This means you will almost always be liable for a deficiency if a motor vehicle is taken.

In addition, if a lender sues you instead of repossessing the property, you are not likely to be liable for any deficiency. If your state is not on the chart above, it means the state does not place additional limits on deficiency balances after repossession.

It is common for creditors to make mistakes in the repossession process. Most states bar creditors from collecting a deficiency balance if they failed to comply with notice requirements (such as notifying you of the right to cure or of the sale) or didn't sell the property in a commercially reasonable manner. If you think the creditor made a mistake, you must raise this defense at the time you are sued for the deficiency balance. Because these cases can be complex, it's a good idea to consult a lawyer.

Some lenders will forgive or write off the deficiency balance if you clearly have no assets. In such a case, the lender will issue you a Form 1099-C or 1099-A and the IRS will expect you to report the forgiven balance as income on your tax return. You can avoid this by proving to the IRS that you are insolvent. (See Chapter 6, Section F.)

If the lender doesn't forgive or write off the balance, expect dunning letters and phone calls, probably from a collection agency. (See Chapter 9, *When the Debt Collector Calls.*)

If the creditor sues you, you should file an answer with the court. Your first line of defense is to review how your repossession was handled. You can argue that the creditor isn't entitled to a deficiency if she didn't inform you about your right to cure the default (if you live in a state where you have this right) or redeem the property, didn't sell the item in a commercially reasonable manner or didn't give you the date and location of the sale.

If you'd rather take the offensive, you can sue the lender for wrongful repossession. For large items, such as cars, you'll probably need a lawyer. But for smaller items, you can probably represent yourself in small claims court. (See Chapter 15.)

D. Pre-Judgment Attachment of Unsecured Property

Prejudgment attachment is a legal procedure which lets a creditor tie up property before obtaining a court judgment. It is the *unsecured creditor's* way of telling the world that you owe money and that the property covered by the attachment can be used to pay the creditor if she wins in court. *Secured creditors* can, under the terms of the security agreement, repossess your property if you don't pay without first suing you. (See Section C, above.) They don't need to attach your property.

Because a prejudgment attachment can make it easy for a creditor to collect what she is owed if she eventually sues you and gets a judgment, a creditor may especially try to attach your property if you live out of state, have fled the state or if the creditor believes you are about to spend, sell or conceal your property.

In most states, a prejudgment attachment works pretty much the same. As the creditor is about to sue you, she prepares a document called a "writ of attachment," in which she lists the property you own that she believes is being held by others. The writ of attachment must be approved by a judge or court clerk (writs are usually approved as long as there is no dispute that the property to be attached is yours), and then the creditor serves it on you and on everyone she thinks has some of your property. Serving means making sure you get a copy. Usually, you must be hand-delivered a copy, but in some cases the creditor can just mail it to you. The most common property to attach is deposit accounts—savings, checking, money markets, certificates of deposit and the like.

Serving the writ freezes your property—the holder of your property can't let you sell it, give it away or, in the case of deposit accounts, make withdrawals. You must be given the opportunity to have a prompt court hearing—this isn't the trial where you argue whether or not you owe the debt. This hearing pertains to only the attachment, and

you'll want to argue that the attached property is exempt (see Chapter 17), you need the property to support yourself and your family or the value of the property attached exceeds what you owe.

If you don't attend the hearing or you lose the hearing, the court will order that the attachment remain on your property pending the outcome of the lawsuit. You won't be able to withdraw or otherwise dispose of any of the attached property. You can get the attachment released by filing a bond for the amount of money you owe. But if you don't file a bond, and the creditor wins the lawsuit, she's almost certain to be paid out of the attached property.

E. Lawsuit

If you don't pay a debt, the most likely consequence is that you will be sued, unless the creditor thinks you are judgment proof or decides not to sue for other reasons. Being judgment proof means that you don't have any money or property that can legally be taken to pay the debt and aren't likely to get any soon. But because most court judgments last many years (up to 20 in some states), and can often be renewed indefinitely, people who are broke may nevertheless be sued on the creditor's assumption that someday they'll come into money or property (and then will no longer be judgment proof). Similarly, very old people or people with terminal illness who are judgment proof may get sued by their creditors simply because the creditors know that it's easier to collect the debt at death (through the probate process) if they have a judgment than if they don't.

Being judgment proof doesn't mean that you have no money or property at all, although many people who are judgment proof have virtually nothing. Being judgment proof means that if a creditor obtains a court judgment, you are allowed to keep all of your property. Each state has declared certain items of property beyond the reach of creditors—these items are called exempt property. (Exempt property is covered in detail in Chapter 17.) Suffice it to say that if you receive no income except government benefits, such as Social Security or unemployment, and have limited personal property and no real property, you are almost always judgment proof, at least right now. There are a few exceptions to this general rule. For example, most government agencies are permitted to collect debts owed to them by taking a percentage of certain federal benefits, such as Social Security.

If a creditor sues you in regular court (as opposed to small claims court) and you fight it, the lawsuit can take time—often several years—to run through the court system. If you don't oppose the lawsuit, or you let the court automatically enter a judgment against you (called a default judgment), however, the case could be over in 30 to 60 days.

If the creditor gets a judgment, he has a number of ways to enforce it. If you are working, the most common method is to attach your wages, meaning that up to 25% of your take-home pay is removed from your paycheck and sent to the creditor before you ever see it. The next most common method to collect a judgment is to seize your deposit accounts. Chapter 15 contains details on getting sued and defending against judgment collections.

F. Lien on Your Property

A lien is a notice attached to your property telling the world that a creditor claims you owe her some money. Liens on real property are a common way for creditors to collect what they are owed. Liens on personal property, such as motor vehicles, are less frequently used but can be an effective way for someone to collect. To sell or refinance property, you must have clear title. A lien on your house, mobile home, car or other property makes your title unclear. To clear up the title, you must pay off the lien. Thus, creditors know that putting a lien on property is a cheap and almost guaranteed way of collecting what they are owed—sooner or later.

A creditor usually can place a lien on your real property—and occasionally on personal property—after she sues you and wins a court judgment. But many creditors need not wait that long. Here are examples of other property liens:

- **Property tax liens.** If you don't pay your property taxes, the county can place a lien on your real property. When you sell or refinance your place, or a lender forecloses on it, the government will stand in line to get paid out of the proceeds.

- **IRS liens.** If you fail to pay back taxes after receiving notices from the IRS, it may place a lien on all of your property, especially if you're unemployed, self-employed or sporadically employed and the IRS would have trouble attaching your wages. Many creditors with property liens simply wait until the house is sold or refinanced to get paid. The IRS, however, doesn't like to wait and may force a sale if the amount you owe is substantial. For more information on dealing with IRS liens, see *Stand Up to the IRS*, by Frederick W. Daily (Nolo).

- **Child support liens.** If you owe a lot in child support or alimony, the recipient may put a lien on your real property. The lien will stay until you pay the support you owe or until you sell or refinance your property, whichever happens first. (See Chapter 14.)

- **Mechanics' liens.** If a contractor works on your property or furnishes construction materials to be used on your property, and you don't pay up, the contractor can record a lien on your property called a mechanic's lien. In most states, the contractor must record the lien within one to six months of when the contractor wasn't paid. The contractor then must sue you to enforce the lien within about one year (the range, depending on the state, is one month to six years) of when the contractor recorded it. If the contractor wins the lawsuit, the contractor may be able to force the sale of your home.

G. Jail

Jailing someone for not paying a debt is prohibited in most instances. In a few situations, however, you could land behind bars.

- You willfully violate a court order. This comes up most frequently when you fail to make court-ordered child support payments, the recipient requests a hearing before a judge and the judge concludes that you could have paid, but didn't. (See Chapter 14.) But imprisonment for willful violation of a court order is not limited to child support situations. In a few states, a court can order you to make periodic payments on a debt. If you don't, the court can hold you in contempt and theoretically put you in jail. That rarely happens, however.

- You are convicted of willfully refusing to pay income taxes.
- You fail to show up for a debtor's examination. A debtor's examination is a procedure where a judgment creditor, with court approval, orders you to come to court and answer questions about your property and finances. (See Chapter 15, Section F.4.)
- You live in a state, such as Rhode Island or Wisconsin, that still has debtors' prisons. In Wisconsin, you may be jailed only if a creditor has a judgment against you for a tort—such as negligence (such as causing a car accident), assault, battery, infliction of emotional distress, false imprisonment, libel and slander—and you refuse to pay. (Statutes Annotated § 898.01.) In both states, poor debtors, after going to jail, may request a hearing before a judge, swear that they have no money or property and get out of jail. In a Rhode Island case, the court held that a debtor who was imprisoned for not paying a $3,100 judgment on a promissory note could be released after swearing that he had no money or property. (General Laws § 10-13-1; *White v. Tenth District Court*, 251 A.2d 539 (1969).)

Debtors' Prisons—A Little History

The mere thought of debtors' prison probably sends shivers up your spine. It should. As unusual and cruel as it seems today, debtors' prison was a major collection method in the 18th and mid-19th centuries of our republic. The legal system of the American colonies included debtors' prisons, which the English Parliament created under the Statute of Merchants in 1285. Creditors who were owed money could simply ask the sheriff to arrest the debtor and throw him (literally him—women were not allowed to own property and therefore couldn't get into debt trouble) in jail. If he couldn't raise the bail, and most couldn't as they had no money, he sat in his cell until someone paid his bill or bailed him out.

Many creditors felt the humiliation of jail was too much to impose on a debtor without first giving him a chance to pay what he owed. Those creditors, rather than having the debtor arrested, sued to obtain a judgment entitling them to payment. If the debtor didn't pay after a judge ordered him to, the creditor then asked the sheriff to arrest the debtor and toss him in jail.

Judicial attitude toward debtors and debtors' prison is reflected in one 17th century English case:

"If a man be taken in execution, and lie in prison for debt, neither the plaintiff at whose suit he is arrested, nor the sheriff who took him is bound to find him meat, drink or clothes, but he must live on his own, or on the charity of others; and if no man will relieve him, let him die, in the name of God, says the law; and so say I." *Manby v. Scott*, 1 Mod. 132, 84 Eng. Rep. 781 (1659).

Local businesses, preachers, butchers and market keepers often felt sorry for these prisoners and would try to help them out, but most sat in their cells until someone paid their debts. Even royalty felt compassion for many imprisoned debtors. Just outside of the Palace at Holyrood in Edinburgh, Scotland, there was (and still is) a small triangular-shaped area in which debtors could stay free from their creditors.

In 1830, an American Indian prisoner lamented on the absurdity of his being imprisoned as punishment for not delivering the payment of beaver skins. "If I was put there to compel me to perform my agreement, my prosecutors have selected a poor place for me to catch beavers."

Public indignation with debtors' prisons found a voice in Silas M. Stillwill, a New York lawyer. In 1831 he introduced the Act to Abolish Imprisonment for Debt. In the federal judicial system, debtors' prisons were gone by 1833. Most American states quickly followed suit, abolishing them in the 1830s and 1840s. And by 1870, nearly 600 years after they were created, England said no more to debtors' prisons.

H. Bank Setoff

A bank setoff happens when a financial institution such as a bank, savings and loan or credit union removes money from a deposit account—checking, savings, certificate of deposit or money market account—to cover a payment you missed on the loan owed that institution.

There are a few limitations on bank setoffs. For instance, most courts have said that banks cannot use setoffs to take income that is otherwise exempt under state or federal law (such as Social Security benefits, unemployment compensation, public assistance or disability benefits). (See Chapter 17, *Property You Get to Keep*, for information on exempt property.) In addition, financial institutions cannot take money out of your account to cover missed credit card payments, unless you previously authorized the bank to pay your credit card bill by automatic withdrawals from your account. (15 U.S.C. § 1666h; Regulation Z of the Truth in Lending Act, 12 C.F.R. § 226.12(d).)

Some states impose limits on bank setoffs as well. For example, California prohibits bank setoffs if the aggregate balance of all your accounts with the financial institution is under $1,000. (Financial Code § 6660.) And in Maryland, all bank setoffs are prohibited unless you have explicitly authorized the setoff or a court has ordered one. (Commercial Law § 15-702.)

I. Collection of Unsecured Debts From Third Parties

If a third person holds property for you or owes you money, most states give creditors the right to sue those third parties to reach your property or the money. Sometimes that third person is a financial institution, such as a bank, savings and loan or credit union, where you have a deposit account. Or, it may be a landlord or utility company to whom you've made a security deposit. Or, it could be a financial adviser, such as a stock broker, with whom you've deposited funds to invest on your behalf.

In a few states, a creditor can't pursue a third person until it has obtained a court judgment against you and tried to collect. In most states, however, the creditor can sue the third person even before getting a judgment against you. If that happens, you will have to be notified of the suit and allowed the opportunity to contest the debt.

J. Interception of Your Tax Refund

If you are in default on your student loan payments, or are behind in your income taxes or child support, the agency trying to collect can request that the IRS intercept your federal income tax refund and apply the money to your debt.

Before the IRS takes your money, it must notify you of the proposed interception. You are given the opportunity to present written evidence or to have a hearing to show that:

- your debt has been paid
- the amount of the proposed intercept is more than you owe, or
- the intercept is not legally enforceable.

If you are married and the intercept is for child support from a previous relationship, your spouse can file a claim for her share of the refund.

Tax refund intercepts are most common in the case of a defaulted student loan. Each year, for example, the federal government pockets over $500,000,000 by grabbing tax refunds from more than 500,000 former students. For more information on student loan collections—including stopping or avoiding future tax refund intercepts—see Chapter 13 and *Take Control of Your Student Loan Debt*, by Robin Leonard (Nolo).

K. Loss of Insurance Coverage

If you miss payments on any insurance policy, your coverage will end. Most insurance companies give you a 30-day grace period—that is, if your payment is due on the tenth of the month and you don't pay until the ninth of the following month, you won't lose your coverage. A few companies may let you get away with 60 days, but don't count on it. After 60 days, your policy is sure to lapse.

If your policy has lapsed, and your lender required you to obtain the insurance as a condition of your loan, you could face more than a canceled insurance policy. Because usually only lenders who make secured loans require insurance coverage, the lender could declare you in default of your loan and either repossess your personal property or foreclose on your house.

However, it is more likely that the lender will get an insurance policy for you and bill you for the premiums. This is called "force placed insurance." Often, lenders will require consumers to pay for coverage that is not actually required by the credit agreement, which can end up being very expensive. The lender may also fail to notify you before it gets this insurance and bills you for it. These types of practices may violate your state Unfair and Deceptive Acts and Practices statute (see Chapter 4, *Debts You May Not Owe*, for an explanation of UDAP laws) and other laws.

L. Loss of Utility Service

If you miss payments on your utility or telephone bill, the utility company will attempt to cut off your service. If the utility company is publicly owned, it must give you notice of the disconnect and the opportunity to discuss it with a representative of the utility company. This is because a publicly owned utility company cannot deprive you of due process of the law, according to the U.S. Supreme Court. (*Memphis Light, Gas & Water Div. v. Craft*, 436 U.S. 1 (1978).) In most states, a private utility company doesn't need to give you any notice. (California is one of a handful of exceptions to this rule.)

In some states, private utilities are also required to give notice or follow other rules before cutting off service. For example, in most northern states, utility companies are not allowed to shut off heat-related utility services to residential customers between November 1 and March 31. In many other states, there are limits to when a utility company can shut off utilities for elderly or disabled residents and occasionally for households with infants.

M. Take a Deep Breath

This chapter has just described many worst-case scenarios. If you ignore all your creditors, have some property and a job, some of these things will happen to you. This is why credit counselors don't recommend sticking your head in the sand. Pull out your list of essential and nonessential debts. After reading this chapter, you should know where you are most vulnerable—that is, where you are most likely to lose some property. If not paying a debt you considered nonessential means you'll probably lose your bank account, move that debt to the essential list and rethink your strategy.

Most important, focus on finding a solution. ■

When the Debt Collector Calls

*The most trifling actions that affect a man's credit
are to be regarded. The sound of your hammer at
five in the morning, or nine at night, heard by a
creditor, makes him easier six months longer; but if
he sees you at a billiard table, or hears your voice at
a tavern when you should be at work, he sends for
his money the next day.*

—Benjamin Franklin, American statesman,
philosopher & inventor, 1706-1790

As recently as 25 years ago, bill collectors
regularly threatened, scared, lied to, harassed,
intimidated and otherwise abused debtors. Debtors
were told they'd go to jail for not paying their bills,
friends and relatives were often interrogated and
threatened with financial and bodily harm if they
didn't tell where runaway debtors were living, and
bill collectors published lists of people who didn't
pay their debts.

The federal Fair Debt Collection Practices Act
(FDCPA), passed in 1977, outlaws unfair collection
practices including debtor harassment. This law has
greatly improved conditions for debtors, although
an unfortunate number of collectors still resort to
abusive practices.

There is one important rule to remember when
dealing with a bill collector. Adopt a plan and stick
with it. One choice—if you have no money, plan to
file for bankruptcy or just don't feel like paying
right now—is to refuse to talk with the collector. As
explained in Section D2, below, you can request
that a debt collector from a collection agency stop
contacting you. Another option, if you really need
more time to pay, is to contact the bill collector to
negotiate a payment schedule.

If you do contact a bill collector, realize that as
nice as a bill collector appears, she is not your
friend and does not have your best interest at heart.
She wants your money. To get it, she may ask you
to take her into your confidence regarding your
personal problems, or she may claim that she's

trying to save you from ruining your credit. Don't
believe her. She doesn't really care about your
problems or your credit rating. Her only goal is to
get you to send her some green bills. Stick to your
plan. If you want extra time to pay or to lower your
payments, insist on it. If you want the bill collector
to go away, tell her not to contact you.

⚠️ **This Chapter Assumes You Have Not Been
Sued.** This chapter focuses on prejudgment
collection efforts. If the creditor or a collection agency
has sued you and obtained a court judgment, the
collection options are different and you will want to
read Chapter 15.

A. Original Creditor or Collection Agency?

To understand your rights when dealing with a bill
collector, you must keep in mind the difference
between the original creditor and a collection agency
(or a "third party collector"). As you read further in
this chapter, this distinction will be important,
primarily because the federal law regulating collection agencies generally doesn't apply to original
creditors, unless they take steps to act like third
party collectors.

Original creditor. An original creditor is a business
or person who first extended you credit or loaned
you money. Sometimes original creditors are called
credit grantors.

Collection agency. A collection agency or third
party collector is someone used by an original
creditor to collect the original creditor's debt. Under
the FDCPA, a collection agency or third party
collector also includes:

- an original creditor that collects its debts
  under a different name or by sending letters
  signed by lawyers
- a lawyer who regularly collects debts owed to
  others (see *Heintz v. Jenkins*, 115 S.Ct. 1489
  (1995)), and
- any company that purchases debts for the
  purpose of collecting them.

Form Letters From an Attorney

If you get what appears to be a form collection letter with a lawyer's mechanically reproduced signature at the bottom (and perhaps her letterhead at the top), the sender of the letter (not necessarily the lawyer) and the lawyer may be violating the FDCPA—and you may have grounds to sue.

Under the FDCPA, a lawyer must be involved in each individual collection case before her name appears on any collection letters. She can't authorize a form letter and then let the bill collector mail out letters bearing her signature without reviewing each particular debtor's file. (See *Masuda v. Thomas Richards & Co.*, 759 F. Supp. 1456 (1991); *Clomon v. Jackson*, 988 F.2d 1314 (2d Cir. 1993).)

If you suspect this is happening, call the law firm on the letterhead and ask to speak with the attorney. If the attorney doesn't exist, or has no recollection of you or your debt, send a letter to the collections manager, president and CEO of the original creditor. Point out the blatant violation of the FDCPA and your right to sue. You might also volunteer to waive your right to sue in exchange for the creditor agreeing that you don't have to pay the debt.

Bill collector or debt collector. The term bill collector or debt collector can refer to either an original creditor or a collection agency. Be sure you know who you are dealing with.

As mentioned above, the difference between an original creditor and a collection agency is important. Original creditors generally are not governed by the FDCPA. Several states, however, have debt collection laws that apply to both original creditors and collection agencies. (These are outlined in Section D5, below.) Also, many states have laws regulating collection agencies more strictly than the FDCPA. (These, too, are outlined in Section D5.)

Efforts to collect past-due bills usually follow a standard pattern. Original creditors first try to collect their own debts. When you initially owe money, you'll receive a series of letters or phone calls from the original creditor's collections or customer service department. Although most creditors make first contact a few weeks after you miss a payment, some more aggressive companies begin hard-core collection efforts within 24 to 36 hours after your payment is due. If you don't respond to the letters or calls within about four months, most original creditors will charge off your account—that is, either send it to a collection agency or write it off as a bad debt.

⚠ Written-Off Debts Could Increase Your Tax Bill. If a creditor writes off a debt, it means that collection efforts will end. That's the good news. The bad news is that the creditor may be obligated to report your windfall to the IRS—and you may have to report it as income and pay taxes on it. See Chapter 6, Section F.

Some original creditors, concerned about their reputations, hire collection agencies known for less aggressive tactics. They realize that you may be a customer again in the future and they don't want to alienate you. Some creditors, however, couldn't care less about what you think of them. They are fed up with you for not paying and will find the most aggressive collection agency around.

B. Original Creditors' Collection Efforts

How an original creditor goes about collecting an outstanding bill will depend on the type of creditor it is. Small local creditors, like a corner store or accountant's office, may have a person on staff who handles delinquent accounts. More often than not, however, the responsibility of collecting overdue money rests with the business owner or manager. Department stores, banks and other creditors with several branches begin their collection efforts with the store or office that handled your transaction. National creditors—for example, banks that issue credit cards—have centrally located, in-house collection departments.

If you've moved since you incurred the debt, many original creditors will still try to find you. Several have access to computer databases compiled (usually by credit bureaus) to help creditors find debtors. You may unknowingly supply information about your new location to these databases when you rent a new place, send your credit card company a change of address or apply for a credit card at your new address.

If the original creditor can't find you, it will probably just send your account to a collection agency.

1. Collection Letters

Original creditors usually begin their collection efforts with collection ("dunning") letters.

One day, several weeks after a bill is past due, you open your mail box and find a polite letter from a creditor reminding you that you seemed to have overlooked the company's most recent bill. "Perhaps it is already in the mail. If so, please accept our thanks. If not, we would appreciate prompt payment," the letter states.

This "past due" form letter is the kind that almost every creditor sends to a customer with an overdue account. If you ignore it, you'll get a second one, also automatically sent. In this letter, most creditors remain friendly, but want to know what the problem is. "If you have some special reason for withholding payment, please let us know. We are here to help." Some creditors also suspend your credit at this point; the only way to get it back is to send a payment.

If you don't answer the second letter, you'll probably receive three to five more form letters. Each will get slightly firmer. The next to last letter will likely contain a veiled threat: "Paying now will protect your credit rating." By the last letter, however, the threat won't be so subtle: "If we do not receive payment within ten days, your credit privileges will be canceled (if they haven't already been), your account sent to a collection agency and your delinquency reported to the national credit reporting agencies. You could face a lawsuit, wage attachment or lien on your property."

Original creditors hate it when collection efforts reach this stage. They want you to pay your bill, but they also want to be nice so that you'll remain a customer. If the original creditor's letter-writing campaign fails or the person assigned to your account prefers direct contact, you'll probably receive a phone call.

EXAMPLES:

"We are not here to beat you up or yell at you. Tell us your problems so we can help you and your family. We want you to remain our customer."

"Oh-no; don't tell me you're considering bankruptcy! It's a big mistake. I'll bet you didn't know that a bankruptcy will stay on your credit record for ten years."

"Is the payment schedule convenient for you? Would it help if we moved your due date up a few days so that your payment is due just a day or two after you get paid?"

"Do you need help planning a budget or paying your bills? Let me suggest that you contact your local Consumer Credit Counseling Service office." [Consumer Credit Counseling Service (CCCS) is a national, nonprofit organization, sponsored and paid for by major creditors. CCCS helps debtors plan budgets and pay their bills. CCCS can be very helpful, but you, not the creditor, should make that decision. See Chapter 20 for a full discussion of CCCS.]

"How would you, if you were a creditor, handle overdue accounts?"

"Do you have $100 a month to pay your debts? I'm sure you realize that our debt is your most important one. We would have to insist that you pay us $75 a month and distribute the rest to your other creditors."

"Did you know that our store's 75th anniversary sale is next month? Everything will be on sale at 50% off. We'll be happy to let you have your $1,000 line of credit back as soon as you clear up this debt."

"Please, why don't you just send the minimum— $20—to prove to me that you are a sincere person."

"I know people who make much less than you do and who pay their bills on time."

If the letters and telephone calls fail, the original creditor will report your delinquency to a credit bureau—which means that it goes on your credit record. Some creditors won't wait until they have exhausted their phone calls and letters to report your account to a credit bureau. These creditors report your default as soon as it becomes obvious (to them) that you aren't planning to pay—that is, after you ignore one letter or call. And if they really want the money, they'll turn your account over to a collection agency.

An increasing number of collectors working for original creditors are abandoning the standard letter/phone call tactic if it is obvious early on that it won't work. Instead, these collectors contact debtors and encourage them to call a toll-free number to set up a repayment plan.

2. How to Respond

When the first overdue notice arrives, your first response may be to throw it away. And if the letter is from a creditor whose debt is on your "nonessential"

debt list (Chapter 5), throwing it away may be your best alternative. Remember, however, that the original creditor won't end its collection efforts with that first letter. Assuming the debt is one you want to pay, but you need a little more time, you're better off writing or calling the creditor and asking for an extension. And if you got a message to call an 800 number and work out a repayment, by all means call back if you can squeeze out a small amount each month and still pay your essential debts.

⚠ Beware of "Urgency-Payment" Suggestions.
If your bill is seriously past due (90 days or more) and you've just agreed to a send a bill collector some money, don't be surprised if he urges you to waste no time. Here are some suggestions the collector may make.

- Send the check by express or overnight mail.
- Wire the money, using Western Union's Quick Collect or American Express's Moneygram.
- Put the payment on a credit or charge card. (If you're having debt problems, the last thing you need to do is incur more debt.)
- Have a bank wire the money.
- Visit the creditor directly and bring the payment.
- The collector will come out to your home to pick up the check.

Your best bet is to resist all urgency suggestions. Many will cost you money (using express or overnight mail, or wiring the money) or time (visiting the collector in person), or are unnecessary incursions into your private life (the collector visiting you in person).

When you get in touch with the collector, you will need to explain your problem, and if possible, suggest an approximate date when you expect to be able to make full payments. Don't give a work phone number unless the creditor already knows where you work and you don't mind calls at your job.

Sending a partial, even token, payment will show that you are earnestly trying to pay. It is not essential, however, especially if it will keep you from paying priority debts. A sample letter asking for more time is below.

Sample Letter Asking for More Time

Collections Department
Rease's Department Store
5151 South Keetchum Place
Chicago, IL 60600

April 18, 20xx

Re: Amy Jones
    Account No. 1294-444-38RD

To Whom It May Concern:

I've received your notice indicating that my account is overdue.

I would like to pay, but a family emergency has prevented me from doing so. My daughter was in a severe automobile accident. She is unable to go to school and I have had to take time off to care for her.

My financial situation will improve in the near future. I will be returning to work in a few weeks and I expect to be able to pay you on July 1, 20xx.

Thank you for your consideration in this matter. If you wish to speak to me, please feel free to call me at my home at (312) 555-9333.

Sincerely,

Amy Jones

Amy Jones

If the creditor rejects your proposal or wants more evidence that you are genuinely unable to pay, consider asking a debt counselor to intervene on your behalf. (See Chapter 20, Section C.) Or, if the debt is quite large, or one of many debts, consider hiring a lawyer to write a second letter asking for additional time. (This is also covered in Chapter 20.) The lawyer won't say anything different than you would, but a lawyer's stationery carries clout. Yes, this will cost some money, but it may be worth it. When a creditor learns that a lawyer is in the picture, the creditor often suspects that you'll file for bankruptcy if he isn't accommodating. So you can often save more in payments than the lawyer costs.

C. When Your Debt Is Sent to a Collection Agency

If you ignore the original creditor's letters and phone calls, or you set up a repayment schedule but fail to make the payments, your bill will most likely be turned over to a collection agency and your delinquency reported to a credit bureau. This will probably take place about four months after you default. By taking some time to understand how collection agencies operate, you'll know how to respond when they contact you so that you can negotiate a payment plan or get the agency off your back.

First, if a collection agency has been hired by an original creditor, it generally must take its cues from the creditor. It can't sue you without the original creditor's authorization. If the original creditor insists that the agency collect 100% of the debt, the agency cannot accept less from you. Before accepting a reduced amount, the collection agency must get the original creditor's okay, or you'll have to contact the original creditor yourself. In recent years, however, original creditors have been giving collection agencies more discretion. Some are authorized to settle a debt for only 75%. Others can decide to drop collection efforts altogether, if it's unlikely the debtor will pay.

Second, you can expect to hear from a collection agency as soon as the original creditor passes on your debt. Professional debt collectors know that the earlier they strike, the higher their chance of collecting.

Third, bill collecting is a serious—and lucrative—business. Collection agents are good at what they do. Some earn well in excess of $100,000 per year. Others pay their collectors meager wages—good collectors augment those wages with high commissions. But paying low wages generally leads to high turnover, low morale and general burnout. For you, it often means you'll be called by a stressed out, rude collector who doesn't care about his job and will often violate the law.

Fourth, a collection agency usually keeps between 10% and 60% of what it collects. The older the account, the higher the agency's fee. Sometimes, the agency charges per letter it writes or phone call it places—usually about 50¢ per letter or $1 per call. In that situation, the collection agencies will be quite aggressive in collecting.

Fifth, before a collection agency tries to collect, it evaluates its likelihood of success. It may carry thousands—or even tens of thousands—of delinquent accounts and must prioritize which ones to go after. If success looks likely, the agency will move full speed ahead. If the chances of finding you are low, the odds of collecting money from you are somewhere between slim and nil or your credit file shows that you've defaulted on 20 other accounts, the agency may give your debt low priority.

1. How Collection Agencies Find People

➡ If You Don't Need to Know How Collection Agencies Find Debtors. Before a collection agency can contact you, it must find you. If you've already been found, you can skip this section. If the agency hasn't found you, however, and you want some tips on minimizing the chances of being found, keep reading.

Collection agencies hunt people down using several possible resources. Some collection agencies use only one or two of the resources described below. Others use more, maybe even all of them. But even agencies that search diligently make mistakes. Most hire fairly low-paid clerks to collect and sift through mountains of data. These clerks can put information about other people into your file and information about you into other files, effectively losing you.

Just because a collection agency calls or writes to you, don't assume that it knows where you live, especially if you've moved since you transacted business with the original creditor. All the bill collector knows is that it mailed a letter or left a phone message that wasn't returned.

Here are the primary resources a collection agency uses to find people.

Information on your credit application. The original creditor provides the collection agency with the information on your credit application—address, phone number, employer, bank, credit references, nearest living relative and the like. If you've moved, someone listed on a credit application may know where you are.

Relatives, friends, employers and neighbors. Collection agents often call relatives, friends, employers or neighbors, posing as a friend or relative. However, the federal fair debt collection law limits these types of calls. For more information on what is legal and what isn't, see Section D.3.

Post office. The agency may check the post office for a forwarding address and is likely to examine several regional phone books. Also, major credit bureaus which have their own collection agencies receive change-of-address information for two million people each month from the U.S. Postal Service.

State motor vehicle department. The collector may contact your state's motor vehicle department in the event you reregistered your car. In most states, collectors can get this information for a few dollars, though a few states restrict motor vehicle records to only people with a legitimate reason for requesting the information. An original creditor collecting a court judgment may be considered to a have a legitimate business need, but a collection agency isn't.

Voter registration records. Some collection agents check voter registration records in the county of your last residence. If you've reregistered in the same county, the registrar will have your new address. If you've moved out of county and reregistered, your new county would have forwarded cancellation information to your old county, and the registrar may make that information available.

Utility companies. Although this process is difficult, an agency collector may be able to find you through the electric or phone company, especially if you are still in the same service area. Even if you move farther, the company may have your new address as a place to send your final bill.

Banks. If you move but leave your old bank account open—even if you don't still do business with the bank—the bank will probably have your new address and may provide it to a collection agency.

Credit bureaus. If a collection agency is associated with a credit bureau (see Chapter 18), the collection agency will have access to all kinds of information, such as your address, phone number, employer and credit history. Even if the collection agency isn't part of a credit bureau, for a small fee the collector can place your name on a credit bureau locate list. In theory at least, if you apply for credit—even if you've moved hundreds or thousands of miles from where you previously lived—your name will be forwarded to the collection agency.

Can a Collection Agency Get Government Records?

Social Security, unemployment, disability, census and other government records are not public documents, so bill collectors can't get them.

In most cases, collectors that try hard will be successful in finding you. Often, your energy is better spent getting your finances in order rather than hiding from a collection agency. Even so, there may be instances when you really don't want to be found. Here are a few tips to avoid detection by collection agencies:

- Don't reveal your new address, city or state (if you have moved) to anyone except a few trusted people.
- Keep your new phone number unlisted.
- Close your old bank accounts; open new ones at different banks.
- Don't apply for new credit.
- Screen your phone calls using caller ID. Be aware that some collection agencies block their own numbers from being displayed, knowing that curious people tend to pick up the phone when no number is displayed.

2. Asking That the Creditor Take Back the Debt

If you are ready to negotiate on a debt, you will probably be better off if the debt is with the creditor, not a collection agency. This is because the creditor has more discretion and flexibility in negotiating with you, and the creditor sees you as a former and possibly future customer. So ask the collector from the collection agency for the phone number of the collections department of the original creditor. Then call the creditor and ask if you can negotiate on the debt.

Here are the possible responses:

- The creditor immediately begins negotiations with you, takes the debt back from the collection agency, and keeps it as long as you make the agreed-upon payments. Only a few creditors will do this.
- The creditor rejects your proposal, but lets you know that if you negotiate with the collection agency, establish a repayment plan and make two or three payments under the plan, the creditor will take your debt back and eventually give you a new line of credit. This helps you

take care of your debt problems and begin to rebuild your credit. Many creditors will do this.

- The creditor rejects your proposal, but negotiates a payment plan with you and requires that its collection agency abide by the plan. A few creditors, including American Express, will do this.
- The creditor rejects your proposal and tells you that your only option is to negotiate with the collection agency. Some creditors will do this.

If You're the Cosigner of a Loan

When you cosign for a loan, you assume full responsibility for paying back the loan in the event the primary borrower defaults. In almost every state, the creditor can go after a cosigner without first trying to collect from the primary borrower. But most creditors try to collect first from the primary borrower, and if you've been contacted by a collection agency, you can assume that the primary debtor defaulted.

Your best bet is to pay the debt if you can (and save your credit rating) and then try to collect yourself from the primary debtor. For more information on cosigned debts, see Chapter 11, Section C5.

---

3. Negotiating With a Collection Agency

Although collection agencies must follow original creditors' instructions, few original creditors put significant restrictions on collection agencies. The original creditor has all but given up on you and will be thrilled if the collection agency can use legal means to collect anything. The collection agency knows you are having debt problems and have been evading your creditors.

a. Unsecured Debts

If the original creditor is flexible, it may be happy to accept a settlement below the full amount to avoid spending months futilely trying to collect the whole thing. As you negotiate, remember two key points:

- The collection agency didn't lend you the money or extend you credit initially. It doesn't care if you owe $250 or $2,500. It just wants to maximize its return, which is usually a percentage of what it collects.
- Time is money. Every time the collection agency writes or calls you, it spends money. The agency has a strong interest in getting you to pay as much as you can as fast as possible. It has less interest in collecting 100% over five years.

Before you contact a collection agency, review your debt priority plan. (See Chapter 5.) If you don't have the cash to make a realistic lump sum offer or to propose a payment plan, don't call—you may make promises you can't keep or give the agency more information than it already has.

1. Offering a Lump-Sum Settlement

If you decide to offer a lump sum, understand that no general rule applies to all collection agencies. Some want 75%–80%. Others will take 50¢ on the dollar. Those that have all but given up on you may settle for one-third of what you owe. Before you make an offer, however, decide your top amount and stick to it. Once the agency sees you will pay something, it will try to talk you into paying more. Don't agree to go any higher than what you can afford.

A collection agency will have more incentive to settle with you if you can pay all at once. If you owe $500 and offer $300 on the spot to settle the matter, the agency can take its fee, pay the balance to the original creditor (who takes as a business loss the amount you don't pay) and close its books.

If the collection agency agrees to settle a debt with you, ask the agency—as a condition of your paying—to have any negative information about the debt removed from your credit files. The collection agency will probably tell you that this is not its decision—that only the original creditor can remove the information. Ask for the name and phone number of the person with the original creditor who has authority to make this decision. Call that person and plead. Let her know that you are taking steps to repay your debts, clean up your credit and be more responsible. Emphasize that a clean credit report will help you achieve your goals. If she refuses, ask her why she is sabotaging your efforts.

2. Offering to Make Payments

If you offer to pay the debt in monthly installments, the agency has little incentive to compromise for less than the full amount. It still must chase you for payment, and experience tells that there's a good chance you'll stop paying after a month or two.

Before a collection agency considers accepting monthly installments, it may have you fill out asset, income and expense statements. These forms must be completed under penalty of perjury—meaning if you lie, you could be prosecuted for perjury, although that is highly unlikely. Nevertheless, if you default on the new agreement, the creditor sues you and you ask a court to knock off interest, late fees or other fees, or to let you pay in installments, the court will not treat you with favor if it knows that you previously lied to the creditor. Filling out these forms will give the collection agency much more information on you than it previously had, something you may want to avoid.

b. Secured Debts

As explained in Chapter 1, a secured debt guarantees repayment because the creditor has the right to take a specific item of property, called the collateral, such as a car or item of furniture. Secured creditors rarely hound you to pay back debts. They don't have to. As long as they comply with state or federal laws that require them to notify you that you are behind on your payments and then follow the proper repossession procedures, they can simply come and take your property.

Can you just give back the collateral and call it even? If you don't need or want the collateral, you can offer to give it back to the creditor or collection agency. They don't have to take it, however, and probably won't if the item has substantially decreased in value or is hard to sell.

Even if the creditor or collection agency takes the property back, in most states you'll be liable for the difference between what you owe and what the creditor is able to sell the property for. This difference is called a deficiency and, as explained in Chapter 8, is often reason enough to avoid having property repossessed.

If you can no longer afford to keep the property, your best strategy in many cases is to offer to give it back in exchange for a written agreement waiving any deficiency. If the creditor refuses, you may be better off trying to sell the item yourself and using the proceeds to pay your debts.

Exemptions won't help you. Chapter 17 covers exempt property—the property your creditors, including collection agencies, can't take even if you file for bankruptcy or get sued. There's one major exception to exempt property—collateral for a secured debt. You can't keep a creditor from repossessing the collateral just because it's exempt.

4. When the Collection Agency Gives Up

If all efforts by the collection agency fail, the agency is likely to send the bill back to the original creditor. The creditor and the collection agency will decide whether or not to pass your debt on to an attorney. No matter what the amount of the debt, before filing a lawsuit the creditor will consider the following:

- **The chances of winning.** Lawyers do not like to lose cases. Most debt collection lawsuits are filed only if they are a sure thing.
- **The chances of collecting.** If you are judgment proof and likely to stay that way (see Chapter 8, Section E), the creditor many not bother suing you.
- **The lawyer's fees.** The older or more difficult your debt will be to collect, the larger the lawyer's fee is likely to be. The creditor doesn't want to have to pay a lot to collect.

Negotiating Tips

- Be honest, but paint the bleakest possible picture of your finances. Explain illnesses and accidents, job layoffs, car repossessions, major back taxes that you owe and the like.

- If you are considering bankruptcy, say so. But be sure you don't incur any more debt after mentioning bankruptcy. If you do, you may not be able to discharge that new debt in your bankruptcy case.

- Never disclose where you work or bank. If you are asked, simply say "no comment"—this isn't the time to worry about being polite. If the collection agency or original creditor later sues you and gets a judgment, knowing where you bank or work will make it easy to collect the judgment.

- If you do make a payment, don't send a check from your bank—get a money order or cashier's check from a different bank or the post office.

- If you're thinking of hiring a lawyer, remember that while a lawyer can carry clout, is probably experienced at negotiating and can convincingly mention bankruptcy, a lawyer costs money. Don't hire one unless you owe a lot and the lawyer has a realistic chance of negotiating a favorable settlement, such as getting a debt reduced to $5,000 from $10,000. After all, if the amount you pay the collection agency and the lawyer totals what you originally owed, you should have just sent the full amount to the collection agency. Also, make sure the lawyer states his fee and doesn't charge more, or you could have one more creditor at your door.

- If you're contacted by more than one collection agency for the same debt, it means the creditor has hired a secondary or even tertiary collection agency. The original creditor and at least one collection agency have given up on you. A collection agency that agrees to take your debt at this time will insist that the original creditor pay a generous fee (usually 50%–60% of what's recovered) and give the agency substantial freedom in negotiating with you. At this point, you can probably settle the bill for far less than you owe. Many secondary and tertiary agencies will take 33¢–50¢ on the dollar. If the agency hasn't been able to reach you by phone but knows that you are receiving its letters, it may even settle for less.

- If the collection agency agrees to settle for less than you owe, be sure it also agrees to indicate "satisfied in full" in your credit report.

- If a debt collector agrees to settle with you for far less than you owe, be sure the deal makes financial sense. Depending on the type of creditor and amount of the debt, you may owe income taxes on the amount waived. See Chapter 5, Section G.

- **If you recently filed for Chapter 7 bankruptcy.** You can't file more than once every six years. If you filed recently, you won't be able to discharge the debt in another Chapter 7 bankruptcy and are a good lawsuit target. Even if you were to file for Chapter 13 bankruptcy, the court would require you to pay back part or all of the debt.
- **The relationship of the lawyer and the creditor.** Sometimes, a lawyer will take small debts along with several large ones to stay in good with the creditor.

If you are sued, the plaintiff (the company suing you) in the court papers will be the original creditor, the collection agency or both. If only the collection agency is named, you may have difficulty figuring out who the original creditor is. For this reason, most collection lawsuits are filed in the name of the original creditor or both the original creditor and the collection agency.

If You Are Sued, Go to Chapter 15. If you ignore any lawsuit, the creditor will quickly get a judgment against you and probably garnish up to 25% of your wages each pay period. If you're not working, you risk having your bank accounts emptied and a lien recorded against your real property. This isn't the time to bury your head in the sand.

D. Debt Collection Practices— Legal and Illegal

The federal Fair Debt Collections Practices Act (FDCPA) requires that a collection agency bill collector make certain disclosures, and also prohibits the collector from engaging in many kinds of abusive or deceptive behavior. (15 U.S.C. § 1692 et seq.) Most important, the FDCPA gives you the right to tell a collection agency bill collector to cease communicating with you.

Not All Creditors—and Debt Collectors—Are Created Equal

The Fair Debt Collection Practices Act applies when a collection agency is seeking to collect a debt, which is defined as an obligation of a consumer to pay money arising out of a transaction which is primarily for personal, family or household purposes. Nothing in the FDCPA requires that the creditor have originally extended credit to the debtor. Most, but not all, courts find that the FDCPA applies to debts that are not the result of an extension of credit, including:

- bounced checks
- payment of condominium and homeowner association fees
- medical bills
- utility bills; and
- judgments.

1. Required Disclosures by a Collection Agency

Normally, the collection agency bill collector's first letter gives you the following information. If it doesn't, by law she has five days from the initial letter to tell you:

- the amount of the debt
- the name of the original creditor
- that you have 30 days to dispute the validity of the debt, and
- that if you dispute the debt's validity, the agency will send you verification of it.

It's wise to request verification of the debt (it must be in writing). A collection agency bill collector cannot resume collection efforts until she double-checks the information on the debt with the original creditor. The results of this check may help you decide whether you have grounds to dispute the debt. Collection agencies and original creditors are busy. While verification may seem like it should take only a simple phone call, it often takes several weeks or months.

If you don't ask the collection agency for verification of the debt within 30 days of receiving the first collection letter, the agency can assume that the debt is valid. This doesn't mean you can't later challenge the collection of the debt, only that you no longer have this particular "automatic" right to verification.

In the first communication, the collection agency must state that it is trying to collect a debt and that any information collected will be used for that purpose. This is often referred to in the collections business as the "mini-Miranda" statement. In all subsequent communications, the collector need only state that the communication is coming from a collection agency.

Collection agencies' bill collectors usually provide the required communications, but often violate the FDCPA anyway through other statements. Often, the first letter states that it is an effort to collect a debt and that you have 30 days to dispute the debt's validity. Then the text of the letter demands payment, usually immediately, or threatens that if payment is not received immediately, the debt will be reported as delinquent to credit bureaus, and that you may be sued. Many courts have held that this kind of statement effectively overshadows or contradicts the debtor's right to dispute the debt for 30 days and therefore violates the FDCPA. (See, for example, *Swanson v. Southern Oregon Credit Services, Inc.*, 869 F.2d 1222 (1988); *Veillard v. Mednick*, 24 F. Supp. 2d 863 (N.D. Ill. 1998).) In such a situation, you are entitled to damages against the agency if you sue. Many cases settle, with the debt erased or greatly reduced in exchange for the debtor dropping his FDCPA violation claim.

2. Actions Debtors Can Take

Your most powerful weapon against a collection agency bill collector is your right to tell her to leave you alone, whether you owe the debt or not. In writing, simply tell her to cease all communications with you. She must do this, except to tell you that:

- collection efforts against you have ended, or
- the collection agency or the original creditor may invoke a specific remedy against you, such as suing you.

Furthermore, if the collection agency bill collector does contact you to tell you that the agency intends to invoke a specific remedy, the agency must truly intend to do so. She cannot simply write to you four times saying "we're going to sue you."

Below is a sample letter you can use to get a collection agency off your back. Although it is not required, you might also want to tell the collector why you are in financial trouble. Be brief. If you are judgment proof, which means you don't have anything that the agency can legally take from you (see Chapter 17 for more on this), you should let the collector know that. If the collection agency knows it can't get anything from you, it is less likely to sue you.

Sample Letter to Collection Agency to Tell It to Cease Contacting You

Sasnak Collection Service
49 Pirate Place
Topeka, Kansas 69000

November 11, 20xx

Attn: Marc Mist

Re: Lee Anne Ito
    Account No. 88-90-92

Dear Mr. Mist:

For the past three months, I have received several phone calls and letters from you concerning my overdue Rich's Department Store account. As I have informed you, I cannot pay this bill.

Accordingly, under 15 U.S.C. § 1692c, this is my formal notice to you to cease all further communications with me except for the reasons specifically set forth in the federal law.

This letter is not meant in any way to be an acknowledgment that I owe this money. I will take care of this matter when I can.

Very truly yours,

Lee Anne Ito
Lee Anne Ito

3. Prohibited Collection Agency Actions

Below are some collection actions prohibited by the FDCPA.

Communications with third parties. For the most part, a collection agency cannot contact third parties about your debt. There are a few exceptions to this general rule. Collectors are allowed to contact:

- Your attorney. If the collector knows you are represented by an attorney, it must only talk to the attorney, not you, unless you give it permission to contact you or your attorney doesn't respond to the agency's communications.
- A credit reporting agency, or
- The original creditor.

Collectors are also allowed to contact your spouse, your parents (only if you are a minor) and your codebtors. But they cannot make these contacts if you have sent a letter asking them to stop contacting you.

There is one other exception. Debt collectors are allowed to contact third parties for the limited purpose of finding information about your whereabouts. In these contacts, the collector:

- must state his name and that he is confirming location information about you
- cannot state his employer's name unless asked
- cannot state that you owe a debt
- cannot contact a third party more than once unless required to do so by the third party, or unless he believes the third party's earlier response was wrong or incomplete and that the third party has correct or complete information
- cannot communicate by post card
- cannot use any words or symbols on the outside of an envelope that indicate he's trying to collect a debt (including a business logo or letterhead) if either would give away the purpose of the letter, and
- cannot call third parties for location information once he knows an attorney represents you.

Communications with a debtor. As mentioned above, a collection agency bill collector must state that the communication is an effort to collect a debt. In addition, he cannot contact you:

- at an unusual or inconvenient time or place—calls before 8 a.m. and after 9 p.m. are presumed to be inconvenient (but, if you work nights and sleep during the day, a call at 1 p.m. may also be inconvenient)
- directly, if he knows or should have known that you have an attorney, or
- at work if he knows that your employer prohibits you from receiving collections calls at work—if you are contacted at work, tell the collector that your boss prohibits such calls.

Harassment or abuse. In general a collection agency cannot engage in conduct meant to harass, oppress or abuse. Specifically, it cannot:

- use or threaten to use violence
- harm or threaten to harm you, another person or your or another person's reputation or property
- use obscene or profane language
- publish your name as a person who doesn't pay bills (child support collection agencies are exempt from this—see Chapter 14, Section D5,
- list your debt for sale to the public
- call you repeatedly, or

- place telephone calls to you without identifying himself as a bill collector.

False or misleading representations. A collection agency bill collector can't lie. For example, he can't:

- claim to be a law enforcement officer or suggest that he is connected with the federal, state or local government (anyone making this kind of claim is probably lying, unless he is trying to collect child support)
- falsely represent the amount you owe or the amount of compensation he will receive
- claim to be an attorney or that a communication is from an attorney
- claim that you'll be imprisoned or your property will be seized, unless the collection agency or original creditor intends to take action that could result in your going to jail or your property being taken (you can go to jail only for extremely limited reasons—see Chapter 8, Section G)
- threaten to take action that isn't intended or can't be taken—for example, if a letter from a collection agency bill collector states that it is a "final notice," he cannot write you again demanding payment
- falsely claim you've committed a crime
- threaten to sell a debt to a third party, and claim that as a result, you will lose defenses to payment you had against the creditor (such as a breach of warranty)
- communicate false credit information, such as failing to state that you dispute a debt
- send you a document that looks like it's from a court or attorney or part of a legal process.
- use a false business name, or
- claim to be employed by a credit bureau, unless the collection agency and the credit bureau are the same company.

Unfair practices. A collection agency bill collector cannot engage in any unfair or outrageous method to collect a debt. Specifically, he can't:

- add interest, fees or charges not authorized in the original agreement or by state law
- accept a check postdated by more than five days unless he notifies you between three and ten days in advance of when he will deposit it

- deposit a postdated check prior to the date on the check
- solicit a postdated check by threatening you with criminal prosecution
- call you collect or otherwise cause you to incur communications charges
- threaten to seize or repossess your property if he has no right to do so or no intention of doing so
- communicate with you by postcard, or
- put any words or symbols on the outside of an envelope sent to you that indicates he's trying to collect a debt.

4. If a Collection Agency Bill Collector Violates the Law

More than a few collection agencies engage in illegal practices when attempting to collect debts. Here are some of the more atrocious acts collection agency bill collectors have committed:

- Sending debtors fake legal papers and then pretending to be sheriffs. They tell debtors to pay immediately or threaten that the debtors will lose their personal possessions.
- Using vulgarity and profanity to threaten debtors.
- Harassing a debtor's parents—in particular, impersonating a government prosecutor before the parent and requesting that the parent ask the debtor to contact the collector.
- Soliciting a postdated check, depositing early and threatening the debtor with prosecution for writing a bad check.
- Suggesting that a debtor take up prostitution to increase income.
- Threatening to report Latino and Asian debtors to the Immigration and Naturalization Service and posing as INS officers.
- Engaging in repeated violations of the law—such as verbal harassment, late night calls and calls to neighbors and friends—especially at the end of each month when collectors are trying to reach their monthly collection quotas.

If a collection agency bill collector violates the law—be it a large or small violation—try to collect

Interest Rate a Collection Agency Can Charge Before Getting a Judgment

This chart gives the interest rates set by state law for situations where the contract or agreement does not set an interest rate. If a contract or agreement does set an interest rate, then that is the one the collection agency can charge, even if it is different from the state rate.

State	Code Section	Rate
Alabama	Ala. Code. § 8-8-1	6%
Alaska	Alaska Stat. § 45.45.010	10.50%
Arizona	Ariz. Rev. Stat. § 44-1201	10%
Arkansas	Ark. Const. Art. 19, § 13(d)(i)	6%
California	Calif. Civil Code § 3289	10%
Colorado	Colo. Rev. Stat. § 5-12-101	8%
Connecticut	Conn. Gen. Stat. § 37-1	8%
Delaware	Del. Code Ann. tit. 6, § 2301	5% above the Federal Reserve discount rate at the time interest is due (www.federalreserve.gov/releases/h15)
District of Columbia	D.C. Code Ann. § 28-3301	6%
Florida	Fla. Stat. Ann. §§ 687.01; 55.03	5% above average Federal Reserve Bank of N.Y. discount rate for preceding year (www.dbf/state/fl.us/interest.html)
Georgia	Ga. Code Ann. §§ 7-4-2, 7-4-18	7%
Hawaii	Haw. Rev. Stat. § 478-2	10%
Idaho	Idaho Code § 28-22-104	12%
Illinois	815 Ill. Comp. Stat. §§ 205/1, 2	5%
Indiana	Ind. Code Ann. § 24-4.6-1-102	8%
Iowa	Iowa Code Ann. § 535.2	5%
Kansas	Kan. Stat. Ann. § 16-201	10%
Kentucky	Ky. Rev. Stat. Ann. § 360.010	8%
Louisiana	La. Civ. Code Art. 2924(c)	12% maximum; must be in writing.
Maine	Me. Rev. Stat. Ann. tit. , § 9A-2-401	$5 on loans up to $75; $15 on loans over $75 and under $250; and $25 on loans of $250 or more.
Maryland	Md. Const. Art. 3, § 57; Md. Code Ann. [Com. Law.] § 12-102	6%
Massachusetts	Mass. Gen. Laws ch. 107, § 3	6%
Michigan	Mich. Comp. Laws § 438.31	5%
Minnesota	Minn. Stat. Ann. § 334.01 (Subd. 1)	6%

Interest Rate a Collection Agency Can Charge Before Getting a Judgment

State	Code Section	Rate
Mississippi	Miss. Code Ann. § 75-17-1 (1)	8%
Missouri	Mo. Rev. Stat. § 408.020	9%
Montana	Mont. Code Ann. § 31-1-106	10%
Nebraska	Neb. Rev. Stat. § 45-102	6%
Nevada	Nev. Rev. Stat. § 99.040	2% above the prime rate at Nevada's largest bank on January 1 or July 1 (www.fid.state.nv.us/ prime%20int.htm)
New Hampshire	N.H. Rev. Stat. Ann. § 336:1(l)	10%
New Jersey	N.J. Stat. Ann. § 31:1-1(a)	6%
New Mexico	N.M. Rev Stat. Ann. § 56-8-3	15%
New York	N.Y. Gen. Oblig. Law § 5-501 (1)	6%
North Carolina	N.C. Gen. Stat. § 24-1	8%
North Dakota	N.D. Cent. Code § 47-14-05	6%
Ohio	Ohio Rev. Code Ann. § 1343.03(A)	10%
Oklahoma	Okla. Const. Art. 14, § 2; Okla. Stat. Ann. tit. 15, § 266	6%
Oregon	Or. Rev. Stat. § 82.010(1)	9%
Pennsylvania	41 Pa. Cons. Stat. § 202	6%
Rhode Island	R.I. Gen. Laws § 6-26-1	12%
South Carolina	S.C. Code Ann. § 34-31-20	8.75%
South Dakota	S.D. Codified Laws Ann. §§ 54-3-4, 54-3-16(3)	12%
Tennessee	Tenn. Code Ann. § 47-14-103(3)	10%
Texas	Tex. Fin. Code Ann. § 302.002	6%
Utah	Utah Code Ann. § 15-1-1	10%
Vermont	Vt. Stat. Ann. tit. 9, § 41a(a)	12%
Virginia	Va. Code Ann. § 6.1-330.53	8%
Washington	Wash. Rev. Code Ann. § 19.52.010(1)	12%
West Virginia	W. Va. Code Ann. § 47-6-5(a)	6%
Wisconsin	Wis. Stat. § 138.04	5%
Wyoming	Wyo. Stat. Ann. § 40-14-106(e)	7%

proof of the violation. Written threats are the best proof, but collectors usually know better than to threaten you in writing. Another effective way to collect evidence is to keep a written log of all calls you get from the agency. Write down the agent's name, date and time of call and any information you remember about what the collection agent told you. In some states, you can tape the conversation without the collector's knowledge. Only do this if you are sure it's legal. To find out, you'll have to do some legal research on your own (see Chapter 20 to learn more about legal research). If it's not legal to do this in your state (or you aren't sure), try to have a witness present during your conversations. If you're loud enough about the abuse you suffered—and you've got proof backing you up—you have a chance to get the whole debt canceled in exchange for shutting up.

To complain, contact the Federal Trade Commission (see Chapter 12, Section F, for the address). Also complain to the state agency that regulates collection agencies for the state where the agency is located. (See "State Consumer Protection Offices" in Chapter 20, Section A.1)

The Federal Trade Commission or the state agency may send you a form to help it process your complaint. Be thorough. Include dates, times and the names of any witnesses to unlawful conversations, and attach copies (keep the originals for yourself) of all offending materials you received.

Also, write to the original creditor and send a copy of this letter to the collection agency, the Federal Trade Commission and the state agency. The original creditor may be concerned about its own liability and offer to cancel the debt at once.

Sample Letter to Original Creditor

Stonecutter Furniture Factory
4500 Wilson Boulevard
Bloomington, IN 47400

April 19, 20xx

Dear Stonecutter:

On May 10, 20xx, I purchased a bedroom set from you for $2,000 ($500 down and the rest at $100 per month). I paid $900 and then lost my job and became ill, and was unable to pay you.

In early 20xx, I was contacted by R. Greene at the Drone Collection Agency. R. Greene called me twice a day for nearly three weeks, used profanity at me, my husband, and my 11-year-old son. In addition, he called my father and threatened him with a lawsuit, even though he is a 76-year-old diabetic with a heart condition and has had no connection with this transaction.

I have contacted the Federal Trade Commission and I am considering seeing an attorney. I am fully prepared to take the steps necessary to protect myself and my family from further harassment. I am writing you in the hope that you have not condoned Drone's practices and can do something to help me.

Very truly yours,

Karen Wood

Karen Wood

cc: Indiana Secretary of State
      Drone Collection Agency
      Federal Trade Commission

You also have the right to sue a collection agency for harassment. You can represent yourself in small claims court or hire an attorney. Attorney fees and court costs are recoverable if you win. You're entitled to any actual damages, including pain and suffering. And, even if you did not suffer any actual damages, you can still recover up to $1,000 for any violation of the FDCPA. You might also be able to

get punitive damages if the collectors' conduct was particularly horrible. But, if you can't document repeated abusive behavior, you'll probably have a tough time winning. For example, if the collector calls five times in one day and then you never hear from him again, you'll probably lose in court.

In truly outrageous cases, consider hiring a lawyer to represent you in regular court. You might especially choose this route if the mental abuse inflicted on you is substantial and you have reports from therapists and doctors documenting your suffering. In 1995, a Texas jury awarded $11 million (this amount was later reduced by an appellate court) to a debtor and her spouse against both a collection agency and creditor after the collection agency called the debtor repeatedly at home and work, and made death threats and bomb threats. The debtor, fearing for her and her husband's safety, moved out of town. (*Driscol v. Allied Adjustment Bureau*, Docket #92-7267 (El Paso, Texas, 1995).)

In addition to bringing a lawsuit against a collector, you can also raise FDCPA violations in a collection lawsuit brought against you by a creditor or collection agency. These are called "counterclaims." See Chapter 15, Section D, for more on counterclaims.

5. State or Local Laws Prohibiting Unfair Debt Collections

Several states have enacted laws prohibiting unfair debt collection practices. A few laws are similar to the federal legislation. Some, however, prohibit additional collection actions. The most valuable prohibit unethical and abusive collection practices by collection agencies and original creditors—remember, the federal law applies only to collection agencies. The specific state laws are described in the chart, below.

State Debt Collection Laws Providing Additional Protections

State	Code Section	Summary
Arizona	Ariz. Admin. Code § R20-4-1512	Collection agency cannot contact debtor at work unless agency has made reasonable attempt to contact debtor at home and such attempt has failed.
	§ R20-4-1514	In the first contact, collection agency must disclose name of original creditor, time and place debt was incurred, merchandise or service purchased and date account was turned over to agency. Debtor has right to see agency's books and records concerning debt and right to copies of all relevant documents in agency's possession.
Arkansas	Ark. Code Ann. § 17-24-307(12)	Collection agency cannot send mail or telephone debtor at work unless agency has made good faith attempt to contact debtor at home and such attempt has failed.
California	Calif. Civil Code §§ 1788.10 to .17	Creditor collecting own debt must comply with all provisions of the Fair Debt Collection Practices Act (FDCPA), except those outlined in Section D.1, above.
Colorado	Colo. Rev. Stat. § 12-14-106(f)	Collection agency collector must identify self within first 60 seconds after the party answering the telephone is identified as debtor.
	§ 12-14-105(3)	Collection agency must notify debtor in writing in its initial communication that debtor has right to: • request that collection agency not contact debtor at home or at work • refuse to pay debt • request that agency cease all communication with debtor.
	4 Colo. Code Regs. § 903-1 (Rule 2.05)	Collection agency must provide debtor with receipt for payments made in cash or by any other means which does not provide evidence of payment. (Check drawn on debtor's bank account would not require receipt.) Receipt must be provided within five days after payment is received (Sundays and holidays excluded).
	(Rule 2.06)	If debtor requests in writing, collection agency must provide at no cost, once per year, statement of up to 12 months' payments within ten days of request. Statement must include debtor's name, creditor's name, amounts paid, dates payments were received, allocation of money to principal, interest, court costs, attorneys' fees and other costs. Collection agency may charge no more than $5 for subsequent statements.
Connecticut	Conn. Gen. Stat. § 36a-646	Creditor collecting own debt cannot use abusive, harassing, fraudulent, deceptive or misleading practices to collect debt.
	§ 36a-801	Individuals or businesses collecting child support debt are subject to the same rules as collection agencies.
District of Columbia	D.C. Code Ann. § 28-3814	Actions prohibited under the FDCPA, outlined in Section D.3, above, apply to creditor collecting own debt.
	§ 22-3401	Collection agency may not use "D.C." or "District of Columbia" in any way that would imply that it is an agency of the government.
Florida	Fla. Stat. Ann. §§ 559.72	Creditor collecting own debt cannot use collection practices prohibited by the FDCPA, as outlined in Section D.3, above.

State Debt Collection Laws Providing Additional Protections (continued)

State	Code Section	Summary
Florida (continued)		In addition, creditor collecting own debt and debt collector cannot: • communicate with debtor's employer before a judgment is obtained unless debtor consents • include the debtor in a "deadbeat" list.
Georgia	Ga. Code Ann. § 7-3-25(5)	Collection agency cannot contact debtor by phone or in person after 10 p.m. or before 5 a.m.
	Ga. Comp. R. & Regs. R. 120-1-14.23(c)	Collection agency cannot attempt to lure debtor into giving information by claiming it has something of value to offer debtor.
	R. 120-1-14.24	Collection agency cannot seek or obtain statement in which debtor agrees: • to pay debt discharged in bankruptcy without clearly disclosing nature and consequence of agreement and fact that debtor is not legally obligated to pay debt • that debt was incurred to pay for necessaries of life when debt was not for that purpose.
Hawaii	Haw. Rev. Stat. Ann. § 443B-19	Collection agency cannot seek or obtain statement in which debtor agrees: • that debt was incurred to pay for necessaries of life when debt was not for that purpose • to pay debt discharged in bankruptcy without clearly disclosing nature and consequence of agreement and fact that debtor is not legally obligated to pay debt • to pay collection agency's fee.
	§ 480D-3	Creditor collecting own debt cannot use collection practices prohibited by the FDCPA, as outlined in Section D.3, above. In addition, creditor collecting own debt and debt collector cannot: • threaten to hire collector who will violate the law • threaten to sell debt to third party, and claim that as a result, debtor will lose defenses to payment debtor had against creditor (such as breach of warranty) • seek or obtain statement in which debtor agrees that the debt was incurred to pay for necessaries of life when debt was not incurred for that purpose • collect or attempt to collect interest or other charges unless authorized by contract or by law.
Idaho	Idaho Code § 26-2229A(2)	If collection agency and creditor have a financial or a managerial interest in the other, that information must be disclosed to the debtor in every communication.
	§ 28-45-109	Creditor collecting own debt cannot use or threaten to use violence or other criminal means to cause harm to the debtor's person, reputation or property.
Illinois	225 Ill. Comp. Stat. § 425/9(14)(19)	Collection agency cannot contact or threaten to contact debtor's employer unless debt is more than 30 days past due; at least five days before contacting employer, agency must notify debtor in writing that it intends to do so. Collection agency cannot engage in conduct which

State Debt Collection Laws Providing Additional Protections (continued)

State	Code Section	Summary
Illinois (continued)		is intended to cause and does cause mental or physical illness to debtor or debtor's family.
	815 Ill. Comp. Stat. § 505/21	Creditor collecting own debt is subject to the same prohibition about contacting debtor's employer (see above).
Indiana	Ind. Code Ann. § 24-4.5-5-107(1)	Creditor collecting own debt cannot use or threaten to use violence or other criminal means to cause harm to the debtor's person, reputation or property.
Iowa	Iowa Code § 537.7103	Creditor collecting own debt cannot use collection practices prohibited by the FDCPA, as outlined in Section D.3, above. In addition, creditor collecting own debt and debt collector cannot: • disseminate information relating to debt to third persons (other than credit bureaus, attorneys and others who may have location information; also, may contact debtor's employer once a month to verify debtor's employment; once every three months may contact debtor's employer or credit union to pass on debt counseling information to debtor; may contact parents of minor debtor or trustee, conservator or guardian of debtor) • include debtor in "deadbeat" list • fail to state name and address of business originally owed money • obtain statement that both husband and wife are liable on debt when only one is • seek or obtain statement in which debtor agrees to pay debt discharged in bankruptcy without clearly disclosing nature and consequence of agreement and fact that debtor is not legally obligated to pay the debt • attempt to collect collection agency's fee • collect or attempt to collect interest or other charges unless authorized by contract or by law.
Kansas	Kan. Stat. Ann. § 16a-5-107(1)	Creditor collecting own debt cannot use or threaten to use violence or other criminal means to cause harm to the debtor's person, reputation or property.
Louisiana	La. Rev. Stat. Ann. § 9:3562	Creditor collecting own debt cannot contact any person not residing in debtor's household other than another creditor or credit bureau, except: • to ascertain location information if creditor believes debtor has moved or changed jobs • to discover property owned by debtor which may be seized to satisfy debt. If debtor has told creditor to cease communicating with debtor, creditor may mail notices to debtor once a month as long as they are not designed to threaten action. Creditor may make four personal contacts with debtor in attempt to settle debt. Creditor may resume contacts if creditor has obtained a judgment against debtor.
Maine	Me. Rev. Stat. Ann. tit. 9-A, § 5-116	Creditor collecting own debt cannot: • threaten or use violence or force • threaten criminal prosecution • disclose information about debt to third persons other than debtor's spouse or person who has a business need for information

State Debt Collection Laws Providing Additional Protections (continued)

State	Code Section	Summary
Maine (continued)		• fail to state to third persons that debtor disputes debt • simulate legal process or government agency • communicate or threaten to communicate with debtor's employer more than twice concerning existence of debt • attempt to collect debt that is legally uncollectable.
	Me. Rev. Stat. Ann. tit. 32, § 11013	Maine has been granted an exemption from the FDCPA. Most of the state law is the same as the FDCPA. Additional laws provide that collection agency cannot: • use shame cards, shame automobiles or similar devices to bring public notice that debtor has not paid debt • falsely state that account was sold to third persons • use notary public, constable, sheriff or other person authorized to serve legal papers to collect debt • hire attorney to collect debt unless authorized to do so by creditor.
Maryland	Md. Code Ann. [Com. Law] § 14-202	Creditor collecting own debt cannot use collection practices prohibited by the FDCPA, as outlined in Section D.3, above. In addition, creditor collecting own debt and debt collector cannot contact debtor's employer before obtaining a court judgment.
Massachusetts	Mass. Gen. Laws ch. 93, § 49	Creditor collecting own debt cannot use collection practices prohibited by the FDCPA, as outlined in Section D.3, above.
	Mass. Regs. Code tit. 209, § 18.09	If debtor sends collection agency more than amount due, excess of $1 or more must be refunded to debtor within 30 days after last day of month in which excess was created.
	§ 18.13	Collection agency must include phone number and office hours on all communications.
	§ 18.15	Collection agency cannot: • communicate with debtor on phone at debtor's home more than twice in a seven-day period or at any location other than debtor's home more than twice in a 30-day period • visit debtor at home other than "normal waking hours," or if they are not known, before 8 a.m. and after 9 p.m. • visit and make contact with anyone at debtor's home more than once in a 30-day period, unless debtor consents in writing to more frequent visits • enter debtor's home unless expressly invited in • visit debtor's work except to repossess collateral or pick up property (including money) • confront debtor in any public place except courthouse, collection agency's office, debtor's attorney's office, place where conversation between collector and debtor cannot reasonably be overheard or any other place agreed to by debtor. Within 30 days after contacting debtor at work, agency must send debtor notice describing debtor's right not to be contacted at work. As long as debtor does not exercise right not to receive calls at work, agency must send notice every six months.
	§ 18.17(2)(b)	Collection agency cannot contact third party in order to find out debtor's current location more than once in any 12-month period.

State Debt Collection Laws Providing Additional Protections (continued)

State	Code Section	Summary
Massachusetts (continued)	§ 18.18(1)(8)	Collection agency cannot: • report information to credit bureau in its own name—must report debt information in name of original creditor • claim it has something of value in its possession to lure debtor.
	§ 18.19	Within five days of first contact with debtor, collection agency must provide debtor with: • name and mailing address of collection agency and creditor • description of debt • statement of alleged default • action required to cure default • name, address and telephone number of person to be contacted for more information.
Michigan	Mich. Comp. Laws § 339.915(m)(q)	Collection agency cannot: • use shame cards, shame automobiles or similar devices to bring public notice that debtor has not paid debt • fail to implement procedures designed to prevent law violations by agency employees
	§ 339.915a(d)(1)	Collection agency cannot: • hire an attorney to collect debt unless authorized by creditor • fail to provide debtor with receipt for cash payments and other payments when specifically requested.
	§ 445.252	Actions prohibited under the FDCPA, outlined in Section D.3, above, apply to creditor collecting own debt.
Minnesota	Minn. Stat. Ann. § 332.37	Collection agency cannot: • communicate in such a way to imply or suggest that health care services will be withheld from the debtor in an emergency • contact a neighbor or other third party (other than a person with whom the debtor lives) to request that the debtor contact the collector when a debtor has a listed telephone number • use shame cards or shame automobiles, advertise or threaten to advertise for sale any claim in order to force payment • transact business or hold itself out as a debt prorater or debt adjuster or someone who will pool, settle or pay the debtor's debts, unless there is no charge to the debtor, or the pooling or liquidation is done pursuant to court order • use an automatic recorded message unless, prior to the message, a live operator tells the debtor that the message is from the collection agency and is intended to solicit payment and gets the debtor's consent to hear the message • fail to provide the debtor with the full name of the collection agency • accept cash without providing a receipt to the debtor • during first mail contact, fail to include a disclosure stating: "This collection agency is licensed by the Minnesota Department of Commerce."
Nebraska	Neb. Rev. Stat. Ann.	Bank lender cannot contact person who does not live in debtor's home

State Debt Collection Laws Providing Additional Protections (continued)		
State	**Code Section**	**Summary**
Nebraska (continued)	§ 45-1043	regarding the debt except for debtor's spouse or attorney, another creditor or a credit bureau.
Nevada	Nev. Admin. Code ch. 649, § 050	Collection agency may not use machine-derived form letter unless it has received prior approval from the state.
New Hampshire	N.H. Rev. Stat. Ann § 358-C:3	Creditor collecting own debt cannot use collection practices prohibited by the FDCPA, as outlined in Section D.3, above. In addition, creditor collecting own debt and debt collector cannot: • communicate with third persons about debt except with others who live in debtor's household, an attorney, a financial counseling organization, another person claiming to represent debtor or a credit bureau • communicate with debtor's spouse, or parent or guardian if debtor is a minor, except to ascertain location information. However, collector must have been unable to locate debtor by any other means for at least 30 days, and collector must not attempt to contact spouse, parent or guardian again • call debtor at work more than once a month unless debtor agrees in writing to more frequent calls.
New York	N.Y. Gen. Bus. Law § 601	Creditor collecting own debt cannot use collection practices prohibited by the FDCPA, as outlined in Section D.3, above. In addition, creditor collecting own debt and debt collector cannot: • contact debtor's employer unless creditor has court judgment, or is seeking wage attachment, or debtor consents • attempt to enforce right collector knows does not exist.
New York City	Rules of the City of N.Y. Tit. 6, § 5-77	Creditor collecting own debt cannot use collection practices prohibited by the FDCPA, as outlined in Section D.3, above. In addition, creditor collecting own debt and debt collector cannot: • contact a third party more than once when trying to locate the debtor • fail to send written notice within five days of initial communication with debtor that states the amount of debt, to whom debt is owed, when debt is due and that the debtor has the right to dispute the validity of the debt • fail to respond in writing if the debtor disputes the validity of the debt • fail to end contact with debtor upon debtor's request (except that creditor can contact debtor one last time to advise debtor that it will invoke a specific remedy, such as bring a lawsuit).
North Carolina	N.C. Gen. Stat. § 58-70-70	Collection agency must provide debtor with receipt for all payments made in cash. Receipt must include name, address and permit number of collection agency, name of creditor, amount and date paid and name of person accepting payment.
	§ 58-70-110(3)	Collection agency cannot claim it has something of value in its possession to lure debtor.
	§ 75-70-115	Collection agency cannot seek or obtain statement in which debtor agrees to: • pay debt discharged in bankruptcy

State Debt Collection Laws Providing Additional Protections (continued)

State	Code Section	Summary
North Carolina (continued)		• pay debt barred by statute of limitations • pay collection agency's fee.
	§§ 75-51 to 55	Creditor collecting own debt cannot use collection practices prohibited by the FDCPA, as outlined in Section D.3, above. In addition, creditor collecting own debt and debt collector cannot: • contact debtor's employer, against debtor's express desire, unless collector does not have phone number to reach debtor during nonworking hours • communicate with third persons other than debtor's attorney unless debtor consents or third person is credit bureau, debt collector or collection agency, spouse of debtor or parent or guardian of minor debtor • claim it has something of value in its possession to lure debtor • seek or obtain statement in which debtor agrees to pay debt discharged in bankruptcy without disclosing nature and consequence of agreement and fact that debtor is not legally obligated to pay debt • sue debtor in county other than that where debt was incurred or debtor lives if distance makes it impractical for debtor to defend claim.
Oklahoma	Okla. Stat. Ann. tit. 14A, § 5-107(1)	Creditor collecting own debt cannot use or threaten to use violence or other criminal means to cause harm to the debtor's person, reputation or property.
Oregon	Or. Rev. Stat. § 646.639	Creditor collecting own debt cannot use collection practices prohibited by the FDCPA, as outlined in Section D.3, above.
Pennsylvania	73 Pa. Cons. Stat Ann § 2270.4	Actions prohibited under the FDCPA, outlined in Section D.3, above, apply to creditor collecting own debt.
South Carolina	S.C. Code Ann. §§ 37-5-107	Creditor collecting own debt cannot use or threaten to use violence or other criminal means to cause harm to the debtor's person, reputation or property.
	§ 37-5-108	Creditor collecting own debt cannot use collection practices prohibited by the FDCPA, as outlined in Section D.3, above. In addition, creditor collecting own debt and debt collector cannot communicate with the debtor or a family member at frequent intervals during a 24-hour period or under other circumstances that make it reasonable to infer that the primary purpose of the communication was to harass the debtor.
Tennessee	Tenn. Code Ann. § 62-20-111(b)	In all written communications collection agency must state that it is licensed by the state collection services board of the Department of Commerce.
Texas	Tex. Fin. Code Ann. §§ 392.303, 392.304(3)	Actions prohibited under the FDCPA, outlined in Section D.3, above, apply to creditor collecting own debt. In addition, collection agency and creditor collecting own debt cannot: • seek or obtain statement in which debtor agrees that debt was incurred to pay for necessaries of life when debt was not for that purpose

State Debt Collection Laws Providing Additional Protections (continued)

State	Code Section	Summary
Texas (continued)		• claim it has something of value in its possession to lure debtor.
Utah	Utah Code Ann. § 70C-7-105	Creditor collecting own debt cannot use or threaten to use violence or other criminal means to cause harm to the debtor's person, reputation or property.
Vermont	Vt. Consumer Fraud Rules CF 104.01 to 104.09	Creditor collecting own debt cannot use collection practices prohibited by the FDCPA, as outlined in Section D.3, above. In addition, debt collector and creditor collecting own debt cannot: • lure the debtor by claiming it has information or something of value in its possession • in the first demand for money, fail to disclose the name and address of the person to whom the claim has been assigned • seek or obtain an affirmation of a debt by a debtor who has received a discharge in bankruptcy, whose debt is barred by the statute of limitations or whose debt is otherwise not collectible, without clearly disclosing to debtor that he is not legally obligated to pay the debt.
Washington	Wash. Rev. Code Ann. § 19.16.250	In all written communications, collection agency must include name and address of agency and name of creditor. In first communication, collection agency must include an itemization showing: • amount owed on original obligation • interest, service charges, collection costs and late fees assessed by creditor • attorneys' fees • any other charges. Collection agency cannot: • threaten debtor with impairment of credit rating if claim is not paid • communicate with debtor more than three times in one week or communicate with debtor at work more than once per week. Collection agency cannot make more than one contact with debtor concerning debts that arise from dishonored checks or ATM transactions if debtor's checkbook was stolen or account information was obtained by fraud, as long as debtor has notified collection agency and sent certified copy of police report.
	Wash. Admin. Code §§ 308-29-070 to -080	Collection agency must disclose interest rate charged. If collection agency reports delinquent debt to credit bureau and debtor later pays, collection agency must notify credit bureau within 45 days that debt has been satisfied.
West Virgina	W. Va. Code Ann. § 46a-2-124 to 128	Actions prohibited under the FDCPA, outlined in Section D.3, above, apply to creditor collecting own debt. In addition, collection agency and creditor collecting own debt cannot: • communicate with debtor's employer before obtaining court judgment except through court process • communicate with relative of debtor other than those in debtor's household except through court process • claim it has something of value in its possession to lure debtor

State Debt Collection Laws Providing Additional Protections (continued)

State	Code Section	Summary
West Virgina (continued)		• seek or obtain statement in which debtor agrees that debt was incurred to pay for necessaries of life when debt was not incurred for that purpose • seek or obtain statement in which debtor agrees to pay debt discharged in bankruptcy without clearly disclosing nature and consequence of agreement and fact that debtor is not legally obligated to pay debt • attempt to collect collection agency's fee.
Wisconsin	Wis. Admin. Code Ch. DFI-Bkg 74.11	Within five days of first communication with debtor, collection agency must notify debtor, in bold face of at least eight-point type, of address of state agency regulating collection agencies.
	Wis. Stat. Ann. § 427.104	Creditor collecting own debt cannot use collection practices prohibited by the FDCPA, as outlined in Section D.3, above.
	§ 425.108(1)	Creditor collecting own debt cannot use or threaten to use violence or other criminal means to cause harm to the debtor's person, reputation or property.
Wyoming	Wyo. Stat. § 40-14-507(a)	Creditor collecting own debt cannot use or threaten to use violence or other criminal means to cause harm to the debtor's person, reputation or property. ■

CHAPTER

Credit, Charge and Debit Cards

Getting along with women,
Knocking around with men,
Having more credit than money,
Thus one goes through the world.

—Johann Wolfgang von Goethe, German poet
and dramatist, 1749-1832

In 1927, Farrington Manufacturing Company in Boston issued the first merchant charge card (it reportedly looked like a dog tag) to be used by American consumers. Following World War II, many more merchants offered charge cards to their customers. In 1950, 22 New York restaurants and one hotel agreed to honor a card to let their customers dine (or sleep) now and pay later. Little did they know that the industry started by their "Diner's Club" card would quickly became an indispensable part of our economy. By 1960, the Diner's Club card had about 1.1 million card holders, and was accepted in all kinds of retail establishments—not just New York restaurants.

Seeing the success of the Diner's Club card, a small number of banks offered credit cards during the 1950s. Few merchants accepted these cards, however, and it wasn't until Bank of America in San Francisco came out with the BankAmericard (now Visa) in 1966 that the idea caught on. East Coast banks quickly followed suit with a credit card that became known as the MasterCard.

Throughout the 1970s, '80s and '90s, the credit card industry grew beyond everyone's wildest expectations. Today, about three-quarters of all families in the United States have one or more credit cards. The average American holds about four retail, three bank, one phone, one gas and one travel and entertainment card (such as Diners Club). Over half of these consumers carry a balance on at least one of these cards.

As consumers are bombarded with more and more solicitations (credit card issuers send out nearly three and one-half billion solicitations each year), it has become increasingly difficult to understand the offers, choose the best deals and use the cards wisely. This chapter explains the key credit card agreement terms, provides tips on how to save money when using credit cards and summarizes laws that apply to credit card use.

A. Credit and Charge Cards

Credit cards can amount to nothing other than very expensive loans made by banks, gasoline companies and department stores. The cards on which you don't pay interest—American Express, Diner's Club and similar cards—are charge cards or travel and entertainment cards, not credit cards, but these can also cost you in the long run.

1. The Credit Card Industry

The way credit cards work is fairly straightforward. The credit card issuer gives you a card. You use the card to pay for items and services up to a certain total amount—your credit limit. The store merchant or service provider collects what you owe from the card issuer, whom you repay. You're allowed to pay off what you owe little-by-little each month, as long as you pay a minimum amount each time. You're charged interest on the balance you owe (sometimes as high as 26% a year) at the end of each period unless you pay the full balance when your bill arrives.

Credit cards yield high profits to their issuers for several reasons. The most important is the high rate of interest—interest on credit cards alone accounts for about 75% of the profits earned by banks that issue credit cards. Credit card companies often charge interest at rates of 20% or higher. The justification for these rates is hard to find. Consider this: banks that offer credit cards often borrow money at an interest rate of 1% to 2%, then turn around and charge interest rates of 20% or more to credit card customers. Some say the big credit card companies charge such high rates because they lack competition. Credit card companies say they must charge high rates in order to compensate for the many people who default on their accounts. Yet despite this claim, defaulted credit card accounts have decreased while profits have increased for most credit card companies. In fact, profits for credit card companies rose by 274% between 1995 and 1999. In addition, credit card companies continue to send out billions of solicitations each year, often to people with marginal credit histories.

In order to profit from high interest rates, the credit card industry is dependent on users who don't pay off their credit card balance each month. Those users are in the majority—between 40% and 60% of credit card users carry a balance of about $2,500 each month (compared to 20% in 1970). As a result, the ten largest card issuers usually earn income from interest alone in excess of $25 billion per year.

Interest is not the only source of profit. Many companies charge an annual fee for issuing a credit card, and most companies charge late fees, over-the-limit fees and other miscellaneous charges. In fact, the annual fee revenue for credit card companies is closing in on $20 billion, up nearly 20% since the early 1990s. Finally, the companies profit by charging merchants and service providers a fee each time a customer uses the company's credit card in the merchant's establishment.

More on the industry and credit card dependency. For an excellent analysis of consumer dependence on credit cards and the consequences, take a look at *Credit Card Nation*, by Robert D. Manning (Basic Books 2000).

2. How to Choose a Credit Card

You may be shopping for a new credit card, or perhaps you want to close all your existing accounts except one. Which card should you choose? Use these guidelines:

If you have more than one credit card account and plan to close all accounts but one, here's how to decide which one to keep. If you're delinquent on any account, close it—otherwise, the credit card issuer may close it for you. If you're delinquent on all your accounts, keep open the account you are least behind on. To close your account, send a letter to the customer service department of the card issuer stating that you wish to close your account, and further stating that your credit report should state "closed by consumer." It's also a good idea to cut up your card. You can do this even if you haven't paid off the balance—the card issuer will close your account, cancel your privileges and send you monthly statements until you pay off your balance.

Soft and Hard Closes

When you ask your credit card company to close your account and cancel your card, you assume that the issuer closes your account and cancels your card. Not so fast. It seems that credit card issuers often have two kinds of closes: soft closes and hard closes. If your card received only a soft close, it means that the issuer will reactivate the account and allow new charges to go through, even though you requested that the account be closed. Asked why they do this, issuers answer: "So that if you're in a store and accidentally try to pay with a card for which you closed the account, you won't be embarrassed by having the merchant reject your card."

Of course, this policy leaves you vulnerable to fraud. If you want to make sure your account is hard closed, call the issuer and demand so. If the issuer refuses, ask how long the soft close will remain and then diligently watch your mail for new charges. If you move, be sure to let the issuer know your new address so you'll get a statement if someone else reactivates your account.

If you still don't know which card to keep (or which to sign up for, if you're looking for a new one), consider how much it will cost you to have a particular card. If you don't carry a monthly balance or only occasionally do, keep (or get) a card with no annual fee, but make sure it has a grace period. If the card issuer later tacks on an annual fee, call and say you'll cancel your card if it doesn't waive the fee. Many will. If you carry a balance each month or most of the time, get rid of (or don't sign up for) the cards that come with the worst of the following features:

- **High interest rates.** If possible, keep the card with the lowest rate. If the only card you plan to hang on to has a high interest rate and you're up to date on your payments, call and ask for an interest rate reduction. Some banks will do this over the phone, but you must be current on your account. According to a 2002 Public Interest Research Group study, 56% of those who called their credit card company and requested a lower interest rate were successful.

- **Early interest posting dates.** Banks used to charge interest from the date a charge was posted. Now, most charge from the date of the purchase, which will be a few days earlier.

- **Unfair interest calculations.** Most banks charge interest on the balance owed. A growing number, however, charge interest based on the average daily balance. For example, say you charge $1,500 on your credit card and pay $1,200 on the due date. When your next bill arrives, a bank using the average daily balance will charge interest on the $1,500 average daily balance from the previous month, not on the $300 you still owe.

- **No grace period.** A few card issuers have done away with grace period—the 24- or 30-day period during which you can pay your bill in full without incurring interest charges. You don't get a grace period, however, if you carry a balance, even on new purchases. This means that not only does interest accrue on the balance carried from the previous month, but it also accrues on new charges from the date of purchase.

- **Nuisance fees.** Banks are looking for new ways to make money. Most now assess late payment fees (as high as $40) and over-the-limit fees (averaging more than $15). Many banks charge a fee if your account is inactive. A few charge fees for not carrying a balance— that is, for paying off your bill—or for carrying a balance under a certain amount. Some charge a monthly fee that's a percentage of your credit limit—the higher your limit, the higher your fee. Others charge fees if you are late on one or two payments during the year. For the most part, state efforts to cap these fees have not been upheld in court. The end result: Credit card companies can pretty much charge what they want.

- **Teaser rates.** Many credit card companies offer a "teaser" rate. This is a temporary low interest rate that lasts for a few months only. Once that period is over, a higher interest rate kicks in. Often, consumers fail to read the fine print and don't realize that the teaser rate is temporary. Others are aware of the rate but forget to switch cards when the new high rate starts. If you want to take advantage of teaser rate offers, keep careful track of the time. Many people forget to switch cards. Juggling cards can end up costing more in the long run.

As a general rule of thumb, avoid having too many credit cards. Usually, two is plenty. If you are searching for a card that matches your needs, you can visit www.cardtrack.com, www.bankrate.com, www.consumer-action.org or www.federalreserve.gov/pubs/shop.

3. Charge Cards

Charge cards, also called travel and entertainment cards, are a little different from credit cards. Charge cards, such as American Express and Diner's Club, have no credit limit. You can usually charge as much as you'd like, but you are required to pay off your entire balance when your bill arrives, with one exception. If you charge air fare, cruise fees, hotel fees for a hotel room booked through a travel agent and a few other large purchases on an American

Express card, you can pay off your balance over 36 months. You'll be charged between 19% and 21% interest and will have to make minimum monthly payments of $20 or 1/36 of your balance, whichever is greater.

If you don't pay your charge card bill in full (and haven't charged travel expenses on an American Express card), you'll get one month's grace, when no interest is charged. After that, you'll be charged interest in the neighborhood of 20%. If you don't pay after about three months, your account will be closed and your bill sent to the collections department.

The charge card company makes its profit by charging very high annual fees—up to $100—and by charging merchants fairly high fees each time a customer pays using the company's charge card.

4. Required Disclosures by Credit and Charge Card Issuers

If You Aren't Concerned About Disclosures. If you aren't concerned that a credit or charge card company failed to disclose the interest rate, grace period, annual fee or other terms, you can skip this section. If you feel you were misled or not informed, however, it is sometimes possible to sue the company and get the debt wiped out.

When a credit or charge card company sends you an application form or pre-approved solicitation letter, it must, under the federal Truth in Lending Act, fully disclose the terms of your agreement. (15 U.S.C. § 1637.)

For credit cards, such as Visa, MasterCard, Sears and Chevron, where the card issuer charges you interest and lets you pay off your charges by taking as long as you'd like as long as you pay the minimum required each billing period, the application or solicitation must give you certain information about the card, including:

- the yearly interest rate (called the annual percentage rate or APR)

- if there is a teaser or introductory rate, the regular rate that will go into effect once the introductory period is over
- how a variable rate is determined (if there is a variable rate)
- penalties for late payments and other circumstances
- any annual, periodic or membership fee, and
- the period of days you have to pay off the entire balance without incurring any interest charge (called the grace period) or state that no grace period is available.

For charge cards such as American Express and Diner's Club, where you are not charged interest but must pay off the entire balance when you get the bill, the application or solicitation must include all the items listed above that apply, and any fee imposed or interest charged for granting an extension to pay.

If a card issuer fails to disclose information or discloses wrong information, you can sue to recover your actual damages, attorneys' fees, court costs and twice the amount of any interest you were wrongfully charged. (15 U.S.C. § 1640.)

Unfortunately, because of a number of loopholes in the law, these cases are hard to win. If a credit card issuer fails to give you the proper disclosures, it is not liable if it notifies you of the error within 60 days. And, as long as the company does not charge interest in excess of the amount it disclosed to you, the company will probably not be held liable for other disclosure errors. In addition, if the card issuer's failure to disclose the proper information was unintentional and resulted from a clerical, calculation, computer, printing or similar error, the card issuer will not be liable.

Suing the card issuer is not the only way to resolve a problem. You can also complain to the appropriate federal agency that regulates the credit card issuer. (See Chapter 12, *Reporting Credit Violations*, for more information.)

5. Unrequested Credit and Charge Cards

A company that issues credit or charge cards cannot legally send you one except in response to your request or application. If a card issuer sends you an unrequested card (except to replace an expiring one), the company assumes full responsibility for its use unless you "accept" the card—use it, sign it or notify the card issuer in writing that you plan to keep it. (15 U.S.C. § 1642.) Once you accept the card, you become liable for all charges made after your acceptance.

If a company wants to issue you a credit card without a detailed application, it can legally send you a letter of congratulations (or something similar) telling you that you have pre-qualified for a certain amount of credit, accompanied by a very simple application form, which usually requires little more than your signature. This is called a pre-approved solicitation.

In the past, credit and charge card issuers asked credit bureaus to compile lists of people with certain credit traits, such as earning over $40,000 and having a mortgage. The card issuer then sent out pre-approval letters to all names given by the credit bureau. Before granting any applicant credit, the card issuer would do one last credit check. The law requires that a pre-approval letter be a "firm" offer of credit. Originally, this meant that the credit card issuer had to grant you credit, without further checking. But, a number of loopholes allow companies that send out pre-approval offers to require further information before granting credit. (15 U.S.C. §1681a(l).) Credit card companies can:

- require that you send back an application indicating that you meet the selection criteria
- verify that you meet the criteria the company used to select the prescreening list, and
- require that you provide collateral for the offered credit (this requirement must be disclosed in the offer).

Card issuers also get around this "firm" offer requirement by pre-approving very low credit limits (such as $500) and then doing a second credit check before offering any increase in credit.

What to Do With Unwanted Credit and Charge Cards

If you receive an unrequested card that you don't want—either for a new account or to replace an expiring card—don't just throw the card away. That doesn't tell the card issuer that you don't want the account or that you want to close it. Your credit file will show that you have an account with an open line of credit for whatever amount you were granted by the card issuer. Today, many creditors refuse credit to people they believe already have too much credit. Having an unused account could be grounds for denying you future accounts you do want or limiting increases on existing accounts. Instead, cut up the card and throw it away, and send a letter to the card issuer telling it to close the account.

6. Lost or Stolen Credit and Charge Cards

Federal law limits your liability for unauthorized charges made on your credit or charge card after it has been lost or stolen. (15 U.S.C. § 1643.) If you notify the card issuer within a reasonable time after you discover the loss or theft, usually 30 days, you're not responsible for any charges made after the notification, and are liable only for the first $50 for charges made before you notified the card issuer. If you don't notify the card issuer within a reasonable time, you could be on the hook for all charges made on your card before the time of your notification.

When you discover that a credit or charge card is lost or stolen, call the customer service department of the card issuer at once. By calling, you provide quick notice. You should be able to call most bank card issuers at any time (many have 24-hour customer service departments), while department stores and gasoline companies probably answer their phones only during regular business hours. If you're away from home, still call at once. Many companies will send you by overnight mail a replacement card with a new account number.

When you call a card issuer, find out who you are speaking to and get an address. Be sure to send a confirming letter and to keep a copy for yourself. You will find the address and phone number of where to report a lost or stolen card on your monthly billing statements or on the disclosures you've received from the card issuer. If you can't find either of those, look in the phone book for local merchants or call toll-free information, 800-555-1212. Many credit and charge card issuers, especially large banks, have toll-free phone numbers. To make things easier, keep a list of the customer service numbers for your credit cards in a safe place. Then, when a card is lost or stolen, you'll have the telephone numbers at your fingertips.

Given that the credit or charge card company is liable for any unauthorized charge over $50, it will act fast. Most likely, the company will cancel your existing account, open a new one for you, issue you a new card and remove all charges above $50 from your statement. (Most companies will remove all charges—even the $50 for which you're legally liable.) Also, many homeowner's insurance policies will cover the $50 if your credit card company doesn't. If the company doesn't respond adequately, refuse to pay the bill and consider having a lawyer write a letter on your behalf. If that doesn't work, you may have to sue.

Below is a sample letter to use to notify a credit or charge card issuer of a lost or stolen card. Be sure to keep a copy for your file.

Letter Confirming Telephone Notice of Lost or Stolen Card

Large Oil Company
Customer Service Department
1 Main Street
Enid, OK 77777

March 2, 20xx

Attn: Natalie Revere

Dear Ms. Revere:

This is to confirm my telephone call of March 1, 20xx, notifying you that I lost my Large Oil Company credit card on February 26, 20xx, while I was on vacation at the Grand Canyon.

I understand that under the law, my telephone call serves as reasonably timely notice to your company. I further understand that I am not liable for any unauthorized use of this card from the time of my telephone call, and the maximum I am liable for on charges made before my notification is $50.

Please contact me immediately if my understandings are not correct.

Sincerely,

Wendy Piter

Wendy Piter

⚠ Credit Card "Protection." Many banks or national credit or charge card companies send letters to their cardholders urging them to buy—for about $40 per year—credit card "protection" to guard against unauthorized use of credit and charge cards. Given that your liability for unauthorized charges is $50 maximum, and then only for charges that are made prior to your notifying the card issuer, this "protection" is a waste of money.

7. Unauthorized Charges

Are you liable when your credit or charge card is not stolen, but used without your permission by someone you know? Maybe. In general, you are not liable if you didn't authorize the person to use the card. But if you gave your card to your 25-year-old son, anything he charges before you take the card away from him is authorized by you—and you owe the bill. This is true even if you told your son that the card was for emergency use only. If he charges beer and pizza on the card, you many have a claim against your son, but not against the credit card company. On the other hand, if your adult daughter took your card without your knowledge and charged a trip to Hawaii, the law limits your liability in the same way as if your card was lost or stolen. (Section 6, above, discusses liability for lost or stolen credit cards.)

Your biggest obstacle will be convincing your card issuer that you did not authorize your son, daughter or any other person to use your card. Your best bet is to send a letter explaining the situation to the card issuer. With your daughter, emphasize that you were not at home and your daughter went to your bedroom, took your card and charged the trip without your ever knowing it.

If the credit or charge card company still claims you owe the bill—that is, that you authorized the charges—you can choose not to pay. The company will no doubt close your account and if the amount is high enough, sue you. If you want to fight it, you'll probably need a lawyer to help you prepare your defense of "unauthorized charges." (See Chapter 20 for tips on finding a lawyer.) You may be best off paying the bill and buying a safe into which you can put your cards—and all papers with the account numbers—to keep them from getting into the hands of people you live with who shouldn't be using them.

Blocked Credit Cards

Have you ever tried using a credit card shortly after checking out of a hotel and been told by the merchant that your card was rejected? It happens because many hotels, when you check in and give the clerk your card for an imprint, put a "hold" on your credit card for the estimated amount you will spend. Hotels claim that they are merely protecting themselves in the event you go on a spending spree during your trip and don't have enough credit left on your account to cover the hotel costs. Unfortunately, they've been known to hold much more than the estimated amount you'll spend and keep the hold on for up to 45 days after you check out.

Hotels have gotten a bad rap for doing this, so the amount they hold is less than in the past. When you check in ask if the hotel will place a hold and if so, for how much. When you check out, insist that the hotel order the hold lifted. Often the hotel will, given that your charges have been put through and you are not going to incur any more expenses at the hotel.

Rental car companies, too, often put a hold on credit cards, fearing that you'll total the car and run off leaving them to pay the bill. If you rent a car, ask the company if it is placing a hold, and if so for how much, before you leave the agency with your rental car. When you return the car, ask that the hold be lifted. And be aware that some gasoline companies put a $50 hold on credit cards when you charge your gas purchases.

8. Billing Errors

Credit and charge card billing errors are governed by the Fair Credit Billing Act (FCBA). (15 U.S.C. § 1666 et seq.) A "billing error" can be more than a mistake in the amount you owe. A "billing error" also includes:

- an extension of credit to someone who was not authorized to use your card
- an extension of credit for property or services that was never delivered to you
- the company's failure to credit your account properly, and
- an extension of credit for items that you returned because they were defective.

If you find an error in your credit or charge card statement, immediately write a letter to the company that issued the card; don't just scribble a note on your bill. Send your letter to the address provided by the credit card company for these types of letters, not to the address where you send your payments. Give your name, account number, an explanation of the error and the amount involved. Also enclose copies of supporting documents, such as receipts showing the correct amount of the charge.

The credit or charge card company must receive your letter within 60 days after it mailed the first bill with improper charges to you. A sample letter is below.

Sample Letter to Notify of Billing Error

Eighteenth Bank of Cincinnati
1 EBC Plaza
Cincinnati, OH 44444

May 20, 20xx

Attn: Customer Service

Re: Bradley Green
     Account Number 123 456 789 0000

To Whom It May Concern:

I have found an error on my MasterCard statement dated May 15, 20xx.

On March 25, 20xx, I purchased with my MasterCard two roundtrip tickets on Skyway Airlines from New York to San Diego, for $1,150. My bill, however, is for $1,510. Obviously, digits were reversed.

I understand that the law requires you to acknowledge receipt of this letter within 30 days unless you correct this billing error before then. Furthermore, I understand that within two billing cycles (but in no event more than 90 days), you must correct the error or explain why you believe the amount to be correct.

I have enclosed a copy of the receipt my travel agent sent me.

Sincerely,

Bradley Green

Bradley Green

Remember to keep a copy of your letter as well as any original receipts or documentation. The credit or charge card company must acknowledge receipt of your letter within 30 days, unless it corrects the bill within that time. Furthermore, the card issuer must, within two billing cycles (but in no event more than 90 days), correct the error or explain why it believes the amount to be correct. If the card company does not comply with these time limits, it forfeits up to $50 of any amount you might owe. In California, if the card company doesn't comply with the 90-day time limit, you don't have to pay any portion of the disputed balance. (Civil Code § 1747.50.)

During the two-billing-cycle/90-day period, the credit or charge card company cannot report the amount to a credit bureau or to other creditors as delinquent. Likewise, the card issuer cannot threaten or actually take any collection action against you for the disputed amount. But it can send you periodic statements. In addition, it can apply the amount in dispute to your credit limit, thereby lowering the amount available for you to charge.

You can withhold payment of the disputed amount and related charges while you are waiting for a response from the credit or charge card company. If the company agrees that there was an error, it must correct the error and credit your account for both the disputed amount and any related charges. It also must report the resolution to all credit agencies that were notified of a delinquency.

If the credit or charge card company disagrees with your complaint, it must send you an explanation and, if you request it, provide you with copies of any evidence. If you still believe you are right, you might consider suing the company for a violation of the Fair Credit Billing Act (15 U.S.C. §1640). Suing a credit card company can be difficult. If the amount is small, you can use small claims court. If you decide not to sue, you should still report the problem to the appropriate government agency. (See Chapter 12, *Reporting Credit Violations.*) You may also want to cancel the card if you don't like the way the company treated you.

9. Disputes Over Credit or Charge Card Purchases

The rights discussed in Section 8, above, apply only to billing errors. Even more common than billing errors are disputes with merchants when you use your credit card to buy a product that is defective. Here too, federal law gives you the right to with-

hold payment in certain circumstances. This is a powerful, but often underused, tool for consumers.

If you buy a defective item or service and pay for it with your credit or charge card, you can often withhold payment if the seller refuses to replace, repair or otherwise correct the problem. (15 U.S.C. §1666i.)

You can stop payment on the credit card if you have a legitimate complaint about the quality of goods or services and you first make a good faith effort to resolve the problem with the merchant directly.

There are a few other requirements:

- The goods or services you bought must have cost more than $50.
- You must have bought the goods or services in your home state or within 100 miles of your mailing address.

These last two conditions don't apply to credit cards issued by the seller (such as a department store card) or if the seller mailed you the advertisement for the goods or services you purchased. But, you still need to make a good faith effort to resolve the problem with the seller in these circumstances.

EXAMPLE: Nan charged a raincoat from Cliff's Department Store on her Cliff's credit card. When she got home, she discovered that the lining was torn. Cliff's refused to replace the coat or refund her money. Nan has the right to refuse to pay her bill as long as she tries to resolve the problem with Cliff's. Had Nan charged the coat on her Visa card, she could refuse to pay only if Cliff's was located in the state where she lived or within 100 miles of her home.

10. Credit Cards, Charge Cards and Merchants

Frequently, when you use a credit card in a store, the merchant takes the card, runs it through a computer and punches in a few numbers or places a phone call. Either way, these merchants are contacting a credit card guarantee company that has a record of your credit status. That information comes directly from your card issuer. If you don't want to be denied use of your credit card, be sure you know how much you've charged and paid for. The guarantee company checks for:

- **Your overall credit limit.** If you've exceeded your line of credit and attempt to make further purchases, the guarantee company will tell the merchant to reject your card.

- **Your daily limit.** Many credit card companies do not let cardholders use their card more than a certain number of times a day or spend more than a certain amount per day. This is meant to protect against the use of stolen cards. If you've exceeded the daily limit, the merchant will be told to reject the card.

- **The amount of the particular purchase.** Merchants must check with the guarantee company for approval on purchases larger than a certain dollar amount (called a "floor limit"), which varies among guarantee companies and merchants.

- **Whether you are late on a payment.** If you often pay late, the guarantee company may tell the merchant to reject your card.

- **Whether the card should be taken away from you.** In some cases, the merchant receives a code on the machine to call the guarantee company directly on the telephone. If the merchant still has the card, the guarantee company will tell her to keep it. This can happen if the card was reported stolen or if you are excessively delinquent in your payments and the credit card company has revoked your card privileges. Some merchants receive rewards for turning in revoked cards. Most merchants, however, refuse to confiscate cards and instead simply tell you your card was not accepted.

Many merchants require a customer to charge a minimum amount on a credit card. But MasterCard and Visa claim that their agreements with merchants prohibit merchants from requiring a minimum purchase. If a merchant refuses to accept your card for a small purchase, send a letter of complaint to the bank that issued the card.

Must You Provide Personal Information When You Use a Credit Card?

When you use your credit card, can the merchant record your address and phone number on the credit card slip? If a merchant correctly processes a credit card transaction, it will be paid even if the charge exceeds the card's credit limit, so it has no reason for the information. In fact, merchants' agreements with Visa and MasterCard prohibit them from requiring a customer to furnish a phone number when paying with Visa or MasterCard. Many merchants who request telephone numbers use that information in direct marketing. Also, several states bar merchants from requiring personal information when you use a credit card.

11. If You Can't Pay Your Credit or Charge Card Bill

If you owe a credit or charge card bill you can't afford, you have a couple of options.

Ignore the bill. You'll get a series of monthly statements and bills. After about four months, your account will be closed and your bill will be sent to a collection agency. Some companies act sooner, especially if you exceeded your credit limit with your charges. Some companies wait a little longer, especially if you have a good payment history. If you still don't pay after being contacted by a collection agency, you may be sued.

Ask to make lower monthly payments. You can write to the credit or charge card company and ask to make lower monthly payments. As explained in Chapter 6, most companies insist that you make the minimum payment. Although the credit card industry used to require that you pay at least 4% of the balance, this is no longer true. For example, if you can convince the company that you're having serious financial problems, your payments may be as low as 2% of the outstanding balance. (Some companies, as a method to simply make a profit, charge a one-time flat fee of around $20 to permanently reduce monthly payment to 2% of the outstanding balance.) Or, the company might accept a half-payment, but it will freeze your credit line in doing so—that is, not let you incur any more charges.

Your delinquent payments—or your arrangement to make reduced payments—will probably be reported to a credit bureau. Most credit card companies send customer information to bureaus once a month. Usually, all accounts more than 60 days past due with a balance over $50 are reported. See Chapter 18, Section B, to understand what it means when negative information is reported to a credit bureau.

⚠ Beware of the minimum payment trap. If you opt to pay only the minimum (or less) each month, you'll need years to get out of debt. To calculate the exact length of time, use one of Nolo's calculators at www.nolo.com; click on "Calculators" in the Free Information and Tools section.

12. If the Card Issuer Closes Your Account or Increases the Fees or Interest Rate

If you're current on your payments, not disputing any charges and otherwise a good customer, can the card issuer close your account anyway, tack on new fees or increase your interest rate? Yes. Can you fight it? Maybe. Is it fair? Definitely not.

A credit card issuer might close your account or increase the cost of using the card if it decides you have become a poor credit risk. For example, a rare company might close your account if you lose a credit card, thinking that you're irresponsible. Although this is unusual, it has been known to happen.

More likely, a card issuer might take action if you've gotten behind on your payments *to other creditor*s or your other credit balances have gone way up. Credit card issuers do periodic checks of the credit reports of their customers, often when deciding whether or not to increase the credit line. If a card issuer sees flags in your credit report, don't be surprised if the credit card bill from the company you're current with comes with any of the following:

- new, higher interest rate (as high as 26%)
- reduced time before the card issuer imposes a late payment fee—many companies give about a ten-day period before slapping on a late payment fee; card holders considered high risk may see that fee if a payment is just a day late
- increased late payment fees (as high as $40)
- elimination of the grace period—that is, interest on your bill even if you pay in full each month, or
- return or introduction of an annual fee.

You can call the company and demand a reversal of the charges, but as long as the terms were disclosed to you, the changes are probably legal. Although usually there is little you can do in this situation, recently some consumers have sued credit card companies arguing that changes in terms such as increased interest rates are against the law. If the credit card company advertised that the initial interest rate would be permanent, a court may hold the company to that rate. Your success will depend on the initial solicitation and the terms of the credit card contract. A simpler route if a credit card company changes the terms of your agreement and won't reinstate the old terms is to close the account.

B. Cash Advances

Many people use their credit cards to obtain cash advances. Similarly, many credit card companies send cardholders convenience checks to use—the amount of the check appears on your credit card statement as a charge. Card issuers usually treat these checks like they treat cash advances.

Cash advances are generally more expensive than standard credit card charges and have fewer protections, including:

- **Transaction fees.** Most banks charge a transaction fee up to 4% for taking a cash advance. Some waive the fee on convenience checks.
- **Grace period.** Most banks charge interest from the date the cash advance is posted, even if you pay it back in full when your bill comes. A few banks give grace periods for convenience checks.

• **Interest rates.** The interest rate is often higher on cash advances than it is on ordinary credit card charges.

C. Automated Teller Machine (ATM) and Debit Cards

ATM cards are issued by banks, essentially to give bank customers flexibility in their banking hours. In most areas, you can use an ATM card to withdraw money, make deposits, transfer money between accounts, find out your balance, get a cash advance and even make loan payments at all hours of the day or night.

Debit cards combine the functions of ATM cards and checks. Debit cards are issued by banks, but are used at stores, not at the banks themselves. When you pay with a debit card, the money is automatically deducted from your checking account. Most banks issue debit cards that can be used wherever a merchant accepts Visa and MasterCard. In fact, most debit cards carry a credit card logo. If you don't have this kind of debit card, many merchants accept ATM cards as debit cards.

Until the early 1990s, technological incompatibility between merchants and banks meant that the use of ATM cards as debit cards was very limited. Once the credit card logo was added, however, debit card acceptance became universal. Many consumers prefer them over checks and credit cards for two reasons:

• They don't have to carry around their checkbook and present identification, but are still able to make purchases direct from their checking account.
• They are paying their bills immediately, unlike when they use credit cards and get the bill later.

Still, there are disadvantages to using debit cards. Many consumers prefer having 20–25 days to pay their credit card bills. Also, consumers using debit cards don't have the right to withhold payment (the money is immediately removed from the account) in the event of a dispute with the merchant over the goods or services paid for. (See Section A.9, above.)

In addition, some banks and some merchants charge transaction fees when you use a debit card. Finally, if your debt card is stolen on the Internet, the thief may drain your bank account before the bank is able to complete its investigation. For this reason, it's best to use credit, rather than debit, cards for online purchases.

1. Statement or Receipt Errors

Although ATM statements and debit receipts are not known for containing errors, mistakes do happen—perhaps more often on bank statements than on receipts. So always check your receipt and bank statement carefully. If you find an error, you have 60 days from the date of the statement or receipt to notify the bank (sometimes longer in extenuating circumstances). (15 U.S.C. § 1693f.) Always call first and follow up with a letter, keeping a copy for your records. If you don't notify the bank within 60 days, it has no obligation to investigate the error and you're probably out of luck.

The financial institution has ten business days from the date of your notification to investigate the problem and tell you the result. If the bank needs more time, it can take up to 45 days, but only if it deposits the amount of money in dispute into your account. If the bank later determines that there was no error, it can take the money back, but it first must send you a written explanation.

2. Lost or Stolen ATM or Debit Cards

If your ATM or debit card is lost or stolen (never, never, never keep your personal identification number—PIN—near your card and always take your ATM receipt after completing a transaction), call your bank immediately, and follow it up with a confirming letter. Under the Electronic Fund Transfer Act (15 U.S.C. § 1693g), your liability is:

• $0—after you report the card missing
• up to $50—if you notify the bank within two business days after you realize the card is

missing unless you were on extended travel or in the hospital

- up to $500—if you fail to notify the bank within two business days after you realize the card is missing unless you were on extended travel or in the hospital, but do notify the bank within 60 days after your bank statement is mailed to you listing the unauthorized withdrawals
- unlimited—if you fail to notify the bank within 60 days after your bank statement is mailed to you listing the unauthorized withdrawals.

If a financial institution violates any provision of the Electronic Fund Transfer Act, you can sue to recover the damages you incurred. You're entitled to your actual damages, twice the amount of any finance charge (but not less than $100 nor more than $1,000), attorneys' fees and court costs. (15 U.S.C. § 1639m.)

In response to consumer complaints about the possibility of unlimited liability, Visa and MasterCard cap the loss at $50, the same as they do for unauthorized credit card charges. And some debit card issuers don't charge you anything in this situation. A few states have capped the liability for unauthorized withdrawals on an ATM or debit card at $50 as well.

3. ATM Fees

Withdrawing money from an ATM can be expensive, especially if you use a machine not associated with the bank that issued your ATM card. You may be hit with two separate fees—one from the bank you are using and another from your own bank for using a financial institution not on your bank's network. If you are lucky, only one of the banks will assess a fee against you. Some banks charge flat fees while others charge a percentage of the amount withdrawn.

Shop around when opening a bank account. Often credit unions or small banks charge the lowest ATM fees. On the other hand, larger banks often have more ATM machines—and usually if you use your bank's ATM machine there is no charge at all. Also, ATMs must disclose any surcharges in a prominent place at the ATM machine and on the ATM screen or on a printout before the customer completes the transaction.

For general information on ATM and other bank fees, check out these websites:

- www.pirg.org (U.S. Public Interest Research Group)
- www.consumersunion.org (Consumers Union)
- www.ftc.gov (Federal Trade Commission)
- www.consumer-action.org (Consumer Action).

■

Consumer Loans

A bank is a place where they lend you an umbrella in fair weather and ask for it back when it begins to rain.

— Robert Frost, American poet, 1875-1963

If you have a loan that you are having trouble paying back, contact the lender and try to work out an arrangement. If you explain that your situation is temporary, the lender will probably grant you an extension, meaning the delinquent payments are put at the end of your loan and your account is brought up to date. Or, the lender may waive interest—that is, have you pay just principal—for a month or two. Some lenders will even rewrite loans, reducing your monthly payments by extending your time to pay. You'll probably pay more interest in the long run, however.

Before contacting your lender, carefully reread your loan agreement to try to understand all of its terms. This will help you intelligently negotiate with the lender. Below is a discussion of the federal law that covers loans—disclosures, applications and fine-print terms. If, after reading these sections, you think that the lender may have violated the law, use the violation as leverage in negotiating with the lender. You should consult with an attorney if you believe the lender violated the law.

Negotiating With a Lender

If you're having trouble paying a loan and need to negotiate with a lender, be sure to read the appropriate sections in Chapter 6. As indicated there, the lender may waive interest, reduce your payments or let you skip a payment but tack it on at the end. But the lender won't do something for nothing. In exchange, you might have to get a cosigner, waive the statute of limitations (see Chapter 15), pay higher interest for a longer period or let the lender take a security interest in your house or car.

You are most vulnerable at this time. Be sure you truly understand any new loan terms and can afford to make the payments under any new agreement.

A. Required Loan Disclosures

If You Aren't Concerned About the Terms of Your Agreement. If you aren't concerned that a lender failed to disclose the interest rate, grace period, annual fee or other terms, you can skip this section.

The federal Truth in Lending Act (TILA) requires lenders to give you specific information about the terms of loans you are considering (15 U.S.C. §1631 et seq). The disclosures required by TILA are different for open-end loans (such as credit card accounts where you continually make new charges and payments) and closed-end loans (fixed purchases such as a home or car that you will pay off over a period of time). Disclosures for open-end loans are discussed in Chapter 10, *Credit, Charge and Debit Cards*.

1. Closed-end Loans

The required disclosures for closed-end loans are extensive. Among other things, the lender must provide you with information about:

- the "amount financed" (the amount of credit provided)
- an itemization of the amount financed or a disclosure of your right to get an itemization
- the "finance charge" (the amount the credit will cost you, including interest and certain fees)
- the annual percentage rate or APR (the cost of the credit on a yearly basis)—in a few situations where the loan amount is very small, this is not required
- the total number of payments needed to pay off the loan, the amount of each payment and the payment schedule
- whether the lender is taking a security interest in the property being purchased
- special disclosures for adjustable rate loans (loans where the interest rate fluctuates) including the maximum interest rate that may be charged; and
- if the creditor is also the seller, the total price of the item or service plus all other charges.

The lender must give you these disclosures before it extends credit to you. For most home mortgage transactions, the lender must give you good faith estimates of this information within three days after the lender receives your loan application. In most cases, if the loan is not being used to finance the purchase of a house (such as second mortgages to finance home improvements), the lender must also give you notice of your right to cancel the loan within three days after you sign the loan documents. This is called a "cooling-off period" and can be longer than three days in some circumstances.

2. Extra Protections for High Rate Loans

In an effort to stop scammers who try to steal the equity from the homes of many older and low-income homeowners, the Home Ownership Equity Protection Act (HOEPA) requires additional disclosures and places many restrictions on secured loans that have the following features:

- closed-ended—meaning it is repayable over a set period of time at set amounts
- secured by your primary residence
- not used to buy or construct the property, and
- an annual interest rate that's at least ten points (eight points for first lien loans after October 1, 2002) above the rate on comparable government securities or the total fees and

charges are at least $400 and greater than 8% of the amount borrowed. The government is considering changing these amounts.

HOEPA requires lenders to provide potential borrowers with the following warning three days before signing the loan papers (additional information will be required beginning October 1, 2002):

> You are not required to complete this agreement merely because you have received these disclosures or have signed a loan application. If you obtain this loan, the lender will have a mortgage on your home. You could lose your home, and any money you have put into it, if you do not meet your obligations under the loan.

HOEPA also prohibits lenders from adding certain features to the loan such as most prepayment penalties (charges for paying the loan back early) and balloon payments if the loan period is for less than five years (see Section C.3, below, for an explanation of balloon payments).

It is complicated to determine if a loan qualifies as a "HOEPA loan" and if it does, whether the lender complied with the law. If you think your loan might qualify as a HOEPA loan, you should consult with an attorney as soon as possible. If you're already in foreclosure, you may be able to use lender violations of TILA and HOEPA as a defense to the foreclosure.

Mortgages for People With Poor Credit

For many years, conventional mortgage lenders wrote only "A" loans. An "A" loan was available to a person with flawless credit—someone who had paid every personal loan, student loan, credit card bill and existing mortgage payment on time. Occasionally, a person with a minor credit blip, such as a one-time late payment on an otherwise perfectly paid loan, would still qualify for an "A" loan. "A" loans typically require as little as 5% to 10% down and charge the most favorable interest rate. Anyone who didn't qualify for an "A" loan had only two choices: forego buying a home for several years (until all the negative marks came off the credit report), or borrow from a lender who required a huge down payment (35% or more) and charged near-credit-card interest rates.

Many mortgage lenders now write "B" and "C" loans for people with somewhat marred credit histories. "D" loans, which require a very large down payment and charge very high interest rates, are still written for people with very bad credit histories. The following describes "B," "C" and "D" loans:

- **"B" loans.** Some lenders require clean credit for the previous 12 months but allow a few missed payments before that. Others permit one or two late mortgage payments, one late personal or student loan payment and few late credit card payments during the previous year. Late payments cannot be more than 60 days late. "B" loans usually require 20% to 25% down; interest rates are usually one or two percentage points higher than "A" loans.
- **"C" loans.** Some lenders require clean credit for the previous 12 months but allow a serious credit problem, such as a bankruptcy or foreclosure, several years before. Others permit three or four late mortgage payments, five or six late loan or credit card payments or late payments more than 60 days past due during the previous year. "C" loans usually require 20% to 35% down; interest rates are usually one or three percentage points higher than "A" loans.
- **"D" loans.** "D" loans are available to people with the worst credit histories—bankruptcy or foreclosure in the past year, or habitual late payments on loans and bills. "D" loans usually require 35% to 60% down; interest rates are usually at least 100% higher than what they are for "A" loans.

Although increased lending to people with shaky credit histories may seem like a good thing, it often isn't. Many "B," "C" and "D" borrowers get loans from predatory lenders—lenders that sell very high-rate loans that borrowers rarely can afford over time. Through tricky dealing, predatory lenders hide the exorbitant cost of the loan. How to tell if a lender is legitimate or predatory? If the lender advertises "easy credit" and low-cost loans to anyone regardless of credit history, beware. If you've already fallen prey to a predatory lender, seek legal help before you default and face foreclosure

For more information on predatory lending, visit the websites of the following organizations: AARP (www.aarp.org), the National Consumer Law Center (www.consumerlaw.org), the Community Reinvestment Association of North Carolina (www.cra-nc.org) and the Federal Trade Commission (www.ftc.gov).

B. Evaluation of Credit Applications

When you apply for credit, creditors use two primary methods to evaluate your request:

- weigh your three "Cs"—capacity, collateral and character, and
- create a "credit score" based primarily, but not exclusively, on information in your credit file.

1. The Three "Cs"

A creditor needs information to determine the likelihood that you will repay a loan or pay charges you incur on a line of revolving credit. This is done by evaluating the three "Cs."

Capacity. This refers to the amount of debt you can realistically pay given your income. Creditors look at how long you've been on your job, your income level and the likelihood that it will increase over time. They also look to see that you're in a stable job or at least a stable job industry. It's important when you fill out a credit application to make your job sound stable, high-level and even "professional." Are you a secretary or are you an executive secretary or the office manager?

Finally, creditors examine your existing credit relationships, such as credit cards, bank loans and mortgages. They want to know your credit limits (you may be denied additional credit if you already have a lot of open credit lines), your current credit balances, how long you've had each account and your payment history—whether you pay late or on time.

Collateral. Creditors like to see that you have assets that they can take from you if you don't pay your debt. Owning a home or liquid assets such as a mutual fund may offer considerable comfort to a creditor reviewing an application. This is especially true if your credit report has negative notations in it, such as late payments.

Character. Creditors develop a feeling of your financial character through objective factors that show stability. These include the length of your residency, the length of your employment, whether you rent or own your home (you're more likely to stay put if

you own) and whether you have checking and savings accounts.

2. Credit Scores

Most credit files include a credit score. Credit scores are numerical calculations that are supposed to indicate the risk that you will default on your payments. High credit scores indicate less risk and lower numbers indicate potential problems. Most credit scores range from lows of 300-400 to highs of 800-900. The biggest credit scoring company, Fair, Isaac and Company, estimates that 40% of Americans have scores over 750. Most lenders consider a score above 750 to be very good.

Lenders use credit scores to help them decide whether you are a good risk for new credit, whether to increase or decrease an existing line of credit, to determine how easy it will be to collect on an account and even to project the likelihood that you will file for bankruptcy. Credit scores are used in about 80% of all mortgages as well as in car loans, credit cards and even insurance policies.

Even though your score may determine whether you can get a loan, credit bureaus are not required to disclose your score to you. However, change is on the horizon. California now requires mortgage lenders to disclose credit scores to a consumer shopping for a mortgage. Similar laws may be passed in other states or even by Congress.

Recently, Fair, Isaac and Company has voluntarily made credit scores available for a fee of $12.95. To get your Fair, Isaac credit score, visit www.equifax.com, www.myfico.com or www.scorepower.com.

A few other companies that create credit scores have followed suit. Trans Union now provides your credit score (at no extra charge) when you order a Trans Union credit report. Experian also offers a credit score product for $12.95.

Although being able to view your credit score is a significant improvement, the jury is still out on how helpful the score will actually be. It is likely that you will get different scores from different companies. And consumer experts are not certain that the score you order from the Internet will be the same one that lenders use to determine whether they will extend credit to you.

Credit scoring companies most likely use the three "Cs" as guidelines for creating scores. Recently, Fair, Isaac and Company disclosed slightly more detailed factors that it uses in generating credit scores. Those factors include:

- your payment history (about 35% of the score)
- amounts you owe on credit accounts (about 30% of the score); Fair, Isaac looks at the amount you owe on all accounts and whether there is a balance. They are looking to see whether you manage credit responsibly. It may view a large number of accounts with balances as a sign that you are over-extended, and count it against you.
- length of your credit history (about 15% of the score)

   In general, a longer credit history increases the score.

- your new credit (about 10% of the score); Fair, Isaac likes to see that you have an established credit history and that you don't have too many new accounts. Opening several accounts in a short period of time can represent greater risk
- types of credit (about 10% of the score); Fair, Isaac is looking for a "healthy mix" of different types of credit. This factor is usually important only if there is not a lot of other information upon which to base your score.

To keep up on credit scoring developments, visit www.creditscoring.com, a private website devoted to credit scoring.

If you do get your credit score, and it seems to be too low, there may be a mistake on your credit report. See Chapter 18 for information on how to clean up your credit report, including getting rid of errors. Your credit score may also be lower than expected for legitimate reasons. Some aspects of your credit history, like having numerous credit accounts, may decrease your score. If your score is good enough to get you the credit you need, don't worry too much about losing a few points here and there.

C. Terms of Loan Agreements

In looking over your loan agreement, these are the terms you may come across.

1. Acceleration Clause

This clause lets the lender declare the entire balance due, "accelerate" the loan, if you default—that is, miss a payment or otherwise violate a term of your loan agreement. If you miss one or two payments, the lender will probably agree to hold off accelerating the loan if you pay what you owe and pay the remaining balance on time. If you miss additional payments, however, you can be sure you'll fall from the lender's good graces.

Once a loan is accelerated, it's very difficult to get the lender to "unaccelerate" and reinstate your old loan.

2. Attorneys' Fee Provision

Many creditors include a provision in a loan contract awarding them attorneys' fees if you default and they have to sue you to get paid. If your contract contains this provision, but says nothing about your right to attorneys' fees, in most states you nevertheless have the right to attorneys' fees in the event you are sued—or you sue—and you win. Several states prohibit the creditor's attorneys from collecting from you a fee in excess of 15% of the amount you owed.

3. Balloon Payment

Many borrowers can't afford the monthly payments when they apply for a loan requiring them to repay the money borrowed in equal monthly installments for a set period. To help them qualify, some lenders will lower the monthly payments and collect the difference at the end of the loan in one large payment called a balloon payment. Balloon payments can be dangerous. Often, those with balloon payments cannot afford the large final payment when it comes due. If you don't pay, the lender may have the right to repossess or foreclose on the property pledged as collateral for the loan—often a house.

Many states prohibit balloon payments in loans for goods or services that are primarily for personal, family or household use. Or, they give borrowers the right to refinance these loans at the lender's prevailing rate when the balloon payment comes due. In practice, many lenders let borrowers refinance balloon payments as long as the borrowers have decent credit at the time of the refinancing.

4. Confession of Judgment

A "confession of judgment" is a provision that lets a lender automatically take a judgment against you if you default, without having to sue you in court. Confessions of judgment are prohibited for any consumer contract (other than for real estate). (16 C.F.R. § 444.2) This type of provision is very anticonsumer and few lenders try to include one in their loans.

5. Cosigner or Guarantor

If you didn't qualify for a loan, a lender may have let you borrow money because you presented a cosigner or guarantor. This person assumed full responsibility for paying back the loan if you don't. The cosigner or guarantor need not benefit from the loan to be liable for it.

If you file for bankruptcy and the cosigner or guarantor is a relative or personal friend, it is possible that the person could be stuck with more than just what you haven't paid on the debt. If you made payments on the loan during the year before you filed for bankruptcy, the cosigner or guarantor may be required to pay to the bankruptcy court the total amount of what you paid during the year. This is because your payments may be considered an "illegal preference" in bankruptcy. (See for example, *In re Finn*, 909 F.2d 903 (6th Cir. 1990).) If this is a concern for you, speak to a bankruptcy lawyer. (See Chapter 20.)

Many young adults with no credit history have their parents cosign or guarantee loans. Other borrowers, who may have had a serious financial setback (repossession, foreclosure or bankruptcy), or simply don't earn enough to get a loan, ask a friend or relative to cosign or guarantee. Cosigners and guarantors should fully understand their obligations before they sign on.

Cosigner Notification

Federal law requires that cosigners be given the following notice:

NOTICE TO COSIGNER

You are being asked to guarantee this debt. Think carefully before you do so. If the borrower doesn't pay the debt, you will have to. Be sure you can afford to pay if you have to, and that you want to accept this responsibility.

You may have to pay up to the full amount of the debt if the borrower does not pay. You may also have to pay late fees or collection costs, which increase this amount.

The creditor can collect this debt from you without first trying to collect from the borrower. The creditor can use the same collection methods against you that can be used against the borrower, such as suing you, garnishing your wages, etc. If this debt is ever in default, that fact may become a part of your credit record.

6. Credit Insurance

Credit insurance guarantees payment of a debt if the borrower is unable to pay. It is sold by credit card companies, car dealers, finance companies, department stores and other lenders who make loans for personal property.

Credit insurance, for the most part, is a rip-off. Insurance companies collect over $2 billion a year in credit insurance premiums, yet pay out only $900 million a year. Consumers spend as much as $8 billion each year on credit insurance, often without knowing what they have bought. In most cases, credit insurance is unnecessary.

There are four main types of credit insurance:

- credit property insurance (insures against damage or loss to the collateral securing the loan)
- credit life insurance (insures that if the consumer dies during the term of the coverage, the remaining debt on a loan or credit card account will be paid off)
- credit disability/accident and health insurance (pays a limited number of monthly payments on a loan or credit card account if the borrower becomes disabled during the term of the coverage); and
- involuntary loss of income insurance (insures against layoff or other causes of involuntary loss of income).

Many lenders will tell you that credit insurance is required as a condition of getting a loan. This is almost always wrong. For the most part, you cannot be required to buy credit insurance. The main exception is for credit property insurance—creditors can require that you buy this type of credit insurance in certain circumstances. But even if property insurance is required, in most states, the creditor cannot force you to buy the insurance from them. It must allow you to shop around and purchase it from another company.

There are also federal and state laws that regulate credit insurance. An important new federal law, applying to most mortgages obtained after July 29, 1999, requires lenders to automatically cancel private mortgage insurance once the homeowner has 22% equity in the property and allows buyers with good payment histories to request cancellation once the equity reaches 20%. (12 U.S.C. § 4901 et seq.)

In a few states, lenders cannot require credit insurance except for loans to buy real estate.

7. Prepayment Penalties

Lenders make money on the interest they charge for lending money. If you pay off your loan early, they don't make as much as they had anticipated. To make up some of the loss, some lenders impose "prepayment penalties"—if you repay the loan before it is due, you have to pay a penalty, usually a percentage of the balance you paid early.

If you're refinancing existing loans or borrowing money to pay off other debts and you have a choice, get a loan without a prepayment penalty.

8. Pyramiding Late Fees

If you're late on a loan payment (such as a car loan or personal loan), the lender normally imposes a late fee. These fees are generally permitted unless the lender engages in an accounting practice known as "pyramiding." Pyramiding takes place when the lender assesses a late fee that you don't pay, and then applies your regular payment first to the late fee and then to partially cover the payment due. You will never fully catch up on the payments due and the lender will therefore impose a late fee every month, even when you pay on time. For the most part, pyramiding is prohibited. (16 C.F.R. § 444.4)

EXAMPLE: Sheila has a bank personal loan that requires her to pay $100 each month by the 5th. On May 6th, when her payment had not yet been received, her lender assessed a $5 late fee. When the lender received Sheila's $100 payment on May 17th, the lender applied the first $5 to cover the late fee and the remaining $95 toward her $100 payment. In June, Sheila was automatically assessed another late fee on the $5 balance due for May, even though her June payment was on time. With this accounting scheme, Sheila will always have a slight balance on which she will continually be assessed a late fee.

9. Security Interest

As described in Chapter 1, when you take out a secured loan you give the creditor the right to take your property or a portion of it if you don't pay. This is called a security interest. The two most common security interests are mortgages, where you give the lender the right to foreclose on your home if you miss payments, and car loans, where the lender can take the car if you default.

Some consumer loans, especially for large appliances and furniture, include a security interest in the item being purchased. Also, some personal loans that are not used to purchase a specific item—and in fact, are often used to pay off other loans—include a security interest in your home, car or important items around your house. These personal loans can be hazardous to borrowers. The interest is usually very high, and if you default, the lender can take the item identified in the contract.

To protect borrowers, lenders are prohibited from taking a security interest in the following, unless you are actually buying the item: your clothing, furniture, appliances, linens, china, crockery, kitchenware, wedding ring, one radio and one television and personal effects. (16 C.F.R. § 444.)

Some states provide borrowers with additional protections. For example, in California, lenders must include a 14-point boldface warning stating "your home could be sold without your permission and

without any court action if you miss any payment as required by the contract." (Cal. Civil Code § 1803.2(3).)

In Kansas, a lender cannot take a security interest in real estate for a consumer loan in which the interest exceeds 12% and the amount financed is $3,000 or less. (Kan. Stat. Ann. § 16a-2-307.) In Virginia, a lender cannot take a security interest in real estate for most consumer loans. (Va. Code Ann. § 6.1-281.)

In North Carolina (N.C. Gen. Stat. § 25A-23) and Wisconsin (Wis. Stat. Ann. § 422.417), creditors may take a security interest in only the following:

- the item being sold
- an item previously sold by that creditor if the creditor has an existing security interest
- personal property in which the item sold is installed or annexed (amount financed must exceed $300 in North Carolina, $500 in Wisconsin)
- real property to which the item sold is affixed (amount financed must exceed $1,000), or
- a motor vehicle (North Carolina only and the amount financed must exceed $100).

10. Wage Assignment

Some lenders, especially credit unions, try to assure your repayment of a loan by suggesting that you voluntarily agree to a wage assignment. This means that each time you are paid, a sum of money is deducted from your paycheck by your employer to pay the lender before you ever see that money. Most people feel that this method of payment is overly intrusive and prefer to pay on their own.

With the exception of real estate loans, a voluntary wage assignment is allowed only if you have the power to revoke it. (16 C.F.R. § 444.) If you are considering agreeing to one, keep in mind that it can help you discipline yourself if you think you won't pay on your own—and you can revoke it if you don't like it.

In many states, if you're married, your spouse must consent before the lender can take a voluntary wage assignment. (See, for example, California (Cal.

Lab. Code § 300(b)(2)); Colorado (Colo. Rev. Stat. § 8-9-104); Indiana (Ind. Code Ann. § 22-2-7-4); Maryland (Md. Code Ann. [Com.Law] § 15-302(b)); Massachusetts (Mass. Gen. Laws ch. 154, § 3); Montana (Mont. Code Ann. § 31-1-306); Virginia (Va. Code Ann. § 6.1-289); and Wyoming (Wyo. Stat. 27-4-111).)

Wage assignments are limited in a number of states. In Kentucky (Ky. Rev. Stat. Ann. § 288.570), Montana (Mont. Code Ann. § 32-5-310) and Virginia (Va. Code Ann. § 6.1.-290), for example, a consumer loan wage assignment can't exceed 10% of your salary. In Illinois, the limit is 15% (740 Ill. Comp. Stat. § 170/4). In Oregon, wage assignments are not allowed on retail installment contracts (Or. Rev. Stat. § 83.150). In Oklahoma they are barred on all consumer contracts (Okla. Stat. Ann. tit. 14A, § 3-403).

11. Waivers of Exemptions

As explained in Chapter 15, if a creditor sues you and gets a court judgment, or you file for bankruptcy, some of your property is protected from your creditors—that is, it can't be taken to pay what you owe. This property is called your exempt property. It usually includes your clothing and personal effects, household goods and some of the equity in your home and car.

Some creditors try to get around the laws that let you keep exempt property by including a provision in a loan agreement whereby you waive your right to keep your exempt property. These provisions are prohibited in any non-real-estate consumer contract (16 C.F.R. § 444).

12. Mandatory Arbitration Clauses

Creditors and other businesses often include a mandatory arbitration clause in many types of consumer contracts, including contracts for employment, credit, insurance and even nursing facility admission. These clauses require you to waive your right to go to court to resolve disputes. Instead, you must resolve any dispute by way of a private, and often costly, arbitration system usually selected by the creditor or business.

Unlike voluntary mediation and arbitration programs, which allow you to sue in court if you cannot resolve a dispute outside of court or if you don't like the arbitration or mediation result, mandatory arbitration clauses waive your right to ever go to court. Watch out for these clauses when you sign contracts.

For more information about mandatory arbitration agreements, contact Public Citizen (www.citizen.org) or the Trial Lawyers for Public Justice (www.tlpj.org). ■

Reporting Credit Violations

Obedience to the law is demanded as a right; not asked as a favor.

—Theodore Roosevelt, 26th President of the United States, 1858-1919

If a creditor violates provisions of the Truth in Lending, Fair Credit Billing or Electronic Fund Transfer Act, report the creditor to the appropriate federal agency. Write a letter giving the identity of the creditor and the name of the particular person who violated the law. Describe the violation in detail. Be sure to keep a copy of your letter for your records.

However, don't assume that these agencies will solve your problem. If you're in trouble and need help fast, you are better off trying to handle the matter yourself or finding a lawyer who can help you. That being said, it is still important to send complaints to these agencies. Consumer complaints help government agencies keep track of creditors and collectors that violate the law.

A. National Banks

National banks will have "National" or "N.A." in their name.

Office of the Comptroller of the Currency
Customer Assistance Group
1301 McKinney Street, Suite 3710
Houston, TX 77010
800-613-6743
customerassitance@occ.treas.gov (email)
www.occ.treas.gov

B. Federal Savings and Loans and Federal Savings Banks

Some federal savings and loans include the initials F.S.L. in their name; some federal savings banks have the initials F.S.B. in theirs.

Office of Consumer Programs
Office of Thrift Supervision
1700 G Street, NW, 5th Floor
Washington, DC 20552
800-842-6929
202-906-6237
consumer.complaint@ots.treas.gov (email)
www.ots.treas.gov

C. National Credit Unions

Public Affairs Division
National Credit Union Administration
1775 Duke Street
Alexandria, VA 22314-3428
703-518-6300
www.ncua.gov

D. State Banks (Members of the Federal Reserve System)

Division of Consumer and Community Affairs
Mail Stop 801
Federal Reserve Board
Washington, DC 20551
202-452-3693
www.federalreserve.gov

E. State Banks (Not Members of the Federal Reserve System)

Office of Compliance and Consumer Affairs
Federal Deposit Insurance Corp.
550 17th Street, NW
Room PA-1730, 17th Floor
Washington, DC 20429
800-934-3342
202-942-3100
consumer@fdic.gov (email)
www.fdic.gov

F. Department Store, Gasoline Company and Other Creditors

Federal Trade Commission
Consumer Response Center
CRC-240
Washington, DC 20580
877-382-4357
www.ftc.gov ∎

Student Loans

Education is our passport to the future, for tomorrow belongs to the people who prepare for it today.

—Malcolm X, 1925-1965

With the cost of education skyrocketing, it's not surprising that student loan borrowing is on the rise. Most graduates these days face not only an uncertain economic future, but also mountains of student loan debt.

Dealing with student loan debt is often a challenge, which is compounded if you're behind in payments. Because the government guarantees most student loans, if you don't pay, it is the government that will try to collect. This is significant because the government can use far more aggressive collection tactics than private collectors. Among other things, the government can take your tax refund and garnish your wages without first getting a court judgment. To make matters worse, there's no time limit for collecting on student loans. The government can keep coming after you ten, 20 or even 30 years after you graduate.

Although you may want to throw this book across the room and try to forget that you owe thousands of dollars in student loans, denial is not the best strategy. One of the worst things you can do is pretend you're not in over your head. One of the best things you can do is learn about the types of student loans you have and the options available to you to pay them back.

Borrowing Is on The Rise

During the 1970s, 1980s and 1990s, the government expanded student loan eligibility to help millions of people. By the late 1990s, the federal government was providing more than $65 billion in student loans each year, compared with less than $10 billion per year just a decade before. In 2000, approximately 64% of students obtained federal student loans—an increase from approximately 42% in the early 1990s. The average undergraduate borrows more than $16,000, the average graduate student borrows more than $25,000 and the average professional school student borrows more than $65,000 (even more for those attending private schools). Nearly one-half of the people who attended professional schools such as law or medical school, have student loan debt in excess of their annual incomes. A 2002 survey by the State Public Interest Research Groups found that about 39% of student borrowers graduate with unmanageable levels of debt. The percentage is much higher for lower-income students and for African-American and Latino students.

There are a number of ways to deal with student loan debt. This chapter reviews the basic types of government student loans and ways to repay them. It also includes a summary of deferment, cancellation and other options to consider if you are having trouble paying your loans.

A. Types of Loans

The first step to managing your student loan debt is understanding what types of loans you have. Because many repayment options and other programs are available for only certain types of loans, knowing what loans you have is essential to making informed decisions about how to handle them.

There is a myriad of student loan types. Here, we discuss the most common ones. If your student loan isn't covered here, get a copy of *Take Control of Your Student Loan Debt*, by Robin Leonard and Deanne Loonin (Nolo). It discusses all types of student loans, including the less common ones.

Student Loan Terminology

As you read this chapter, you may see unfamiliar terms or terms with meanings that may not be obvious. Here's what you need to know:

Guaranty agency. A state or private nonprofit company that is essentially an insurance company. Guaranty agencies must insure your loans and pay the holder if you default. If that happens, the guaranty agency will receive reinsurance money from the federal Department of Education. Information about each state's guaranty agency, including how to contact it, is available at www.ed.gov/Programs/bastmp/SGA.htm or by calling 800-433-3243.

Holder. The owner of your loan or company hired by the owner to service it (that is, collect and process payments). Your loan holder may be your lender or a company that has purchased your loan from the lender. If you're in default, the holder will be a guaranty agency, the Department of Education or a collection agency working for the Department.

Lender. The institution from which you obtained your loan. This may be a bank, savings and loan, credit union, your school or the federal government.

---

1. Federal Student Loans

Most student loans are guaranteed by the federal government, meaning that the government will reimburse your lender or the state or private guaranty agency if you don't pay what you owe. The government does this so that private lenders will have incentives to offer student loans. Other federal loans, called direct loans, are provided directly by the government to students. Through these various programs, the government provides about 70% of all student aid.

Here are the most common types of federal loans:

Stafford and Direct loans. Most federal loans are either Stafford (previously called Guaranteed Student Loans or GSLs) or Direct loans. Stafford loans are made directly by the government or by a financial institution to help pay for college or graduate school education. These loans have been around in one form or another since the 1960s. The Direct loan program is newer, beginning only in 1993. Under this program, the government makes loans directly to students, eliminating the role of banks.

Perkins loans, National Direct Student loans and National Defense Student loans. A Perkins loan is a low-interest loan for undergraduate or graduate students with very low incomes. These loans were previously known as National Direct Student Loans, and before that, National Defense Student Loans. The federal government guarantees repayment of Perkins loans, but unlike other loans, Perkins loans are made by the school with a combination of federal and school funds. This means that the school, and not a bank or the government, is the lender.

PLUS loans. Loans for parents are called PLUS loans. These loans are also federally guaranteed and are made to creditworthy parents to pay for their dependent children's education.

Other federal loans. There are many other types of federal loans including loans for independent students, professionals and nursing students. To find out more, contact your lender or the Federal Student Aid Information Center (800-433-3243). The Center offers a free booklet, *The Student Guide,* that explains many of the basic terms and rules governing federal loans (to get a copy, call the Center or visit its website at www.ed.gov/prog_info/SFA/ StudentGuide).

2. Private Loans

Many students have private loans—loans made by banks and other financial institutions without being guaranteed by the federal government. Private loans are closely linked with federal loans, however. Many graduate students and some undergraduates apply for federally guaranteed loans and private loans with one application package.

Many loans are made by the Student Loan Marketing Association (Sallie Mae) or by the New England Loan Marketing Association (Nellie Mae). For more information on these loans, contact Sallie Mae at 800-222-7183 (or visit its website at www. salliemae.com) and Nellie Mae at 800-634-9308 (or visit its website at www.nelliemae.com). For more information about other types of private loans, see *Take Control of Your Student Loan Debt*, by Robin Leonard and Deanne Loonin (Nolo).

3. State Loans

Many states have their own student loan programs. To find out about these programs, contact your state department of higher education or state guarantee agency. The Department of Education's website (see Section G) has contact information for each state guarantee agency.

B. Figuring Out Who Holds Your Student Loan

If you want to set up a repayment plan, postpone payments, consolidate your loans, cancel a loan or apply for some other government program, you not only need to know what type of loan you have, but also who holds your loan. If you're in default, you've probably heard from the holder because it's trying to collect the loan. If you're not in default, it's often more difficult to find out who holds your loan. Try these sources:

- The Department of Education (800-621-3115; 800-730-8913 (TYY)). Department representatives are trained to assist borrowers in default.
- The National Student Loan Database (www.nslds.ed.gov). This is the Department of Education's central database for student aid. You can get information about loan or grant amounts, outstanding balances, loan status and disbursements. Identification information is required to access the database, including a personal identification number (PIN) that you can obtain online. You can also access the database by calling the Federal Student Aid Information Center.
- Federal Student Aid Information Center (800-4-FED-AID). Center representatives can help you access the National Student Loan Database and find information about the holder of your loan.
- If you've tried all of these places and are still having trouble, consider calling the student loan ombudsman office at 877-557-2575. (See Section G for more information on the ombudsman office.)

C. Repaying Student Loans

If you're struggling to repay your loans, you have good reason to feel hopeful. Many lenders, daunted by the number of students defaulting on their loans, have come up with new, flexible repayment options for student loan borrowers. Some of these plans apply only if you're not in default. Other repayment plans were created specifically to help you get out of default.

The best advice is this: Don't stick your head in the sand. If you let your loan payments slip, you'll most likely hear from the loan holder right away. If you ignore them completely, the government has all kinds of ways to come after you for collection. (See Section F for more on collection.) It's best to deal with the problem early by learning about the options available to you and taking action.

1. Repayment Plans

There are many flexible options for repaying federal loans. The options are more limited for private loans. This section focuses on federal loans only. If you have a private loan, you should contact your loan holder for more information about repayment plans.

Standard plan. This is the basic payment plan for federal loans. These plans carry the highest monthly payments, but cost less in the long run because you pay less interest. About 90% of all borrowers either choose this plan or end up with it because they fail to choose something else. In most cases, a standard plan requires that you pay your student loans back in ten years.

Graduated plan. In a graduated plan, payments start out low and increase every few years. This may be your best option if you are just starting a career or business and your income is low but likely to increase over time.

Extended repayment plan. This plan allows you to stretch your payments over a longer period of time, from 12 to 30 years, depending on the loan amount. Your monthly payments will be lower, but you'll pay more interest over the long-term.

Plans for low-income borrowers. There are other plans available for low-income borrowers. You may be eligible for these plans even if your financial difficulties are only temporary. If you have a Direct loan, you can apply for an Income Contingent Repayment Plan (ICRP). Under the ICRP, your monthly payments can be as low as five dollars or even zero. The ICRP may be your only choice if you are in dire financial straits, but use it as a last resort. Because the low monthly payments often don't pay even the accruing interest, you won't make a dent in the principal balance. You must renew the plan every year and the monthly payment amount will change if your financial circumstances change. If you make payments pursuant to an ICRP plan for 25 years, the government will cancel the remaining balance.

⚠ **You may owe taxes if the government cancels your loan.** If a government agency cancels the balance of your loan, you may owe taxes on the amount cancelled. For more on this, see Chapter 6, Section F.

If you have a federal loan other than a Direct loan, you may be eligible for an income-sensitive repayment plan. Under this plan, you pay a monthly amount that is affordable for you, based on your annual income, family size and total loan amount. This plan must be renewed every year and the monthly payment changes if your financial circumstances change.

2. Loan Consolidation

Consolidation is a good option if you are having trouble paying your loans. You can consolidate loans even if you're already in default. In fact, consolidation is one good way to get out of default. (See Section E for more on getting out of default.)

When you consolidate, you refinance several loans or even just one loan with better interest rates and payment terms. Often, the result is lower monthly payments. You may want to consolidate your loans if:

- you can't afford the monthly payments on your federal student loans, don't qualify for a postponement and aren't eligible for any of the payment plans for low-income borrowers described in Section C.1
- you qualify for some of the payment plans for low-income borrowers described in Section C.1, but you are so deep in debt that you still can't afford your monthly payments
- you can afford substantial monthly payments and intend to pay off your loans under a standard plan, but you want to refinance at a lower interest rate
- you are in default, but can make low monthly payments, or
- you don't qualify for loan cancellation (see Section D.1).

The vast majority of loans can be consolidated, but there are some restrictions. For example, usually you cannot consolidate private loans. Also, although you can consolidate your loans jointly if you are married, you and your spouse must agree to pay the entire loan if you later get a divorce. And you may lose certain benefits if you consolidate jointly.

There are two main loan consolidation programs. The FFEL Consolidation Program requires you to find a lender who will offer you a consolidated loan. Not all lenders in this program will consolidate loans that are already in default.

A second, and usually much better program, particularly for low-income borrowers, is the Direct Consolidation Loan Program. In this program, you consolidate your loans directly with the federal government. To get a Direct Consolidation Loan, contact the Department of Education (see Section G). The Department's website has lots of information about consolidation, including an online calculator that tells you what your monthly payments would be under a Direct Consolidation Loan. You can even apply for the loan online.

There are many advantages to consolidation including the possibility of getting out of default and making only small monthly payments. There are also disadvantages. If you have old loans, your interest rate will probably go up, not down, with consolidation. Consolidation will not completely clean up your credit report either. Your report will reflect that your previous loans were in default but are now paid in full through the new loan.

D. Strategies When You Just Can't Pay

If you can't make payments on your student loans, even with one of the payment plans discussed above, don't give up. You may have other options. For example, in limited circumstances, you may be able to cancel your student loans altogether. Or, if you can't cancel your loans, postponing payments by obtaining a deferment or forbearance may be an option. Eliminating your student loan debt in bankruptcy is another possibility, although remote—recent changes to the law make it very difficult to get rid of student loan debt this way.

1. Canceling Student Loans

You may be able to cancel your student loan under certain circumstances. If you qualify for cancellation, it is always your best option because it completely wipes out the remaining loan balance and allows you to get reimbursement for any payments you have made or that have been taken from you through tax intercepts or wage garnishments.

Below are several ways to cancel your loan. Keep in mind that the first three—cancellation due to school closure, false certification and unpaid refunds—apply primarily to students who attended trade schools.

School closure. Many former students were lulled into taking out student loans to attend a school (usually a trade school), only to have the school close before they could finish the program. You can cancel a Stafford, Direct, Perkins, PLUS or the portion of a consolidation loan used to pay off any of these loans if (1) the loan was made after January 1, 1986, and (2) you were unable to complete the program because the school closed during one of the following time periods:

- before you began attending classes
- while you were enrolled and attending classes (and you were not able to complete your studies), or
- within 90 days of when you left the school.

The Department of Education has a list of closed schools. In order to get a closed school cancellation, your school must be on the list and you must meet the above time period requirements using the Department of Education's school closure date. You can get the closed school list and application forms by calling the Department or visiting its website. (See Section G for contact information.)

False certification. If the school did not make sure you were qualified to attend the program, you may be able to cancel your loans based on "false certification." This program applies to Stafford, Direct, PLUS or the portion of a consolidation loan used to pay off one of these loans. The grounds for false certification are:

- you did not have a high school diploma or GED at the time of admission and the school did not properly test your ability to benefit from the program

- at the time of enrollment, you could not meet the licensing requirements for employment in the field for which you were to receive training (for example, you had a felony record and enrolled in a security guard course, but your state doesn't permit prior felons to work as security guards), or
- your signature was forged on the loan papers.

Only loans made after January 1, 1986, qualify. You can get false certification application forms from the Department of Education (see Section G for contact information).

Unpaid refunds. This program is newer—it went into effect on July 1, 2000. It allows you to cancel all or a portion of a loan if the school failed to pay you a refund that it owed you. Loans must be Stafford, PLUS or Direct and must be made after January 1, 1986. In addition, some states have funds to reimburse students who didn't get refunds due them.

Permanent disability. You can cancel any federal loan if you are unable to work because of an illness or injury that is expected to continue indefinitely or result in your death. In most cases, to qualify for this cancellation, you cannot have had the injury or illness at the time you signed up for the loan. If you did have the disability at the time you got the loan, you might be able to cancel your loans if you can show substantial deterioration of your disability. To qualify for loan cancellation due to disability, you will need to get a statement from your treating physician on a form provided by the holder of your loan. You can get a copy of the application form from the Department of Education (see Section G for contact information).

Parents who took out PLUS loans together cannot both get disability cancellations unless both are disabled. If only one parent is disabled and both parents took out the loan, the nondisabled parent is still obligated to pay.

Participation in a volunteer program, teaching program or military service. Different federal loans have different cancellation programs that apply if you are engaged in a particular type of work, such as volunteering for the Peace Corps, teaching needy populations or serving in the military. Some programs allow you to postpone payments on your loans only while you are engaged in the service, others allow you to cancel all or a portion of the loan. For more information about these cancellation programs, see *Take Control of Your Student Loan Debt*, by Robin Leonard and Deanne Loonin (Nolo).

2. Postponing Payments

If you can't afford to make any payments right now, you may be able to postpone student loan payments for a certain period of time through either a deferment or forbearance.

Deferments. Each type of federal loan program has different rules that allow you to postpone paying your loan in certain circumstances. These postponements are called "deferments." If you get a deferment, you will still have to pay the loan back at some point, but you can wait a while. Most important, interest on the loan will not accrue during the deferment period. Deferments are only available if you are not yet in default and if you meet the specific criteria for your type of loan.

The most common deferments are available if you are:

- enrolled in school at least half-time
- unemployed and seeking employment
- suffering an economic hardship (only for certain loans obtained after June 30, 1993), or
- a parent with young children.

For more information about deferments, see *Take Control of Your Student Loan Debt*, by Robin Leonard and Deanne Loonin (Nolo). Application forms for deferments are available from the Department of Education (see Section G for contact information).

Forbearances. If you don't qualify for a deferment, but are facing hard times, your loan holder may still allow you to postpone payment on your loans or temporarily reduce your payments. An arrangement of this sort is called a forbearance. You may be able to get a forbearance even if your loans are in default.

Forbearances are less attractive than deferments because interest continues to accrue when you are not making payments. But if you can't make your loan payments, a forbearance will at least keep you out of default. In the long run, the cost of default is much higher than the interest that accrues during a forbearance. Even if you can't get a forbearance on all of your loans, a forbearance on some of them may give you enough breathing room to catch up financially.

3. Discharging Student Loans in Bankruptcy

Before October 1998, you could get rid of student loans in bankruptcy if your payments had become due more than seven years prior to the bankruptcy or if repaying the loans would be a severe hardship for you. Congress eliminated the seven-year rule in 1998. However, you can still discharge student loans if repayment would cause you "undue hardship." This is a difficult, although not impossible, standard to meet.

The Bankruptcy Code does not define "undue hardship," but in general, it means that your present income is inadequate to pay the loan and your future earning potential will not change the situation. In determining undue hardship, bankruptcy courts look to several factors, discussed below. If you can show that all or most factors are present, the court will discharge your loans. If you meet only some of the factors, the court does not have to discharge any of your student loans. However, some courts might discharge a portion of your loans if doing so would help you repay the remaining portion of your loans.

In deciding whether it would be an undue hardship for you to repay your student loans, most bankruptcy courts look at the following factors:

- **Poverty.** Based on your current income and expenses, you cannot maintain a minimal living standard and repay the loans.
- **Persistence.** It is not enough that you can't currently pay your loan. You must also demonstrate to the court that your current financial condition is likely to continue for a significant portion of the repayment period.
- **Good faith.** The court will look at whether you've made a good faith effort to repay your debt.

Recently, a few courts have used a more flexible standard for determining whether student loans should be discharged based on undue hardship. Those courts look to the "totality of the circumstances." (*In re Kopf*, 245 B.R. 731 (Bankr. D. Me. 2000); *In re Coutts*, 263 B.R. 394 (Bankr. D. Mass. 2001)).

Even if bankruptcy is unlikely to erase your student loans, it may help you get rid of other debts, freeing up money to repay your student loans. Another option is to file for Chapter 13 bankruptcy (see Chapter 16) and pay your student loan arrears in a court approved payment plan over three to five years.

Student Loans and School Transcripts

Your school may refuse to turn over your transcripts if you don't pay your student loans. Many students need their transcripts to supplement job applications, and virtually all former students need their transcripts to enroll in school again.

Filing for bankruptcy may solve the problem. If your student loan is discharged in bankruptcy (which, as discussed above, may be difficult), the school must provide you with your transcript. (*In re Gustafson*, 111 B.R. 282 (9th Cir. BAP 1990).) Even better, some courts have held that a school must release your transcripts upon the mere act of filing for bankruptcy, regardless of whether the loans are eventually discharged or not. (*Loyola University v. McClarty*, 234 B.R. 386 (1999).)

E. Getting Out of Default

Getting out of default is key to dealing with student loans. Many repayment plans (see Section C.1) and most postponement options (see Section D.2) require that you not be in default. In addition, as long as you're in default, you are not eligible to get new loans or grants. You can get out of default by canceling your loan or discharging it in bankruptcy. Here are a few additional ways to get out of default:

1. Reasonable and Affordable Payment Plans

One way to renew eligibility for new loans is to set up a "reasonable and affordable payment plan" with your loan holder. This plan allows you to make payments in an amount that you can afford based on your financial circumstances. But beware. You can only take advantage of this plan once. If you don't live up to the payment agreement, you can't get another reasonable and affordable payment plan.

If you make six consecutive and timely payments under a reasonable and affordable payment plan, you become eligible to apply for new federal student loans or grants if you want to return to school. In order to get out of default, you must make at least 12 consecutive and timely payments. At that point, the guaranty agency or Department of Education can sell your loan to a new lender. This is called loan rehabilitation. Once your loan is rehabilitated, you will be put on a standard ten-year repayment plan or you can request one of the more flexible options discussed in Section C.1, above. Loan rehabilitation also wipes out the default notation on your credit report.

2. Loan Consolidation

Loan consolidation is discussed in Section C.2 above. Usually, consolidation is a faster way to get out of default than a reasonable and affordable payment plan. Once you go through the application process and get a Direct Consolidation Loan, you will immediately be taken out of default status. You will stay this way as long as you keep making payments.

F. Consequences of Ignoring Student Loan Debt

Although student loans are not secured debt and therefore you will not lose your home or car if you don't pay them, they are also different from most other unsecured debts. (See Chapter 1 for a discussion of secured and unsecured debts. See Chapter 5 for information on prioritizing debts.) If you don't pay your student loans, you won't be able to get additional student loans or grants in the future. In addition, you will be subjected to a number of "special" debt collection tactics that only the government can use. These government collection tools can have very severe consequences.

First, the government can charge you hefty collection fees, often far in excess of the amount you originally borrowed. Second, unlike almost every other kind of debt imaginable, there is no statute of limitations for collection of student loans. This means that even 20 or 30 years after you went to school, the government can continue to try to collect your loans.

If you don't pay your student loans, the government can also:

- seize your income tax refund
- garnish up to 10% of your wages without first getting a court judgment (the government is currently attempting to increase that to 15%), and
- attach some federal benefits that are usually exempt from collection, such as Social Security income, although the government must let you keep a certain amount of this income. Advocates are currently challenging the ability of the government to take Social Security benefits to collect on older student loans. The outcome of this challenge remains to be seen.

If you get notice of a wage garnishment or tax intercept, you have the right to challenge it by requesting a hearing. Sometimes just the act of requesting a hearing prompts the collector to agree to a payment plan. If you can pay a small amount, you should consider the various affordable payment plans that can get you out of default (see Section E).

Will the Department of Education Sue You to Collect Your Student Loans?

The Department of Education has had the power to sue defaulted borrowers for quite some time. For a long time, they rarely used this power. Those days are definitely over. Since the mid-1990s, the Department has become very aggressive in suing borrowers to collect student loans. There was a 55% increase in student loan lawsuits filed by the Justice Department from 1997 to 1998. By 1998, the government had filed over 14,000 student loan collection cases. The Department of Education expects the numbers to grow as it gets more and more aggressive in trying to collect defaulted student loans.

G. Where to Go for Help

Here are a few good resources for learning about and dealing with student loan debt:

The student loan ombudsman office. The Department of Education's student loan ombudsman assists borrowers with student loan problems. The ombudsman office will informally research your complaint, and if it finds that it is justified, will work with you, the Department of Education and your loan holder to resolve the problem. It if decides that your complaint is not justified, it will provide you with an explanation as to why it arrived at that decision. The ombudsman office is a "last resource"—usually it will help you only if you have first tried to resolve the problem on your own.

You can contact the student loan ombudsman office at 877-557-2575. Assistance is available in both English and Spanish. It also has an excellent website (www.sfahelp.ed.gov) where you can complete an online request for assistance.

The Department of Education. The Department of Education also has lots of information about student loans as well as application forms for all of the various repayment, cancellation, postponement and other programs discussed in this chapter. You can reach the Department at 800-621-3115 (voice) or 800-848-0983 (TDD). Or, visit its website at www.ed.gov to get both information and downloadable forms.

Take Control of Your Student Loan Debt. *Take Control of Your Student Loan Debt,* by Robin Leonard and Deanne Loonin (Nolo) has detailed information about managing your student loan debt, including a comprehensive description of the many types of student loans, repayment plans and cancellation programs. In addition, it has sample forms and contact information for all the state and private guaranty agencies. ■

Child Support and Alimony

The fundamental evil of the world arose from the fact that the good Lord has not created money enough.

— Heinrich Heine, German poet
and critic, 1797-1856

Benjamin Franklin once said that only two things in life are certain: death and taxes. Of course, Franklin's remark was made in the 18th century. If he were alive today and a parent with a child support obligation, he would undoubtedly add child support to the list.

If You Are Owed Child Support or Child Support and Alimony

This chapter addresses the concerns of debtors who pay child support or alimony, not those entitled to receive it. Many people, of course, have debt problems because they aren't receiving support to which they are entitled. While this chapter doesn't explain how to get the support to which you are entitled, reading it will nevertheless help you understand your rights and the strategies available to you.

Your first step is to contact the local child support enforcement agency in your county. That agency may be located in the courthouse, at the local prosecuting attorney's office, at the welfare department or at some other location. You might increase the likelihood of getting your support by contacting a national nonprofit organization that helps custodial parents collect child support. One group to contact is ACES—Association for Children for Enforcement of Support, 800-738-ACES, www.childsupport-ACES.org. ACES helps custodial parents work with their local enforcement agency and provides specific advice on how to be heard and get your case processed, or if necessary, file a complaint with the agency.

In addition, private collection agencies have sprung up around the country which try to collect child support for custodial parents. Two such collection agencies increasing their presence are Children's Support Services and Child Support Investigations. Be aware that a collection agency will charge an application fee (as much as $50) and will keep a percentage of what it collects—perhaps as much as 25%–33%. Some of these agencies have been criticized for taking the application fee and then not doing anything else. If you're interested, look in your local phone book to find an office near you. Before signing up, find out exactly how much it will cost and the agency's rate of success. Then call the local Better Business Bureau to see if any complaints have been filed.

Whether parents live together or apart, they are legally obligated to support their children. When they live together, a court rarely involves itself with how the parents raise or support their children—unless someone claims that the children are being abused or neglected.

As soon as the parents split up, however, or one of the parents applies for welfare, the law gives the state the right to involve—perhaps over-involve—itself in how the children are supported. Sweeping laws enacted by Congress during the 1980s and 1990s have resulted in greatly stepped-up state child support collection efforts. These laws have changed the way child support is established, paid and collected when past due.

Explained below are child support enforcement techniques used in most states and some strategies for dealing with your child support debt when you can't pay. Before getting into that material, however, take this advice to heart: Pay your child support obligation unless you will starve or go homeless. No children—not yours, not anybody's—should grow up poor. Obviously, you can do little about the poverty endured by millions of children in this country. But you can do everything humanly possible to see that your own kids are adequately supported.

It's true that many parents who don't pay child support believe they have a good reason for not doing so:

- they have a new family to support
- their ex won't let them see their kids
- their ex moved their kids far away
- their ex misuses the support
- their ex plays all day while they have to work, or
- the court ordered them to pay too much.

But your reason makes no difference to a judge. If you owe child support and have the ability to pay, a judge will use a variety of harsh legal techniques to see that you do, and may lock you up if all else fails.

Child Support and Visitation

If your ex is interfering with your visitation rights, you generally don't have the right to withhold support. But you can schedule a court hearing (see Section C, below) to show substantial interference with your visitation right and ask the judge to rectify the situation. You'll need to document a persistent pattern of being denied access to your children. A good way to do this is to take notes on a calendar. Missing a weekend or two won't fly. If you've seen the kids once in eight months, however, a court may well hold your ex in contempt of court for violating the court order allowing you visitation. In addition, some judges will order your child's other parent to reimburse you for expenses you incur trying to exercise your visitation rights. And a judge may suspend your obligation to pay child support if your child's other parent and the child have disappeared altogether, leaving no one to whom you can send the support.

A. How Child Support Is Determined

The federal Family Support Act of 1988 requires all states to use a formula or guidelines to calculate child support. You or your child's other parent can request that a court review an existing order to see if it is in accordance with the formula or guideline. Don't request a review unless you know you are paying above what is required. If you're not, you might wind up being ordered to pay more. Section C, below, describes how you go to court to have the judge review the support order.

In addition to your obligation to make monthly child support payments, a court may require you to pay some of the following expenses as a part of child support:

- health and dental insurance for your children, or your child's health and dental costs if neither parent has insurance covering the children—in fact, many states mandate that a parent pay for medical insurance if the costs are reasonable

- life insurance naming your child's custodial parent as the beneficiary
- child care so that the custodial parent can work or go to school
- education costs for your children.

B. Enforcement of Child Support Obligations

This section describes the methods used to collect child support as it becomes due. Section D, below, discusses the methods used to collect past due child support, called arrears.

If your child support order was issued by a judge fifteen years ago, it probably just requires you to send a certain amount of money each month to your child's other parent. If your order was issued more recently, however, it may be very different. Today, you may have money withheld from your paycheck, or may be required to send money to a court clerk or state agency which in turn sends a check to the custodial parent.

1. Automatic Wage Withholding

The federal Family Support Act requires that all states implement an automatic wage withholding program. For child support orders made or modified on or after January 1, 1984, wage withholding is automatic unless the parties agree otherwise (for example, your ex-spouse agrees that you pay her directly) or there is good cause not to require immediate withholding. The way the second exception is carried out varies by state. For example, in some states if the parent has a reliable history of paying child support, wage withholding is not automatic. In others, regardless of payment history, automatic wage withholding is ordered.

For pre-1994 child support orders, wage withholding may also be ordered if you are in arrears. These automatic wage withholding provisions also apply to orders which combine child support and alimony, but not to orders for alimony only. And, if wage withholding is ordered in one state (for example, where your child lives), but you live in another, your state's court will enforce the wage garnishment.

An automatic wage withholding order works quite simply. After a court orders you to pay child support, the court—or your child's other parent—sends a copy of the court order, along with the custodial parent's name and address, to your employer. At each pay period, your employer withholds a portion of your pay and sends it on to the custodial parent. If you and your child's other parent agree—and the court allows it—you can avoid the wage withholding and make payments directly to the custodial parent or through a third party.

If you don't receive regular wages, but do have a regular source of income, such as income from a pension, retirement fund, annuity, Social Security, unemployment compensation or other public benefits, the court can order the child support withheld. Instead of forwarding a copy of the order and the custodial parent's name and address to an employer, the court sends the information to the retirement plan administrator or public agency from whom you receive your benefits.

If your income is from Social Security or a private pension governed by either ERISA (Employee Retirement Income Security Act) or REA (Retirement Equity Act), the administrator might not honor the court order. This is because Social Security and many private pensions have "anti-alienation" clauses which prohibit the administrator from turning over the funds to anyone other than the beneficiary (you).

2. Establish Paternity

As an additional effort to find fathers and make them pay child support, the Family Support Act requires states to meet certain standards for establishing paternity. To help states foot the bill, the Act authorizes the federal government to reimburse states up to 90% of the costs spent on paternity lab tests.

If you've got a kid you're not paying child support for and you never married the child's mother, you may find yourself hauled into court on a paternity and child support action—up to 18 years after the child was born. If the court declares that you are the father, you are likely to be ordered to pay support until the child turns 18, and, in many states, will probably be required to pay back support covering up to three years. In other states, you aren't responsible for support until the date that the custodial parent files in court.

To establish your paternity, the mother of the child, or a county attorney if the mother receives welfare, will sue you as the alleged father. To successfully fight it, you will have to refute the following kinds of evidence:

- **Access.** That you and the mother had an opportunity to engage in sexual intercourse during the period of conception.
- **Potency and fertility.** That you are neither impotent nor sterile.
- **Blood tests.** Blood tests are used to rule out the possibility of paternity. Initially, your blood will be compared for types (A, B, AB, O) and Rh factor. If you are not excluded by those two tests, your blood will be HLA tested. HLA tests can disprove paternity with nearly 98% accuracy.
- **Genetic typing.** DNA "fingerprinting" tests your cells against the child's and can prove or disprove paternity with 99.99% accuracy, when the tests are administered correctly.
- **Acknowledgment of paternity.** If you paid for the mother's hospital costs, had your name put on the birth certificate, ever acknowledged that the child is yours, voluntarily sent support or took other steps that would make you seem like the father, you'll have a large obstacle to overcome.
- **Resemblance.** If you look like the child, the mother or county attorney will probably march the kid past you while you are sitting in the court for the judge to see.

3. Other Efforts to Collect Support As It Becomes Due

Below are a few other efforts being undertaken to help collect child support payments as they become due. What these efforts point out is how much the states are getting into the act of collecting child support.

- Computers are used to track parents and make sure they pay.
- States are theoretically required to collect the Social Security numbers of both parents when a child is born, and must pass those numbers on to the state agency that enforces child support.
- Judges sometimes order noncustodial parents to pay child support to the county child support enforcement agency, which in turn pays the custodial parent. This method is often used when the noncustodial parent is without regular income (perhaps he is self-employed) or when parents agree to waive the automatic wage withholding.
- Judges sometimes order noncustodial parents to make payments to court clerks or court trustees who in turn pay the custodial parents.

C. Modifying the Amount of Child Support

If you owe child support you can't afford, you must take the initiative to change your child support order. This requires that you go to court, request a modification and show the judge that you have inadequate income and cannot afford the ordered support. If you don't get the order modified and child support you cannot pay builds up, a court won't retroactively decrease it, even if you were too sick to get out of bed during the affected period. To repeat—once child support is owed and unpaid, it remains a debt until it is paid.

In most states, filing a motion to modify child support requires you to fill out and file court papers, schedule a hearing and present evidence to a judge. To do this, you'll probably need the help of a lawyer. (See Chapter 20.) The kind of evidence to show the court includes:

- a sworn statement from your most recent employer, if you were recently let go
- records of your job search, if you've been looking unsuccessfully, and
- sworn statements from all medical and healing professionals, if you are sick, injured, depressed or whatever.

1. Legal Reasons to Justify a Support Change

To get a judge to reduce a child support order, you must show a significant change of circumstance since the last order. What constitutes a significant change of circumstance depends on your situation. Generally, the condition must not have been considered when the original order was made and must affect the current standard of living of you, your child or the custodial parent. Changes that qualify as significant include the following:

- **Your income has substantially decreased.** The decrease must be involuntary or for the ultimate benefit of your child. If you quit your job to become a basket weaver, the court probably won't modify your support obligation. If you quit your job to attend business school, however, the court may temporarily decrease the amount, expecting to increase it significantly when you graduate.

- **The custodial parent's income has substantially increased.** Not all increases in the custodial parent's income will qualify. For example, if your child's needs have increased as the

custodial parent's income has risen, you probably won't get a reduction. Or, if the custodial parent's income increase is from a new spouse's earnings, few courts will consider that money because the new spouse has no obligation to support your child.

- **Your expenses have increased.** You may be entitled to a reduction, for example, if you have a new child.

- **Your child's needs have decreased.** You may be entitled to a reduction, for instance, if your child is no longer attending private school. Be warned, however, that the older children get, the more often their financial needs increase.

- **The children spend more time in your custody than when the court initially ordered the support.** In this situation, you're entitled to a reduction because the other parent needs less money for the children.

As you can see, the judge won't be inclined to modify your support order if your financial condition —or the financial condition of your child or your child's other parent—hasn't changed substantially since the order was initially issued. If you just feel the court was wrong the first time, you're probably out of luck.

If your child support obligation is old and exceeds what you would now owe under your state's mandatory child support guidelines, you may be able to get a modification on that basis. The Family Support Act specifically requires that a child support order be reviewed to determine its accordance with the guidelines. Be aware, however, that the effect of the Act has been to raise child support amounts nationwide, not to lower them. If your current payment isn't what is required by the Act, it's probably too low, not too high.

2. Negotiate With Your Child's Other Parent

Your request to modify the amount of child support you have to pay will be either contested or uncontested. Contested means your child's other parent opposes it, files formal papers with the court in opposition and shows up at the hearing with evidence refuting what you say. Uncontested means that your child's other parent does not file a response in court.

Child support modification hearings can be time-consuming, costly and unpleasant. If at all possible, avoid a contested hearing. Before you file the court papers, call your child's other parent and let her know of your changed circumstance. She may voluntarily agree to reduce the amount. If you were laid off or in an accident, she knows the court will probably order some change in the amount and may agree ahead of time.

If your child's other parent agrees to reduce the amount of child support you owe, make sure you get your new agreement in writing. Then bring it to the court for its approval. You may need the help of a lawyer or legal typing service to do this. (See Chapter 20.) Keep in mind that once a court sets support, only a court can change it. If you make an informal modification and your ex changes her mind, you won't have any recourse.

3. File Modification Papers If Negotiations Fail

If your child's other parent won't agree to a reduction in child support, you will have to take your dispute to court. If the judge denies your request, you will have to reassess your position. If you can't come up with the necessary payments by reducing your living expenses, you may need to consider filing for bankruptcy. This will allow you to get rid of some of your debts—such as those typically owed to credit card companies and health care providers—and free up some money to meet your child support obligation.

4. When You Can Stop Paying Child Support

You must pay child support for as long as your child support court order says you must pay, unless the court changes the order. If the order does not contain an ending date, depending on the state, you must support your children:

- until they reach 18
- until they are 19 or finished with high school, whichever occurs first
- until they reach 21
- as long as they are dependent, if they are disabled, or
- until they complete college.

To find out exactly what your state law requires, you'll need to do a little legal research or talk to a lawyer. (See Chapter 20.)

In addition, your child support obligation will probably end early if your child joins the military, gets married or moves out of the house to live independently, or a court declares your child emancipated.

Once you are no longer liable for support, it doesn't mean that unpaid child support disappears. If the custodial parent went to court and had the back support made into a judgment, that judgment can be collected for as long as your state lets a creditor enforce a judgment. This typically covers a period of between 10 and 20 years (see Chapter 15, Section F), which can be extended if the judgment is renewed. In most states, judgments for back child support can easily last your entire life. Also, as mentioned earlier, child support judgments collect interest, and the amount frequently becomes larger than the child support arrearage.

D. How Unpaid Child Support Is Collected

To you, unpaid child support is unpaid child support. You owed it but didn't pay it. But unpaid child support takes two forms, and the difference is important in how that support can be collected.

The first type of unpaid child support is the money that accumulates when you don't pay what you owe under a court order to pay child support. This child support is generally called arrears. If you owe a lot in arrears, your child's other parent may go to court and ask a judge to issue a judgment for the amount of the arrears. This second type of unpaid child support is generally called a judgment for child support.

Under the Family Support Act and various state laws, states' child support enforcement agencies, custodial parents, judges and district attorneys use nearly ten different methods to collect arrears. To use a few of the methods, the custodial parent must have a court judgment.

> **EXAMPLE:** Al was ordered to pay his ex-wife Cindy $550 per month in child support. He lost his job and hasn't made the last three payments. He is in arrears under the order a total of $1,650. Cindy can try to collect the arrears owed under the child support order, or she can go ask a judge to grant her a judgment for the amount he owes. Then she can use some additional techniques for collecting.

You Can Run but You Cannot Hide. You may think that by moving frequently, you can avoid paying child support. It's possible for a while, but unlikely if your ex is persistent. Each state and the federal government maintains a parent locator service that searches federal, state and local records to find missing parents. The federal parent locator service has access to Social Security, IRS and all other federal information records except census records. The state locator services check welfare, unemployment, motor vehicle and other state records. And, last but not least, every employer is required to provide identifying information on all new employees, which is entered in a federal database maintained for the specific purpose of locating "deadbeat dads."

Child Support Arrearages: The Debt That Won't Go Away

Back child support is a debt that almost never goes away unless it is paid in full. In addition, the interest on this debt can become greater than the debt itself. Courts are usually prevented by law from considering the circumstances that gave rise to the debt, and may not reduce it for any purpose. Nor is back child support affected by bankruptcy. In a word, do what you can to pay your child support on time, or go to court to have it reduced if you are legitimately unable to make the current payments. (See Section C, above, for information on modifying the amount of child support due).

1. Intercept Your Income Tax Refunds

One of the most powerful collection methods available is an interception of your federal income tax refund. If you owe more than $150 and the custodial parent receives welfare, the county attorney who collects child support where the custodial parent lives (see Section 9, below) will notify the U.S. Department of the Treasury. Similarly, if the custodial parent doesn't receive welfare but asks the county attorney for help in collecting what's owed, the county attorney can call on the Treasury Department.

Before your refund is taken, you'll receive a written intercept notice which will give you a chance to request a hearing to object to the intercept. But the claims you can make at a hearing are limited. Judges only want to hear that the support has been paid or that the notice requests more than you owe. If the intercept notice incorrectly states an amount you owe, and is based on information given by the custodial parent, you need to ask her to attend the hearing, or ask the court to order her to attend if she won't on her own.

Only in rare cases will a judge listen to a hard-luck story and a claim of a desperate need for the funds. To most judges, adult hard-luck stories are not as heartbreaking as kids not being supported.

If you are now married to someone other than the custodial parent to whom you owe support, your spouse should attend the hearing and file a claim for her share of the refund. The IRS cannot send her portion to your child's other parent to satisfy a child support debt of yours, even in community property states. (See for example, *Sorenson v. Secretary of the Treasury,* 557 F. Supp. 729 (W.D. Wash. 1982), *aff'd,* 752 F.2d 1433 (9th Cir. 1985), *rev'd on other grounds,* 475 U.S. 851 (1986).)

If all or a part of your refund is intercepted wrongly—for example, the IRS took too much or your spouse's share was taken with your share—you can request a reimbursement. You do this by filing an amended tax return (Form 1040X). If you're requesting the refund because your spouse's share was taken, you must also complete Form 8379, Injured Spouse Claim and Allocation. You can obtain copies of both forms—and directions for filling them out—by calling 800-829-3676. Or you can download them from the Internet by visiting the IRS's website at www.irs.ustreas.gov.

States with income taxes also intercept tax refunds to satisfy child support debts. In Nebraska, for example, court clerks report all child support arrears to the state for an interception of the state tax refund. As with federal intercepts, you must be sent a notice and given the chance to schedule a hearing. And your spouse can file a claim to have her share withheld from what is sent to your child's other parent.

2. Place Liens on Your Property

In some states, a custodial parent owed child support can place a lien—a notice that tells the world that the custodial parent claims you owe her some money—on your real or personal property. The lien remains until your child is no longer entitled to support and you've paid all the arrears, or until the other parent agrees to remove the lien. The custodial parent can force the sale of your property, or can wait until the property is sold or refinanced. Some states require that the custodial parent obtain a judgment for the arrears before putting a lien on

property; other states allow liens to be imposed on property when you miss payments under the court order for support.

Your best defense is to schedule a hearing before a judge and claim that the lien on your property impairs your ability to pay your current support. If the lien, for example, is on your house and impairs your ability to borrow money to pay the child support arrears, make that clear to the judge. You'll probably need to bring copies of loan rejection letters specifically stating that your poor credit rating—due to the lien—was the reason for the rejection.

3. Require You to Post a Bond or Assets to Guarantee Payment

Some states allow judges to require parents with child support arrears to post a bond or assets, such as stock certificates, to guarantee payment. In some states, for example, if a self-employed parent misses a child support payment and the custodial parent requests a court hearing, the court can order the noncustodial parent to post assets (such as putting money into an escrow account).

Most states' Child Support Enforcement Agencies have the power to require parents to post bonds or assets. But not all agencies use this measure and others use it for extreme cases only. In practice, few bond companies will write bonds for child support debts. Most parents will find that they must put property into an escrow account, or, as is done in some states, such as Montana and Wyoming, into a trust account that is managed and invested for the child's benefit.

You must be given notice of the possible action and an opportunity to contest. Your best defense is that posting the assets or bond impairs your ability to pay your current support or to borrow money to pay the arrears.

4. The Arrears May Be Reported to Credit Bureaus

The law requires credit bureaus to include information about overdue child support in your credit report. Creditors and lenders often deny credit based on this information. In addition, sometimes creditors and lenders report the whereabouts of missing parents to child enforcement agencies.

Child support arrears remain on your credit report for up to seven years unless you can make a deal with the child support enforcement agency. Sometimes, an agency will agree not to report negative information to the credit bureau if you pay some or all of the overdue support. But, few child support enforcement agencies will agree to eliminate all negative information. Most will at least report that you were delinquent in the past. (See Chapter 18 for information on how to correct your report if information reported is wrong or obsolete).

Many states require child support enforcement agencies to notify you before reporting overdue child support information to the credit bureaus. Usually, the enforcement agency must give you a reasonable opportunity to dispute the information. Many states only require agencies to report overdue amounts over $1,000. (For information on how to find your state law, see Chapter 20.)

5. You May Be Publicly Humiliated

Congress is encouraging states to come up with creative ways to embarrass parents into paying the child support they owe. One method used nationwide by an association of state child support enforcement agencies is the publishing of "most wanted" lists of parents who owe child support.

In some areas, for example, the family court lists the names of parents not paying child support on cable television 300 times a week and in a full-page newspaper advertisement once a month. One county claims to have located over 50% of the parents owing support. Similarly, the Iowa attorney general reports that 90% of missing fathers who owe child support have been located through the state's "most wanted" poster program.

If your name is included on a most wanted list, your only recourse to get your name off the list (unless you don't mind being a local "celebrity") is to turn yourself in. You'll be ordered to make monthly payments henceforth—possibly your wages will be attached—and the court will take steps to see that you pay your back child support. But that may be better than having your Andy Warhol 15 minutes of fame 43 times a day or all over town.

6. You May Be Denied a State License

In several states, a parent with child support arrears will be denied an original or renewed driver's or professional license—doctor, lawyer, contractor and the like. And in some states, parents who owe child support are at risk of having their driver's licenses suspended.

7. You May Be Held in Contempt of Court

Failing to follow a court order is called contempt of court. A parent owed child support can schedule a hearing before a judge and ask that you be held in contempt of court. You must be served with a document ordering you to attend the hearing, and then must attend and explain why you haven't paid the support you owe. If you don't attend, the court can issue a warrant for your arrest. Many courts do issue warrants, so county jails have become resting stops for fathers who don't pay child support and fail to show up in court.

If you attend the hearing, the judge can still throw you in jail for violating the order to pay the support. And the judge may very well do so, depending on how convincing your story is as to why you haven't paid. A particularly nasty lawyer might schedule the hearing for late Friday afternoon before a judge known for putting parents behind on child support into jail. By the time the hearing is over, it will be too late in the day for you to hire a lawyer to help you fight the order. Most likely, you'll spend the weekend in the county jail. (A U.S. Supreme Court case upholding the right of a state to jail a parent for failing to pay child support is *Hicks on behalf of Feiock v. Feiock*, 485 U.S. 624 (1988).)

To stay out of jail, you may have to convince the judge that you're not as irresponsible as the judge probably thinks you are. Preparing evidence is a must. Your first step is to show why you didn't pay. If you've been out of work, get a sworn statement from your most recent employer stating why you were let go. If you went job searching but with no luck, provide records of when you interviewed or filled out an application, and with whom you spoke. Remember—disputes with your ex about custody or visitation are never an acceptable excuse for not paying child support.

Next, you want to explain why you didn't request a modification hearing. If you've been in bed or otherwise immobilized—depressed, sick or injured—get sworn statements from all medical and healing professionals who treated you. Also, get statements from friends or relatives who cared for you. Emphasize that you couldn't get out of bed.

If you spoke to lawyers about helping you file a modification request, but couldn't afford their fees, be sure to bring a list of the names of lawyers you spoke to, the date you spoke to each one and the fee the lawyer wanted to charge. If you tried to hire a Legal Aid lawyer to help you but you made too much money to qualify for such assistance, the office had too many cases and couldn't take yours or the office doesn't handle child support modifications, make sure you note the name of the lawyer and the date you spoke to her.

If the judge isn't inclined to put you behind bars, the judge will instead order you to make future payments and will set up a payment schedule for you to pay any back support still owed. The judge won't reduce the amount of your back support—arrears cannot be modified retroactively—but may decrease your future payments. The judge may also order your wages withheld or a lien placed on your property, or may order you to post a bond or other assets.

Holding a parent in contempt of court and throwing him in jail used to be the primary method of enforcing child support orders. Today, the technique is still used, but usually only if a wage withholding order (see Section B.1, above) and a wage garnish-

ment (see Section D.8, below) won't work. This is because courts recognize that a jailed parent cannot take the necessary steps (like holding a job) to make child support payments.

8. Your Wages May Be Garnished and Other Assets Seized

Child support arrears made into a court judgment can be collected by the various methods of collecting judgments described in Chapter 15. Even if the judgment was obtained in one state and you have since moved to another state, various state laws allow the custodial parent to register the judgment in the second state and enforce it there.

The most common method of collecting a judgment for support is a wage garnishment. A wage garnishment is similar to a wage withholding—a portion of your wages is removed from your paycheck and delivered to the custodial parent before you ever see any of it. In many states, the arrears need not be made into a judgment to be collected by way of a wage garnishment.

To garnish your wages, the custodial parent obtains authorization from the court in a document usually called a writ of execution. Under this authorization, the custodial parent directs the sheriff to seize a portion of your wages. The sheriff in turn notifies you and your employer of the garnishment.

Wage withholdings and wage garnishments differ in one way: The amount of a wage withholding is the amount of child support you have been ordered to pay each month. The amount of a wage garnishment, however, is a percentage of your paycheck. What you were once ordered to pay is irrelevant. The court simply wants to take money out of each of your paychecks—and leave you with a minimum to live on—until the owed back support is made up.

If a court orders that your wages be garnished to satisfy any debt except child support or alimony, a maximum of roughly 25% of your net wages can be taken. With unpaid child support, however, up to 50% of your net wages can be garnished and up to 60% if you are not currently supporting another dependent. If your check is already subject to a wage withholding for your future payments or a garnishment by a different creditor, the total amount taken from your paycheck cannot exceed 50% (or 65% if you are not currently supporting another dependent and are more than 12 weeks in arrears).

To put a wage garnishment into effect, the court, custodial parent or county attorney must notify your employer. Once your employer is told to garnish your wages, your employer tells you of the garnishment. You can request a court hearing, which will take place shortly after the garnishment has begun. At the hearing, you can make only a few objections:

- the amount the court claims you owe is wrong
- the amount will leave you with too little to live on
- the custodial parent actively concealed your child, as opposed to merely frustrating or denying your visitation (not all states will allow this objection), or
- you had custody of the child at the time the support arrears accrued.

If the wage garnishment does not cover the amount you owe, or you don't have wages or other income to be garnished, the custodial parent may try to get the debt for the back support paid out of other items of your property. For example, many states with lotteries let custodial parents apply to the state for an interception of the other parent's winnings. In addition, Keith M. Clemens, a lawyer who spent many years with the Center for Enforcement of Family Support in Los Angeles, described what property he and his colleagues went after for their clients:

> *Bank accounts are an easy target if you know where the debtor banks. We also take cars, motorcycles, boats and airplanes, houses and other real property, stock in corporations, horses, rents payable to the debtor and accounts receivable. It's harder to do, but we also successfully attack trusts, even spendthrift trusts, and the debtor's interest in partnerships. [A spendthrift trust contains a clause prohibiting the trust funds from being paid out to anyone other than the trust beneficiary—the debtor.] We were even able to take the debtor's community property share of the television game show winnings of his new wife.*

9. The Arrears May Be Sent to County Attorney Collections

If the custodial parent receives welfare, the county attorney (such as the district attorney or state's attorney) is required to help collect unpaid child support. In addition, in most states a county attorney will help—and may be required to help—a custodial parent who doesn't receive welfare. If you've moved out of state, state laws require that when the custodial parent contacts a county attorney in her state, that county attorney calls a county attorney in your state. The county attorney in your state contacts you, and orders you to pay a sum of money. If you pay that money to the county attorney in your state, he sends it to the county attorney in the custodial parent's state.

When the county attorney is involved, you'll receive a notice requesting that you attend a conference. If you don't show up, the county attorney may initiate criminal charges against you for failure to appear. The purpose of the conference is to establish your income, expenses, including support for other children, and how much you should pay. The county attorney is likely to propose that you pay a lot. You must emphasize your other necessary expenses—food, shelter, clothing, other kids and the like—to get that amount reduced. Bring receipts, bills and all other evidence of your monthly costs.

10. You May Be Criminally Prosecuted

In many states, it's a misdemeanor to fail to provide support for your child. While criminal prosecution isn't all that likely, the involvement of a county attorney increases the possibility. Also, if you have violated a judge's order enough times, the judge may contact buddies in the police department and county attorney's office and let your crimes be known.

E. Alimony

Alimony, sometimes called spousal support or maintenance, is money paid by one ex-spouse to the other for support, after a marriage is over. No federal law requires states to have guidelines for setting the amount of alimony. In some courts, however, judges have adopted informal written schedules to help them determine the appropriate level of support. Mostly, judges consider:

- the age, health, earnings and obligations of each spouse
- whether a spouse contributed to the education, training or career advancement of the other
- the length and standard of living of the marriage
- who will have custody
- the time needed for a supported spouse to become self-sufficient, and
- the tax consequences to each person.

If you cannot pay the amount of alimony you've been ordered to pay, you must file a motion for modification. You must show a material change in circumstances since the last court order. Your ex-spouse's cohabitation with someone of the opposite sex may qualify you for a reduction in alimony in some states.

Your ex-spouse's remarriage is also a good change of circumstance. Your divorce decree probably states that alimony terminates on your ex-spouse's remarriage. Even if it doesn't, in most states a recipient spouse's remarriage ends your obligation to pay alimony.

Other common reasons for changes in alimony include your decreased income or your ex-spouse's substantially increased income. Where you have voluntarily decreased your income, however, the judge may instead consider your ability to earn, not just your actual earnings.

If child support and alimony are lumped together in one payment, the collection techniques discussed in Sections B and D, above, may be used against you. If they are kept separate, however, only the following techniques can be used to collect alimony:

- interception of income tax refunds (for ex-spouses receiving welfare)
- court hearings, and
- wage garnishments and other judgment collection methods, such as property liens.

As with child support, alimony arrearages can be reduced by judgment and collected while the judgment is in effect (which may be for your life if the judgment is properly renewed). Also, back alimony generates interest payments that cannot be eliminated in bankruptcy.

F. Bankruptcy

Bankruptcy is covered more thoroughly in Chapter 16. Bankruptcy is discussed here, however, because many debtors consider filing for bankruptcy to get rid of child support or alimony debts. As discussed already, bankruptcy won't cancel arrears or a support judgment. But it may help in some limited situations.

If you file a Chapter 7 bankruptcy, collection efforts must cease while the case is open—typically between three and six months—but once the case is closed, collection may be resumed as if the bankruptcy was never filed. The primary advantage of filing a Chapter 7 bankruptcy is that you can typically get rid of many of your other debts, thus freeing up money to meet your current support obligation as well as pay off the arrearage.

If you file a Chapter 13 repayment plan bankruptcy, you also can get rid of many of your debts, but you will have to pay off the entire support arrearage over the life of your plan—typically between 3 and 5 years—as well as remain current on your support obligation during that period. However, since your repayment arrangements will be made under the protection of the bankruptcy court, you will not be subject to the harsh collection techniques that are normally available to a judgment creditor. (For more information on how Chapter 7 and Chapter 13 bankruptcies work, see Chapter 16.)

How Bankruptcy Affects Marital Debts

We have explained that child support and alimony are not discharged in bankruptcy. However, other types of debt that are created in the course of a divorce or separation may be discharged as long as they are not "in the nature of support," and as long as the other spouse doesn't raise a successful objection to the discharge of the debt in the bankruptcy court. An example of a debt "in the nature of support" would be one spouse agreeing to pay for the children's school tuition as part of a divorce settlement agreement. A debt that typically would not be considered "in the nature of support" would be an agreement by one spouse to pay off the other spouse's credit card debts as part of an overall division of the marital assets and liabilities.

If your ex-spouse objects to the discharge of a marital debt in the bankruptcy court, the court will only allow the debt to be discharged if it determines either of the following:

- After you pay all necessary expenses to support yourself and your dependents and to run any business you own, you will not have enough money to pay the marital debt.
- The benefit you would receive by the obligation being discharged would outweigh any detriment to your ex-spouse or children.

Importantly, the rules on discharging marital debt only apply to obligations owed to the debtor's spouse, ex-spouse or children. For instance, if you have taken on the obligation to pay a marital debt as part of your marital settlement agreement, and you list that debt in your bankruptcy papers, the debt will be discharged as to the third-party creditor. However, assuming your ex-spouse successfully objects to your discharging the debt, you will still owe it to him or her even if you no longer owe it to the third-party creditor.

If You Are Sued

Lawsuits consume time and money, and rest and friends.

— George Herbert, English poet,
1593-1633

If you don't pay your debts, you'll probably be sued unless any of the following are true:

- **The creditor or collection agency can't find you.** See Chapter 9, Section C.1.
- **You're judgment proof.** As explained in Chapter 8, Section E, being judgment proof means that you have no property or income that the creditor can legally take to collect on a judgment, now or in the foreseeable future.
- **You file for bankruptcy.** One way to prevent a lawsuit is to file for bankruptcy. (See Chapter 16.) Filing for bankruptcy stops most collection efforts, including lawsuits, dead in their tracks and you will probably be able to erase (discharge) the debt in your bankruptcy case.

Being sued is not the end of the world. It doesn't make you a bad person—millions of people are sued each year. Yes, it can be scary and may cause sleepless nights, but in large part that's because few people actually know what goes on in a lawsuit. Our perceptions, which typically have been shaped by television shows, movies and famous (or infamous) trials, are usually off the mark.

As this chapter explains, if you are sued on a debt you do owe and you have no good defenses, the lawsuit usually takes very little time and money. And if you do have a good defense, depending on how complicated it is, you may be able to assert it without hiring a lawyer.

The premise of this chapter is that you owe someone money and haven't paid. Usually this is considered a breach of a contract. Therefore, this chapter explains negotiating and the types of defenses you can raise in response to being sued for breaching a contract.

You may, however, be sued for any number of other reasons—for example, you allegedly caused a car accident, defamed someone or infringed a copyright. Before you are sued, you do not owe those

people money. If you are sued and you have a defense to the allegations made against you (see Chapter 4 for information on debts you may not owe), you will have to consult a source beyond this book for help. (See Chapter 20.) If the other side wins, you will owe a debt (in the form of a money judgment), and this chapter explains what you can expect.

A. How a Lawsuit Begins

A lawsuit starts when a lawyer for a creditor or collection agency or the creditor herself prepares a document called a complaint or petition, claiming that you owe money. The lawyer or creditor files the document with a court clerk and pays a filing fee. She then has a copy of the complaint, along with a summons, served on you. The summons is a document issued by the court, notifying you that you are being sued.

The complaint identifies:

- the plaintiff—that's the creditor or collection agency, or possibly another third party the creditor sold the debt to
- the defendant—that's you and anyone else liable for the debt, such as your spouse, a cosigner or a guarantor
- the date the complaint was filed (this is important if you have a statute of limitations defense—see Section D.1, below)
- the court in which you are being sued
- why the creditor is suing you, and
- what the creditor wants out of the lawsuit.

1. Where the Lawsuit Is Filed

The creditor must normally sue you in the state where you live or where the transaction took place. The creditor usually selects the state where you live if it's different from where the transaction took place because the court requires a substantial connection between you and the state in which you are sued. For example, if you send a check from your home in South Carolina to a mail-order business in Wisconsin, and your check bounces, the creditor

Being Sued in Small Claims Court

Virtually every state has a small claims court to hear disputes involving modest amounts of money. The range is from $1,000 to $10,000, with most states falling between $2,000 and $3,500. Small claims courts handle matters without long delays and formal rules of evidence, and are intended for people to represent themselves. If you owe the creditor a few thousand dollars or less, you may be sued in your state's small claims court. Even if the amount you owe is above your state's limit, the creditor may opt to sue you in small claims court and give up (waive) the excess.

In most states, you don't need to file a written response to a lawsuit in small claims court. You simply show up on the date of the hearing. If, however, you plan to file your own claim against the creditor for money—for example, if the creditor breached a warranty—you have to file a Claim of Defendant before the hearing so that both the creditor's claim and your claim are heard together.

Be sure you show up at the hearing. If you don't, most of the time you will lose the case. At the hearing, just be yourself and tell your side of the dispute. You don't normally need to hire a lawyer, even if your state allows them in small claims court and the creditor has one. Small claims court is designed to operate without lawyers and most small claims judges feel that people do as well or better without them. If you lose the case, the judge may let you set up a schedule to pay off the judgment in monthly payments—but don't count on it.

If you're sued in small claims court, an excellent resource is *Everybody's Guide to Small Claims Court,* by Ralph Warner (Nolo). Use that book as a guide to representing yourself. The rest of this chapter assumes that you are sued in your state's regular civil court, not in small claims court.

can sue you in South Carolina, but probably not in Wisconsin. Your connections with Wisconsin—even assuming the transaction took place there—are too insubstantial to sue you there.

After selecting the state, the creditor must select a county within the state. This is called the venue for the case. In most states, the creditor can choose the county where you live, the county where the transaction took place or the county where the creditor is located. If your home, the location of the transaction and the location of the creditor's business aren't all in one county, most creditors will choose the county where they are located simply because that is more convenient for them. If the creditor has chosen a county that is terribly inconvenient for you, you can file a motion to have the case transferred to somewhere else. You'll almost certainly need the help of a lawyer to do this.

Once the creditor has selected the state and county, the creditor must choose the court—small claims court or regular civil court. You'll probably be sued in your state's regular civil court if:

- the amount of money you owe exceeds your state's small claims limit
- a collection agency has your debt and is prohibited from suing in small claims court, or
- the creditor simply chooses not to use small claims court—no plaintiff is obligated to use small claims court, even on a $10 debt.

The exact name of the regular civil court depends on your state, and possibly the amount of money involved. It may be a Circuit Court, City Court, County Court, District Court, Justice Court, Justice of the Peace Court, Magistrate's Court, Municipal Court or Superior Court. Although the names differ, what goes on in each court is pretty much the same. You might also be sued in a federal district court if you owe money to the federal government—for example, on a federally guaranteed student loan.

In regular civil court, a lawsuit can be time-consuming and expensive, although routine debt collection cases rarely are. In theory, you are required to follow formal (and often absurd) procedural and evidentiary rules, but many judges are flexible when dealing with a person representing himself. While it can be extremely difficult to represent yourself in regular civil court, more and more people are doing it.

Resources for Representing Yourself in Court. Californians will want to obtain a copy of *How to Sue for Up to $25,000 … and Win!* by Judge Roderic Duncan (Nolo), which contains information on defending a lawsuit. People who decide to handle their own case—in any state—will find *Represent Yourself in Court,* by Paul Bergman and Sara Berman-Barrett (Nolo), to be indispensable.

2. Service of Court Papers

After the creditor files papers with the court, she must serve them on you. In most regular civil courts, you must be handed the papers personally. If you can't be found, the papers can be left with someone over 18 at your home or business, as long as another copy is mailed to you. The creditor himself cannot serve the papers on you because a party to a lawsuit can't do the actual serving. Most creditors hire professionals called process servers or have a local sheriff or marshal do the job.

Sometimes, a creditor will mail you a copy of the summons and complaint with a form for you to sign and date, acknowledging that you have received the papers. If you sign and date the form, you are deemed to have been served on that date.

It's often a good idea to sign the form and send it back promptly because you can save money. If you refuse to sign and the creditor can later prove that you declined the opportunity to do so, you may have to pay whatever costs—frequently between $35 and $150—the creditor incurred in hiring a process server or sheriff to serve the papers on you personally.

If Service Was Done Wrong

Suppose the creditor has a friend serve you, and the friend simply slides the papers under your door. Sure, you got the papers, but service was technically improper because they were not handed to you or left with a responsible person at your home or office, followed by a mailed copy. You now have two choices. You can either ignore the impropriety or complain about it in court. Unless you complain, the court won't know that service was improper, and it will proceed as if service was fine. If you don't formally respond, a default judgment will probably be entered against you.

Should you complain? In most cases, no. Fighting an improper service will probably require your hiring a lawyer. That gets expensive. The creditor's friend (or other process server) will simply serve you again—most likely on the day you show up in court to fight the initial improper service. All you buy is a little time. And you might pay a lot for it.

3. Understanding the Complaint

Complaints are usually written in hyped-up legalese. You may be referred to as the "party of the second part," not simply "the defendant," and almost never just by your name. The document will probably include "heretofores," "thereafters," "saids" and much more.

To find out what exactly the plaintiff wants from you, turn to the final pages. Find the word "WHEREFORE" and start reading. You'll not only learn how much the creditor says you owe, but most of the time you'll also find out that the creditor is claiming you must pay interest, court costs incurred, possibly attorneys' fees and "whatever other relief the court deems appropriate." This last phrase is a somewhat meaningless catchall added in the unlikely event the court comes up with another solution.

4. When Is Your Response Due?

In regular civil court, you will probably have between 20 and 30 days to respond in writing (in a document usually called an answer) to the creditor's complaint. The summons tells you precisely how much time you have. If you don't respond in time, the creditor can come into court and ask that a default judgment be entered against you. Usually the default judgment is granted for the amount the creditor requested. Some judges, however, will scrutinize the papers. If the judge feels that the creditor's claim for interest or attorneys' fees is excessive, the judge may not allow it. Other judges will require the creditor to present evidence of actual damages before awarding any money.

When There's a Judgment Against You. Often the defendant has no real defense or the money to hire a lawyer to put up a fight. In fact, in most routine debt cases (80%–90%), a default judgment is taken against the defendant. If you owe money and decide to default, skip ahead to Section F on what to do when the creditor has a judgment. If you are unsure as to whether you have a defense, see Chapter 4.

B. Negotiate

Even if you've avoided your creditor or a collection agency up to this point, it's never too late to try to negotiate. If you call and offer to settle the matter,

the collector may agree to suspend, though not withdraw the lawsuit, while you are negotiating. Unless the creditor gives you an extension of time, in writing, to respond to the lawsuit, you should file an answer, even while you are negotiating. For tips on negotiating, see Chapter 6. If your efforts to negotiate with the collector are unsuccessful, consider contacting a nonprofit debt counseling agency that will work with you to set up a repayment plan by contacting your individual creditors. (See Chapter 20, Section C.)

1. Lump Sum Settlement

You will be in the best position with a collector if you can offer a lump sum of cash to settle the case. Usually, the collector will insist that you pay between one-half and three-fourths of what you owe. The collector, not wanting to start all over if you miss the payments, is unlikely to stop a lawsuit in exchange for a promise to pay in installments.

If the collector agrees to take your lump sum offer, make sure he also agrees to do so in complete settlement of what you owe and further agrees to dismiss (withdraw)—and in fact *does* dismiss—the lawsuit filed against you. Of course, get all agreements in writing. You can check to see that the lawsuit has been dismissed by visiting the courthouse filing office and asking to see the case file. Bring the papers that were served on you to the filing office; these papers include the case number, which you will need to request the file. The file should contain a paper called a request for dismissal, or something similar.

If the collector hasn't filed a request for dismissal, you may have to take some action yourself. Ask the court clerk if your state has a form used for requesting dismissals. If it does, get a copy and fill it out, but don't sign it. If your state doesn't have such a form, you may have to visit a law library, find a form book, and prepare a request for dismissal yourself. Once your request is completed, make a copy and send the original to whoever sued you. Ask that the form be signed and sent back to you. Once it comes back, file it with the court clerk yourself.

2. Settlement Involving Installment Payments

Assuming the collector does agree to settle the case on the basis of your promise to make installment payments, chances are she will probably insist that you agree ("stipulate") to having a court judgment entered at the courthouse against you if you fail to make payments. If you agree to this, sign the stipulation, but make sure the collector commits in writing not to file it with the court unless you fail to make the installment payments. This way, your credit file won't show that there's a judgment against you. Of course, if you stop making the agreed-upon installment payments at some point, the creditor or collector can sue you again to enforce the payment plan.

3. If the Negotiations Hit a Sour Note

If your negotiations are going nowhere, or you're uncomfortable handling them yourself, consider hiring an attorney to negotiate for you. An attorney carries clout that might lead the collector to settle for a good deal less than what you owe. But don't hire an attorney unless it's cost-effective. If an attorney charges $250 to negotiate a $700 debt down to $500, you've actually lost $50. (See Chapter 20 for information on finding an attorney.)

C. Alternative Dispute Resolution

Alternative dispute resolution (ADR) is a phrase referring to methods used to settle a disagreement short of going to court. If you clearly owe a debt and are looking for some way to avoid court, most creditors won't agree to using ADR. If you really don't think you owe the money or have some other credible defense to the creditor's lawsuit, however, the creditor may agree to resolve the lawsuit through ADR.

ADR can be informal, fast and inexpensive. Because of the informality of ADR, you are often not constrained by formal procedural and evidentiary rules. You just tell your story. However, generally you should use ADR only if it is nonbinding (meaning you can still go to court if you don't like the result) or if you are confident that the process will be fair. These are the main ADR options:

Arbitration. This is the most formal type of ADR. You and the creditor or collector agree to submit your dispute to at least one neutral third person—often a lawyer or judge. Where a lot of money is at stake, arbitrators usually let the parties use attorneys at arbitration hearings, and impose formal rules of evidence. In other disputes, arbitration is less formal and can take place without lawyers. You often have to pay the arbitrator's fees in advance, and they can be high. If you win, however, you're frequently refunded the amount.

If arbitration is voluntary and nonbinding (meaning you can appeal the decision in court if you don't like it), it can be a good thing. However, more and more creditors and businesses include clauses in contracts that require you to submit to nonbinding arbitration. In these types of arbitration, you can rarely challenge a bad arbitration decision in court, even if the arbitrator decides not to follow the law.

If your contract requires that you go to arbitration, you may be able to get out of arbitration and go to court instead—but to do so is often complicated. You'll have to get help from a lawyer. If you are stuck with arbitration, find out as much as you can about the panel of arbitrators (the group from which your arbitrator will be selected). Look for any that might be sympathetic to consumers rather than

Sample Settlement Agreement or Release

This Agreement is entered into on the date below between   Christopher's Contracting Company , Creditor, and   Donna Markell , Debtor.

Whereas Creditor has alleged that   Debtor owes him $7,745 for construction work he did on Debtor's home ;

Whereas Debtor agrees that   she has not paid Creditor any money for the work done but alleges that Creditor damaged her home while doing the construction work ;

Whereas Creditor has filed   Civil Action No. C49903 in the Superior Court for the County of Fairfield, State of Connecticut, seeking a money judgment ; and

Whereas Creditor and Debtor desire to settle their differences and end the above-identified litigation.

Therefore, in consideration of the undertakings set forth below, Creditor and Debtor hereby agree as follows:

1. Within 20 days of the date this agreement is entered into, Creditor will file in the Superior Court for the County of Fairfield, State of Connecticut, a Dismissal With Prejudice in the above-identified litigation.

2. Creditor further agrees not to make any future claim or bring any future action against Debtor for the acts alleged, or which could have been alleged, in   Civil Action No. C49903 , occurring up to the time of the entry of the Dismissal With Prejudice identified in Paragraph 1 of this Agreement.

3. Debtor agrees not to make any future claim or bring any future action against Creditor for acts alleged, or which could have been alleged as a counterclaim, in   Civil Action No. C49903 .

4. Debtor will, at the time of executing this Agreement, pay to Creditor the sum of $5,000   as full settlement of any claim of Creditor against Debtor.

5. Creditor agrees to remove all negative information related to this debt from the files maintained by the major credit reporting agencies.

6. *[California; other states may have similar provisions]* The releases recited in this Agreement cover all claims under California Civil Code Section 1542 and Creditor and Debtor hereby waive the provisions of Section 1542 which read as follows:

"A general release does not extend to claims which the creditor does not know or suspect to exist in his favor at the time of executing the release, which if known by him must have materially affected his settlement with the debtor."

7. Creditor and Debtor will bear their own costs, expenses and attorneys' fees.

8. This Agreement embodies the entire understanding between Creditor and Debtor relating to the subject matter of this Agreement and merges all prior discussions between them.

Dated: May 30, 20xx

Creditor's signature, address and phone number:
Stephen Christopher

 1782 Main Street, Fairfield, CT 06500

 (203) 555-9993

Debtor's signature, address, and phone number:
Donna Markell

 98 South Acorn Ave., Bridgeport, CT 06000

 (203) 555-0081

creditors and businesses. For example, many arbitrators are also practicing lawyers—find out if they represent mostly creditors or mostly consumers.

Mediation or conciliation. This is the second most common type of ADR. You and the creditor or collector work with a neutral third party to come up with a solution to your dispute. Mediation is informal, and the mediator does not have the power to impose a decision on you. An excellent resource on mediation is *Mediate Your Dispute*, by Peter Lovenheim (Nolo).

Mini-trial. You and the creditor or collector present your positions to a neutral third person who listens as a judge would and then issues an advisory opinion. You can agree to be bound by that opinion. A growing number of states have "rent-a-judge" programs to encourage the use of mini-trials to settle disputes.

Several states encourage mediation or arbitration and encourage the court to make ADR available. These are usually not binding and can provide a quick way to resolve problems without battling it out in court.

If your state doesn't assign cases to mediation or another form of ADR, you can find someone to resolve your dispute yourself. Many people are listed in the phone book. Before hiring someone, ask for references. Call and find out if they were satisfied with the service. Also, the National Council of Better Business Bureaus operates a nationwide system for settling consumer disputes through arbitration and mediation. Local BBB offices handle over two million consumer disputes each year. One advantage to BBB arbitration over more formal arbitration is that it is free to consumers and is geared toward operating without lawyers.

If you would like to use ADR instead of going to court, write to the creditor and emphasize the advantages of ADR. (See the "Sample Letter to Creditor Requesting ADR," below.) Even if you send a letter requesting ADR, file a response to the complaint. The creditor may say no, may say yes and then decide not to participate or may say yes but some time after the time limit has passed for

you to file an answer. As explained in Section A.4, above, if the deadline passes and you haven't filed a response, the creditor can ask the court to have a default judgment entered against you. If that happens, you will automatically lose.

Sample Letter to Creditor Requesting ADR

Merrily Andrews, Esq.
Legal Department
Presley Hospital
900 Hollis Boulevard
Carson City, NV 88888

March 15, 20xx

Re: Shawn Smith
    Account # 7777-SMI
    Civil Case # 93-0056

Dear Ms. Andrews:

I have just been served with the Summons and Complaint for the lawsuit filed by Presley Hospital against me for $7,400. I would very much like to resolve this matter and suggest that we mediate the dispute with the help of a mediator from the Nevada Consumer Council. I know that the Consumer Council has helped many people resolve their differences quickly, informally and inexpensively.

Although I did not respond to your earlier collection efforts, it was not because I did not want to settle the matter. My wife and I were both very ill and hospitalized at Presley. My wife died, and taking care of my debts was not my highest priority. I admit that I owe you some money, but nowhere near $7,400.

I hope you'll agree to mediate this dispute. If so, please contact me by April 10, 20xx.

Thank you,

Shawn Smith

Shawn Smith

D. Respond in Court

If you want to respond to the lawsuit, you must do so in writing, within the time allowed. (See Section A.4, above.) This means you must file formal legal papers, and the task can be difficult. Regular civil court is designed and operated by lawyers. Arcane rules dominate and the language is often indecipherable. Clerks may be rude and hostile, and many don't answer simple questions, such as "Where do I file the forms?" Instead, they often stonewall even the most routine request for information with the claim that they "can't give legal advice."

This doesn't mean you can't or shouldn't represent yourself in court. You can, but you will have to educate yourself and do some legal research.

You'll also need patience to play the game according to the lawyers' and judges' rules. For example, if you raise an argument or a defense completely unsupported by the facts of your case or by the law, the judge could fine you for filing frivolous papers. It's an extreme measure and rarely invoked, but judges who get angry and frustrated by people who represent themselves have been known to do it.

You can also hire a lawyer to represent you in court. (See Chapter 20.) As you know, lawyers are expensive. But you may be able to hire a lawyer and keep your expenses down by doing some of the work yourself. Also, if you have a strong claim against the creditor (see Section D.2, below) that could generate substantial money for you if you win, the lawyer may take your case on a contingent fee basis—you don't pay the lawyer unless you win.

In going to court, you want to raise any possible defenses you have, such as that the statute of limitations has expired or the goods you received were defective.

1. Statute of Limitations

The creditor has a limited number of years to sue you after you fail to pay your debt. This is called the statute of limitations. The time allowed varies greatly from state to state and for different kinds of debts—written contracts, oral contracts, promissory notes and open-ended accounts, such as credit card payments. The statute of limitations begins to run from the day the debt—or payment on an open-ended account—was due.

Is the Account Open- or Closed-End Credit?

The statute of limitations for open-end and closed-end credit is often different. Unfortunately, determining whether an account is open-end or closed-end is not always easy. Generally, if you can use the account repeatedly, it is open-end credit (also called "revolving credit"). Your payments vary, depending on how much credit you have used in a certain period of time. The most common example of open-end credit is a credit card. Closed-end credit usually involves a single transaction, such as the purchase of a house or car, and the payments are fixed in amount and number.

Many transactions fall somewhere in between open- and closed-end credit. Also, many creditors try to characterize a closed-end account as open-end, either to take advantage of a longer statute of limitations or to avoid providing the more extensive disclosures required with closed-end credit.

To complicate matters even more, the statute of limitations for an open-ended account is not always clear. Some states specify limits for credit card accounts only. In others, if you have a written contract with the credit card company, the statute of limitations for written contracts applies to credit card accounts. In still other states, the statute of limitations for oral contracts governs open-ended accounts. In order to find the statute of limitations for an open-ended account in your state, you'll have to do some legal research or check with a local attorney. (See Chapter 20 for help finding an attorney or for tips on doing legal research.)

If the creditor has waited too long to sue you, you must raise this as a defense in the papers you file in response to the creditor's complaint.

EXAMPLE: Bart lives in Delaware, where the statute of limitations on open-ended accounts is three years. Bart had a large balance on his Visa card, made a small payment in July 1997, and then paid no more. His August Big Bank Visa statement included a payment due date of August 15, 1997. Bart was sued in September of 2000, three years and a few days after he first missed the payment. Bart has a statute of limitations defense. Bart must raise this defense in the papers he files opposing Big Bank's lawsuit. If Bart doesn't, he loses the defense.

Be diligent if you think the creditor has sued you when the statute of limitations has already run. It's common for banks that issue credit cards to sell their uncollected debts to collection agencies. Those agencies then aggressively try to collect, ignoring the fact that the statute of limitations may have expired. If the collection agency sues you once the statute of limitations has run, the agency has probably violated the federal Fair Debt Collection Practices Act (FDCPA). (See Chapter 9, Section D, and *Kimber v. Federal Financial Corp.*, 668 F. Supp. 1480 (M.D. Ala. 1987).)

In response to your claim that the statute of limitations prevents the creditor or collector from going forward with the lawsuit, he might claim that you waived, extended or revived the statute of limitations in your earlier dealings.

a. Waiving the Statute of Limitations

If you waive the statute of limitations on a debt, it means you give up your right to assert it as a defense later on. The law makes it very difficult for a consumer to waive the statute of limitations by accident. A court will find it waived only if you understood what you were doing when you told a creditor you would waive the statute of limitations for your debt. In many cases, even if you knew what you were doing, the court will still find the waiver unenforceable. If you think you may have waived the statute of limitations, you should still raise it as a defense (and force the creditor to demonstrate that you waived it).

b. Extending or Reviving the Statute of Limitations

Extending and reviving the statute of limitations are two different things. Extending the statute is often called "tolling." Tolling or extending the statute temporarily stops the clock for a particular reason, such as the collector agreeing to extend your time to pay.

EXAMPLE: Emily owes the Farmer's Market $345. The statute of limitations for this type of debt in her state is six years. Normally the statute would begin to run when Emily stopped paying the debt, but Farmer's gave her an additional six months to pay (and therefore tolled or extended the statute of limitations for six months). After six months, Emily still cannot pay the debt. The six-year statute of limitations begins to run at this point.

Reviving a statute of limitations means that the entire time period begins again. Depending on your state, this can happen if you make a partial payment on a debt or otherwise acknowledge that you owe a debt that you haven't been paying. In some states, partial payment will only "toll" the statute rather than revive it.

EXAMPLE: Ethan owes Memorial Hospital $1,000. The statute of limitations for medical debts in his state is four years. He stopped making payments on the debt in 1997. The four-year statute began to run at this point. In 1999, Ethan made a $300 payment and then stopped making payments again. In Ethan's state, his partial payment of $300 revived the statute of limitations. The hospital now has four years from the date of the $300 payment to sue Ethan for the remainder of the debt.

A new promise to pay a debt may also revive the statute of limitations in some circumstances. In most states, an oral promise can revive a statute of limitations, although in a few states the promise must be in writing.

Statutes of Limitations			
State	Written Contracts	Oral Contracts	Promissory Notes
Alabama	6 years	6 years	6 years
Alaska	3 years	3 years	3 years
Arizona	6 years	3 years	6 years
Arkansas	5 years	3 years	5 years
California	4 years	2 years	4 years
Colorado	6 years	6 years	6 years
Connecticut	6 years	3 years	6 years
Delaware	3 years	3 years	6 years
District of Columbia	3 years	3 years	3 years
Florida	5 years	4 years	5 years
Georgia	6 years	4 years	6 years
Hawaii	6 years	6 years	6 years
Idaho	5 years	4 years	5 years
Illinois	10 years	5 years	10 years
Indiana	10 years	6 years	6 years
Iowa	10 years	5 years	10 years
Kansas	5 years	3 years	5 years
Kentucky	15 years	5 years	15 years[+]
Louisiana	10 years	10 years	5 years
Maine*	6 years	6 years	6 years
Maryland	3 years	3 years	3 years
Massachusetts*	6 years	6 years	6 years
Michigan	6 years	6 years	6 years
Minnesota	6 years	6 years	6 years
Mississippi	3 years	3 years	3 years

* The applicable statute of limitations in Maine and in Massachusetts on a debt owed to a bank or on a promissory note signed before a witness is 20 years. Me. Rev. Stat. Ann. tit.14, § 751; Mass. Gen. Laws ch. 260, § 1.

[+] Five years if promissory note is added to a bill of sale.

Statutes of Limitations			
State	**Written Contracts**	**Oral Contracts**	**Promissory Notes**
Missouri	10 years	5 years	10 years
Montana	8 years	5 years	8 years
Nebraska	5 years	4 years	5 years
Nevada	6 years	4 years	6 years
New Hampshire	3 years	3 years	3 years
New Jersey	6 years	6 years	6 years
New Mexico	6 years	4 years	6 years
New York	6 years	6 years	6 years
North Carolina	3 years	3 years	3 years
North Dakota	6 years	6 years	6 years
Ohio	15 years	6 years	15 years
Oklahoma	5 years	3 years	5 years
Oregon	6 years	6 years	6 years
Pennsylvania	4 years	4 years	4 years
Rhode Island	10 years	10 years	10 years
South Carolina	3 years	3 years	3 years
South Dakota	6 years	6 years	6 years
Tennessee	6 years	6 years	6 years
Texas	4 years	4 years	4 years
Utah	6 years	4 years	6 years
Vermont	6 years	6 years	6 years**
Virginia	5 years	3 years	6 years
Washington	6 years	3 years	6 years
West Virginia	10 years	5 years	10 years
Wisconsin	6 years	6 years	6 years
Wyoming	10 years	8 years	10 years

** Vermont's statute of limitations on a promissory note signed before a witness is 14 years.

2. Other Defenses and Claims

If you file a response in court, you'll want to state any reason why the creditor should not recover all or part of what he asked for in the complaint. You bring up each reason either as an affirmative defense in your answer or as a separate claim, called a counterclaim, in a complaint that you file against the creditor.

An affirmative defense goes beyond simply denying the facts and arguments in the complaint. It sets out new facts and arguments. If you prove your affirmative defense, even if what is in the complaint is true, you will win, or at least reduce the amount you owe.

A counterclaim is the basis of a lawsuit you have against the creditor or collector. It may be based on different issues than are in the complaint. You may even be asking for more money than the creditor or collector wants from you. The counterclaim, however, must arise out of the same transaction for which you are being sued.

Listed below are some affirmative defenses you might be able to list in your answer:

- You never received the goods or services the creditor claims to have provided.
- The goods or services were defective. (See Chapter 4.)
- The creditor damaged your property when delivering the goods or services.
- The creditor lied to you to get you to enter into the agreement. (See Chapter 4.)
- You legally canceled the contract and therefore owe nothing. (See Chapter 4.)
- You cosigned for the loan and were not told of your rights as a cosigner. (See Chapter 11.)
- The creditor was not permitted to accelerate the loan. (See Chapter 11.)
- The contract was too ambiguous to be enforced. (See Chapter 4.)
- After repossessing your property, the creditor did not sell it in a "commercially reasonable manner." (See Chapter 8.)

Here are some counterclaims you might want to make against the creditor or collector. As mentioned, to raise a counterclaim, you will usually have to serve and file your own complaint and pay a filing fee within the time you have to respond to the complaint. (See Sections A.2 and A.4, above.) If you succeed on a counterclaim, you may be entitled to monetary damages from the creditor or collector, or at least to rescind (cancel) the contract with the creditor.

- The creditor breached a warranty. (See Chapter 4.)
- The creditor violated the Fair Credit Reporting Act (see Chapter 18), Truth in Lending Act (see Chapter 11), Electronic Fund Transfer Act (see Chapter 10) or Equal Credit Opportunity Act (see Chapter 18). If you want to get a copy of your original agreement with the creditor, just ask. Most will provide you with a copy for a small fee of around $5.
- A collection agency debt collector violated the Fair Debt Collections Practices Act or a state debt collection law. (See Chapter 9.)

3. Responding Formally

To avoid having the creditor or collector ask the court to enter a default judgment against you, you must file formal papers in response to the lawsuit. If you don't have access to a law library and can't afford a lawyer, just file any paper with the court saying why you oppose the lawsuit. In many states, as long as you file a paper resembling an answer, the court cannot enter a default judgment against you. Also, you can amend your paper after you have learned more about the process.

If you can get into the courtroom, the judge may be sympathetic to someone representing himself. If all you want is the right to pay in installments, the judge may have a harder time saying no to you when you're standing in the courtroom than if you let the creditor get a default. Unfortunately, many judges have little patience for individuals who represent themselves. For this reason, it is important to be as prepared and organized as possible.

Here's how to respond; a sample follows these instructions.

- Get yourself a stack of plain white, 8½" x 11" unlined paper or turn on your computer and follow the steps below.
- Have the complaint in front of you.
- Take a sheet of paper. In the upper left corner, type your name, address, phone number and the words "Defendant in Pro Per" (also called "Defendant in Pro Se" in some states) single spaced. Look at the way this is done on the complaint.
- Type the name of the court and the caption—the caption contains the name(s) of the plaintiff(s), the word "Plaintiff(s)," "v.," your name and any other defendants, the word "Defendant(s)" and the case number. Copy all of this information off of the complaint. Place this information at approximately the same place on the page that it is on the complaint.
- On the next line in the center of the page, type the word "Answer."

Now stop typing. Go back to the complaint and read through it. Write the word "admit" near the paragraphs where you agree with absolutely everything said in it, such as "Plaintiff's sporting goods store is located at 74 Hollis Road, Cranston, Rhode Island."

Next, write the word "deny" near each paragraph in which you deny all or a part of what was said. For instance, if the paragraph says "Defendant bought a gym set and has refused to pay for it for no good reason" and you agree that you bought a gym set but haven't paid because it doesn't do what you want and the store won't refund your money, deny the whole paragraph.

For each paragraph where you are not sure what the truth is, but you believe the plaintiff's statement is probably more false than true write "deny on information and belief." An example is if the plaintiff wrote that you bought the gym set at night, but you think it was in the afternoon.

Finally, if you have no idea whether or not the allegation in a paragraph is true, for example, a paragraph saying that plaintiff is a corporation, write "deny because no information."

- Start typing again, this time double-spaced. Type what follows; following each colon, type the corresponding paragraph numbers for the

paragraphs in the complaint you just marked up:

1. Defendant admits the allegations in the following paragraphs:
2. Defendant denies the allegations in the following paragraphs:
3. Defendant denies on information and belief the allegations in the following paragraphs:
4. Defendant denies because no information the allegations in the following paragraphs:

- Next, type your statute of limitations defense (if applicable) and any affirmative defenses. Use Sections 1 and 2, above, for the appropriate language, but feel free to add a sentence or two if you feel further explaining is needed. List each defense and affirmative defense separately, and be sure you are still typing double-spaced. Don't worry about how many pieces of paper you need.
- Type your name, sign your name and date it at the bottom.

E. What to Expect While the Case Is in Court

Once you type up your answer and any counterclaim, you'll have to serve it on the plaintiff. You can usually have the plaintiff served by having a friend over the age of 18 send the plaintiff your papers through the mail. However, sometimes it must be done in person. Details on serving your answer and counterclaim vary considerably from state to state, but you can ask a court clerk or check a local law library for the rules. (See Chapter 20.)

After your papers are served, you must file the papers at the court. You must also file a "proof of service," a document that shows that the plaintiff was served in the proper manner. After your papers are filed, you will receive written notification of all further proceedings in your case. If yours is a routine debt collection case, the next paper you will probably receive is a notice of the plaintiff's request for a trial and date. The paper after that will probably be a notice of the trial date. In some courts, how-

Sample Answer

Judith Morrison
355 Bryce Avenue
Hackensack, NJ 07123
(201) 555-7890
Defendant in Pro Per

Municipal Court for the County of Bergen

In and For the State of New Jersey

Bergen Bank, Inc.,	)
Plaintiff,	)
v.	) Case No. BC—455522
Judith Morrison,	)
Defendant.	)

ANSWER

1. Defendant admits the allegations in the following paragraphs: 1, 2, 3, 4, 7, 9, 16, 22 and 23.

2. Defendant denies the allegations in the following paragraphs: 5, 6, 8, 12, 13, 14, 15, 17, 24 and 26.

3. Defendant denies on information and belief the allegations in the following paragraphs: 10, 11, 19, 20, 21 and 25.

4. Defendant denies because no information the allegations in the following paragraphs: 18, 27 and 28.

5. Defense: Plaintiff is not entitled to the money it claims because the applicable statute of limitations has run.

6. First Affirmative Defense: I canceled the contract as I was entitled to and therefore I owe nothing.

7. Second Affirmative Defense: Clause 14 of my loan agreement prohibits the creditor from accelerating the loan. In violation of Clause 14, the creditor has accelerated the loan and now claims the entire balance is due.

Judith Morrison   _June 17, 20xx_
Judith Morrison   Date

ever, you will be sent a notice of a settlement conference before the trial date. Be sure to attend the settlement conference or trial. If you move, make sure you notify the plaintiff and court of your address change.

If yours isn't a routine debt collection case, or the creditor's lawyer wants to play the litigation game, a whole lot can go on between the time you file your answer and any counterclaim and the time you get a notice of the trial. You may want to take the offensive with some of this, especially if you filed a counterclaim. Below is a brief description of the most common of these proceedings. It's difficult for someone without a lawyer to undertake them, but it's not impossible. These descriptions are not meant to be a detailed account of how to cope with court procedures. For that, you'll want to look at *Represent Yourself in Court*, by Paul Bergman and Sara Berman-Barrett (Nolo).

1. Discovery

Discovery refers to the formal procedures used by parties to obtain information from each other and from witnesses. The information is meant to help the party prepare for trial or settle the case. In routine debt collection cases where you don't have any defense, don't expect the plaintiff to engage in discovery. Discovery can be expensive, and quite frankly, there is nothing for the plaintiff to "discover." You owe the money. You haven't paid.

If you raise a strong affirmative defense or file your own counterclaim, however, the plaintiff may want to engage in discovery. These are the primary discovery methods.

Deposition. A proceeding in which a witness or party is asked to answer questions orally under oath. A court reporter is present and takes down the entire proceeding.

If you receive papers ordering you to appear at a deposition, get a copy of *The Deposition Handbook*, by Paul Bergman and Albert Moore (Nolo).

Interrogatories. Written questions sent by one party to the other to be answered in writing under oath.

Sample Proof of Service

Judith Morrison
355 Bryce Avenue
Hackensack, NJ 07123
(201) 555-7890
Defendant in Pro Per

Municipal Court for the County of Bergen

In and For the State of New Jersey

Bergen Bank, Inc.,	)
	)
Plaintiff,	)
	) Case No. BC—455522
v.	)
	)
Judith Morrison,	)
	)
Defendant.	)
_____	)

PROOF OF SERVICE

I, Gordon Freed, declare that:

I am over the age of 18 years and not a party to the within action. I reside [or am employed] in the County of Bergen, state of New Jersey. My residence [or business] address is 56 Trainor Court, Englewood, New Jersey.

On June 22, 20xx, I served the within ANSWER on the plaintiff by placing a true and correct copy of it in a sealed envelope with first-class postage fully pre-paid in the United States mail at Englewood, New Jersey, addressed as follows:

Deb Miles, Esq.
Bergen Bank, Inc.
1400 Fort Lee Circle
Fort Lee, New Jersey 07333

I declare under penalty of perjury that the foregoing is true and correct. Executed on June 23, 20xx, at Englewood, New Jersey.

Gordon Freed
_____
Gordon Freed

Request for production of documents. A request from one party to the other to hand over certain defined documents. If you are adamant in your defense of a lawsuit that you paid the debt, the other side will most likely request that you produce a check, money order receipt or other document supporting your assertion.

Request for admissions. A request from one party to the other to admit or deny certain allegations in the lawsuit.

Request for inspection. A request by one party to look at tangible items (other than writings) in the possession of the other party. For instance, if you raise as an affirmative defense that the painter who sued you spilled paint on your rug and it cannot be removed, the painter may request to inspect the rug.

Request for physical examination. A request by one party that the other party be examined by a doctor if the other party's health is at issue.

Subpoena. An order telling a witness to appear at a deposition.

Subpoena duces tecum. An order telling a witness to turn over certain documents to a specific party.

In some states, the trend is toward limiting discovery. For example, parties to a lawsuit can ask only a limited number of questions in their interrogatories. Also, a party or witness can be deposed only once. If the creditor sends you volumes of interrogatory questions or schedules your deposition after it's already been taken, you can ask the court to issue a "protective order" to stop the harassment.

If you don't respond to a discovery request, the creditor will probably schedule a court hearing and ask the judge to order you to comply. The creditor will also ask the court to fine you whatever amount it cost the creditor, including the attorneys' fees the creditor had to pay, to get the hearing. If you still don't comply, the judge may eventually order that judgment be entered for the plaintiff and that you lose the case.

2. Summary Judgment

The creditor may try to convince the judge that none of the facts of the case are in dispute—for example, that you signed a legal loan agreement, made no payments and have no defense as to why you're not paying. The creditor does this by filing a summary judgment motion. If the judge agrees with the creditor, the judge can enter a judgment against you without any trial taking place. The creditor should not win if there are any facts in dispute (for example, if you claim you didn't sign the agreement).

You usually must file papers opposing the creditor's summary judgment motion if you want to fight it. If you don't, you'll probably lose. Because responding to a summary judgment motion can be complicated and because the entire lawsuit is at stake, you may want to consult with an attorney. Of course, remember what we said earlier: if it costs more to hire a lawyer than what the creditor seeks in the lawsuit, it makes little sense to seek attorney assistance.

3. Settlement Conference

Several states and the federal court system require that the parties come together at least once before the trial and try to settle the case. To assist you in settling, you'll be scheduled to meet with a judge or attorney who has some familiarity with the area of law your case involves. You don't have to settle, but the judge or attorney will usually give you an honest indication of your chance of winning in a trial.

4. Trial

If you are not overwhelmed by discovery and any summary judgment motion, and you don't settle your case, you will eventually find yourself at a trial. In a trial, a judge makes all the legal decisions, such as whether or not a particular item of evidence can be used. At the same time, either a judge or a jury makes the factual decisions, such as whether or not the item sold to you was defective.

At the trial, you will be required to present your case according to very specific rules of procedure and evidence. As mentioned before, the book that can help you in any trial is *Represent Yourself in Court*, by Paul Bergman and Sara Berman-Barrett (Nolo). Or, you may want to consult with a lawyer before the trial to get some help.

Some Guidelines on Presenting Evidence

- You can testify only as to facts in your knowledge. You can't testify that "someone told you" something; this is hearsay. There are many exceptions to the general rule against hearsay evidence. To find out more, do some legal research on your own or contact a lawyer (see Chapter 20).
- Bring all relevant documents—receipts, bills, letters, warranties, advertisements and the like. Try to bring originals (and make a few copies of each before the trial), but if you only have copies, bring them.
- Your witnesses can testify only to facts in their knowledge—that is, something they saw or heard. For example, if a bill collector threatened to have you jailed, a witness testifying about the truth of this statement can testify only that she heard the threat, not that you called and told her about the threat.

F. If the Creditor Gets a Judgment Against You

Your creditor will get a judgment against you in the following situations:
- you don't respond to the complaint
- you don't comply with a judge's order to respond to a discovery request
- you lose a summary judgment motion, or
- you lose a trial.

The judgment is a piece of paper issued by the court stating that the plaintiff wins the lawsuit and is entitled to a certain sum of money. The judgment must be "entered"—that is, filed with the court clerk, and this usually happens a day or two after the judge issues it. After it is filed, the court or the creditor's attorney sends you a copy.

1. Components of a Money Judgment

When you get a copy of the judgment, your first step is to understand the amount of money to which the plaintiff is entitled, and what each portion represents. Keep in mind that the judge may have knocked off some money in response to a defense or counterclaim you raised.

A judgment usually consists of the following components.

The debt itself. This is the amount of money you borrowed from the creditor, charged on a credit card or owe on a repossession deficiency balance.

Interest. Part of the judgment will be the interest the creditor is entitled to collect under the loan agreement or contract. If you defaulted on a $1,000 loan at 9% annual interest and the creditor obtains a judgment a year later, the court will award the creditor $90 in "prejudgment" interest ($1,000 x .09 = $90).

Interest can be added after judgment from the time the judgment is entered into the court clerk's record until you pay the judgment in full. The post-judgment interest rate is set by your state's law. (See below.)

Court costs. Almost every state awards the winner of a lawsuit the costs incurred in bringing the case, including filing fees, service costs, discovery costs and jury fees.

Attorneys' fees. If your original contract with the creditor includes the creditor's right to collect attorneys' fees in the event the creditor sues you and wins, these fees will be added to the judgment. They can add up to thousands of dollars. Even without an attorneys' fees provision in a contract, the creditor may be entitled to attorneys' fees if a state law allows it—although a few states provide for attorneys' fees in these types of cases.

Post-Judgment Interest Rates

This chart gives the interest rates set by state law for judgments where the contract or agreement does not set an interest rate. If a contract or agreement does set a post-judgment interest rate, then that is the one that generally applies, even if it is different from the state rate. The rate is usually written in the judgment.

State	Code Citation	Post-Judgment Interest Rates
Alabama	Ala. Code. § 8-8-10	12%
Alaska	Alaska Stat. § 09.30.070	3% above the 12th Federal Reserve District discount rate on January 2 of the year judgment is entered. If contract calls for a different rate, it must be written in the judgment. Rate posted at www.state.ak.us/courts/int.htm
Arizona	Ariz. Rev. Stat. § 44-1201(A)	10%
Arkansas	Ark. Stat. § 16-65-114	Whichever is greater, 10% or contract rate
California	Cal. Civ. Proc. Code § 685.010	10%
Colorado	Colo. Rev. Stat. § 5-12-102	8%
Connecticut	Conn. Gen. Stat. § 37-3a	10%; 12%
Delaware	Del. Code Ann. tit. 6, § 2301(a)	5% above the Federal Reserve Discount rate at the time interest is due. Rate posted at www.federalreserve.gov/releases/h15
District of Columbia	D.C. Code Ann. § 28-3302	70% of the penalty rate for underpayment of federal taxes. Underpayment penalty is published in IRS publication 505, Withholding and Estimated Tax, available at www.irs.gov
Florida	Fla. Stat. Ann. § 55.03	5% above average Federal Reserve Bank of N.Y. discount rate for preceding year. Posted at www.dbf.state.fl.us/interest.html
Georgia	Ga. Code Ann. § 7-4-12	12%
Hawaii	Haw. Rev. Stat. § 478-3	10%
Idaho	Idaho Code § 28-22-104	5% above weekly average yield on U.S. Treasury bills for one year. Set July 1 by State Treasurer. Find under "Judgment Rate" at www2.state.id.us/treasur
Illinois	735 Ill. Comp. Stat. § 5/2-1303	9%
Indiana	Ind. Code Ann. § 24-4.6-1-101	8%
Iowa	Iowa Code Ann. § 535.3	10%
Kansas	Kan. Stat. Ann. § 16-204	4% above Federal Reserve Bank of New York average discount rate for preceding year. Secretary of State posts rate on July 1 at www.kssos.org/rates.html
Kentucky	Ky. Rev. Stat. Ann. § 360.040	12%
Louisiana	La. Rev. Stat. Ann. § 13:4202	3¼% above the Federal Reserve Board discount rate published on the first business day of October in the Wall Street Journal. Effective for the following calendar year. Posted at state Office of Financial Institutions at www.ofi.state.la.us. Click on "Judgment Interest Rates."
Maine	Me. Rev. Stat. Ann. tit. 14, § 1602-A	7% above weekly average for one-year Treasury constant maturities, for the first calendar week of the month just before the date on which interest is calculated. Posted at www.federalreserve.gov/releases/h15

Post-Judgment Interest Rates		
State	**Code Citation**	**Post-Judgment Interest Rates**
Maryland	Md. Code Ann. [Cts. & Jud. Proc.] §§ 11-106, 107	10%
Massachusetts	Mass. Gen. Laws ch. 107, § 3; ch. 235, § 8	6%
Michigan	Mich. Comp. Laws § 600.6013	Judgments based on a written contract: 12% unless contract had a higher legal rate; may not exceed 13%. All other money judgments: 1% above the average interest rate paid at auction of five-year Treasury notes for the 6 months preceding January 1 and July 1.
Minnesota	Minn. Stat. Ann. § 549.09	Set annually in December for the following year. Based on one-year Treasury constant maturities yield for most recent month. Posted at www.courts.state.mn.us/cio/story/ 2002_interest_rate.htm
Mississippi	Miss. Code Ann. § 75-17-7	Rate stated in contract; if contract is silent, rate set by judge
Missouri	Mo. Rev. Stat. § 408.040(1)	9%
Montana	Mont. Code Ann. § 25-9-205	10%
Nebraska	Neb. Rev. Stat. § 45-103	2% above the bond investment yield of average auction price of 26-week U.S. Treasury bills at first auction of each quarter; takes effect two weeks after price published. Posted at http:// court.nol.org/community/interestrate.htm
Nevada	Nev. Rev. Stat. § 17.130	2% above the prime rate at Nevada's largest bank on January 1 or July 1 preceding the judgment. Posted at http:// fid.state.nv.us/prime%20int.htm
New Hampshire	N.H. Rev. Stat. Ann. § 336:1(II)	2% above discount interest rate on 26-week U.S. Treasury bills at the last auction prior to September 30. Rate in effect January 1 through December 31. Posted at www.state.nh.us/ courts/aoc/interest.htm
New Jersey	N.J. Ct. Rule 4:42-11	For judgments of $10,000 or less: Interest equals the average rate of return of the N.J. state cash management fund for preceding fiscal year, ending June 30; if over $10,000, same rate plus 2%. Posted at www.state.nj.us/treasury/doinvest/rate1.html
New Mexico	N.M. Rev. Stat. Ann. § 56-8-4	8.75%
New York	N.Y. C.P.L.R. Law § 5004	9%
North Carolina	N.C. Gen. Stat. §§ 24-1, 24-5	8%
North Dakota	N.D. Cent. Code §§ 28-20-34	12%
Ohio	Ohio Rev. Code Ann. § 1343.03(A)	10%
Oklahoma	Okla. Stat. tit. 12, § 727(1)	4% above the average U.S. Treasury bill interest rate for the preceding year. Effective the first business day in January. Rate posted at Oklahoma State Courts Network: www.oscn.net/ applications/oscn/index.asp?ftdb=STOKIN&level=1

Post-Judgment Interest Rates

State	Code Citation	Post-Judgment Interest Rates
Oregon	Or. Rev. Stat. § 82.010(2)	9%
Pennsylvania	42 Pa. Cons. Stat. Ann. § 8101; 41 Pa. Cons. Stat. Ann. § 202	6%
Rhode Island	R.I. Gen. Laws §§ 6-26-1; 9-21-8	12%
South Carolina	S.C. Code Ann. § 34-31-20	12%
South Dakota	S.D. Codified Laws §§ 54-3-5.1, 54-3-16(2)	10%
Tennessee	Tenn. Code Ann. § 47-14-121	10%
Texas	Tex. Fin. Code Ann. § 304.002	18% or the contract rate, whichever is less
Utah	Utah Code Ann. § 15-1-4	2% above federal post-judgment interest rate as of January 1. Posted at www.uscourts.gov/postjud/postjud.html
Vermont	Vt. Stat. Ann. tit. 12, § 2903; Vt. R. Civ. Proc. Rule 69	12%
Virginia	Va. Code Ann. §§ 8.01-382, 6.1-330.54	Judge or jury sets interest, unless there is a rate set by contract; if no court or contract rate, then 9%
Washington	Wash. Rev. Code Ann. §§ 4.56.110, 19.52.020	Contract rate as long as rate is set out in the judgment; or whichever is higher: 12% or 4% above average price for 26-week (6-month) U.S. Treasury bills in month prior to judgment. Posted in the Washington State Register at http://slc.leg.wa.gov/wsr
West Virginia	W. Va. Code Ann. § 5-6-31	10%
Wisconsin	Wis. Stat. §§ 814.04(4), 815.05(8)	12%
Wyoming	Wyo. Stat. Ann. § 1-16-102	10%

2. How Long Judgments Last

Depending on the state, a creditor may have as many as 20 years to collect a court judgment. In addition, in most states the judgment can be renewed indefinitely if it is not collected during the original period, thus giving the creditor an unlimited amount of time to collect a judgment.

3. Enforcing Judgments in Different States

Sometimes a creditor obtains a judgment against you in a state that is not where you live. This can happen if you have moved since the debt was incurred or if you signed a contract in another state. You may also own property or have assets outside the state where the judgment was obtained. The creditor can go into court in the state where you now live or where you have assets and register the original out-of-state judgment. This means the creditor now has the right to use all the judgment remedies available in the second state.

If the creditor goes into the second state to make the original judgment into a judgment of that state, you will be sent a notice and are given the opportunity to object. You can object if you don't have any property in that state, but it's usually not worth the bother. If you do have property in the other state, however, you may want to object if you don't reside in that state, didn't sign the contract that forms the basis of the lawsuit in that state or the property you own in that state isn't real estate. (See *Fox v. Citicorp Credit Services, Inc.*, 15 F.3d 1507 (9th Cir. 1994), where the court did not permit the registration of an out-of-state judgment for these very reasons.)

4. How Judgments Are Enforced

Once a judgment is entered against you, the creditor is now called a judgment creditor and you are called a judgment debtor. Judgment creditors have many more collection techniques available to them than do creditors trying to collect debts before getting a court judgment. For example, in some states a judgment creditor can order you to come to court and answer questions about your property and finances. Also, a judgment creditor can direct a sheriff to seize some of your property to pay the judgment.

What property the creditor can take varies from state to state. Usually, the creditor can go after a portion of your net wages (up to 25%, more if the judgment is for child support), bank and other deposit accounts, and your valuable personal property, such as cars and antiques.

Not all of your property can be taken, however. Every state has certain property it declares "exempt." This means it is off limits to your creditors, even judgment creditors. Just because you owe money, you shouldn't have to lose everything. You still need to eat, keep a roof over your head, clothe yourself and provide for your family. If you have very few possessions you may find that most of what you own is exempt. Exempt property is covered in Chapter 17. Note that exemption laws do not apply to income tax debts.

a. Debtor's Examination

Most states let a judgment creditor question you about your property and finances. Basically, the judgment creditor is looking for money or property that can be legally taken to pay the debt. High on the list of property the creditor looks for are deposit accounts (such as savings, checking, certificate of deposit and money market), tax refunds due and other easy cash. The procedure is usually called a debtor's examination or order of examination.

1. Written Questions

In some states, a judgment creditor sends you a form and asks you to fill it out, listing your employer's name and address, your assets and other financial information. You must do this under penalty of perjury. If you don't comply or the judgment creditor believes you're lying or not disclosing all relevant information, the judgment creditor can ask the court to issue an order requiring you to come to court and answer the questions.

Time Limit to Collect Court Judgment
(Judgments Can Be Renewed in Most States)

State	Time Limit	State	Time Limit
Alabama	20 years	Missouri	10 years
Alaska	10 years	Montana	10 years
Arizona	5 years	Nebraska	5 years
Arkansas	10 years	Nevada	6 years
California	10 years	New Hampshire	20 years
Colorado	6 years	New Jersey	20 years
Connecticut	20 years (10 years if small claims court judgment)	New Mexico	14 years
Delaware	10 years	New York	20 years
District of Columbia	12 years	North Carolina	10 years
Florida	20 years	North Dakota	10 years
Georgia	7 years	Ohio	21 years
Hawaii	10 years	Oklahoma	5 years
Idaho	6 years	Oregon	10 years
Illinois	7 years	Pennsylvania	4 years
Indiana	10 years	Rhode Island	20 years
Iowa	20 years	South Carolina	10 years
Kansas	5 years	South Dakota	20 years
Kentucky	15 years	Tennessee	10 years
Louisiana	10 years	Texas	10 years
Maine	20 years	Utah	8 years
Maryland	12 years	Vermont	8 years
Massachusetts	20 years	Virginia	20 years
Michigan	10 years	Washington	10 years
Minnesota	10 years	West Virginia	10 years
Mississippi	7 years	Wisconsin	20 years
		Wyoming	5 years

*If judgment debtor does not live in Mississippi, the period for collection is extended to 7 years.

2. Court Appearance

In other states, the creditor serves you with a paper ordering you to show up in court and bring certain financial documents, such as bank statements or pay stubs. You may be sent the questions and given a chance to answer them in writing first. If you receive an order to appear in court and you don't show up, the court can declare you in contempt and issue a warrant for your arrest.

In a few states, if the judge issues an order for you to come to court, serving that order on you creates a lien on your personal property. The lien may make it difficult for you to sell the property without first paying the judgment. Also, if the judgment creditor believes you are about to leave the state or conceal your property to avoid paying the judgment, the creditor can ask the judge to issue a warrant for your immediate arrest. This is quite drastic, but it's been known to happen when a lot of money is owed.

If you receive an order to appear but can't take the time off from work or otherwise can't make it, call the judgment creditor or her lawyer and explain your situation. Tell her you're willing to answer questions over the phone or even in person but at another time. If the creditor hasn't already sent you a form about your finances and property, and she thinks you're telling the truth, she may be happy to get the information over the telephone.

If the judgment creditor agrees to change the date or to let you answer the questions over the phone, ask her to send you and the court a letter verifying that you need not appear at the hearing. If the creditor refuses, write your own letter to the creditor confirming your conversation. Send a copy to the court as well.

If you can attend the hearing, or you reschedule it to a convenient time, do not take any money or expensive personal items with you. The judgment creditor can ask you to empty your pockets or purse and can ask the court to order you to turn over any nonexempt money or valuable personal property in your possession, such as a college ring or leather jacket.

b. Wage Attachments

The first item of your property most judgment creditors will go after is your paycheck through a wage attachment (or wage garnishment). A wage attachment is an easy technique if you receive a regular paycheck. Your employer takes a portion of your wages out of your net pay each pay period and sends that money to your creditor before you ever see it.

In most states, the judgment creditor can't take more than the lesser of 25% of your net earnings or the amount by which your weekly net earnings exceed 30 times the federal minimum wage, which is currently $5.15 an hour. Net earnings are your gross earning less all mandatory deductions such as withheld income taxes and unemployment insurance.

A few states offer greater protections for judgment debtors about to lose their wages. In Delaware, for example, a judgment creditor cannot take more than 15% of your net wages. (Del. Code Ann. § 10-4913.)

The wage attachment laws and limitations described in this section do not apply to three specific debts:

- student loans—if you are in default on a federally guaranteed student loan, the holder of your loan can attach 10% of your wages without first suing you (the government is currently seeking to increase this amount to 15%)
- child support—up to 50% of your wages may be taken to pay support arrears (more if you don't currently support another dependent or are in arrears), and your child's other parent usually does not have to first sue you, and
- income taxes—if you ignore all attempts by the IRS to collect taxes you owe, the government can grab virtually all of your wages and leave you with about $100 a week.

To attach your wages, a judgment creditor obtains authorization from the court in a document usually called a writ. Under this authorization, the judgment creditor directs the sheriff to seize a portion of your wages. The sheriff in turn notifies your employer of the attachment and your employer notifies you. Unless you object, your employer sends the amount withheld at each pay period to the sheriff, who deducts his expenses and sends the balance to the judgment creditor.

You can object to the wage attachment by requesting a court hearing. (See Section G, below.) In some states, the attachment can't begin until after the hearing, unless you give up your right to a hearing. In most states, however, as long as you have the opportunity to have your objection promptly considered, the attachment can take effect immediately.

Can You Be Fired for a Wage Attachment?

Your employer may consider a wage attachment a hassle and may threaten to fire you if you don't settle the debt right away. Under the law, however, an employer cannot fire you because your wages are attached to satisfy a single debt. (15 U.S.C. § 1674(a).) If two judgment creditors attach your wages or one judgment creditor attaches your wages to pay two different judgments, however, this law does not protect you from being fired.

In Washington state, an employer can't fire you unless your wages are attached by three different creditors or to satisfy three different judgments within a year. (Wash. Rev. Code Ann. § 6.27.170.) In Connecticut, you can't be fired unless your employer has to deal with more than seven creditors or judgments in a single year. (Conn. Gen. Stat. Ann. § 52-361a(j).)

Most employers will work with employees who are honestly trying to clear up their debt problems. If your wages are attached, talk with your employer and explain that you are working hard to settle the matter as soon as possible. If, however, you are fired because your employer was not aware of the law or because your employer was "suddenly" unhappy with your work, consider filing a complaint or lawsuit. (See Chapter 20 for tips on finding a lawyer.)

---

c. Property Liens

One collection device commonly used by judgment creditors is the property lien. In just under half the states, a judgment entered against you automatically creates a lien on the real property you own in the county where the judgment was obtained. In the rest of the states, the creditor must record the judgment with the county, and then the recorded judgment creates a lien on your real property. In a few states, the lien is on your real and personal property.

If a judgment creditor does not get a lien on personal property after the judgment is entered or recorded, the judgment creditor may be able to get a lien on your personal property by recording the judgment with the Secretary of State. This usually applies only to property with title, such as a car, or a business's assets. If, for example, you tried to sell your car, the lien would appear and you'd have to pay off the judgment creditor before selling.

Once the judgment creditor has a lien on your property, especially your real property, he can safely assume he'll eventually be paid. When you sell or refinance your property, title must be cleared—that is, all liens must be removed by paying the lienholder—before the deal can close.

Instead of waiting for you to sell your property, the creditor can "execute" on the lien, that is, have the sheriff seize your property, typically a house, and arrange for a public sale from which the creditor is paid out of the proceeds. However, if your property is exempt (see Section G, below), the creditor cannot do this. Even if your property is not exempt, many creditors don't want to go through the expense and hassle of a public sale. This is especially true if the creditor won't get much money through the sale. Any mortgage holder, government taxing authority or other creditor who has placed a lien on your property before the judgment creditor will be paid first. Then you get any homestead exemption to which you are entitled. (See Chapter 17.) Only then does the judgment creditor get her share.

EXAMPLE: Lin lives in Wisconsin and owns a house worth $200,000. Child-Aid Medical Clinic obtained a judgment against Lin for emergency treatment of his daughter for $2,500 and, consequently, got a lien on Lin's house. Child-Aid considers seizing his house to sell it and be paid, but realizes that it won't get any money because:

- Lin owes $125,000 on his first mortgage
- Lin owes $23,000 on a home equity loan
- Lin owes the IRS $17,000
- Lin's homestead exemption is $40,000.

These items total $205,000, more than the value of Lin's house.

d. Property Levies

A judgment creditor can go after your personal property by "levying" on it. If you have money in a bank account or safe-deposit box that isn't exempt, the sheriff can usually take it. Or, if you own valuable personal property such as a car or antique, the judgment creditor might send a sheriff or marshal to take it, sell it at a public auction and apply the proceeds toward the debt. You do not have to let the sheriff into your home, however, unless she has a special court order allowing entry. The judgment creditor won't be interested in any other property, as it usually has little value.

Here's is how the levying process generally works.

1. The judgment creditor gets a court order letting him levy on your property. This order is usually called a writ of execution.
2. The judgment creditor directs the sheriff to seize a particular asset, such as your car.
3. The sheriff comes to your home. If you are present, he explains that he has an order to take a particular item of your property to sell to pay off your debt.
4. If you aren't home or don't cooperate, the sheriff can use a duplicate car key or hotwire a car, as long as it is not in a locked garage. Stay calm; in most states you can be arrested for interfering with the sheriff. The sheriff can't enter your house without your authorization to take other property, unless he has a special court order allowing entry. But again, if the sheriff insists on entering anyway, don't interfere.
5. The sheriff puts the item into storage.

6. If you don't file an objection within the time allowed by your state, the sheriff will put the item up for sale (see Section G, below).
7. After the sale, the proceeds are used to pay whatever you still owe the original lender, then to pay the sheriff's costs (seizing, storage and sale), and then to pay the judgment. If the sale doesn't cover all of what you owe, the judgment creditor can still come after you for the rest.

e. Assignment Orders

An assignment order lets creditors go after property you own that can't be subjected to a levy, such as an anticipated tax refund, the loan value of an unmatured life insurance or an annuity policy. Independent contractors and other self-employed people who have no regular wages to be garnished are particularly susceptible to an assignment order against their account receivables.

An assignment order is straightforward. The judgment creditor applies to the court for an order prohibiting you from disposing of money you have a right to receive—such as a tax refund, insurance loan, royalties, dividend payments or commissions. You are given the date and time of the court hearing and an opportunity to contest. If the creditor gets the order, the creditor serves it on whomever holds your money. When payment to you comes due, the money is sent to the judgment creditor instead.

f. Contempt Proceedings

Sometimes, a judgment issued by the court will include a schedule of when the judgment debtor is to make payments. In a few states, if a judgment doesn't include such a schedule, the judgment creditor can go back to the court and ask the judge to make an order requiring periodic payments on a debt.

Violating a court order is generally referred to as contempt of court. In a handful of states, if a judge issues an order requiring periodic payments on a debt and you miss any payments, the judge can hold you in contempt. In theory, at least, the judge could issue a warrant for your arrest and you could be jailed.

Liens on Your Property After Judgment
(In Most States Liens Can Be Extended or Renewed)

State	Code Section	Property	How Creditor Obtains Lien	How Long Lien Lasts
Alabama	Ala. Code. §§ 6-9-210 to -211	Real & personal	Creditor registers judgment with office of probate court in any county where debtor has property now or may have property in future	10 years
Alaska	Alaska Stat. § 09.30.010	Real	Creditor files judgment with county recorder in any county where debtor has property now or may have property in future	10 years
Arizona	Ariz. Rev. Stat. Ann. § 33-964	Real	Creditor files and records judgment with county recorder in any county where debtor has property now or may have property in future	5 years
Arkansas	Ark. Code Ann. § 16-65-117	Real	Automatic on property in county where judgment entered; otherwise creditor must file judgment with clerk of circuit court in county where property located	10 years
California	Cal. Civ. Proc. Code §§ 697.310, 697.340	Real	Creditor records judgment with county recorder in any county where debtor has property now or may have property in future	10 years
Colorado	Colo. Rev. Stat. § 13-52-102	Real	Creditor files judgment with country recorder in any county where debtor has property now or may have property in future	6 years
Connecticut	Conn. Gen. Stat. Ann. § 52-355a	Personal	Creditor files judgment with Office of Secretary of State	5 years
	Conn. Gen. Stat. Ann. § 52-380a	Real	Creditor must attach property during lawsuit; within four months of judgment creditor must file lien certificate with town clerk where property located	20 years
Delaware	Del. Code Ann. tit. 10, §§ 4710 to 4711	Real	Automatic on property located in county of superior court where judgment rendered; for other property creditor must file judgment with superior court in county where property is located	10 years
District of Columbia	D.C. Code Ann. §§ 15-101 to -102	Real	Creditor files judgment with District of Columbia Recorder of Deeds	12 years
Florida	Fla. Stat. Ann. §§ 55.202 to .205	Personal	Creditor files judgment with Florida Department of State	5 years
	Fla. Stat. Ann. §§ 55.081, 55.10	Real	Creditor records judgment with any county recorder where debtor has property nor or may have property in future	10 years
Georgia	Ga. Code Ann. §§ 9-12-81 to -82; 9-12-60	Personal	In county of debtor's residence, creditor enters judgment in execution docket kept by clerk of superior court	7 years
	Ga. Code Ann. §§ 9-12-83; 9-12-86; 9-12-60	Real	Creditor records judgment with superior court clek in county where debtor has property or may have property in future	7 years
Hawaii	Haw. Rev. Stat. § 636-3	Real	Creditor records judgment with Hawaii Bureau of Conveyances	10 years

Liens on Your Property After Judgment
(In Most States Liens Can Be Extended or Renewed)

State	Code Section	Property	How Creditor Obtains Lien	How Long Lien Lasts
Idaho	Idaho Code § 11-101 to -102(1)	Real	Creditor records judgment with county clerk in any county where debtor has property now or may have property in future	5 years
Illinois	735 Ill. Comp. Stat. §§ 5/12-101, 105, 106, 108	Real	Creditor files judgment with recorder in county where property located; to enforce against property in another county creditor files copy with circuit court clerk	7 years
Indiana	Ind. Code Ann. § 34-55-9-2	Real	Automatic on property in county where judgment handed down; for property in another county, creditor files copy with circuit court clerk	10 years
Iowa	Iowa Code Ann. §§ 624.23 to .24	Real	Automatic on property in county where judgment is entered; creditor files judgment with district court clerk for property outside county where judgment entered	10 years
Kansas	Kan. Stat. Ann. §§ 60-2202; 60-2403	Real	Automatic on property in county where judgment is entered; creditor files judgment with district court clerk for property outside county where judgment entered	5 years
Kentucky	Ky. Rev. Stat. Ann. §§ 426.720; 413.090	Real	Creditor records judgment with county clerk in any county where debtor has property now or may have property in future	15 years
Louisiana*	La. Rev. Stat. Ann. § 9:2721 La. Civ. Code Art. 3299 to 3303	Real	Creditor files judgment in registry of mortgages and conveyances in office of parish recorder in any parish where debtor has or may have property in future	10 years
Maine	Me. Rev. Stat. Ann. tit. 14, §§ 3132, 4651-A(9)	Real & Personal	Creditor must have attached debtor's property during the lawsuit; then automatic when judgment entered	20 years
Maryland	Md. Code Ann. [Cts. & Jud. Proc.] § 11-402; Md. Ct. Rule 3-601, 3-622	Real	Automatic on property in county where judgment entered; to enforce in another county creditor files copy with circuit court clerk	12 years
Massachusetts	Mass. Gen. Laws ch. 223, §§ 42, 59, 63; ch.260, § 20	Personal Real	Creditor files copy with city or town clerk Creditor files judgment with registrar of deeds in any county where debtor has property now or may have property in future	30 days 20 years
Michigan	Mich. Comp. Laws §§ 600.4035, .6004, .6017, .6018	Real & personal	Judgment must first be satisfied from personal property; if insufficient, then real property may be attached; copy of attachment must be filed with registrar of deeds in county where property located	10 years
Minnesota	Minn. Stat. Ann. § 548.09	Real	Automatic on present and future property in county where judgment entered; for property in another county, creditor files copy with that county's court administrator	10 years
Mississippi	Miss. Code Ann. §§ 11-7-189 to -197	Real & personal	Automatic on property in county where judgment is enrolled; to enforce in another county, creditor files copy with circuit court clerk	7 years

*In Louisiana, a lien is known as a "judicial mortgage" and real property is known as "immovables."

State	Code Section	Property	How Creditor Obtains Lien	How Long Lien Lasts
	Liens on Your Property After Judgment (In Most States Liens Can Be Extended or Renewed)			
Missouri	Mo. Rev. Stat. §§ 511.350 to .360; Mo. Civ. Proc. Rule 74.08, 74.13	Real	Automatic on property in county where judgment is entered; creditor files judgment with county circuit clerk for property outside county where judgment entered	10 years
Montana	Mont. Code Ann. § 25-9-301	Real	Automatic on present and future property in county where judgment entered	10 years
Nebraska	Neb. Rev. Stat. §§ 25-1303, 25-1542	Real	Automatic on property in county where judgment is entered; creditor files judgment with district county clerk for property outside county where judgment entered	5 years
Nevada	Nev. Rev. Stat. Ann. § 17.150	Real	Creditor files judgment with county recorder in any county where debtor has property now or may have property in future	6 years
New Hampshire	N.H. Rev. Stat. Ann. §§ 511:5, 511:55; 511-A:5		Creditor must attach debtor's property during lawsuit.	
		Real	Creditor files order of attachment with register of deeds in any county where debtor has property now or may have property in future	6 years
		Personal	Creditor files order with town or city clerk or with secretary of state	6 years
New Jersey	N.J. Stat. Ann. §§ 2A:26-9 to -11	Real	Automatic on debtor's present and future property anywhere in the state	20 years
New Mexico	N.M. Stat. Ann. § 39-1-6	Real	Creditor files judgment with county clerk in any country where debtor has property now or may have property in future	14 years
New York	N.Y. C.P.L.R. §§ 211(b), 5016 to 5018	Real	Automatic on property in county where judgment entered; for property in another county, creditor files transcript with that county's clerk	20 years
North Carolina	N.C. Gen. Stat. § 1-234	Real	Automatic on property in county where judgment is entered; creditor files judgment with county clerk for property outside county where judgment entered	10 years
North Dakota	N.D. Cent. Code § 28-20-13	Real	Automatic on property in county where judgment is entered; creditor files judgment with county clerk for property outside county where judgment entered	10 years
Ohio	Ohio Rev. Code Ann. §§ 2329.02, 2329.07	Real	Creditor files judgment with clerk of court of common pleas in any county where debtor has property now or may have property in future	5 years
Oklahoma	Okla. Stat. tit. 12, §§ 706, 735	Real	Creditor files Statement of Judgment with county clerk in any county where debtor has property now or may have property in future	5 years
Oregon	Or. Rev. Stat. §§ 18.320 to 18.360	Real	Automatic on property in county where judgment entered; for property in another county, creditor records judgment in County Clerk Lien Record	10 years

			Liens on Your Property After Judgment (In Most States Liens Can Be Extended or Renewed)	
State	**Code Section**	**Property**	**How Creditor Obtains Lien**	**How Long Lien Lasts**
Pennsylvania	42 Pa. Cons. Stat. Ann. §§ 4303, 5526(1)	Real	Creditor records judgment with clerk of the court of common pleas in county where debtor has property now or may have property in future	5 years
Rhode Island	R.I. Gen. Laws §§ 10-5-2. 10-5-9 10-5-42, 10-5-46	Real & personal	Creditor must attach debtor's property during lawsuit. Judge issues writ that court officer leaves with town clerk or recorder of deeds in town where debtor's property is located	personal, 4 months real, 20 years
South Carolina	S.C. Code Ann. §§ 15-35-510 to -540, 15-35-810	Real	Automatic on property in county where judgment entered; for other counties creditor files transcript of judgment with clerk of the court of common pleas	10 years
South Dakota	S.D. Codified Laws Ann. § 15-16-7	Real, except debtor's home	Automatic on debtor's present and future property in county where judgment entered; for other counties, creditor files judgment with clerk of circuit court	10 years
Tennessee	Tenn. Code Ann. §§ 25-5-101 to -107	Real	Creditor files certified copy of judgment with register of deeds in any county where debtor has property now or may have property in future	10 years
Texas	Tex. Prop. Code Ann. §§ 52.001 to .006	Real	Creditor files judgment with county clerk in any county where debtor has propety now or may have property in future	10 years
Utah	Utah Code Ann. §§ 78-22-1 to -1.5; 78-5-119	Real	Creditor records judgment in Registry of Judgments in the office of the district court clerk in any county where debtor has property now or may have property in future; creditor must supply information about debtor when recording the judgment	8 years
Vermont	Vt. Stat. Ann. tit. 12, §§ 2901 to 2904	Real	Creditor records judgment with town clerk in any town where debtor has property	8 years
Virginia	Va. Code Ann §§ 8.01-251, 8.01-458	Real	Creditor records judgment on county recorder's lien docket in any county where debtor has property now or may have property in future	10 years
Washington	Wash. Rev. Code Ann. § 4.56.190	Real	Automatic on property in county where judgment is entered; creditor files judgment with county clerk for property outside county where judgment is entered	10 years
West Virginia	W. Va. Code Ann. §§ 38-3-5 to -7	Real	Automatic on property in county where judgment is entered; for property in other counties, creditor records abstract of judgment with clerk of county court	10 years
Wisconsin	Wis. Stat. Ann. §§ 806.14 to .15	Real	Automatic on property in county where judgment is entered; for property in other counties, creditor records copy of judgment with clerk of circuit court	10 years
Wyoming	Wyo. Stat. Ann. §§ 1-17-301 to 307; 5-9-138	Real	Automatic on property in county where judgment is entered; for property in other counties, creditor files judgment with clerk of court of same jurisdiction, and records judgment with county clerk	5 years

As you might hope, arresting a debtor on this kind of warrant is usually a very low priority, and in most situations the warrants become old and moldy without anyone being arrested. But the threat of arrest and jail can be a serious incentive for many judgment debtors to send a check ASAP.

G. Stopping Judgment Collection Efforts

Having your property taken or your wages attached can be devastating. It's miserable enough to owe money; it's worse to have your creditors take what little property you may have left.

Fortunately, in many situations you can still take steps to try to head off collection efforts. The process of trying to grab property to pay a judgment can be quite time-consuming and burdensome for a judgment creditor. Also, the creditor might fear that your employer will fire you if the creditor sets up a wage attachment or that you'll quit your job or file for bankruptcy.

It's never too late to negotiate. A judgment creditor who receives a reasonable offer to pay will often stop a lien, levy, wage attachment, garnishment suit or assignment order. (For tips on negotiating, see Chapter 6.) Or consider contacting a debt counseling agency for help in negotiating and setting up a repayment plan. (See Chapter 20.)

Most important, just because a judgment creditor levies on your property or attaches your wages, it doesn't mean that the creditor is entitled to take the property. Every state exempts certain property from creditors. This means that creditors simply cannot have that property, even if you owe $100,000 and have no other resources. In addition, you may be able to keep property that isn't exempt if you can prove to the court that you need it to support yourself or your family.

Exempt property is described in detail in Chapter 17. In most states, your clothing, furniture, personal effects and public benefits can't be taken to pay a debt. Nor can some of the equity in your car and house, most of your wages and most retirement pensions. Charts for each state are in Appendix 2. What follows is a discussion on how to claim that your property is exempt (or that you need non-exempt property) when the judgment creditor pursues a lien, levy, wage attachment or assignment order.

Any time the judgment creditor seeks to take your property you must be notified. You can request a hearing, called something like a claim of exemption, to argue that it will be a financial hardship on you if the property is taken, or that your property is exempt under state law. If you lose that hearing and your wages are attached, you can request a second hearing if you suffer a hardship and your circumstances have changed—for example, you have sudden medical expenses or must make increased support payments.

Debts for Necessities

In most states, you cannot request a claim of exemption hearing to protect your wages from being attached to pay for a debt for basic necessities, such as rent or mortgage, food, utilities or clothing. The law is clear that you should pay for your necessities, even if you suffer a hardship in doing so.

This doesn't mean that you shouldn't request a claim of exemption hearing if the debt (now part of the judgment) was for a basic necessity. The creditor may not challenge your claim. Or, the judge might not care whether the debt was for a basic necessity and may consider only whether or not you need the money to support your family.

Here is an overview of how a claim of exemption hearing normally works.

1. When your employer notifies you of a wage attachment request, or you are notified of a property levy (such as a bank account attachment) or assignment order, you will be told in writing how to file a claim of exemption—that is, how to tell the judgment creditor you consider the property unavailable. The time period in which you must file your claim is usually strictly enforced—don't miss it.

2. Complete and send a copy of your claim of exemption to the judgment creditor. Some-

times you'll also have to serve it on the levying officer, such as the Sheriff. The judgment creditor will probably file a challenge to your claim. She may abandon her attachment, levy or assignment order, however, if it's too expensive or time-consuming to challenge you. If she does abandon it, your withheld wages or taken property will be returned to you.

3. If she doesn't abandon her attachment, levy or assignment order, she'll schedule a hearing before a judge. If you don't attend, you'll probably lose. On the day of the hearing, come early and watch the way the judge handles other cases. If you're nervous, visit the court a day earlier to get accustomed to the surroundings.

4. At the hearing, you'll have to convince the judge that your property is exempt or that you need it to support yourself or your family. This is your opportunity to defend yourself from having your wages or other property taken. You must do all that you can to prepare for this hearing if you want to keep your property.

   For example, if the creditor tries to take your "tools of trade," which are exempt to a certain value in most states, bring along someone who works in your occupation. A supervisor, union boss or shop leader can say that you use the items in your job. You'll need to add the fact that the items' value does not exceed the exemption amount. If you have high income one month, bring in pay stubs to show that you usually make less. Or if your bills are higher than average, bring copies. Be creative.

5. The judge will listen to both you and the judgment creditor, if the judgment creditor shows up. Sometimes the judgment creditor relies on the papers he filed with the court. The judge may make a ruling, or may set up an arrangement for you to pay the judgment in installments. ■

CHAPTER 16

Bankruptcy—The Ultimate Weapon

Thou whom avenging powers obey.
Cancel my debt (too great to pay).
Before the sad accounting day.

—Wentworth Dillon,
English poet and translator, 1633-1685

Bankruptcy might be the ultimate solution to your debt problems. For a court filing fee of $185–$200 and the cost of a self-help law book, most people can wipe out (discharge) all—or a good portion—of their outstanding debts. Your creditors know this, and try hard to keep you from filing for bankruptcy. But deciding whether or not to file for bankruptcy isn't easy. You need to understand the different types of bankruptcies and what bankruptcy can and cannot do for you.

Bankruptcy Law May Change for the Worse

For the past five years, the United States Congress has batted around legislation that would drastically change bankruptcy law—mostly to the detriment of debtors. In 2001, Congress passed the bill. But, as congresspersons were ironing out a few minor differences between the House and Senate versions of the bill, September 11 happened. Congress halted its efforts to make the bill into law, only to revisit those efforts in 2002. Now, the legislation is dangerously close to becoming law. The only snag is a disagreement over language regarding the treatment of debts incurred by anti-abortion protestors who block access to abortion clinics. If Congress can work out an agreement on that provision, both Houses are posed to pass the bill, and President Bush has indicated he will sign it into law.

The bill is backed by the credit card industry and is unfriendly to debtors. Among other things, the bill would prohibit some people from filing for bankruptcy, add to the list of debts that people could not wipe out in bankruptcy, make it harder for people to come up with manageable repayment plans and limit the protection to bankruptcy filers from collection efforts while the bankruptcy case is pending.

If the legislation becomes law, most of the new rules will become effective 180 days later. If you are planning to file for bankruptcy, keep close watch on this bill. If it does become law, it might benefit you to file for bankruptcy before the new rules take effect. To learn about the status of this legislation and the details of its provisions, check Legal Updates on Nolo's website (www.nolo.com). The websites of the American Bankruptcy Institute (www.abiworld.org) and the Commercial Law League of America (www.clla.org) also have up-to-date information on the legislation.

Nolo's Bankruptcy Resources. Nolo publishes several bankruptcy aids; this chapter contains only an overview of the bankruptcy process.

Bankruptcy: Is It the Right Solution to Your Debt Problems?, by Robin Leonard, contains all the information you need to figure out if bankruptcy is right for you, and if so, which type of bankruptcy case you should file. Bankruptcy answers questions such as "Will I lose my house?," "Can I keep my car?," "Will I lose my job?" and "Will I get rid of all my debts?"

How to File for Chapter 7 Bankruptcy, by Stephen Elias, Albin Renauer, Robin Leonard and Kathleen Michon, contains all the forms and instructions necessary for you to file for Chapter 7 bankruptcy.

Nolo's Law Form Kit: Personal Bankruptcy, by the same authors, is a streamlined bankruptcy guide for people who are certain they want to file a simple Chapter 7 bankruptcy.

Chapter 13 Bankruptcy: Repay Your Debts, by Robin Leonard, contains all the information needed to file for Chapter 13 bankruptcy on your own.

Congress has devised two kinds of bankruptcy: liquidation and reorganization. The liquidation bankruptcy is called Chapter 7, and can be filed by either individuals or businesses. There are three different reorganization bankruptcies:

- Chapter 13 bankruptcies for individuals
- Chapter 11 bankruptcies for businesses and for individuals with unusually high debts, and
- Chapter 12 bankruptcies for family farmers

This chapter addresses only Chapter 13 bankruptcies and Chapter 7 bankruptcies for individuals.

In a Chapter 7 bankruptcy, you ask the court to erase your debts completely. In exchange, you must give up your nonexempt property or its equivalent in cash or other property. (See Section F.2, below, for a discussion on exempt property.)

In a Chapter 13 bankruptcy, you set up a court-approved plan to repay your debts. Under the plan, you make monthly payments to the bankruptcy court—usually for three years. The court in turn pays your creditors a percentage of the money they are owed. Under the plan, you must use all of your disposable income to pay off your debts. In addition, your creditors must receive at least as much as they would have received had you filed for Chapter 7 bankruptcy—that is, the value of your nonexempt property. Some creditors, however—such as a former spouse to whom you owe alimony—are entitled to receive 100% of what you owe. (You can either pay it in full through your plan or come out of bankruptcy still owing some.) In Chapter 13 bankruptcy, you are not required to give up any property.

If you're deeply in debt, bankruptcy may seem like a magic wand. It often is. But it has its drawbacks too. First, it's intrusive. A court-appointed person, the bankruptcy trustee, must approve almost all financial transactions you make while your bankruptcy case is open. For a Chapter 7 bankruptcy, this period can last several months. For a Chapter 13 bankruptcy, it can be as long as five years. Second, bankruptcy can cause practical problems, especially if you must surrender property you desperately want to keep. Finally, bankruptcy can be depressing—some people would rather struggle along under mountains of debt than be labeled bankrupt.

You may also be concerned about your credit rating. Credit bureaus can report bankruptcies on your credit record for ten years. But you can take steps to start rebuilding your credit almost immediately. (See Chapter 18 to learn how to do this.) And you'd be surprised at how quickly new credit cards will come in the mail after your bankruptcy. Some credit card companies are more than willing to extend credit to people who have recently completed a bankruptcy—they assume that given your track record, you're likely to carry a balance on the card (which means more money for them in the form of interest) and won't be able to discharge any debt for another six years (see Section A.1.). It will take longer to qualify for other types of credit, like mortgages or car loans. But most people who pay their bills on time for two to three years after completing a bankruptcy are able to get other types of loans.

Go Slow With Getting New Credit. Before you fill your wallet with new credit cards, stop and reconsider. Although you're likely to get lots of credit card offers in the mail, it's a good bet that the cards will charge exorbitant rates (since your credit rating will be less than stellar after the bankruptcy). And, especially if high credit card bills are what caused you trouble before the bankruptcy, the last thing you need to do is start charging things you can't afford and carrying large balances on your cards. (See Chapter 10 for more on how to choose credit cards and use them wisely.)

A. Don't Feel Guilty

Some people feel ashamed at the prospect of filing for bankruptcy. Don't. Bankruptcy has been around for a long time, for good reason. Bankruptcy is a necessary safety net for people who need to regain their footing. It prevents individuals and families who are over their heads in debt (often due to unemployment, illness or injury) from being pushed out of the economy altogether.

Consider who files for bankruptcy: The average person filing for bankruptcy earns just $22,000 per year (according to a 1999 study by federal bankruptcy judges). Most have suffered a significant period of unemployment before filing. According to Consumers Union, among elderly debtors, 85% cite medical or job problems as the reason for bankruptcy. Consumers Union also says that single moms trying to make ends meet make up a large portion of bankruptcy filers—divorced women raising children are 500% more likely to end up in bankruptcy than married or single women without children.

Consider also the American consumer economy. Aggressive salespeople, finance companies and even banks bombard us every day with special deals, credit card solicitations, home equity loan packages and more. We are encouraged to buy on credit now, and worry about payment later. If we default, we are then bombarded with letters and phone calls demanding payment.

In one form or another, aggressive creditors demanding to be paid have been around for a long time. Not surprisingly, so has bankruptcy, which originates in the Hebrew Bible. (See Deuteronomy 15:1-2—"Every seventh year you shall practice remission of debts. This shall be the nature of the remission: Every creditor shall remit the due that he

claims from his neighbor; he shall not dun his neighbor or kinsman.")

More than one million people each year file for bankruptcy. Hundreds of companies—often the same ones that hound you for payment—themselves file bankruptcy each year. Bankruptcy is here to stay, and creditors know it. You have no reason to feel guilty.

Famous Bankruptcy Filers

Among the over one million people who file for bankruptcy each year are some familiar faces:

Samuel Clemens (aka Mark Twain), author.

Oscar Wilde, poet and author.

Milton Hershey, filed for bankruptcy for each of his first four candy companies. His fifth is now known as the Hershey Foods Corp.

Henry Ford, filed for bankruptcy for his first company. He later founded Ford Motor Co.

Mickey Rooney, actor.

Burt Reynolds, actor.

B. Filing for Bankruptcy Stops Your Creditors

When you file for bankruptcy, a protection called the automatic stay immediately stops any lawsuit filed against you and virtually all other actions against your property by a creditor or collection agency. Especially if you are facing eviction or foreclosure, or losing your utility service, the temporary protection of the automatic stay may seem like a powerful reason to file for bankruptcy.

There are some notable exceptions to the automatic stay. The following proceedings can continue:

- **Criminal proceedings.** A criminal proceeding that can be broken down into criminal and debt components will be divided, and only the criminal component will continue. For example, if you were convicted of writing a bad check and sentenced to community service and ordered to pay a fine, your obligation to do community service won't be stopped by the automatic stay.

- **Enforcement of child support or alimony and paternity actions.** The automatic stay will not halt a lawsuit seeking to establish your paternity. And, if you owe child support or alimony, bankruptcy will not interrupt your obligation to make current payments. Nor does the automatic stay stop proceedings to establish, modify or collect back support. Also, these debts will survive bankruptcy intact and will have to be paid once the case is closed. In Chapter 13 bankruptcy, you can include the back support in your repayment plan.
- **Certain tax proceedings.** The automatic stay stops the IRS from issuing a tax lien or seizing property. But it does not stop an audit, the issuance of a tax deficiency notice, a demand for a tax rerun, the issuance of a tax assessment or the demand for payment of such an assessment.

Bankruptcy Isn't Necessary to Stop Bill Collector Harassment

Usually, you don't need to file for bankruptcy just to get annoying collection agencies off your back. As discussed in Chapter 9, they cannot threaten you, lie about what they can do to you or invade your privacy. Also, you can legally stop collection agencies from phoning or writing you simply by demanding that they stop, even if you owe them a bundle and can't pay a cent.

These rules only apply to debt collection agencies, not to creditors collecting their own debts. However, many states have fair debt collection laws that cover creditors as well. If most or all of your income and property is exempt (that is, the debt collectors and creditors cannot take it from you, see Chapter 17 for more on this), it usually makes little sense to file for bankruptcy. If you want to stop the calls and letters, simply tell them to stop. (Chapter 9 tells you how to do this.)

The bankruptcy court may lift the automatic stay as it applies to a particular creditor if that creditor convinces the court that the stay isn't serving its intended purpose. The stay can be lifted within a week or two, though a few months is more common.

Here is how the automatic stay affects some common emergencies.

Foreclosure. If your mortgage is in foreclosure, the automatic stay temporarily stops the proceedings. If you face foreclosure, Chapter 13 bankruptcy is almost always better than Chapter 7 bankruptcy if you want to keep your house. You can make up mortgage arrears as part of your Chapter 13 repayment plan, and get back on track with your regular payments. In Chapter 7 bankruptcy, the creditor will be able to get the stay lifted and continue the foreclosure.

Eviction. If you're being evicted, the automatic stay can buy you a few days or a few weeks. But if the landlord asks the court to lift the stay, the court will probably agree, reasoning that eviction won't affect the bankruptcy. Despite the attractiveness of even a temporary delay, filing for bankruptcy solely because of an eviction is almost never a good idea. In fact, some courts may view it as an abuse of the bankruptcy system. You're better off looking for a new place to live or fighting the eviction in state court if you have a defense.

Utility disconnects. If you're behind on a utility bill and the company is threatening to disconnect your water, electric, gas or telephone service, the automatic stay will prevent the disconnection for at least 20 days (11 U.S.C. § 366). Bankruptcy will probably discharge past due debts for utility service.

Public benefit overpayments. If you receive public benefits and were overpaid, normally the agency is entitled to collect the overpayment out of your future checks. The automatic stay prevents this collection. Furthermore, the overpayment you owe can be wiped out in bankruptcy unless the agency convinces the court it resulted from fraud on your part.

Loss of driver's license. In some states, your driver's license may be suspended until you pay a court judgment for damages resulting from an automobile accident. The automatic stay can prevent this suspension if it hasn't already occurred. If you are absolutely dependent on your ability to drive for your livelihood and family support, keeping your driver's license can be a powerful reason to file for bankruptcy.

If your driver's license has already been suspended, you'll probably be able to get it back after bankruptcy. This is because after bankruptcy, a federal, state or local government agency cannot deny, revoke, suspend or refuse to renew a license, permit, charter, franchise or other similar grant solely because you filed for bankruptcy. If your license was also suspended because you didn't have state-required insurance, however, you won't get your license back until you meet your state insurance requirement.

Multiple wage attachments. Although no more than 25% of your net wages may be taken to satisfy a court judgment (up to 50% for child support or alimony, more if you're in arrears or not currently supporting anyone and everything but about $100 a week to the IRS), many people file for bankruptcy especially when creditors threaten to attach their wages for more than one debt. For some people, *any* loss of income is devastating. Also, some employers get angry at the expense and hassle of taking money out of an employee's wages for a succession of attachments and may take it out on the employee. (For information on wage attachments and getting fired, see Chapter 15, Section F.4.) Filing for bankruptcy stops wage attachments dead in their tracks. Not only will you take home a full salary, but chances are you can discharge the debt in bankruptcy.

C. Bankruptcy Might Not Help You

Bankruptcy is a powerful legal proceeding meant to give debtors a fresh financial start in facing the world. Many people with overwhelming debt problems find that bankruptcy helps, because the majority of their debts can be discharged. Even if some of your debts are nondischargeable (that is, you cannot wipe them out in bankruptcy), getting rid of other debts may better enable you to pay the nondischargeable ones.

But please understand that:

- bankruptcy won't always help, and
- bankruptcy isn't always available to you.

1. You Previously Received a Bankruptcy Discharge

You cannot file for Chapter 7 bankruptcy if you obtained a discharge of your debts under Chapter 7 or Chapter 13 in a case begun within the past six years. The six-year period runs from the date you filed the earlier bankruptcy case, not the date of your discharge. Chapter 13 bankruptcy has no such restriction; you can file for it at any time, assuming you have the income to fund a repayment plan.

Also, you cannot file for bankruptcy if a court dismissed a previous bankruptcy case within the past 180 days because you violated a court order, the court ruled that your filing was fraudulent or an abuse of the bankruptcy system, or you requested the dismissal after a creditor asked the court to lift the automatic stay.

2. You Don't Want to Stick a Codebtor With a Debt

A friend, relative or anyone else who guarantees or cosigns a debt or otherwise takes on a joint obligation with you can be held wholly responsible for the debt if you don't pay it.

If you discharge the debt in Chapter 7 bankruptcy, you will no longer be liable for the debt, but the guarantor or cosigner will be left on the hook. If you don't want to subject the cosigner to this liability, explore other alternatives discussed in this book (like negotiating with creditors). Or, consider filing for Chapter 13 bankruptcy. By arranging to pay the cosigned debt over time, you can keep creditors from going after the cosigner for payment. However, keep in mind that if you don't pay the debt in full during the course of your Chapter 13 bankruptcy, your liability for the remaining balance will be wiped out at the end of the bankruptcy, but the creditor can then seek payment from the cosigner.

3. You Could Pay Your Debts Over Three to Five Years

A bankruptcy judge can dismiss a Chapter 7 bankruptcy if the judge decides that you have enough assets or income to repay most of your debts either in a Chapter 13 bankruptcy or outside of bankruptcy altogether. The judge may lean toward dismissing your case if all of the following are true:

- a substantial majority of your debts are consumer (not business) debts
- you have an adequate and steady income, and
- with a modification of lifestyle, you could pay off all or most of your debts over three to five years.

Even if a bankruptcy judge wouldn't throw out your Chapter 7 bankruptcy case, if you can repay your debts over time you may be better off negotiating with your creditors than filing for bankruptcy. (See Chapter 6.)

4. You Want to Prevent Seizure of Wages or Property

You may not need to file for bankruptcy to keep creditors from seizing your property and wages. Normally, a creditor's only legal means of collecting an unsecured debt is to sue you, win a court judgment and then try to collect the amount of the judgment out of your property and income. If a debt is secured by collateral, however, the creditor can usually repossess it without first getting a court judgment.

However, the law prevents a creditor from taking much of your property, including food, clothing, personal effects and furnishings. Such property is called "exempt." (See Chapter 17 for more on exempt property.) Often, the creditor won't go after your nonexempt property, either, if its value won't cover the creditor's costs of seizure and sale of the property.

Creditors usually start by going after your wages and other income. But a creditor can take only 25% of your net wages to satisfy a court judgment, unless the judgment is for alimony or child support.

And in some states, you can keep more than 75% of your wages if you show that you need the extra amount to support yourself and your family. Income from a pension or other retirement benefit is usually treated like wages. Usually, creditors cannot touch public benefits such as public assistance, unemployment insurance, disability insurance or Social Security. (See Chapter 17 for more on exempt property.)

5. You Defrauded Your Creditors

Bankruptcy is geared toward the honest debtor who got in too deep and needs a fresh start. A bankruptcy court will not help someone who has played fast and loose with creditors.

Certain activities are red flags to bankruptcy courts and trustees. If you have engaged in any of them, do not file for bankruptcy unless you first consult a bankruptcy lawyer. These no-no's are:

- unloading assets or cash to your friends or relatives to hide the assets or cash from creditors or from the bankruptcy court—for example, if you owned a house and you simply transferred title (ownership) from yourself to your child
- incurring debts for nonnecessities when you were clearly broke—for instance, if you charged a month-long trip to Tahiti when you were earning nothing and couldn't even pay your rent
- concealing property or money from your spouse during a divorce proceeding, and
- lying about your income or debts on a credit application—such as stating your income as $28,000 when you earn only $18,000.

6. You Recently Incurred Debts for Luxuries

If you've recently run up large debts for a vacation, hobby or entertainment, filing for Chapter 7 bankruptcy probably won't help you, at least with regard to those debts. Most luxury debts incurred just before filing are not dischargeable if the creditor objects. And running up unnecessary debts shortly before filing casts a suspicion of fraud over your entire bankruptcy case. Luxury debts can, however, be included in a Chapter 13 bankruptcy case.

Last-minute debts presumed to be nondischargeable in Chapter 7 bankruptcy include debts to any one creditor of $1,150 or more for luxury goods or services purchased within 60 days before filing and debts for cash advances in excess of $1,150 obtained within 60 days of filing for bankruptcy.

To discharge last minute luxury debts in Chapter 7 bankruptcy—assuming a creditor objects to their discharge—you'll have to prove that extraordinary circumstances required you to make the charges and that you really weren't trying to put one over on the creditor. It's an uphill job. Judges often assume that people who incur last minute charges for luxuries were on a final buying binge and had no intention of paying.

If You Expect to Incur Debts Soon

If you expect to incur more debts for necessities, you should consider delaying filing for bankruptcy. Most debts you incur before you file will be discharged, but debts incurred after you file won't be. Waiting to file until after you incur these debts will allow you to include them in your bankruptcy papers. Creditors rarely argue that expenses incurred for necessities (such as additional medical costs you anticipate because of an existing illness, the cost of buying your children new school clothes or substantial heating costs during the upcoming winter) were fraudulent.

D. An Overview of Chapter 7 Bankruptcy

The Chapter 7 bankruptcy process takes about three to six months, currently costs $200 in filing and administrative fees (which may be waived in certain circumstances) and commonly requires only one or two trips to the courthouse. To begin a Chapter 7 bankruptcy case, you fill out several forms and file them with the bankruptcy court in your area. If you need the automatic stay immediately and don't have time to fill out all of the forms, you can file just a few of the forms, obtain the benefit of the automatic stay, and then file the rest of the forms within 15 days.

The forms ask you to describe:

- your property and income
- your debts and monthly living expenses
- the property you claim is exempt, and
- any transactions involving your property in the past two years.

Until your bankruptcy case ends, the trustee assumes legal control of the nonexempt property you own as of the date you file, and the debts you owe as of that date. You cannot sell or pay for anything without the trustee's consent. You have control over only your exempt property and the property you acquire and the income you receive after you file for bankruptcy.

If you are entitled to receive property when you file for bankruptcy but haven't yet received it, you must turn the property over to the trustee when you eventually get it, assuming it's nonexempt—even if it's after your case has closed. Examples include proceeds of a divorce settlement, tax refunds, inheritances and life insurance from someone who has died and personal injury recoveries.

The trustee's primary duty is to see that your unsecured creditors are paid as much as possible of what you owe them. Because the trustee is paid a percentage of the assets recovered for your creditors, the trustee is usually very interested in what property you claim as exempt.

The trustee goes through the papers you file and asks you questions at a short hearing, called the creditors' meeting, held 20–40 days after you file. For example, if your list of property is sparse, the trustee might ask you if you've forgotten anything. You must attend the creditors' meeting, though few of your creditors will. Most creditors' meetings last no more than five minutes.

After this hearing, the trustee collects your non-exempt property, sells it and pays your creditors. You don't have to surrender nonexempt property if you pay the trustee the property's value in cash, or the trustee is willing to accept exempt property of roughly equal value instead. Generally, very few debtors give up any property in a Chapter 7 bankruptcy case.

If you file for bankruptcy and then change your mind, you can ask the court to dismiss your case. However, not all courts will allow you to do so.

At the end of your bankruptcy case, most of your debts are discharged by the court, which means you no longer owe anything to the creditor.

Are Secured Debts Dischargeable?

As explained in Chapter 1, secured debts are linked to specific items of property, called collateral. The property guarantees payment of the debt. Common secured debts include personal loans from banks, car loans and home loans.

Bankruptcy eliminates your personal liability for your secured debts—the creditor can't sue you for the debt itself. But bankruptcy doesn't eliminate the creditor's lien on the secured property. To eliminate the lien, you'll have to give the secured property to the creditor or pay the creditor its current value or the debt amount, whichever is less. In a few situations, you can file papers with the court to request that a lien be wiped out. And usually, you can agree to have the debt survive bankruptcy, keep the collateral and make payments under the original loan agreement.

E. An Overview of Chapter 13 Bankruptcy

Chapter 13 bankruptcy is similar in many ways to Chapter 7 bankruptcy, but there are substantial differences. Chapter 13, like Chapter 7, immediately

stops your creditors from taking further action against you. Currently, Chapter 13 costs $185. In a Chapter 13 bankruptcy, you keep your property. In exchange, you pay off your creditors (sometimes in part, sometimes fully) over three years, although some repayment plans last as long as five years. Also, you cannot file for Chapter 13 bankruptcy if your unsecured debts exceed $290,525 or your secured debts exceed $871,550.

Chapter 13 Bankruptcy and Debt Counseling Agencies

Filing for Chapter 13 bankruptcy and using a debt counseling agency to help repay your debts has one primary feature in common: you devise a repayment plan, under which you make one monthly payment to a third person who in turn pays your creditors.

But there are major differences. First, Chapter 13 bankruptcy costs $185 plus any fee you must pay if you hire a lawyer or typing service to help you. A counseling agency may charge you a small monthly fee, but will waive it if you can't afford it. Second if you miss a payment, Chapter 13 protects you from creditors who would start collection actions. A debt counseling plan has no such protection. Third, a debt counseling plan usually requires that your debts be repaid in full; in Chapter 13 bankruptcy, you usually pay less than the full amount.

To begin a Chapter 13 bankruptcy, you fill out a packet of forms—much like the forms in a Chapter 7 bankruptcy—listing your income, property, expenses and debts, and file them with the bankruptcy court. In addition, you must file a realistic plan to repay your debts, given your income and expenses. Under the plan, you must pay your creditors an amount that is at least the value of your nonexempt property within three years. You may have to pay certain creditors the full value of your debt. You do this by paying to the trustee all of your disposable income each month. Disposable income is the amount of money left after you have paid for reasonable living expenses.

The income you use to repay creditors need not be wages. You can use benefits, pension payments, investment income or receipts as an independent contractor. At the end of the three- or five-year period, the court will wipe out the remaining un-paid balance on your dischargeable debts.

As in Chapter 7 bankruptcy, you are required to attend a creditors' meeting. You must also attend a confirmation hearing where the judge reviews your plan and then confirms or denies it. Once your plan is confirmed, you make payments directly to the bankruptcy trustee, who in turn distributes the money to your creditors. If your plan is denied, you can modify it, refile it and try again.

If, for some reason, you cannot finish a Chapter 13 plan—for example, you lose your job—the trustee can modify your plan. The trustee can give you a grace period if the problem looks temporary, reduce your total monthly payments or extend the repayment period. As long as you're acting in good faith, the trustee will try to help you through rocky periods. If it's clear that you won't be able to complete the plan because of circumstances beyond your control, the court might let you discharge the remainder of your debts on the basis of hardship.

If the bankruptcy court won't let you modify your plan or give you a hardship discharge, you can:

- convert to a Chapter 7 bankruptcy unless you are prohibited from filing for Chapter 7 because of an earlier Chapter 7 discharge, or
- dismiss your Chapter 13 case, which means you'll owe what you owed before filing for Chapter 13, less the payments you made, plus interest from the date you filed (which had stopped accruing while your case was ongoing).

F. Does Bankruptcy Make Economic Sense?

In evaluating whether or not bankruptcy makes economic sense, answer these questions:

- Will bankruptcy discharge enough of your debts to make it worth your while?
- Will you have to give up property you desper-ately want to keep?

1. Will Bankruptcy Discharge Enough of Your Debts?

Most debts are dischargeable. If the majority of your debts are the ones listed below, you have little to worry about—these debts are normally wiped out in bankruptcy:

- back rent
- utility bills
- deficiency balances (see Chapter 8, Sections B and C.4)
- court judgments
- credit and charge card bills
- department store and gasoline company bills
- loans from friends and relatives
- newspaper and magazine subscriptions
- legal, medical and accounting bills, and
- other unsecured loans.

Several types of debts (listed below), however, cannot be discharged if you file for Chapter 7 bank-ruptcy. These nondischargeable debts can be in-cluded in your Chapter 13 repayment plan. If you don't pay the entire amount owed in your Chapter 13 plan, you may owe a balance at the end of your case. But that shouldn't necessarily deter you from filing for Chapter 13 bankruptcy. Including these debts as part of your repayment plan may give you room to breathe.

Some of the debts that are nondischargeable in both Chapter 7 and Chapter 13 bankruptcy are:

- debts you forget to list in your bankruptcy papers, if the affected creditor doesn't other-wise learn of the bankruptcy
- child support and alimony
- debts for personal injury or death caused by your intoxicated driving
- student loans, unless you can prove to the court it would be an undue hardship for you to repay the loans
- some condominium or cooperative assess-ments
- fines and penalties imposed for violating the law, such as traffic tickets, criminal court penalties, criminal fines and restitution, and
- recent taxes.

Bankruptcy and Income Taxes

The only time you can discharge income taxes—and the penalties and interest assessed for failing to pay income taxes—in bankruptcy is if all of the following are true:

- You didn't file a fraudulent return or try to evade paying taxes.
- The liability is for a tax return (not a Substitute for Return filed by the IRS) filed at least two years before you file for bankruptcy.
- The tax return was due at least three years ago.
- The taxes were assessed at least 240 days (eight months) before you file for bankruptcy.

Even if all of the above are true and bankruptcy erases your obligation to pay your back taxes, the IRS may still get paid if it recorded a lien against your real estate before you filed for bankruptcy. This is because the lien is untouched by the bankruptcy. Once your case is over, the IRS can force the sale of your property (if you have equity in it) or get paid when you sell or refinance the property.

Don't despair if you have a tax debt and want to file for bankruptcy. Chapter 13 bankruptcy might help. Although you may have to pay your entire tax bill, you can include your tax debt in your repayment plan. During that period, the IRS must cease all collection efforts, including adding penalties and interest, enforcing liens and taking your wages. The reprieve from IRS collection efforts during the pendency of your case may be a great relief.

A debt you couldn't discharge in a previous bankruptcy is dischargeable in Chapter 13 bankruptcy but not in Chapter 7 bankruptcy.

In addition, if a creditor objects to the discharge of certain debts, the judge may refuse to discharge them. The debts in this category, however, are dischargeable in a Chapter 13 bankruptcy. These debts are:

- debts the creditor proves you incurred on the basis of fraud, such as writing a bad check or lying on a credit application
- credit purchases of $1,150 or more for luxury goods or services made within 60 days of the bankruptcy filing
- loans or cash advances of $1,150 or more obtained within 60 days of the bankruptcy filing
- debts from willful or malicious injury to another or another's property, including assault, battery, false imprisonment, libel and slander
- debts from embezzlement, larceny or breach of trust, and
- debts arising out of a marital settlement agreement or divorce decree that aren't otherwise automatically nondischargeable as support or alimony, such as credit card debts you agree to pay or payments you owe to an ex-spouse to even up the property division.

There is no formula to determine whether the amount of debt that you are able to discharge in bankruptcy makes filing worthwhile. Each situation is individual. If bankruptcy will wipe out all or almost all of your major debts, the decision to file may be easy. If bankruptcy won't get rid of your largest debt, you may choose not to file. Or, maybe filing makes sense if, by wiping out other debts, bankruptcy will free up money to pay that large nondischargeable debt. Likewise, if the court is unlikely to discharge most of your debts upon a creditor objection, it still might be worthwhile to file in the hope that your creditors won't file objections. Or, in this case, you could file for Chapter 13 bankruptcy and wipe out those debts at the end of your repayment plan.

2. How Much Property Will You Have to Give Up?

Very few people lose property in Chapter 7 bankruptcy. Only if you have the kind of property listed below—and you don't want to lose it—should you be concerned:

- substantial equity in a house or motor vehicle
- a second house or motor vehicle
- expensive musical instruments
- stamp, coin and other collections
- cash, deposit accounts, stocks, bonds and other investments
- valuable artwork
- expensive clothing and jewelry, or
- family heirlooms.

Exempt property—or a portion of a partially exempt item—is the property you can keep during a Chapter 7 bankruptcy. (Remember, in a Chapter 13 bankruptcy you keep all your property whether or not it is exempt.) Nonexempt property (or its equivalent in value) is the property you must surrender to the bankruptcy trustee, who will use it to pay your unsecured creditors. The more you can claim as exempt, the better off you are.

Each state has laws that determine which items of property are exempt in bankruptcy, and in what amounts. A list of each state's property exemptions is in Appendix 2; also, Chapter 17 covers the subject of exempt property in detail.

If you are inclined to file for bankruptcy but have mostly nonexempt property, consider Chapter 13 bankruptcy or negotiating with your creditors. If you prefer Chapter 7 bankruptcy, you need to evaluate exactly how much of your property is not exempt and take steps to preserve its value by selling some of it and buying exempt property before you file. Converting your nonexempt property into exempt property is introduced in Chapter 17 and covered extensively in *How to File for Chapter 7 Bankruptcy,* by Stephen Elias, Albin Renauer, Robin Leonard and Kathleen Michon (Nolo). ■

Property You Get To Keep

The reason why men enter into society is the preservation of their property; and in the end, they choose and authorize a legislature so that there may be laws made, and rules set, as guards and fences to the properties of all the society.

— John Locke, English philosopher,
1632-1704

As mentioned throughout this book, and specifically in Chapters 15 and 16, if a creditor gets a judgment against you or you file for bankruptcy, much of your property cannot be taken to pay your debts. The items you are allowed to keep are called your exempt property or exemptions.

A. What Property Is Exempt?

Worksheet 3, below, helps you determine what property you own, which property is exempt and the value of that exempt property. Instructions for completing Worksheet 3 immediately follow it. The information on Worksheet 3 is important for two reasons.

First, you are considered to be "judgment proof" if your property and wages cannot be taken by a creditor who gets a judgment against you. Being judgment proof may not be a permanent state. It just means that for now, your property and wages are exempt from collection by your creditors. If you are judgment proof, writing a letter to a creditor explaining your status may convince the creditor not to sue you.

Second, the information in Worksheet 3 will help you to decide whether bankruptcy is appropriate in your situation. If much of your property is exempt from being taken by creditors and your debts are large, bankruptcy may be the best solution.

Exemptions and Secured Debts

As explained in Chapter 1, secured debts are linked to specific items of property, called collateral. The property guarantees payment of the debt. Common secured debts include personal loans from finance companies, car loans and home loans. Common items of collateral are houses, cars, large furniture and major appliances.

In general, the fact that an item of property otherwise qualifies as exempt doesn't mean you can keep it if it has been pledged as collateral on a secured debt and you are behind on your payments. Rather, you stand to lose the property unless you file for bankruptcy, which may allow you to hang on to it.

Instructions for Completing Worksheet 3

1. Your Property

When you complete Column 1 of the worksheet, you will have a complete inventory of your property. List everything you own that could bring in more than $50 at a garage sale. Lump together low valued items, such as kitchen utensils. Keep in mind that many items you originally paid hundreds of dollars for are now worth much, much less.

1. Real estate
- ☐ Residence
- ☐ Condominium or co-op apartment
- ☐ Mobile home
- ☐ Mobile home park space
- ☐ Rental property
- ☐ Vacation home or cabin
- ☐ Business property
- ☐ Undeveloped land
- ☐ Farm land
- ☐ Boat/marina dock space
- ☐ Burial site
- ☐ Airplane hangar

2. Cash on hand
- ☐ In your home
- ☐ In your wallet
- ☐ Under your mattress

3. Deposits of money
- ☐ Bank deposit
- ☐ Brokerage account (with stockbroker)
- ☐ Certificates of deposit (CDs)
- ☐ Credit union deposit
- ☐ Escrow account
- ☐ Money market account
- ☐ Money in a safe deposit box
- ☐ Savings and loan deposit

4. Security deposits
- ☐ Electric
- ☐ Gas
- ☐ Heating oil
- ☐ Prepaid rent
- ☐ Security deposit on a rental unit
- ☐ Rented furniture or equipment
- ☐ Telephone
- ☐ Water

5. Household goods, supplies and furnishings
- ☐ Antiques
- ☐ Appliances
- ☐ Carpentry tools
- ☐ China and crystal
- ☐ Clocks
- ☐ Dishes
- ☐ Food (total value)
- ☐ Furniture
- ☐ Gardening tools
- ☐ Home computer (for personal use)
- ☐ Lamps
- ☐ Lawn mower or tractor
- ☐ Microwave oven
- ☐ Radios
- ☐ Rugs
- ☐ Sewing machine
- ☐ Silverware and utensils
- ☐ Small appliances
- ☐ Snow blower
- ☐ Stereo system
- ☐ Telephones and answering machines
- ☐ Televisions
- ☐ Vacuum cleaner
- ☐ Video equipment (VCR, Camcorder)

6. Books, pictures, art objects; stamps, coin and other collections
- ☐ Art prints
- ☐ Bibles
- ☐ Books
- ☐ Coins
- ☐ Collectibles (such as political buttons, baseball cards)
- ☐ Compact disks, records and tapes
- ☐ Family portraits
- ☐ Figurines
- ☐ Original artworks
- ☐ Photographs
- ☐ Stamps
- ☐ Video tapes

7. **Apparel**
   - ☐ Clothing
   - ☐ Furs

8. **Jewelry**
   - ☐ Engagement and wedding ring
   - ☐ Gems
   - ☐ Precious metals
   - ☐ Watches

9. **Firearms, sports equipment and other hobby equipment**
   - ☐ Board games
   - ☐ Bicycles
   - ☐ Camera equipment
   - ☐ Electronic musical equipment
   - ☐ Exercise machine
   - ☐ Fishing gear
   - ☐ Guns (rifles, pistols, shotguns, muskets)
   - ☐ Model or remote cars or planes
   - ☐ Musical instruments
   - ☐ Scuba diving equipment
   - ☐ Ski equipment
   - ☐ Other sports equipment
   - ☐ Other weapons (swords and knives)

10. **Interests in insurance policies**
    - ☐ Credit insurance
    - ☐ Disability insurance
    - ☐ Health insurance
    - ☐ Homeowner's or renter's insurance
    - ☐ Term life insurance
    - ☐ Whole or universal life insurance

11. **Annuities**

12. **Pension or profit-sharing plans**
    - ☐ IRA
    - ☐ Keogh
    - ☐ Pension or retirement plan
    - ☐ 401(k) account

13. **Stocks and interests in incorporated and unincorporated companies**

14. **Interests in partnerships**
    - ☐ General partnership interest
    - ☐ Limited partnership interest

15. **Government and corporate bonds and other investment instruments**
    - ☐ Corporate bonds
    - ☐ Deeds of trust
    - ☐ Mortgages you own
    - ☐ Municipal bonds
    - ☐ Promissory notes
    - ☐ U.S. savings bond

16. **Accounts receivable**
    - ☐ Accounts receivable from business
    - ☐ Commissions already earned

17. **Family support**
    - ☐ Alimony (spousal support, maintenance) due under court order
    - ☐ Child support payments due under court order
    - ☐ Payments due under divorce property settlement

18. **Other debts owed you where the amount owed is known and definite**
    - ☐ Disability benefits due
    - ☐ Disability insurance due
    - ☐ Judgments obtained against third parties you haven't yet collected
    - ☐ Sick pay earned
    - ☐ Social Security benefits due
    - ☐ Tax refund due under returns already filed
    - ☐ Vacation pay earned
    - ☐ Wages due
    - ☐ Worker's compensation due

19. **Powers exercisable for your benefit other than those listed under real estate**
    - ☐ Right to receive, at some future time, cash, stock or other personal property placed in an irrevocable trust
    - ☐ Current payments of interest or principal from a trust
    - ☐ General power of appointment over personal property

20. **Interests due to another person's death**
    - ☐ Property you are entitled to receive as a beneficiary of a living trust, if the trustor has died
    - ☐ Expected proceeds from a life insurance policy, if the insured has died

☐ Inheritance from an existing estate in probate (the owner has died and the court is overseeing the distribution of the property) even if the final amount is not yet known

☐ Inheritance under a will that is contingent upon one or more events occurring, but only if the will writer has died

21. All other contingent claims and claims where the amount owed you is not known, including tax refunds, counterclaims and rights to setoff claims (claims you think you have against a person, government or corporation but haven't yet sued on)

☐ Claims against a corporation, government entity or individual

☐ Potential tax refund but return not yet filed

22. Patents, copyrights and other intellectual property

☐ Copyrights

☐ Patents

☐ Trade secrets

☐ Trademarks

☐ Tradenames

23. Licenses, franchises and other general intangibles

☐ Building permits

☐ Cooperative association holdings

☐ Exclusive licenses

☐ Liquor licenses

☐ Nonexclusive licenses

☐ Patent licenses

☐ Professional licenses

24. Automobiles and other vehicles

☐ Car

☐ Mini-bike or motorscooter

☐ Mobile or motor home if on wheels

☐ Motorcycle

☐ Recreational vehicle (RV)

☐ Trailer

☐ Truck

☐ Van

25. Boats, motors and accessories

☐ Boat (canoe, kayak, rowboat, shell, sailboat, pontoon, yacht, etc.)

☐ Boat radar, radio or telephone

☐ Outboard motor

26. Aircraft and accessories

☐ Aircraft radar, radio and other accessories

☐ Aircraft

27. Office equipment, furnishings and supplies

☐ Artwork in your office

☐ Computers, software, modems, printers (for business use)

☐ Copier

☐ Fax machine

☐ Furniture

☐ Rugs

☐ Supplies

☐ Telephones

☐ Typewriters

28. Machinery, fixtures, equipment and supplies used in business

☐ Military uniforms and accoutrements

☐ Tools of your trade

29. Business inventory

30. Livestock, poultry and other animals

☐ Birds

☐ Cats

☐ Dogs

☐ Fish and aquarium equipment

☐ Horses

☐ Other pets

☐ Livestock and poultry

31. Crops—growing or harvested

32. Farming equipment and implements

33. Farm supplies, chemicals and feed

34. Other personal property of any kind not already listed

☐ Church pew

☐ Country club or golf club membership

☐ Health aids (for example, wheelchair, crutches)

☐ Portable spa or hot tub

☐ Season tickets

Worksheet 3: Your Property

1 Your property	2 Value of property (actual dollar or garage sale value)	3 Your ownership share (%, $)	4 Amount of liens	5 Amount of your equity	6 Exempt? If not, enter non- exempt amount
1. Real estate					
2. Cash on hand (state source of money)					
3. Deposits of money (indicate sources of money)					
4. Security deposits					
5. Household goods, supplies and furnishings					
6. Books, pictures, art objects; stamp, coin and other collections					

Worksheet 3: Your Property (continued)

1 Your property	2 Value of property (actual dollar or garage sale value)	3 Your ownership share (%, $)	4 Amount of liens	5 Amount of your equity	6 Exempt? If not, enter non-exempt amount
7. Apparel					
8. Jewelry					
9. Firearms, sports equipment and other hobby equipment					
10. Interests in insurance policies					
11. Annuities					
12. Pension or profit-sharing plans					
13. Stocks and interests in incorporated and unincorporated companies					

Worksheet 3: Your Property (continued)

1 Your property	2 Value of property (actual dollar or garage sale value)	3 Your ownership share (%, $)	4 Amount of liens	5 Amount of your equity	6 Exempt? If not, enter non- exempt amount
14. Interests in partnerships					
_____	_____	_____	_____	_____	_____
_____	_____	_____	_____	_____	_____
_____	_____	_____	_____	_____	_____
15. Government and corporate bonds and other investment instruments					
_____	_____	_____	_____	_____	_____
_____	_____	_____	_____	_____	_____
_____	_____	_____	_____	_____	_____
_____	_____	_____	_____	_____	_____
_____	_____	_____	_____	_____	_____
_____	_____	_____	_____	_____	_____
16. Accounts receivable					
_____	_____	_____	_____	_____	_____
_____	_____	_____	_____	_____	_____
_____	_____	_____	_____	_____	_____
_____	_____	_____	_____	_____	_____
17. Family support					
_____	_____	_____	_____	_____	_____
_____	_____	_____	_____	_____	_____
_____	_____	_____	_____	_____	_____
18. Other debts owed you where the amount owed is known and definite					
_____	_____	_____	_____	_____	_____
_____	_____	_____	_____	_____	_____
_____	_____	_____	_____	_____	_____
_____	_____	_____	_____	_____	_____
19. Powers exercisable for your benefit, other than those listed under real estate					
_____	_____	_____	_____	_____	_____
20. Interests due to another person's death					
_____	_____	_____	_____	_____	_____
_____	_____	_____	_____	_____	_____

Worksheet 3: Your Property (continued)

1 Your property	2 Value of property (actual dollar or garage sale value)	3 Your ownership share (%, $)	4 Amount of liens	5 Amount of your equity	6 Exempt? If not, enter non- exempt amount

21. All other contingent claims and claims where the amount owed you is not known

_____ _____ _____ _____ _____ _____

_____ _____ _____ _____ _____ _____

22. Patents, copyrights and other intellectual property

_____ _____ _____ _____ _____ _____

_____ _____ _____ _____ _____ _____

23. Licenses, franchises and other general intangibles

_____ _____ _____ _____ _____ _____

_____ _____ _____ _____ _____ _____

24. Automobiles and other vehicles

_____ _____ _____ _____ _____ _____

_____ _____ _____ _____ _____ _____

_____ _____ _____ _____ _____ _____

25. Boats, motors and accessories

_____ _____ _____ _____ _____ _____

_____ _____ _____ _____ _____ _____

_____ _____ _____ _____ _____ _____

26. Aircraft and accessories

_____ _____ _____ _____ _____ _____

_____ _____ _____ _____ _____ _____

27. Office equipment, furnishings and supplies

_____ _____ _____ _____ _____ _____

_____ _____ _____ _____ _____ _____

_____ _____ _____ _____ _____ _____

_____ _____ _____ _____ _____ _____

28. Machinery, fixtures, equipment and supplies used in business

_____ _____ _____ _____ _____ _____

_____ _____ _____ _____ _____ _____

_____ _____ _____ _____ _____ _____

_____ _____ _____ _____ _____ _____

Worksheet 3: Your Property (continued)

1 Your property	2 Value of property (actual dollar or garage sale value)	3 Your ownership share (%, $)	4 Amount of liens	5 Amount of your equity	6 Exempt? If not, enter non- exempt amount
29. Business inventory					
30. Livestock, poultry and other animals					
31. Crops—growing or harvested					
32. Farming equipment and implements					
33. Farm supplies, chemicals and feed					
34. Other personal property					

Subtotal (column 6): _____

Wild Card Exemption   - _____

Total Value of NONEXEMPT Property _____

2. Value of Your Property

In Column 2, enter a value for each item of property listed in Column 1. For your cash, deposits, publicly traded stock holdings, bonds, mutual funds and annuities, enter the cash amount. For shares of stock in small business corporations, any ownership share in a partnership, business equipment, copyrights, patents or other assets that may seem hard to sell, do your best to assign a reasonable dollar amount.

If you own an item jointly, put its entire value here. In Column 3 you'll enter your share.

Here are some suggestions for valuing specific items:

Real estate. If your interest is ownership of a house, get an estimate of its market value from a local real estate agent or appraiser. If you own another type of real estate—such as land used to grow crops— put the amount it would bring in at a forced sale.

If you don't know how to arrive at a value, or if you have an unusual asset such as a life estate (a current right to live in a house until you die) or a lease, leave this column blank.

Older goods. Want ads in a local flea market or penny-saver newspaper are a good place to look for prices. If an item isn't listed, use the garage sale value—that is, begin with the price you paid and then deduct about 20% for each year you've owned the item. For instance, if you bought a camera for $400 three years ago, subtract 20% ($80) for the first year (down to $320), $64 for the second year (down to $256), and $51 for the third year (down to $205). If you paid top dollar for the item, begin with the price you could have paid had you bought it at a discount outlet, not the actual price you paid.

Jewelry, antiques, and other collectibles. Any valuable jewelry or collection should be appraised.

Life insurance. Put the current cash surrender value; call your insurance agent to find out. Term life insurance has a cash surrender value of zero. Don't put the amount of benefits the policy will pay, unless you're the beneficiary of an insurance policy and the insured person has died.

Stocks, bonds, etc. You can check the stock's current value by looking it up in a newspaper business section. If you can't find the listing, or the stock isn't traded publicly, call your broker and ask.

If you have a brokerage account, use the value from your latest statement.

Cars. Start with the low *Kelley Blue Book* price. You can find this book at the public library or online at http://www.kbb.com. If the car needs substantial repairs, reduce the value by the amount it would cost you to fix the car.

Total Column 2 and enter the figure in the space provided.

3. Your Ownership Share

In Column 3, enter two amounts: the percentage of your separate ownership interest in the property and the dollar value of your ownership interest in the property.

If you own an item alone, your percentage is 100%. If you are married and own an item together, your ownership share depends on several factors, including the form of title (for example, joint tenancy or tenancy by the entirety) and the laws in the state where you live or where the property is located. Whether a collector or creditor can get property held by your spouse depends on the type of debt. For example, usually a creditor cannot take the separately owned property of one spouse to pay the separate debts of the other spouse. (See Chapter 3 for more on property rights and debt liability of married, divorced or separated people.)

> **EXAMPLE:** Audrey and her brother jointly bought a music synthesizer currently worth $10,000. They still owe the music store $3,000; but that is not subtracted in this column. Audrey's ownership share is one half, or $5,000.

4. Value of Liens

In Column 4, put the value of any legal claim (lien) against the property. For example, if you owe money on your house or car, the creditor probably has a security interest in that item of property. The property is collateral for the debt. If you didn't sign a security agreement or the creditor has not put a lien on your property, there is no lien, even if you still owe money. Even if you own only part of the property, for example, your spouse or partner owns a share, enter the full value of the lien.

> **EXAMPLE:** Marian owns a house, and owes her mortgage lender $135,000. Last winter Marian had a new roof put on her house. She was not satisfied with the roofer's work and therefore didn't pay him all of his bill. He recorded a mechanic's lien on her house for $5,000. Marian also owes the IRS $25,000, and so the IRS recorded a lien on her house. In Column 4, Marian enters the total of all her liens: $135,000 + $5,000 + $25,000 = $165,000.

Liens must be paid off before property can be transferred to a new owner—such as a creditor with a judgment against you or the bankruptcy trustee. If the value of the lien exceeds the property's value, you're probably in luck. The creditor or trustee won't want the property; once the lienholders are paid, there won't be anything for the creditor or trustee.

Include all of the following:

- mortgages and home equity loans
- personal loans where you pledge items of property that you already own as security for your repayment
- security agreements when you buy from a department store which specifically takes a security interest in items purchased
- motor vehicle loans
- liens held by contractors who worked on a house without getting paid what they claim you owe (mechanic's lien)
- liens placed by the IRS after you fail to pay a bill for past taxes, and
- judgment liens recorded against you by someone who won a lawsuit.

5. Amount of Your Equity

Your equity is the amount you would get to keep if you sold the property. If you own the property alone, calculate your equity by subtracting the amount in Column 4 from the property's total value. Put the

amount in Column 5. If you get a negative number, enter "0."

If you own the property with your spouse and the two of you are considering filing for bankruptcy or you together owe a creditor, calculate your equity by subtracting the amount in Column 4 from the property's total value. If you co-own the property with someone other than a spouse, use the following formula:

1. If the liens in Column 4 are from debts jointly incurred by you and the other owner of the property, figure the total equity (Column 2 less Column 4). Then multiply that number by your ownership share (the percentage you figured in Column 3). Enter this figure in Column 5.

> **EXAMPLE:** Bill and Lee, brother and sister, inherited their parents' $150,000 house in equal proportions. Bill and Lee owe $100,000 on the house's mortgage. Bill owes money to several creditors and wants to figure out his equity in the house. It's $25,000—the total value of the house ($150,000) less what he and Lee owe on the mortgage ($100,000), multiplied by Bill's percentage share (50%).

2. If the liens in Column 4 are from debts incurred solely by you, then deduct the total amount of the lien from the figure in Column 2. Only your assets—not a co-owner's—are calculated to pay your secured creditors.

> **EXAMPLE:** Now assume that Bill and Lee inherited the $150,000 house free and clear of any mortgage. Bill owes the IRS $30,000, however, and the IRS placed a lien for that amount on the property. Now Bill's equity is $45,000—the total value of the house ($150,000), multiplied by Bill's percentage share (50%), less the lien ($30,000).

6. Is the Property Exempt?

By this time, you may be ready to put down the book and quit thinking about all these technicalities. Don't. Figuring out exactly what property you're legally entitled to keep if a creditor has a judgment against you or you file for bankruptcy takes work, but it is not inherently difficult. And it is often critical to determining what your next step should be.

a. Exemption Overview

Each state has laws that determine which items of property can't be taken away from people with debt problems, and what amounts are protected. The list for each state is in Appendix 2. For instance, many states exempt health aids, personal effects (things such as electric shavers, hair dryers and tooth-brushes), ordinary household furniture and clothing without regard to their value.

Other kinds of property are exempt up to a limit. For example, in Massachusetts, furniture is exempt to $3,000. Cars, too, are exempt up to a certain amount—such as $2,500 in Washington. These exemption limits mean that any equity you have in the property above the limit isn't exempt. The judgment creditor or bankruptcy trustee can take the property and sell it, pay off any lienholders, give you the exemption amount and keep the rest.

Many states also provide a general-purpose exemption, called a "wild card" exemption, which can be applied to any type of nonexempt property. For example, Washington has a $2,000 wild card exemption, so you could add it to the $2,500 vehicle exemption and exempt up to $4,500 equity in a car, or use it to exempt up to $2,000 of any other property.

If You Are Married

If you are married, and you and your spouse are jointly planning to file for bankruptcy or jointly owe judgment creditors, you are entitled to double your exemptions, except in a few states, for a few exemption types.

In addition, "tenancy by the entirety" is a property ownership form available only to married couples in about 14 states and the District of Columbia. Property held as tenancy by the entirety is exempt, but only for debts incurred by one spouse. (States that allow or prohibit doubling, and states that exempt tenancy by the entirety property are listed in Appendix 2.)

If you are married but only one of you owes a judgment creditor or is considering filing for bankruptcy, your spouse's separate property cannot be taken by the judgment creditor or bankruptcy trustee to pay your debts.

---

b. Determining Which of Your Property Is Exempt

Step 1: Choose an exemption system. If you care about your exemptions only with respect to your judgment creditors, turn to your state exemption list. (In California, use System 1.) If you want to figure out what property you can keep if you file for bankruptcy, you may have to choose between two exemption lists. In Arkansas, Connecticut, Hawaii, Massachusetts, Michigan, Minnesota, New Hampshire, New Jersey, New Mexico, Pennsylvania, Rhode Island, South Carolina, Texas, Vermont, Washington, Wisconsin or the District of Columbia, you must choose either your state exemptions or the federal bankruptcy exemptions. In California, you must choose between two state exemption lists.

If you must choose between two exemption systems in bankruptcy, locate these exemption lists from Appendix 2:

- the federal bankruptcy exemptions (this list appears after all the states), and
- your state's exemptions plus the federal *non-bankruptcy* exemptions.

If you live in California, take out the System 1 exemptions, the System 2 exemptions and the federal *nonbankruptcy* exemptions.

Compare the federal bankruptcy exemptions to your state exemptions (or compare the two California exemption systems) for large items, such as your home and car.

- **Your home.** If the equity in your home is your major asset, your choice may be dictated by the homestead exemption alone. Compare your state's homestead exemption to the federal $16,150 exemption. In some states, the homestead exemption is $20,000 or more, so you'll get greater protection by using your state exemption. By contrast, in other states, the homestead exemption is less than $16,150, and so the federal exemptions may offer greater protections.
- **Your valuable property.** If the equity amount in your home isn't a factor in your decision, identify the most valuable items you own. Look at the federal bankruptcy exemptions and your state and the federal *nonbankruptcy* exemptions. Which lets you keep the most?
- **Small items.** If you're still having trouble choosing, look for small differences. For example, federal bankruptcy exemptions limit most personal property exemptions to $425 per item, $8,625 total. Some states have no such limit. On the other hand, if you don't have a house, the federal bankruptcy system has a wild card exemption of up to $8,075 (depending on how much homestead exemption you use), allowing you to claim anything you want.

Step 2: Decide which items you listed on Worksheet 2 might be exempt under the exemption system you're using. Use the Glossary (Appendix 1) if you need more information or an explanation of terms.

> **EXAMPLE:** The exemption system you're using exempts "furnishings and household goods." You could argue that all of your household furniture, fixtures, appliances, kitchenware and electronic equipment are exempt.

In evaluating whether or not your cash on hand and deposits of money are exempt, look to the source of the money, such as welfare benefits, disability benefits, insurance proceeds or wages.

Step 3: Decide which items you listed on Worksheet 2 might be exempt under the federal nonbankruptcy exemptions, if available. If you use your state exemptions—this includes all Californians—you may also select from a list of federal nonbankruptcy exemptions, mostly military and other federal benefits, as well as 75% of wages you have earned but have not yet been paid. You cannot, however, stack your exemptions if the federal nonbankruptcy exemptions duplicate your state's exemptions. For example, if you're using your state's exemptions and your state exempts 75% of unpaid wages, that's all you can claim.

Step 4: Double your exemptions if you're married and state law allows it. If you are married and filing jointly, you can double all exemptions unless your state expressly prohibits it. Look in your state's listing in Appendix 2 to see whether or not doubling is allowed. If you're using the federal bankruptcy exemptions, you may double all exemptions. If your state's chart doesn't say doubling is prohibited, go ahead and double.

Step 5: Use any wild card exemption to which you are entitled. If the exemption system you are using has a wild card exemption, apply it to property you couldn't otherwise exempt, such as property whose value exceeds the exemption limit or an item that isn't exempt at all.

Step 6: Determine the value of all nonexempt items. If an item (or group of items) is exempt to an unlimited amount, put "0" in Column 6.

If an item (or group of items) is exempt to a certain amount (for example, household goods to $4,000), total up the value of all items that fall into the category using the values in Column 5. Subtract from the total the amount of the exemption. What is left is the nonexempt value. Enter that in Column 6.

If an item (or group of items) is not exempt at all, copy the amount from Column 5 to Column 6.

Step 7: Total up Column 6. This is the value of your nonexempt property.

Exemption Rules for Pensions When You File for Bankruptcy

If your pension is covered by the federal law called ERISA, pay special attention to these rules.

Rule 1: Your ERISA pension is exempt if you use the federal bankruptcy exemptions.

Rule 2: Your ERISA pension is yours to keep if you use state exemptions, even if your state exemption list doesn't refer to ERISA pensions. The reason is somewhat complex, involving both ERISA law and bankruptcy law. (See *Patterson v. Shumate*, 112 S.Ct. 2242 (1992).)

If your pension is not covered by ERISA, it is exempt only if:

- you use your state's exemptions, and
- the pension is listed in either your state exemption list or the federal *nonbankruptcy* exemption list.

If it looks like you might lose your pension in bankruptcy, see a lawyer before filing.

B. Turning Nonexempt Property Into Exempt Property

If you have an asset that is not exempt, you may want to sell it before you file for bankruptcy or before a judgment creditor has a chance to grab it.

Converting property is not only sensible, it's legal in most circumstances, but it requires careful planning.

1. If a Creditor Has a Judgment Against You

Unless you file for bankruptcy, you remain indebted to your judgment creditors. This doesn't mean, however, that you must willingly turn over your property to your creditors, unless a court orders you to. Thus, you can convert your nonexempt property into exempt property, even if the judgment creditor is on your tail.

> **EXAMPLE:** Charlie, a carpenter, lives in Alaska. He has a savings account of $1,500. He also owes a judgment creditor $1,300. Charlie's bank account isn't exempt. But Alaska's tools of trade exemption is $3,360. Charlie closes his account and buys new carpenter's tools, fully protecting his $1,500 from his judgment creditor.

There is one big caveat to converting property. If you give away nonexempt property, or sell it for less than it is worth, a creditor may claim that you were fraudulently trying to hide assets. Selling property to close friends and relatives is especially suspicious. The creditor can sue the recipient of the property, and ask the court to order the recipient to turn the property over to her. If this happens, the recipient, especially if she bought the item from you (even for a ridiculously low amount), could sue you for compensation. And if the judge is anti-debtor, you could be fined severely.

If you plan on unloading—or have already unloaded—some nonexempt property, you probably should see a lawyer. (See Chapter 20.)

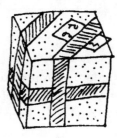

2. If You Plan to File for Bankruptcy

Converting nonexempt property into exempt property in contemplation of bankruptcy is more difficult because bankruptcy rules prohibit some types of conversions assumed to be fraud on your creditors. (See Section 3, below.) Still, if you understand the rules, it can be done.

There are two ways to reduce your nonexempt property. You can replace nonexempt property with exempt property or use your nonexempt property to pay debts.

a. Replace Nonexempt Property With Exempt Property

There are several ways to replace your nonexempt property holdings with exempt property. You can:

- Sell a nonexempt asset and use the proceeds to buy an asset that is completely exempt. For example, you can sell a nonexempt coin collection and purchase clothing, which in most states is exempt without regard to its value.
- Sell a nonexempt asset and use the proceeds to buy an asset that is exempt up to the amount received in the sale. For example, you can sell a nonexempt coin collection worth $1,200 and purchase a car that is exempt up to $1,200 in value.
- Sell an asset that is only partially exempt and use the proceeds to replace it with a similar asset of lesser value. For example, if jewelry items are only exempt up to a value of $200 each, you could sell your $500 watch and buy one for $200, putting the remaining cash into other exempt assets such as clothing or appliances.
- Use cash (which isn't exempt in most states) to buy an exempt item, such as furniture or tools.

b. Pay Debts

If you choose to reduce your nonexempt property by using the money from the sale of your non-exempt property to pay debts, keep the following points in mind.

Don't pay off a debt that could be discharged in bankruptcy. Dischargeable debts such as credit card bills can almost always be completely discharged in bankruptcy. The main reasons to pay a dischargeable debt would be to:

- keep good relations with a valued creditor, such as a department store that you rely on for necessities, or
- pay a debt for which a relative or friend is a cosigner, because the friend or relative will be stuck with paying the whole debt if you get it discharged.

In either case, if the payment is more than $600 you must wait at least 90 days—one year if the creditor is a friend, relative or close business associate—after you pay that creditor before filing for bankruptcy. Otherwise, the payment is considered a "preference," and the trustee can set it aside and take back the money for your other creditors.

You can, however, pay regular monthly bills right up until bankruptcy. So keep paying monthly phone bills, utilities, rent and mortgage payments.

3. Fraudulent Transactions in Anticipation of Bankruptcy

There's one major limitation on selling nonexempt property and using it to purchase exempt property before filing for bankruptcy. You can't do it to defraud your creditors. The two main factors a judge looks at are:

Your motive. The bankruptcy court will probably approve your conversion if your primary motive is to buy property that will help you make a fresh start after bankruptcy. You probably can sell a second car and buy some tools needed in your business or clothing for your kids. But if you sell your second car and buy a diamond ring or new stereo system, a court might consider it a greedy attempt to cheat your creditors, even if the item is legally exempt.

The amount of property involved. If the amount of nonexempt property you get rid of before you file is enough to pay off a healthy portion of your debts, the court may dismiss your bankruptcy case.

If you make pre-bankruptcy conversions that the bankruptcy court questions, the burden will be on you to justify your actions. Here are important guidelines to keep in mind in making pre-bankruptcy conversions and then dealing with the court.

- **Be honest.** If the subject comes up, freely admit that you arranged your property holdings to exempt the maximum property and get a better fresh start. If you attempt to cover up your actions, the court may consider it evidence of fraudulent intent.

- **Sell and buy for equivalent value.** If you sell a $500 nonexempt item and purchase an exempt item worth $100, the court will want to know where the other $400 went.

- **Sell property at reasonable prices.** When you sell nonexempt property to purchase exempt property, make the price as close to the item's market value as possible.

- **Don't make last-minute transfers or purchases.** The longer you can wait to file for bankruptcy after making these kinds of property transfers, the less likely the court will disapprove.

- **Don't merely change the way you hold title to property.** Merely changing the way property is held from a nonexempt form to an exempt form usually arouses suspicion. For example, if tenancy by the entirety property is exempt in your state, but you and your spouse hold your house in joint tenancy (not exempt), don't just change the title from joint tenancy to tenancy by the entirety.

C. Claiming Your Exemptions

In a few states, to take advantage of the state exemptions, you must file a declaration with the court clerk, county recorder, county clerk or similar official. The declaration is a simple form in which you describe (or list) your property and give its location. If a creditor has already sued you or you've filed for bankruptcy, don't despair. In the states where you must file a declaration, you can sometimes file it after you've been sued or after you file for bankruptcy. If you don't know what is required in your state, call the court clerk, county recorder or county clerk and ask if the office has an exemption declaration form. If it does, fill it out and file it. If it doesn't, ask if people file these forms anyway. If they don't, you probably don't have to either. If they do, check with a stationery store or form typing service (see Chapter 20) for help in completing one.

In most states, any real estate or personal property in which you reside, such as a mobile home or boat, will qualify for the homestead exemption. And, to take advantage of the homestead protection, you usually must be living in the homestead when you claim it exempt.

When you file a property exemption declaration, you put your creditors on notice that they shouldn't bother to go after that particular property. If they do, you need only point out your filed declaration for protection.

If you don't have to file an exemption declaration, it doesn't mean that you need not do anything to take advantage of your state's exemptions. If you file for bankruptcy, you must list all of the exemptions you claim on your bankruptcy forms. And, as pointed out in Chapter 15, if a judgment creditor goes after your exempt property, you must file a claim of exemption. ∎

Rebuilding Your Credit

Credit is like a looking-glass, which, once sullied by a breath, may be wiped clear again.

—Sir Walter Scott, Scottish poet
and novelist, 1771-1832

If you've gone through a financial crisis—bankruptcy, repossession, foreclosure, history of late payments or something similar—you may think that you'll never get credit again. Not true. Although, in general, a bankruptcy filing can be reported on your credit record for ten years, and all other negative information can be reported for seven, in about two years you can probably rebuild your credit to the point that you won't be turned down for a major credit card or loan (assuming your financial troubles are behind you). Even in the limited situations in which negative information can be reported indefinitely (see Section B.2, below), if you successfully rebuild your credit, creditors will ignore old, negative information.

When reviewing a credit application by someone with poor credit, most creditors look for steady employment, a recent history of making and paying for purchases on credit and maintaining a checking and savings account since the financial setback. And many creditors disregard a bankruptcy discharge, often thought of as the most devastating of all financial setbacks, after about five years.

This chapter provides a thorough overview of cleaning up your credit. For more detailed information, including 30 sample forms, see *Credit Repair,* by Robin Leonard & Deanne Loonin (Nolo).

A. Avoid Overspending

To rebuild your credit, you must understand where your money goes. With that information in hand, you can make intelligent choices about how to spend your money. If you'd rather not create a budget yourself, you can contact a nonprofit debt counseling agency. These organizations primarily help debtors negotiate with creditors; they can also help you set up a budget for free or a nominal fee.

(See Chapter 20, Section C, for more information on finding a reliable debt counselor.)

1. Figure Out Where Your Money Goes

Before you put yourself on a budget that limits how much you spend, take time to figure out exactly how much money you spend now. To do this, make at least four copies of the Daily Expenditures form, below, and fill them out for a month. Write down every cent you spend—50¢ for the paper, $2 for your morning coffee and muffin, $7 for lunch, $2 for the bridge or tunnel toll and so on. Be sure to include the money you lay out maybe only once a month, such as $20 for your child's swim class, $5 for an office party gift or a $10 donation to a local charity.

Be sure to also include monthly payments such as your rent or mortgage, educational loans, credit card payments, car payments, insurance payments, utility, telephone and cable bills and other similar expenses.

Be tough-minded—if you omit any money, your picture of how much you spend, and your budget, will be inaccurate.

At the end of the 30 days, review your Daily Expenditure forms. Are you surprised at the total or the number of items you purchased? Are you impulsively spending your money or do you tend to consistently spend it on the same types of things?

Daily Expenditures for Week of _____

Sunday's Expenditures	Cost	Monday's Expenditures	Cost	Tuesday's Expenditures	Cost	Wednesday's Expenditures	Cost
Daily Total:		Daily Total:		Daily Total:		Daily Total:	

Thursday's Expenditures	Cost	Friday's Expenditures	Cost	Saturday's Expenditures	Cost	Other Expenditures	Cost
Daily Total:		Daily Total:		Daily Total:		Weekly Total:	

2. Make a Spending Plan

After you've kept track of your expenses for a month, you're ready to create a spending plan, or budget. Your twin goals in making a spending plan are to control your impulses to overspend and to help you start saving money—an essential part of rebuilding your credit.

Begin with a blank piece of paper. At the top, write down your monthly income from all sources —such as wages, receipts if you're an independent contractor, child support or alimony and interest or dividends on investments. For your income, list the net—the amount after taxes and other mandatory deductions have been taken out.

At the left, create broad categories of expenses based on the items you listed in your Daily Expenditures forms. For example, if you spend money on coffee at work, lunch out and groceries, you can combine that into "food." Or you can separate groceries from the rest, and use two categories— "food at home" and "food out." Here are some suggested categories:

- rent/mortgage (including taxes and insurance)
- telephone and utilities (water, gas, electric, cable, garbage)
- household supplies
- furnishings and furniture
- food/groceries
- clothing
- personal care (haircut, cosmetics, toiletries)
- health care (insurance, medications, doctors, therapist)
- transportation (car payment, car insurance, gasoline, tolls)
- entertainment
- dependent care
- vacation and travel
- educational expenses
- insurance (other than homeowner's, car and health), and
- business expenses (out of your own pocket).

Be sure to include a category for any bank or other deposit accounts you deposit money into, and any loans on which you make payments.

To the right of each category, write down the amount of money you spend, deposit or pay each month—using the figures you entered on your Daily Expenditures forms. Add any expenses you usually incur but did not during the month you were keeping track. (Look back through your check register and credit card statements to help yourself figure out any expenses you might have missed.) Also, add in the monthly equivalent for expenses you incur less often, such as bimonthly or yearly. For example, divide your annual car registration by 12 and put down the amount.

Finally, total up the amount. If it exceeds your monthly income, you will need to make some changes—eliminate or reduce expenditures for non-necessities—and start over.

Once you are able to break even, go one step farther. Think about the changes you need to make to put away a few dollars at the end of every week. If you think there's nothing to spare, try to set a small goal—even $5 a week. It will help. If you spend $2 per day on coffee and a muffin, that adds up to $10 per week and at least $40 per month. Eating breakfast at home might save you most of that amount.

If you buy the newspaper at the corner store every day, consider subscribing. A subscription doesn't involve extending credit; if you don't pay, the newspaper company simply stops delivering. And you can usually get clothes for your kids at a thrift shop.

If you'd rather not create a budget yourself, you can contact a nonprofit debt counseling agency. These organizations can help you set up a budget for free or a nominal fee. (See Chapter 20, Section C, for more information.)

3. Prevent Future Financial Problems

There are no magic rules that will solve everyone's financial troubles. But the following suggestions should help you stay out of financial hot water. If you have a family, everyone will have to participate —no one person can do all the work alone. So make sure your spouse or partner, and the children, understand that the family is having financial difficulties and agree together to take the steps that will lead to recovery.

- **Create a realistic budget and stick to it.** This means periodically checking it and readjusting your figures and spending habits.
- **Don't impulse buy.** When you see something you hadn't planned to buy, don't purchase it on the spot. Go home and think it over. It's unlikely you'll return to the store and buy it.
- **Avoid sales.** Buying a $500 item on sale for $400 isn't a $100 savings if you didn't need the item to begin with. It's spending $400 unnecessarily.
- **Get medical insurance if at all possible.** Even a stopgap policy with a large deductible can help if a medical crisis comes up. You can't avoid medical emergencies, but living without medical insurance is an invitation to financial ruin.
- **Charge items only if you can afford to pay for them now.** If you don't currently have the cash, don't charge based on future income—sometimes future income doesn't materialize. An alternative is to get rid of some or all of your credit cards and commit to living without credit for a while. (See Chapter 10, Section A.2 for information on which credit card accounts to close and how to properly close them.)
- **Avoid large rent or house payments.** Obligate yourself only for what you can now afford and increase your mortgage payments only as your income increases. Consider refinancing your house if your payments are unwieldy. (See Chapter 6, Section A.2 for information on avoiding rip-offs when refinancing.)
- **Avoid cosigning or guaranteeing a loan for someone.** Your signature obligates you as if you were the primary borrower. You can't be sure that the other person will pay.
- **Avoid joint obligations with people who have questionable spending habits**—even a spouse or partner. If you incur a joint debt, you're probably liable for it all if the other person defaults.

- **Don't make high-risk investments.** Opt for certificates of deposit, money market funds and government bonds over speculative real estate, penny stocks and junk bonds.

Should You Rebuild Your Credit?

Habitual overspending can be just as hard to overcome as excessive gambling or drinking. If you think you may be a compulsive spender, one of the worst things you can do is rebuild your credit. Instead, you need to get a handle on your spending habits.

Debtors Anonymous, a 12-step support program similar to Alcoholics Anonymous, has programs nationwide. If a Debtors Anonymous group or a therapist recommends that you stay out of the credit system for a while, follow that advice. Even if you don't feel you're a compulsive spender, paying as you spend may still be the way to go—because of finance charges, transaction fees and other charges, buying on credit costs between 15% and 20% more than paying with cash.

Debtors Anonymous groups meet all over the country. If you can't find one in your area, send a self-addressed, stamped envelope to Debtors Anonymous, General Services Office, P.O. Box 920888, Needham, MA 02492-0009. Or call their office and speak to a volunteer or leave your name, address and a request for information. Their number is 781-453-2743. You can also visit their website at www.debtorsanonymous.org.

B. Clean Up Your Credit File

If you have serious debt problems, you are probably concerned about what's in your credit file. There's no question that your credit rating will suffer if you don't pay your bills. Bankruptcies, repossessions, foreclosures, lawsuits to collect debt, and even missed payments get into credit files. Potential creditors see the negative information and often use it to deny you a loan or credit card.

What exactly is a credit file? Few people know or have ever seen one. Yet, to understand the credit world and how to rebuild your credit, you need to know how credit is established and how credit information is used.

Establishing credit involves taking steps to make sure that when you apply for a loan or credit card, or even for an apartment or job, the lender, landlord or employer will find favorable information on you when she runs a credit check. A credit check is a search of information found in a computer file assembled and maintained by a credit bureau. (See Section 1, below.) If the information indicates that you are a good risk—you'll probably pay the loan (or your rent) on time or will be a reliable employee —you have "good credit." If it shows that you have a history of paying bills late or not at all, you have "bad credit."

If the prospective lender, landlord or employer finds no credit file, she cannot assess your trustworthiness one way or the other, and may hesitate to lend you money or let you open up a credit card account. Similarly, without a credit history, a landlord may decide against renting to you. An employer, too, may conclude that a 35-year-old applicant doesn't have a stable life if the employer finds no credit file.

Many of us first established credit in our late teens or early twenties when we accepted the steady stream of gasoline and local department store pre-approved credit card applications we received after high school graduation. Or, perhaps we were lured by the credit card companies that set up shop on our college's campus and offered all kinds of perks for signing up. With many of these first credit cards, our parents were guarantors—meaning if we missed the payments, they would foot the bill.

Others may have waited until buying a first car or getting a first job. And anyone who financed his college education with student loans established a credit history the day he made (or missed) his first loan payment.

A few of us believe we've never taken steps to establish credit. We have no credit cards and pay cash for everything. But as stated above, we don't establish credit just by taking out a loan or buying items with a credit card. Often, by applying for a job, apartment or insurance policy, we start down the road to having credit. Employers, landlords and insurance companies often request copies of credit files from credit bureaus. For this reason, nearly every adult in the United States has a credit file.

1. Credit Bureaus and Credit Files

Credit bureaus are private, profit-making companies that gather and sell information about a person's credit history. Credit bureaus sell credit files to banks, mortgage lenders, credit unions, credit card companies, department stores, insurance companies, landlords and employers. They in turn use the credit files to supplement applications for credit, insurance, housing and employment.

If the bureau has no information on you, it has nothing to sell. Thus, credit bureaus are always searching for more information.

There are three major credit bureaus—Equifax, Trans Union and Experian (formerly known as TRW). Together they have over 1,000 branches throughout the country. Each company maintains a file on nearly every U.S. adult—about 190 million people.

Credit bureaus get most of their data from creditors such as department stores, banks and credit card issuers. Credit bureaus also search court records, looking for lawsuits, judgments and bankruptcy filings. And they go through county records offices to find recorded tax, judgment, mechanic's or other liens (legal claims).

To create a credit report for a given person, a bureau searches its computer files until it finds entries that match the name, Social Security number and any other available identifying information. All matches are gathered together and constitute a credit report or credit file.

Data gathered in a credit file usually includes your name (and any former names), past and present addresses, Social Security number, employment history, marriages, divorces, lawsuits to which you are a party and liens, legal claims on your property. If you've been through bankruptcy, it will show up in your credit file. Sometimes, credit reports include outstanding child support payments.

The bulk of information in a credit file is your credit history—positive and negative. Each credit entry in a credit file typically contains the name of the creditor, the type of account (such as revolving credit line, student loan, mortgage), your account number, when the account was opened, your credit limit or the original amount of the loan, whether anyone else is obligated on the account, your current balance and your payment pattern for the previous 24–36 months (whether you pay on time or have been 30, 60, 90 or 120 days past due). The file will show if any accounts have been turned over to a collection agency, if you are disputing a charge or if you've wiped out the debt in bankruptcy.

> **EXAMPLE:** Martin visits Cars for Less and finds a used Porsche for $20,000. Martin plans to put one-third down, and to use the dealer's financing for the rest. Although Martin brought $6,000 cash, Cars for Less wants to be sure that he can make payments of about $300 per month on the balance.
>
> The salesclerk at Cars for Less calls up her Equifax computer database. She searches the database for Martin's file by entering his name, address and Social Security number.
>
> The computer digests the information and pulls up Martin's file. It shows that he makes his credit card payments within 30 days, is current on his mortgage, but does owe the county property tax office about $250. The salesclerk decides that Martin's property tax is of no concern—it will be paid when Martin sells his house, if not before—and lends him the money for the car.

Most credit files also contain a credit score. For an explanation and discussion of credit scores, see Chapter 11, Section B.2.

2. Laws Regulating Credit Bureaus

Credit bureaus are regulated by the Federal Trade Commission under the provisions of the 1971 federal Fair Credit Reporting Act (FCRA) (15 U.S.C. § 1681 and following) and by state law.

a. The Fair Credit Reporting Act

The FCRA was passed to address consumers' concerns about the proliferation of credit bureaus and the information in credit files. The law is designed to bar inaccurate or obsolete information from credit files, and it requires that credit bureaus adopt reasonable procedures for gathering, maintaining and disseminating information.

The FCRA also regulates who can look at your credit report and how long creditors can report negative information. In general, only people or businesses with a "permissible purpose" can access your credit report. The most common are:

- **Creditors.** Creditors can look at your report whenever you apply for credit or for a loan.
- **Employers.** Employers can look at your report, but only under certain circumstances and only if you give them written authorization.
- **Government Agencies.** Government agencies can request your report to determine whether you are eligible for public assistance. State and local government officials can also get reports to help determine whether you can make child support payments. But many other agencies are not allowed to access your report. For example, the Immigration and Naturalization Service (INS) cannot look at your credit report for immigration proceedings or to review citizenship applications.
- **Judgment Creditors.** Judgment creditors are allowed to look at credit reports in order to decide whether to begin collection efforts.
- **Landlords and Mortgage Lenders.** These people and businesses are also allowed to review your report.

- **Utility Companies.** Utilities can request your credit report. However, in many circumstances, utility companies cannot deny you service due to bad credit.

The FCRA also regulates the type of information that can be reported, how consumers can get copies of their reports and how long information can appear on your credit report. (For more on these rules, see Sections 4 and 5, below).

More on credit repair and credit bureaus. Nolo's *Credit Repair,* by Deanne Loonin & Robin Leonard, is a complete guide to repairing your credit. Among other things, it discusses in detail the credit reporting system, how to read your credit report and the laws regulating credit bureaus. In addition, it provides all the plain-English instructions and forms you need to clean up your credit report and build good credit.

b. State Credit Bureau Laws

All states have laws governing credit reporting agencies. Only some of those laws, however, impose more limitations on creditors and credit bureaus and provide more protections to consumers than does the Fair Credit Reporting Act. To find out if your state imposes more restrictions than does the FCRA, you'll have to do some legal research on your own. Your state consumer protection office may also be able to provide you with this information. (See Chapter 20 for information on how to do legal research and for a list of state consumer protection offices.)

3. Get a Copy of Your Credit File

Under the FCRA, a credit bureau must provide you with a copy of your credit file if you present proper identification. And it's free in these circumstances:

- You've been denied credit because of information in your credit file. You are entitled to a free copy of your file from the bureau that reported the information; even if you request it from a different bureau, that bureau will probably provide you with a copy. A creditor

that denies you credit in this situation will tell you the name and address of the credit bureau reporting the information that led to the denial. You must request your copy within 60 days of being denied credit.

- You can get a free copy of your credit report once a year from any credit bureau if you live in Colorado, Georgia, Maryland, Massachusetts, New Jersey or Vermont.
- You can get a free copy once in any 12-month period if you are unemployed and planning to apply for a job within 60 days following your request for your credit report. You must enclose a statement swearing that this is true information. It might also help to include a copy of a recent unemployment check, layoff notice or similar document verifying your unemployment.
- You receive public assistance. Enclose a statement swearing that this is true information and a copy of your most recent public assistance check as verification.
- You believe your credit file contains errors due to someone's fraudulent use of your credit cards, Social Security number, name or something similar. Here, too, you will need to enclose a statement swearing that this is true information.

To obtain a report in any other situation, you'll have to pay a fee of about $9.00 unless you are in a state that has lowered the fee. Expect to receive your report in a week to ten days.

It's best to order a credit report from all three credit bureaus. If you've been denied credit, at the very least, get a copy of your credit report from the bureau that reported the information leading to the denial. If you choose to order only one report and you haven't been denied credit, request a copy from the company closest to where you live. If you find errors in the first credit file, be sure to obtain copies of your file from the other two bureaus.

Call the credit bureaus and ask if they have a file on you. Under the FCRA, a credit bureau *must* do a search for a credit file if you offer "proper identification." The credit bureau needs little beyond your name (and former names), address (and former addresses), phone number, Social Security number and year of birth to establish your identification. If the clerk searches while you're on the phone, she'll tell you only whether or not the bureau has a file. She won't tell you what is in it. For that, you'll have to put your request in writing or order a report online.

If you are in a hurry, you may want to visit a local credit bureau (look in the Yellow Pages). Local companies get all of their information from the big three bureaus.

The credit bureau must provide you with all information in your file (except medical information—usually placed by insurance companies), the sources of the information and the names of people who requested copies of your file during the past year or two. It is not required to tell you your credit score, but a few are starting to reveal them anyway. See Chapter 11, Section B.2, for more on credit scores.

Obtaining Medical Information

Getting a copy of medical information on file is possible for some people. The for-profit Medical Information Bureau, Inc., collects data—mostly about major illnesses—on about 5% of all people in the U.S. MIB files contain data requested by life insurance companies from a person who applies for coverage. To obtain a copy of your file, contact MIB (P.O. Box 105, Essex Station, Boston, MA 02112, 617-426-3660, infoline@mib.com (email)), and ask for a copy of the Request for Disclosure of MIB Record Information form. Then complete it and return it to MIB. You will not have to provide your Social Security number. You will have to pay a fee unless you received an "adverse action" notice from an MIB member insurance company. For general information about MIB, visit their website at www.mib.com.

To request a copy of your credit report by mail, you will need to include the following information in a letter.

Full name. A credit bureau cannot process your request without your name. It's important that you provide your full name, including generations (Jr., Sr., III).

Date of birth. A credit bureau may provide your report without your date (or at least year) of birth. But this information helps distinguish you from anyone else with a similar name.

Social Security number. Many people refuse to give out their Social Security numbers to anyone other than their employers, banks and the IRS. That's fine, but realize that most credit bureaus require this in order to pull your report. This is because credit bureaus use Social Security numbers to help distinguish between people with the same or similar names.

Spouse's name. It's not absolutely necessary, but again, it helps distinguish you from anyone else with a similar name.

Telephone number. You may not get your report if you don't include your telephone number. You may hesitate to include it, knowing that bill collectors can get it by getting a copy of your credit file. But unless it's unlisted, they can also call Directory Assistance and get it. If you're trying to rebuild your credit, you will want to make sure your phone number is in your file. This is one sign of stability your future creditors look for.

Current address. You won't get a copy of your credit report if you don't include your address. You should also include proof of your current address, such as a photocopy of your driver's license, a current billing statement or other document showing your address. (This is required to avoid someone fraudulently requesting a copy of your report.)

Previous addresses and dates there. Credit bureaus ask for this if you've been at your current address less than two years. Again, it helps distinguish you from other people with similar names. If you don't want the bureau to have this information, you can leave it off, but your request may be rejected.

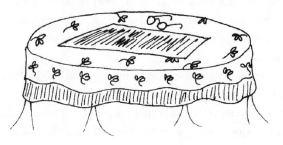

**Credit Bureaus' Addresses
and Phone Numbers**

Equifax
P.O. Box 740241
Atlanta, GA 30374
800-685-1111
www.equifax.com

Experian
National Consumer Assistance Center
P.O. Box 2002
Allen, TX 75013
www.experian.com

Trans Union
Consumer Disclosure Center
P.O. Box 2000
Chester, PA 19022
800-888-4213
www.tuc.com

4. Review the Contents of Your Credit File

A credit bureau will provide you with the data in your file, the sources of the data and the names of people who requested copies of your file—called inquiries—within the last two years.

Review your report carefully. One of the biggest problems with credit files is that they contain incorrect or out-of-date information. According to a 1998 investigation by the U.S. Public Interest Research Group, 70% of the credit reports examined contained an error.

Sometimes credit bureaus confuse names, addresses, Social Security numbers or employers. If you have a common name, say John Brown, your file may contain information on other John Browns, John Brownes or Jon Browns. Or your file may erroneously contain information on family members with similar names.

Because consumers are generally not told when information is placed in their files, they usually discover errors only when they are denied credit and then request a copy of their credit file. The conse-

quences of such errors can be serious. Each year, people are wrongfully denied mortgages, student loans, car loans, insurance policies, employment or a place to live because of credit bureau mistakes. It can be a bureaucratic nightmare to try to clear up the file, delaying by months, and sometimes years, the time it takes to get the loan. A cautious consumer could avoid some problems by requesting a copy of his credit file before applying for credit.

As you read through your credit report, make a list of everything that is incorrect, misleading or not authorized to be in your file. In particular, look for the following:

- incorrect or incomplete name, address, phone number, Social Security number or marital status
- incorrect, missing or outdated employment information
- bankruptcies not identified by the specific chapter of the bankruptcy code
- credit inquiries older than two years
- credit inquiries by automobile dealers when you simply test drove a car or from other businesses when you were only comparison shopping (creditors cannot pull your credit report without your permission until you indicate a desire to enter into a sale or lease)
- credit accounts that are not yours, even if the account is current
- lawsuits you were not involved in
- incorrect account histories—look especially for late payments when you've paid on time
- a missing notation when you disputed a charge on a credit card bill (some agencies require you to file a written statement of dispute)
- collection agency listed separate from the original creditor, making it appear that you are delinquent on more than one debt
- closed accounts incorrectly listed as open—it may look as if you have too much open credit, and
- any account you closed that doesn't have a "closed by consumer" notation; if it's not there, you'll want it added, otherwise it looks like the creditor closed the account.

You should also review your credit report for old information. Credit bureaus are prohibited from reporting certain kinds of negative information after certain periods of time. Here are the basic rules:

- Bankruptcies can be reported for no more than ten years from the date of the last activity. Although the date of the last activity for most bankruptcies is the date you receive your discharge or the date your case is dismissed, credit bureaus usually start counting the ten-year period from the earlier date of filing.
- Lawsuits and judgments may be reported from the date of the entry of judgment against you for up to seven years or until the governing statute of limitations has expired, whichever is longer.
- Paid tax liens may be reported from the date of the last activity for up to seven years.
- Most criminal records, such as information about indictments or arrests, may be reported for only seven years. But records of criminal convictions may be reported indefinitely.
- Accounts sent for collection, accounts charged off or any other similar action may be reported from the date of the last activity on the account for up to seven years. The date of last activity is no later than 180 days from the delinquency itself. Creditors must include the date of the delinquency when they report past due accounts to credit bureaus. The clock does not start ticking again if the account is sold to another collection agency.
- Bankruptcies, lawsuits, paid tax liens, accounts sent out for collection, criminal records and any other adverse information may be reported beyond the usual time limits if you apply for $150,000 or more of credit or insurance, or if you apply for a job with an annual income of at least $75,000. However, as a practical matter, credit bureaus usually delete all items after seven or ten years.
- Positive information may be reported indefinitely.

5. Take Action If Someone Steals a Credit Card or Your Identity

If, by reviewing your credit report, you discover that someone has stolen a credit card or, worse, your identity, you should take immediate action. Identity theft has become a national epidemic. Government agencies and consumer organizations estimate the number of identity theft victims in the United States alone to be 900,000 per year—and that number is increasing.

If you believe someone has stolen your credit card or identity, ask the credit bureaus to add a "fraud alert" to your credit file and a "victim's statement" asking that creditors call you before opening any new accounts or changing your existing accounts. Here's how the different credit bureaus handle it:

Experian. Experian lets you put a security alert in your credit file for 90 days (during which time no new credit will be approved) and a victim statement for seven years. In the statement, you can ask that a creditor call you for oral confirmation of your application before approving further credit. To put a fraud notation in your credit file, call Experian at 888-397-3742.

Trans Union. Trans Union's fraud alert lets you specify that no new credit should be approved until the creditor calls you to verify the application. It lasts for seven years unless you ask that it be removed earlier. To put a fraud notation in your credit file, call Trans Union at 800-680-7289.

Equifax. Like the other bureaus, Equifax's fraud alert lets you specify that no new credit should be approved until the creditor calls and obtains a verification from you that the application is legitimate. Contact Equifax at 800-525-6285.

If someone steals your identity, you should take additional steps to clean up the mess. For example, contact the Social Security Administration to see if your Social Security number has been used fraudulently. You'd notice this if your earnings records lists earnings for jobs you've never held. You can get a copy of your earnings report by calling 800-772-1213 (or by visiting the SSA's website at www.ssa.gov). If you notice fraudulent use of your

Social Security number, call the SSA's fraud hotline at 800-269-0271.

You should also contact any creditors that have reported the fraudulent information on your credit report. Ask to speak with someone in the security or fraud department and follow up with a letter.

Immediately close any accounts that have been tampered with and open new ones with new personal identification (PIN) numbers and passwords. When choosing a password, don't use one based on easily available information such as your mother's maiden name or your birth date.

Finally, file a report with the local police department or the police department in the community where the identity theft took place. Even if the police don't do anything, it will help to have a copy of a police report when you are explaining the situation to creditors. Identity theft is a serious crime. Federal law makes identity theft a crime (18 U.S.C. § 1028) as do many state laws.

To find out more about identity theft, call the Federal Trade Commission's Identity Theft Hotline at 877-438-4338 or 202-326-2502 (TDD). Or visit it's website at www.consumer.gov/idtheft. You can also get information from www. identitytheft.org or www.privacyrights.org.

6. Dispute Incorrect, Outdated and Misleading Information in Your Credit File

Once you've compiled a list of all information you want changed or removed, complete the request for reinvestigation form which was enclosed with your credit report. If the bureau did not enclose such a form, send a letter to the address provided by the credit bureau for disputing information. List each incorrect item and explain exactly what is wrong. Also, enclose copies of documents that support your claim. You should also send a copy to the creditor who furnished the incorrect or incomplete information to the credit bureau. These "furnishing" creditors have a duty to correct and update the information that they send to credit bureaus. Be sure to keep a photocopy of your request for reinvesti-

gation and letter to the furnishing creditor. Requesting a reinvestigation shouldn't cost you anything.

Once the credit bureau receives your letter, it must reinvestigate the matter and get back in touch with you within 30 days. Some states require a faster reinvestigation. These requirements are not hard for a credit bureau to meet. Credit bureaus and 6,000 of the nation's creditors are linked by computer, which speeds up the verification process. Furthermore, if you let a credit bureau know that you're trying to obtain a mortgage or car loan, they can do a "rush" verification.

You might be concerned that if information is incorrect with one credit bureau it will be wrong with the others. That may be the case, and it's one reason you should get copies of your files from all three bureaus if you find errors in a credit report.

If you don't hear from the bureau within the deadline, send a follow-up letter. To get someone's attention, send a copy of your second letter to the Federal Trade Commission (see Section B.7, below, for more information), the agency that oversees credit bureaus. Again, keep a copy for your records.

If you are right, or if the creditor who provided the information can no longer verify it, the credit bureau must remove the information from your file. Often credit bureaus will remove an item on request without an investigation if rechecking the item is more bother than it's worth.

> **EXAMPLE:** Jim's credit file with Credit Gatherers reporting agency shows that he has not paid a $275 bill from Acrelong Drug Store. But Jim has never done business with Acrelong. Credit Gatherers contacts Acrelong for verification. Acrelong has no information showing that Jim owes $275 and cannot verify the debt. Credit Gatherers removes the information from Jim's file.

If the credit bureau responds that the creditor reporting the information verified its accuracy, call the credit bureau at its toll free 800 number listed in Section B.4, above.

Credit bureaus must do much more than simply contact the creditor reporting the information to verify its accuracy. Specifically, credit bureaus must do the following:

- complete its investigation within 30 days of receiving your complaint
- contact the creditor reporting the incorrect information within five days of receiving your complaint
- review all relevant information supplied by you
- remove all inaccurate and unverified information
- adopt procedures to keep the information from reappearing
- reinsert removed information only if the provider of the information certifies its accuracy and the credit bureau notifies you within five days of the reinsertion, and
- provide you with the results of its reinvestigation, including a new credit report, within five days of completion.

If you receive a favorable decision from a credit bureau, you should take the following steps:

- obtain another copy of your credit report to make sure that the bureau made the corrections
- find out whether other credit bureaus' files contain the same error and if so, send the results of the investigation to those agencies as well, and
- get a copy of the report three to six months later to make sure that the credit bureau has not reinserted the information.

If the credit bureau responds that the information you dispute is accurate and will remain in your file, you will have to take more aggressive action. Start by contacting the creditor that is reporting the information and demand that it be removed. Write to the customer service department, vice president of marketing and the president or CEO. If the information was reported by a collection agency, send the agency a copy of your letter, too. Under the Fair Credit Reporting Act, the creditor must do the following:

- refrain from reporting information they know is incorrect
- refrain from ignoring information they know contradicts what they have on file

- refrain from reporting incorrect information when they learn that the information is incorrect, and
- provide credit bureaus with correct information when they learn that they are reporting incorrect information.

If the creditor will not remove the information from your file, you will have to contact the credit bureau for additional help. Call the credit bureau at:

Experian:	888-397-3742
Trans Union:	800-888-4213
Equifax:	800-685-1111 or 800-525-6285.

If all else fails, consider calling your congressional representative or senator. That person can call an official at the Federal Trade Commission, the federal agency that regulates credit bureaus, and demand action. (See Chapter 12, Section F.)

7. Consider Adding a Brief Statement to Your Credit File

If you feel a credit bureau is wrongfully including information in your file, or you want to explain a particular entry, you have the right to put a brief statement in your file. If the reporting agency helps you write the summary, it must be limited to 100 words. Otherwise, there is no word limit, but it is a good idea to keep the statement very brief.

The credit bureau is only required to provide a summary of your statement (not your actual statement) to anyone who requests your file. If your statement is short, the credit bureau is more likely to pass on your statement, unedited. If your statement is long, the credit bureau will probably condense your explanation to just a few sentences. To avoid this problem, keep your statement clear and concise and as short as possible.

If you request it, the bureau must also give the statement or summary to anyone who received a copy of your file within the past six months—or two years if your file was given out for employment purposes.

This is not an unlimited right. Credit bureaus are only required to include a statement in your file if you are disputing the completeness or accuracy of a particular item. If that is the case, they must do it for free. The bureau does not have to include a statement if you are only explaining extenuating circumstances or other reasons why you haven't been able to pay your debts. If the bureau does allow you to add such a statement, it can charge you a fee.

Don't assume that adding a brief statement is the best approach. It's often wiser to simply explain the negative mark to subsequent creditors in person than to try to explain it in such a short statement. Many statements or summaries are simply ineffective. Few creditors who receive credit files read them. In any David (consumer) vs. Goliath (credit bureau) dispute, creditors tend to believe Goliath. To make matters worse, your statement might stay in your file even longer than the disputed information.

Sample Statements

As mentioned, be judicious in your use of explanatory statements. But if the information in your file is clearly wrong and can be simply explained, consider adding a statement. Here are a few samples:

"I am not unemployed. Since 20xx, I have worked as a freelance technical writer, and have earned an average of $35,000 per year.

"Although I was sued by Randy Roofer, I did not pay her because the roof she put on my house is not sealed and she refuses to fix it. I refuse to pay Randy until she repairs the roof. I filed a complaint with the state contractor's board, which is pending."

"It is technically accurate that I was sued by Jones and Jones Department Store on June 11, 20xx, but the lawsuit was a mistake. Jones and Jones dismissed the lawsuit when they realized that they had confused my account with another customer's. My account with Jones and Jones has never been delinquent."

"I was hospitalized following a car accident. I sent the medical bills to my insurance company, but the company took over six months to pay the bills. In the meantime, the hospital began collection efforts against me. Those efforts ended when the insurance company paid the bill."

8. Complaints About a Credit Bureau

If a credit bureau employee violates the law, you can complain to the Federal Trade Commission. (See Chapter 12, Section F.) For the best result, complain in writing. Include the name of the credit bureau, its address and phone number, the name of the employee you dealt with, the nature of the problem, the dates of your contact with the credit bureau and copies of documents that pertain to the problem. Be sure to send a copy of this letter to the credit bureau.

If a credit bureau insists on reporting out-of-date or wrong information, complaining to the FTC may put a stop to it. Also, if you paid an unreasonable fee, for example, $50 for a copy of your file, complaining could help you get a refund.

Sample Complaint Letter

---

78 Marshall Street
Burlington, VT 00011

April 12, 20xx

To Whom It May Concern:

Under 15 U.S.C. § 1681s, I wish to lodge the following complaint about the following credit reporting agency:

Collect-O Credit Services
503 Grand Avenue, Montpelier, Vermont,
802-555-1234

On March 29, 20xx, I visited Collect-O Credit Services to see my credit file. I paid $10, after complaining that this exceeds the state's limit of $7.50. After waiting almost 30 minutes, Maggie Beach brought me to a small room. She pulled out my file and started going through it.

I noticed that Ms. Beach refused to show me certain pages. I asked her why she was skipping those pages. She just said she didn't have to show them to me.

Ms. Beach also refused to let ask me ask questions about some of the entries she did show me. And when I asked her to double-check some inaccurate information, she told me it had just come into their office and therefore must be correct.

Please investigate this matter and inform me of the results.

Thank you,

Alex Stewart

Alex Stewart

cc: Collect-O Credit Services

In many states, you should also complain to the state agency that regulates credit bureaus' illegal or unethical conduct. If the credit bureau is associated with a collection agency, see Chapter 9 on complaining about collection agencies. The addresses of state agencies that regulate credit bureaus are in Chapter 20, Section A.1.

If you were seriously harmed by the credit bureau —for example, it continued to give out false information after you requested corrections—you may want to sue. The FCRA lets you sue a credit bureau for negligent or willful noncompliance with the law within two years after the bureau's harmful behavior first occurred. You can sue for actual damages, such as court costs, attorneys' fees, lost wages and, if applicable, intentional infliction of emotional distress. In the case of truly outrageous behavior, you can recover punitive damages—damages meant to punish for malicious or willful conduct. Consider representing yourself in court or hiring a lawyer. (See Chapter 20.)

C. Add Positive Account Histories to Your Credit File

Often, credit reports don't include accounts that you might expect to find. Some creditors don't report account statuses to credit bureaus. Others report only infrequently. If your credit file is missing credit histories for accounts you pay on time, send the credit bureaus a copy of a recent account statement and copies of canceled checks (never originals) showing your payment history. Ask the credit bureaus to add the information to your file. Although credit bureaus aren't required to do so, they often will, although they may charge a fee.

D. Add Information Showing Stability to Your Credit File

Your credit history is only one thing lenders consider in deciding whether to extend credit. They also want to see stability in your life. If any of the items listed below are missing from your file, you may want to send a letter to the credit bureaus asking that the information be added.

- **Your current employment**—employer's name, employer's address and your job title. You may wisely decide not to add this if you think a creditor may sue you or a creditor has a judgment against you. Current employment information may be a green light for a wage garnishment.

- **Your previous employment,** especially if you've had your current job less than two years. Include your former employer's name and address and your job title.

- **Your current residence,** and if you own it, say so. Not all mortgage lenders report their accounts to credit bureaus. Again, don't do this if you've been sued or you think a creditor may sue you. Real estate is an excellent collection source.

- **Your previous residence;** especially if you've lived at your current address less than two years.

- **Your telephone number,** especially if it's unlisted. If you haven't yet given the credit bureaus your phone number, consider doing so now. A creditor who cannot verify a telephone number is often reluctant to grant credit.

- **Your date of birth.** A creditor will probably not grant you credit if it does not know your age. However, creditors cannot discriminate based on age (see Chapter 19).

- **Your Social Security number.** (See discussion in Section B.3, above.)

- **Bank checking or savings account number.** It's an excellent sign of stability. Again, however, you won't want to add this information if you've been sued or you think a creditor may sue you. A creditor with a judgment against you will likely use this information to try to collect.

Credit bureaus aren't required to add any of this information, but they often do. They are most likely to add information on jobs and residences, as that information is used by creditors in evaluating applications for credit. They will also add your telephone number, date of birth and Social Security number

because those items help identify you and lessen the chances of "mixed" credit files—that is, getting other people's credit histories in your file.

Enclose any photocopies of documentation that verifies information you're providing, such as your driver's license, a canceled check, a bill addressed to you, a pay stub showing your employer's name and address or anything else similar. Remember to keep photocopies of all letters you send.

E. Build Credit in Your Own Name

Getting credit in your own name is an excellent strategy for rebuilding your credit if:

- all of most of your financial problems can be attributed to your spouse, or
- you and your spouse have gone through financial difficulties together, but most credit was in your spouse's name only.

Whether you are married, separated, divorced or single, your credit file should contain information about you only. Information about both spouses should appear in both files only if both spouses use or are obligated to use an account. Information on joint accounts, for example, should appear on both spouses' credit reports.

This is usually good news if you are worried that your spouse's negative credit history may reflect badly on you. However, this may be bad news if you are now divorced or separated and had relied primarily on your spouse's credit when you applied for loans or other credit.

The Equal Credit Opportunity Act (15 U.S.C. §1691-1691f) and most state credit discrimination statutes can help you build up credit in your own name. If you're still married, these laws require creditors to report information about joint accounts to both your file and your spouse's file. Creditors must report this information to your file even if your spouse is listed as the primary signer or obligor on the account.

If you're already divorced or separated and trying to get credit on your own, these laws also require creditors to at least consider any information you present from past accounts with your former spouse that reflect on your own creditworthiness. For example, you may be able to show that you and your spouse made payments on an account with joint checks even though the account was in your spouse's name only.

F. Ask Creditors to Consider Your Spouse's Credit History

A credit bureau cannot include information from your spouse's credit file in your credit file with two exceptions: (1) you and your spouse have a joint account (that is, both of you can use it), or (2) you are obligated (responsible for paying) on an account belonging to your spouse. In those situations, the credit bureau must report that information on your credit report.

Although a credit bureau is not required to include your spouse's good credit information on your account (unless it meets one of the two exceptions above), you may be able to get a creditor to consider information on your spouse's credit report when applying for a loan, credit card or other type of extension of credit. If any of your spouse's accounts reflect on your own creditworthiness, ask the creditor to consider them. For example, if you and your spouse make payments on your spouse's account with joint checks, bring this to the creditor's attention.

G. Use Existing or New Credit Cards

If your financial problems are behind you and you managed to hold onto one of your credit or charge cards, use it and pay your bills on time. Your credit history will improve quickly. Most credit reports show payment histories for 24–36 months. If you charge something every month, no matter how small, and pay at least the minimum required every month, your credit report will show steady and proper use of revolving credit.

Don't Overuse Your Credit Cards. Charge only a small amount each month and pay it in full. By paying in full, you will avoid interest charges (assuming your card has a grace period). Consumer groups point out that the average consumer who pays the minimum each month ends up paying hundreds of dollars in interest charges alone. Their example: If you charge $1,000 on a 19.8% credit card and pay it off by making the minimum payments each month, you'll take over eight years to pay off the loan and will pay almost $850 in interest. This is crazy. Rebuilding your credit might cost you some money, but you don't have to throw it away in the process. (See Chapter 10 for more on credit cards.)

1. Applying for Credit Cards

The best way to develop a positive credit history is to obtain credit and make timely payments. But, don't try to do this while you are steeped in financial trouble. You'll be more likely to get credit from a predatory lender (see "Mortgages for People With Poor Credit," above) and be in danger of getting into deeper debt. Getting a new credit card before you're on your feet may send you down the same path that got you into trouble in the first place.

However, if you are ready to start using credit again, go ahead and apply for a credit card. It's often easiest to obtain a card from a department store or gasoline company. They'll usually open your account with a very low credit line. If you start with one credit card, charge items and pay the bill on time, other companies will issue you cards. When you use department store and gasoline cards, try not to carry a balance from one month to the next. The interest rate on these cards is as high as 26%.

Next, apply for a regular credit card from a bank, such as a Visa card, MasterCard or Discover card. Competition for new customers is fierce among card issuers, and you may be able to find a card with relatively low initial rates. Depending on how bad your credit history is, however, you may qualify only for a low credit line or a card with a high interest rate and high annual fee. If you use the card and make your payments, however, after a year or so you can apply for an increase in your line of credit and possibly a reduction in your annual fee.

As outrageous as it sounds, you might even apply for an American Express card. If you have a very high income—even if you have horrible credit—you may very well be approved for an American Express card.

Many people who have had serious financial problems misused or overused their credit cards. The following tips will help you when you apply for credit cards or an increased credit limit:

Be consistent with the name you use. Either use your middle initial always or never. Always use your generation (Jr., Sr., II, III, etc.).

Take advantage of preapproved gasoline, department store and bank credit cards. If your credit is shot, you may not have the luxury of shopping around.

Be honest, but appear sympathetic. On applications, paint a picture of yourself in the best light. Lenders are especially apt to give less weight to past credit problems that were out of your control, such as a job layoff, illness or death in the family, recent divorce or new child support obligation. Don't emphasize how you forgot to write checks because you were too busy or on an extended vacation.

Apply for credit when you are most likely to get it. For example, apply when you are working, when you've lived at the same address for at least a year and when you haven't had an unusually high number of inquiries on your credit report in the last two years. A lot of inquiries is a sign that you are either desperate for credit or preparing to commit fraud.

Apply for credit from creditors with whom you've done business. For example, if you had a Sears charge card from a store in New Jersey and you moved to Hawaii, apply for a Sears card from a store near your new home.

Don't get swept up by credit card gimmicks. Before applying for a credit card that gives you rebates, credit for future purchases or other "benefits," make sure you will benefit by the offer. Some are good deals, especially if you like to travel and can get a card that helps you build up frequent flyer miles. But in general, a card with no annual fee and/or low interest usually beats the cards with deals.

Look carefully at preapproval solicitations for non-bank cards. A gold or platinum card with a very high credit limit (as much as $10,000) may be nothing more than a card that lets you purchase items through catalogues provided by the company itself. No other merchant accepts these cards and the company won't report your charges and payments to the credit bureaus. You usually have to pay a fee for the card and then another one for the catalogue. And the items in the catalogues are usually high priced and of low quality.

Once you receive a credit card, protect yourself and your efforts to repair your credit by following these suggestions:

Send your creditors a change of address when you move. Many creditors provide change of address boxes on their monthly bills. For your other creditors, you can send a letter, call the customer service phone number or use a post office change of address postcard.

If you need an increase in your credit limit, ask for it. Many creditors will close accounts or charge late fees on customers who exceed their credit limits. But pay close attention; if you're charging to the limit on your credit card, you may be heading for financial trouble.

Take steps to protect your cards. Sign your cards as soon as they arrive. If you have a personal identification number (PIN) that allows you take cash advances, keep the number in your head and never write it down near your credit card. Make a list of your credit card issuers, the account numbers and the issuer's phone numbers so you can quickly call if you need to report a lost or stolen card.

Don't give you credit card number to anyone over the phone unless you placed the call and are certain of the company's reputation. Never, never, never give your credit card number to someone who calls you and tries to sell you something or claims to need your credit card number to send you a "prize." *These are scam artists.*

2. Cosigners and Guarantors

A cosigner is someone who promises to repay a loan or credit card charges if the primary debtor defaults. Similarly, a guarantor promises the credit grantor that he will pay if the primary debtor does not. Usually, neither the cosigner's nor the guarantor's name appears on the credit account.

Although getting a cosigner or guarantor will help you get credit, it may not help you build credit in all situations. On some cosigned accounts, the creditor will report the information on the cosigner's credit report only. For this reason, ask the creditor if you can use a guarantor instead of a cosigner. It should make no difference to the creditor.

Cosigners and guarantors must understand their obligations before signing on. If you don't pay or you erase the debt in bankruptcy, the cosigner or guarantor remains fully liable. See Chapter 11, Section C.5, for more information.

| **Must a Cosigner Live Nearby?** |

Many people who apply for credit and provide a cosigner are told that their cosigners don't qualify because "it's against the law to accept an out-of-state cosigner." Hogwash. This may be the lender's policy, but it isn't the law.

The lender is concerned that if the primary borrower defaults, the lender will have to run all over the country to collect from the cosigner. Your best bet is to have the cosigner talk directly to the lender, stating something like the following:

I am fascinated that there's a law requiring that a cosigner be from the same state as the primary borrower. Can you tell me a little more about this law—like the citation? I'd like to get a copy of the law and read it. [At this point, the loan officer will admit it is a policy, not the law.]

I can understand your concern that if the primary borrower (my aunt, my brother, my friend, etc.) defaults, you will have to run all over the country to collect from me. How about if I agree in the contract to inform you of any changes in my address. Furthermore, I'll submit to the jurisdiction of your state—that is, if you have to sue me to collect this debt, I'll agree that you can sue me in your state, not just mine. [By now, the loan officer will see that the cosigner is serious about paying the debt if the primary borrower defaults and should accept the cosigner.]

3. Secured Credit Cards

Many people with poor credit histories are denied regular credit cards. If your application is rejected, consider whether you truly need a credit card. Millions of people get along just fine without them. If you decide that you really need a card—for example, you travel quite a bit and need a card to reserve hotel rooms and rent cars—then you can apply for a secured credit card. With a secured credit card, you deposit a sum of money with a bank and are given a credit card with a credit limit for a percentage of the amount you deposit—as low as 20% and as high as 120%. Depending on the bank, you'll be required to deposit as little as one hundred dollars or as much as a few thousand.

Unfortunately, secured credit cards can be expensive. Many banks charge application and processing fees in addition to an annual fee. Also the interest rate on secured credit cards is often close to 22%, while you earn only 2% or 3% on the money you deposit. And some banks have eliminated the grace period—that is, interest on your balance begins to accrue on the date you charge, not 25 days later. If you find a card with a grace period and pay your bill in full each month, you can avoid the interest charges.

Many secured credit cards have a conversion option. This lets you convert the card into a regular credit card after several months or a year, if you use the secured card responsibly. Because regular credit cards typically have lower interest rates and annual fees than secured credit cards, it's usually preferable to obtain a card with a conversion option.

Avoid 900 number advertisements for "instant credit" or other come-ons. Obtaining a secured credit card through one of these programs will probably cost you a lot—in application fees, processing fees and phone charges. Sometimes you call one 900 number and are told you must call a second or third number. These ads also frequently mislead consumers into thinking their line of credit will be higher than will be available. If you have to deposit $5,000 to get a card, your credit line may only be $2,500 to $4,000 (50% to 80%).

Shop around before getting a secured card. You may be able to get a less expensive, unsecured car just as easily. Even if you've had credit problems or filed for bankruptcy, you may still get lots of offers for unsecured cards in the mail, often with much better terms than secured cards.

Don't Get a Card Secured by Your Home. Some secured credit cards require that you put your home up as collateral. If you default, your home is in jeopardy. Avoid these cards at all costs.

Limit the Number of Credit Cards You Carry

Once you succeed in getting a credit card, you might be hungry to apply for many more cards. Not so fast. Having too much credit may have contributed to your debt problems in the first place. Ideally, you should carry one bank credit card, maybe one department store card and one gasoline card. Your inclination may be to charge everything on your bankcard and not bother using a department store or gasoline card. When creditors look in your credit file, however, they want to see that you can handle more than one credit account at a time. You don't need to build up interest charges on these cards, but use them and pay the bill in full.

Creditors frown on applicants who have a lot of open credit. So keeping many cards may mean that you'll be turned down for other credit—perhaps credit you really need. And if your credit applications are turned down, your file will contain inquiries from the companies that rejected you. Your credit file will look like you were desperately trying to get credit, something creditors never like to see.

H. Open Deposit Accounts

Creditors look for bank accounts as a sign of stability. Quite frankly, they also look for bank accounts as a source of how you will pay your bills. If you fill out a credit application and cannot provide a checking account number, you probably won't be given credit.

A savings or money market account, too, will improve your standing with creditors. Even if you never deposit additional money into the account, creditors assume that people who have savings or money market accounts use them. Having an account reassures creditors of two things: You are making an effort to build up savings, and if you don't pay your bill and the creditor must sue you to collect, it has a source from which to collect its judgment.

Just because you've had poor credit history, you shouldn't be denied an account. Shop around and compare fees, such as check writing fees, ATM fees, teller transaction fees, monthly service charges, the minimum balance to waive the monthly charge (many banks waive the minimum if you have your paycheck or other income directly deposited into the account) and the interest rates on savings. To learn more about ATM and other bank fees, visit the following websites: www.uspirg.org (U.S. Public Interest Research Group), www.consumersunion.org (Consumers Union), www.consumer-action.org (Consumer Action) and www.ftc.gov (Federal Trade Commission).

I. Work With Local Merchants

Another way to rebuild your credit is to approach a local merchant (such as a jewelry or furniture store) and arrange to purchase an item on credit. Many local stores will work with you in setting up a payment schedule, but be prepared to put down a deposit of up to 30% or to pay a high rate of interest. If you still don't qualify, the merchant might agree to give you credit if you get someone to cosign or guarantee the loan. Or you may be able to get credit by first buying an item on layaway.

Even if a local merchant won't extend you credit, she may very well let you make a purchase on a layaway plan. When you purchase an item on layaway, the seller keeps the merchandise until you fully pay for it. Only then are you entitled to pick it up. One advantage of layaway is that you don't pay interest. One disadvantage is that it may be months before you actually get the item. This might be fine if you're buying a dress for your cousin's wedding that is eight months away. This isn't so fine if your mattress is so shot that you wake up with a backache every morning.

Layaway purchases are not reported to credit bureaus. If you purchase an item on layaway and make all the payments on time, however, the store may be willing to issue you a store credit card or store credit privileges.

J. Obtain a Bank Loan

One way to rebuild your credit is to take some money you've saved and open a savings account. You ask the bank to give you a loan against the money in your account. In exchange, you have no access to your money—you give your passbook to the bank and the bank won't give you an ATM card for the account—so there's no risk to the bank if you fail to make the payments. If the bank doesn't offer these loans, called passbook loans, apply for a personal loan and offer either a cosigner or to secure it against some collateral you own.

No matter what type of loan you get, be sure you know the following:

- **Does the bank report these loan payments to credit bureaus?** This is key; the whole reason you take out the loan is to rebuild your credit. If a bank doesn't report your payments to a credit bureau, there's no reason to take out a loan.
- **What is the minimum deposit amount for a passbook loan?** Some banks won't give you a loan unless you have $3,000 in an account; others will lend you money on $50. Find a bank that fits your budget.
- **What is the interest rate?** The interest rate on the loan is usually much higher than what people with good credit pay. You will probably pay between 8% and 12% interest on the loan. Yes, this means you'll lose a little money on the transaction, but it can be worth it if you're determined to rebuild your credit.
- **What is the maximum amount you can borrow?** On passbook loans, banks won't lend you 100% of what's in your account; most will lend you between 80% and 90%. On other loans, you will face a maximum on how much you can borrow.
- **What is the repayment schedule?** Banks usually give you one to three years to repay the loan.

Some banks have no minimum monthly repayment amount on passbook loans; you could pay nothing for nearly the entire loan period and then pay the entire balance in the last month. Although you can pay back the loan in only one or two payments, don't. Pay it off over at least 12 months so that monthly installment payments appear on your credit file.

K. Don't Use a Credit Repair Clinic

You've probably seen ads for companies that claim they can fix your credit, qualify you for a loan or get you a credit card. Their pitches are tempting, especially if your credit is bad and you desperately want to buy a new car or house.

You will want to avoid these outfits, however. Many of their practices are fraudulent, deceptive and even illegal. Some have been caught stealing the credit files or Social Security numbers of people who are under 18, have died or live in out-of-the-way places like Guam or the U.S. Virgin Islands, and substituting these for the files of people with poor credit histories.

Other credit clinics break into credit bureau computers and change or erase bad credit files. Still others suggest that you create a new credit identity by applying for a nine-digit employer identification number and using it in place of your Social Security number. These schemes are just the beginning. Credit repair clinics devise new illegal methods just as soon as consumer protection agencies catch onto their old ones.

Even assuming that a credit repair company is legitimate, don't listen to its come-ons. These companies can't do anything for you that you can't do yourself. What they will do, however, is charge you between $250 and $5,000 for their unnecessary services.

Here's what credit repair clinics claim to be able to do for you:

Remove incorrect information from your credit file. You can do that yourself under the Fair Credit Reporting Act. See Section B.5, above.

Remove correct, but negative, information from your credit file. Negative items in your credit file can legally stay there for seven or ten years, as long as they are correct. No one can wave a wand and make them go away. One tactic of credit repair services is to try and take advantage of the law requiring credit bureaus to verify information if the customer disputes it. Credit repair clinics do this by challenging every item in a credit file—negative, positive or neutral—with the hope of overwhelming the credit bureau into removing information without verifying it. Credit bureaus are aware of this tactic and often dismiss these challenges on the ground that they are frivolous, a right credit bureaus have under the Fair Credit Reporting Act. You are better off getting your file and selectively challenging the outdated, incorrect and ambiguous items.

Even if the credit bureau removes information that a credit bureau had the right to include in your file, it's no doubt only a temporary removal. Most correct information reappears after 30–60 days when the creditor that first reported the information to the credit bureaus reports it.

Get outstanding debt balances and court judgments removed from your credit file. Credit repair clinics often advise debtors to pay outstanding debts if the creditor agrees to remove the negative information from your credit file. This is certainly a negotiation tactic you want to consider, but you don't need a credit repair clinic for this advice.

Get a major credit card. Credit repair clinics can give you a list of banks that offer secured credit cards. While this information is helpful in rebuilding credit, it's not worth hundreds or thousands of dollars—you can find it out for little or nothing. (See Section G.3, above.)

Federal law regulates for-profit credit repair clinics. (15 U.S.C. § 1679.) Some dubious credit repair clinics have tried to get around these regulations by setting themselves up as nonprofits, but still take your money and provide poor results. Before using any organization that claims to be a nonprofit, carefully check the company's fees, claims of what it can do and its reputation. Call the Better Business Bureau or ask for the names of satisfied customers.

Under the federal law, a credit repair clinic must:

- inform you of your rights under the Fair Credit Reporting Act
- accurately represent what it can and cannot do
- not collect any money until all promised services are performed
- provide a written contract, and
- let you cancel the contract within three days of signing.

Any lawsuit you bring against a credit repair clinic for violation of this law must be filed within five years of the violation. A court may award actual damages, punitive damages (meant to punish) and attorneys' fees.

A few states provide additional protections to consumers who use credit repair clinics. For example, some states give you more than three days to cancel the credit repair contract, require the credit repair clinic to perform the promised services within a specific amount of time and require that the credit repair clinic inform you about available nonprofit credit counseling services. The chart below lists the states that provide additional protections. To find out the details of the additional protections in your state, look up the code section listed in the chart. For information on how to do this, see Chapter 20.

In at least two states, the law limits who can provide credit repair services. In Georgia, only attorneys, nonprofit agencies, regulated lenders or banks, licensed credit bureaus or real estate brokers may provide credit repair services. (Ga. Code Ann. § 16-9-59.) In New Jersey, only nonprofit social service organizations or nonprofit credit counseling agencies may provide credit repair services. (N.J. Stat. Ann. §§ 17:16G-1, 2.)

State Laws Providing Additional Protections Concerning Credit Repair Clinics

State	Code Section	State	Code Section
Arizona	Ariz. Rev. Stat. Ann. §§ 44-1701 to 1712	Michigan	Mich. Comp. Laws §§ 445.1821 to 1826
California	Cal. Civ. Code §§ 1789.1 to .26	Minnesota	Minn. Stat. Ann. § 332.52 to .60
Colorado	Colo. Rev. Stat. § 12-14.5-101 to 113	Missouri	Mo. Ann. Stat. § 407.635 to .644
Connecticut	Conn. Gen. Stat. § 36a-700	Nebraska	Neb. Rev. Stat. §§ 45-801 to 815
Delaware	Del. Code Ann. tit. 6, §§ 2401 to 2414	Nevada	Nev. Rev. Stat. § 598.281 to .289
D.C.	D.C. Stat. §§ 28-4601 to 4608	New Hampshire	N.H. Rev. Stat. Ann. § 359-D:1 to 11
Florida	Fla. Stat. Ann. §§ 817.701 to 706	New York	N.Y. Gen. Bus. Law §§ 458-a to k
Georgia	Ga. Code Ann. § 16-9-59	North Carolina	N.C. Gen. Stat. §§ 66-220 to 226
Hawaii	Haw. Rev. Stat. § 481B-12	Ohio	Ohio Rev. Code Ann. §§ 4712.01 to .99
Idaho	Idaho Code §§ 26-2221 to 2251	Oklahoma	Okla. Stat. tit. 24, § 131 to 147
Illinois	815 Ill. Comp. Stat. Ann. § 605	Oregon	Or. Rev. Stat. Ann. §§ 646.380 to 396
Indiana	Ind. Code Ann. § 24-5-15-1 to 11	Pennsylvania	Pa. Stat. Am. tit. 73, §§ 2181 to 2192
Kansas	Kan. Stat. Ann. §§ 50-1101 to 1115	Tennessee	Tenn. Code Ann. §§ 47-18-1001 to 1011
Louisiana	La. Rev. Stat. Ann. §§ 9:3573.1 to .16	Texas	Tex. Fin. Code Ann. § 303.001 to 505
Maine	Me. Rev. Stat. Ann. Tit. 9-A, §§ 10-101 to 401	Utah	Utah Code Ann. § 13-21-1 to 9
Maryland	Md. Code Ann. Com. Law §§ 14-1901 to 1916	Virginia	Va. Code Ann. §§ 59.1-335.1 to 335.12
		Washington	Wash. Rev. Code § 19.134.010 to 900
Massachusetts	Mass. Gen. Laws Ann. Ch. 93, §§ 68A to E	West Virginia	W. Va. Code Ann. §§ 46A-6C-1 to 12
		Wisconsin	Wis. Stat. §§ 422.501 to 506

Credit Discrimination

... prejudice marks a mental land mine.

—Gloria Steinem, feminist and author,
1934-

Several powerful federal laws prohibit discrimination in credit transactions. Two of those laws, the Equal Credit Opportunity Act (ECOA) and the Fair Housing Act (FHA), cover most situations in the credit area. However, others, such as the Community Reinvestment Act, are useful as well. And, state anti-discrimination laws often provide even more protection than do federal laws.

A. The ECOA and the FHA

The ECOA (15 U.S.C. § 1691 et seq.) is quite broad in scope. It prohibits discrimination in any part of a credit transaction, including:

- applications for credit
- credit evaluation
- restrictions in granting credit such as requiring collateral or security deposits
- credit terms
- loan servicing
- treatment upon default, and
- collection procedures.

The ECOA requires a creditor to give you notice when it denies your credit application or changes the terms.

The ECOA prohibits a creditor from refusing to grant credit because of your:

- sex
- marital status
- race or color
- religion
- national origin
- age, and
- public assistance income.

The federal Fair Housing Act (FHA) (42 U.S.C. § 3601 et seq.) prohibits discrimination in residential real estate transactions. It covers loans to purchase, improve or maintain your house or loans in which your home is used as collateral. Other provisions of the FHA prohibit discrimination in the rental housing market. Like the ECOA, the FHA prohibits discrimination based on race, color, religion, national origin and sex. In addition, the FHA prohibits discrimination based on:

- familial status, and
- disability.

B. Sex Discrimination

The ECOA, FHA and many state laws prohibit credit discrimination based on sex. This category often overlaps with the "marital status" category.

Specific examples of prohibited sex discrimination include:

- rating female-specific jobs (such as waitress) lower than male-specific jobs (such as waiter) for the purpose of obtaining credit
- denying credit because an applicant's income comes from sources historically associated with women—for example, part-time jobs, alimony or child support
- requiring married women who apply for credit alone to provide information about their husbands while not requiring married men to provide information about their wives, and
- denying credit to a pregnant woman who anticipates taking a maternity leave.

However, a creditor is allowed to ask your sex when you apply for a real estate loan. The federal government collects this information for statistical purposes. A proposal by the Federal Reserve Board would allow other creditors to ask for this information as well, although provision of the information would be optional. This proposal is not yet final law.

C. Marital Status Discrimination

The ECOA and many state laws prohibit discrimination based on marital status. The FHA has a similar provision which prohibits discrimination based on familial status.

These laws prohibit a creditor from requiring an applicant's spouse to cosign on an individual account as long as no jointly held or community property is involved and the applicant meets the creditor's standards on her own.

These laws also prohibit a creditor from asking about your spouse or former spouse when you apply for your own credit, unless:

- your spouse will be permitted to use the account
- your spouse will be liable for the account
- you are relying on your spouse's income to pay the account
- you live in a community property state (Arizona, California, Idaho, Louisiana, Nevada, New Mexico, Texas, Washington or Wisconsin) or you are relaying on property located in a community property state to establish your credit worthiness, or
- you are relying on alimony, child support or other maintenance payments from a spouse to repay the creditor. (You are not required to reveal this income if you don't want the creditor to consider it in evaluating your application.)

The prohibition against marital status discrimination also means that a creditor must consider the combined incomes of an unmarried couple applying for a joint obligation. (*Markham v. Colonial Mortgage Service Co.*, 605 F.2d 566 (D.C. Cir. 1979).)

No federal law specifically prohibits credit discrimination based on sexual orientation. However, a few states prohibit this type of discrimination.

D. Race Discrimination

In general, lenders are prohibited from asking a person's race on a credit application or ascertaining it from any means (such as a credit file) other than the personal observation of a loan officer. There is one important exception to this law: A mortgage lender *must* request a person's race for the sole purpose of monitoring home mortgage applications. A proposal by the Federal Reserve Board would allow other creditors to ask for this information. This is not yet final law.

Unfortunately, prohibiting race discrimination doesn't mean it has disappeared. In fact, lenders are accused of getting around race discrimination prohibitions by redlining—that is, denying credit to residents of predominantly black neighborhoods.

In one attempt to stop redlining, Congress enacted the Home Mortgage Disclosure Act. (12 U.S.C. § 2801 et seq.) Under that law, mortgage lenders must maintain and disclose their lending practices for certain areas. Critics complain, however, that the data lenders must disclose is inadequate to analyze discrimination.

Congress also enacted the Community Reinvestment Act to address redlining and other types of discrimination. (12 U.S.C. § 2901 et seq.) The CRA requires that bank mortgage lenders demonstrate that they serve the needs of the communities which they are chartered to serve. If the bank fails to do so, bank regulators can deny the bank the right to establish branches or other activity requiring regulatory approval.

More recently, credit discrimination laws have been used to challenge what is known as "reverse redlining." In "reverse redlining," instead of avoiding certain neighborhoods, creditors target low-income, often minority neighborhoods to sell loan products with extremely high interest rates and other costly terms.

E. National Origin Discrimination

Discrimination based on national origin is prohibited under the ECOA, the FHA and most state credit discrimination laws. The exact definition of "national origin" is often unclear, but it generally refers to an individual's ancestry. A creditor might be discriminating based on national origin if he treats people with Latino or Asian surnames differently than people with European names. This category has also been interpreted to include discrimination against non-English speakers. However, it does not necessarily include noncitizens. A creditor is allowed to consider an applicant's residency status in the United States in certain circumstances.

F. Age Discrimination

The ECOA and many state laws prohibit credit discrimination based on age. This is mostly meant to protect the elderly (defined in the ECOA as people aged 62 or over). Creditors are allowed to consider age in order to give more favorable treatment to an older person (for example, considering an older person's long payment history that a younger person hasn't had time to build yet). However, age cannot be used to an older person's detriment. For example, a creditor cannot automatically refuse to consider income often associated with the elderly such as part-time employment or retirement benefits.

G. Other Discrimination Prohibited by State Law

A few states have enacted laws barring credit discrimination on grounds other than those covered by the federal laws (such as sexual orientation, mental disability or political affiliation). Check with your state consumer protection office (see Chapter 20, Section A.1) or do some research on your own (see Chapter 20, Section A) to see if there are additional grounds in your state. If you feel that a creditor has discriminated against you on one of these grounds, complain to the federal agency that regulates the particular creditor. (See Chapter 12.) Also, register your complaint with your state consumer protection office. (See Chapter 20, Section A.1.)

H. Post-Bankruptcy Discrimination

If you're considering filing for bankruptcy or you've been through bankruptcy, you may be worried that you'll suffer discrimination. Bankruptcy laws prohibit discrimination by the government. All federal, state and local governmental entities are prohibited from denying, revoking, suspending or refusing to renew a license, permit, charter, franchise or other similar grant solely because you filed for bankruptcy. (11 U.S.C. § 525(a).) In interpreting this law, judges have ruled that the government cannot:

- deny you a job or fire you
- deny or terminate your public benefits
- deny or evict you from public housing
- deny or refuse to renew your state liquor license
- exclude you from participating in a state home mortgage finance program
- exclude you from participating in a student loan program
- withhold your college transcript
- deny you a driver's license, or
- deny you a contract, such as a contract for a construction project.

In general, once any government-related debt has been canceled in bankruptcy, all acts against you that arise out of that debt also must end. For example, if a state university has withheld your transcript because you haven't paid back your student loan, once the loan is discharged (or, according to some courts, even once you file for bankruptcy, see *Loyola v. McClarty*, 234 B.R. 386 (1999)), you must be given your transcript.

Keep in mind that only government denials based on your bankruptcy are prohibited. You may be denied a loan, job or apartment for reasons unrelated to the bankruptcy (for example, you earn too much to qualify for public housing), or for reasons related to your future creditworthiness (for instance, the government concludes you won't be able to repay a student loan).

In addition, private employers may not fire you or otherwise discriminate against you solely because you filed for bankruptcy. (11 U.S.C. § 525(b).) It is unclear, however, whether or not the act prohibits employers from not hiring you because you went through bankruptcy.

Unfortunately, other forms of discrimination in the private sector aren't necessarily illegal. If you seek to rent an apartment and the landlord does a credit check and refuses to rent to you because you filed for bankruptcy, there's not much you can do other than try to show that you'll pay your rent and be a responsible tenant. If a bank refuses to give you a loan because it perceives you as a poor credit risk, you may have little recourse.

If you suffer illegal discrimination because of your bankruptcy, you can sue in state court or in the bankruptcy court. You'll probably need the assistance of an attorney.

I. What to Do If a Creditor Discriminates Against You

Although this chapter provides an overview of your rights, you may want to learn more. Chapter 20 explains how to do legal research. Also, the following websites provide information about credit discrimination:

- www.innercitypress.org
- www.aclu.org (American Civil Liberties Union)
- www.communitychange.org (nonprofit Center for Community Change), and
- www.usdoj.gov (U.S. Department of Justice).

If you think that a creditor has discriminated against you on a prohibited basis, you should complain to the Federal Trade Commission (see Chapter 12, Section F, for contact information) and the federal agency that regulates the particular creditor. If the discrimination is related to housing, contact the Department of Housing and Urban Development (http://www.hud.gov). You may also want to contact an attorney for help. ■

Help Beyond the Book

It takes nearly as much ability to know how to profit by good advice as to know how to act for one's self.

— François de La Rochefoucauld, French writer and moralist, 1613-1680

Money Troubles gives you strategies for coping with your debts. But the suggestions outlined in this book may not be enough—a bill collector might continue to harass you even after you tell her to stop, you might want help in negotiating with your creditors, you might be sued, you may want to sue a creditor or you may decide to file for bankruptcy.

This chapter suggests some ways to get more information or advice than this book provides. Before discussing the methods in more detail, here's a general piece of advice: Make all decisions yourself. By reading this book, you've taken the responsibility of getting information necessary to make informed decisions about your legal and financial affairs. If you decide to get help from others, apply this same self-empowerment principle—shop around until you find an advisor who values your competence and intelligence, and recognizes your right to make your own decisions.

A. Do Your Own Legal Research

Often, you can handle a legal problem yourself if you're willing to do some research. The trick is to know where to turn for the type of information you need. One obvious source is a lawyer. But lawyers aren't the only source for legal help. There's a lot you can do on your own. Both the Internet and law libraries are full of valuable information, such as state and federal statutes. For example, you could read the Fair Debt Collection Practices Act, find out that harassment by collection agencies is illegal, and then read court cases that have decided what types of behavior constitute harassment by a bill collector.

If you decide to take the library route, you must first find a law library that's open to the public. You might find such a library in your county courthouse or at your state capitol. Publicly funded law schools generally permit the public to use their libraries, and some private law schools grant access to their libraries—sometimes for a modest fee.

Don't overlook the reference department of the public library if you're in a large city. Many large public libraries have a fairly decent legal research collection. Also, ask about using the law library in your own lawyer's office. Some lawyers, on request, will share their books with their clients.

We don't have space here to show you how to do your own legal research in anything approaching a comprehensive fashion. To go farther, get a copy of *Legal Research: How to Find & Understand the Law*, by Stephen Elias and Susan Levinkind (Nolo). This nontechnical book gives easy-to-use, step-by-step instructions on how to find legal information. Also visit the Legal Research Center on Nolo's website at www.nolo.com.

1. State and Federal Laws

In many states, debt collection and credit reporting are governed by state and federal law. Generally, when laws overlap, the stricter laws will apply. In practical terms, this usually means that the laws that give debtors the most protection will prevail over less protective laws.

a. State Statutes

Your state consumer protection agency or attorney general's office may provide publications at little or no cost explaining state laws on debt, credit and general consumer matters. A list of state consumer protection offices appears below.

State Consumer Protection Agencies

Alabama
Consumer Affairs Division
Office of Attorney General
Alabama State House
11 South Union Street, Third Floor
Montgomery, AL 36130
334-242-7335
800-392-5658
www.ago.state.al.us

Alaska
Consumer Protection Unit
Fair Business Practices Section
Attorney General's Office
1031 West 4th Ave., Suite 200
Anchorage AK 99501
907-269-5100
www.law.state.ak.us/consumer

Arizona
Consumer Information and Complaints
Office of Attorney General
1275 West Washington Street
Phoenix, AZ 85007-2026
602-542-5763
800-352-8431
602-542-5002 (TTY)
www.ag.state.az.us

Arkansas
Consumer Protection Division
Office of the Attorney General
323 Center Street, Suite 200
Little Rock, AR 72201
501-682-2341
800-482-8982
501-682-6073 (TTY)
www.ag.state.ar.us/consumer/
home.htm

California
Public Inquiry Unit
Office of the Attorney General
Department of Justice
P.O. Box 944255
Sacramento, CA 94244-2550
916-322-3360
800-952-5225
http://caag.state.ca.us/consumers/
index.htm

Colorado
Consumer Protection Section
Office of Attorney General
1525 Sherman Street, Seventh Floor
Denver, CO 80203
303-866-5189
800-222-4444
www.state.colorado.gov

Connecticut
Consumer Credit Division
Department of Banking
260 Constitution Plaza
Hartford, CT 06103-1800
860-240-8200
800-831-7225
www.state.ct.us/dob/pages/
ccdiv.htm

Delaware
Consumer Protection Unit
Office of the Attorney General
820 North French Street, Fourth Fl.
Wilmington, DE 19801
302-577-8600
800-220-5424
www.state.de.us/attgen/
consumer.htm

District of Columbia
Department of Consumer and
Regulatory Affairs
941 North Capitol Street, N.E.
Washington, DC 20002
202-442-4400
www.dcra.dc.gov

Florida
Division of Consumer Services
Department of Agriculture and
Consumer Services
407 South Calhoun St., Mayo Building
Tallahassee, FL 32399-0800
850-488-2221
800-435-7352
http://doacs.state.fl.us/consumer

Georgia
Governor's Office of Consumer
Affairs
2 Martin Luther King, Jr. Drive,
Suite 356
Atlanta, GA 30334
404-651-8600
800-869-1123
www2.state.ga.us/gaoca

Hawaii
Office of Consumer Protection
235 S. Beretonia St., Suite 801
Leiopapa A Kamehameha Building
Honolulu, HI 96813
808-587-3222
www.state.hi.us/dcca/ocp

Idaho
Consumer Protection Unit
Office of Attorney General
P.O. Box 83720
Boise, ID 83720-0010
208-334-2424
800-432-3545
www.state.id.us/ag

Illinois
Consumer Protection Division
Office of Attorney General
100 W. Randolph Street
Chicago, IL 60601
312-814-3000
800-386-5438
800-964-3013 (TTY)
www.ag.state.il.us/consumer/
consumer.htm

State Consumer Protection Agencies (cont'd)

Indiana
Consumer Credit Division
Department of Financial Institutions
402 West Washington St., Room W066
Indianapolis, IN 46204
317-232-3955
800-382-4880
www.dfi.state.in.us/conscredit

Iowa
Consumer Protection Division
Office of Attorney General
1305 E. Walnut Street
Des Moines, IA 50319
515-281-5926
www.state.ia.us/government/ag/consumer.html

Kansas
Consumer Protection Division
Office of Attorney General
120 S.W. Tenth Street, 2nd Floor
Topeka, KS 66612-1597
785-296-3751
800-432-2310
785-291-3767 (TTY)
www.ink.org/public/ksag/contents/consumer/main.htm

Kentucky
Consumer Protection Division
Office of Attorney General
1024 Capitol Center Drive
Frankfort, KY 40601
502-696-5389
888-423-8257
www.law.state.ky.us/cp

Louisiana
Consumer Protection Section
Office of Attorney General
P.O. Box 94005
Baton Rouge, LA 70804-9005
225-342-9638
800-351-4889
www.ag.state.la.us/consumer.shtml

Maine
Consumer Information and Mediation Service
Public Protection Division
Office of the Attorney General
State House, Station No. 6
Augusta, ME 04333-0006
207-626-8849
207-626-8865 (TTY)
www.state.me.us./ag/consumer.htm

Maryland
Consumer Protection Division
Office of Attorney General
200 St. Paul Pl., 6th Floor
Baltimore, MD 21202-2022
410-576-6550
888-743-0023
www.oag.state.md.us/consumer

Massachusetts
Office of Consumer Affairs and Business Regulation
10 Park Plaza, Suite 5170
Boston, MA 02116
617-727-7780 (hotline)
617-727-7755
888-288-3757
www.state.ma.us/consumer

Michigan
Consumer Protection Division
Office of Attorney General
P.O. Box 30213
Lansing, MI 48909
517-373-1140
877-765-8388
www.ag.state.mi.us/cp

Minnesota
Consumer Connection
Office of Attorney General
1400 NCL Tower
445 Minnesota Street
St. Paul, MN 55101-2130
651-296-3353
800-657-3787
651-297-7206 (TTY)
800-366-4812 (TTY)
www.ag.state.mn.us/consumer

Mississippi
Consumer Protection Division
Office of Attorney General
P.O. Box 22947
Jackson, MS 39225-2947
601-359-4230
800-281-4418
www.ago.state.ms.us/divisions/consumer/consumer-protection.html

Missouri
Consumer Protection Division
Office of Attorney General
P.O. Box 899
Jefferson City, MO 65102
573-751-3321
800-392-8222
www.ago.state.mo.us/fraud.htm

State Consumer Protection Agencies (cont'd)

Montana
Legal and Consumer Affairs
Department of Commerce
1424 Ninth Ave.
P.O. Box 200501
Helena, MT 59690
406-444-3553
www.mtfinanceonline.com

Nebraska
Consumer Protection Division
Office of Attorney General
2115 State Capitol Building
P.O. Box 98920
Lincoln, NE 68509-8920
402-471-2682
800-727-6432
www.nol.org/home/ago

Nevada
Consumer Affairs Division
Department of Business and Industry
1850 E. Sahara Ave., Suite 101
Las Vegas, NV 89104
702-486-7355
www.fyiconsumer.org

New Hampshire
Consumer Protection and Antitrust
  Bureau
Department of Justice
33 Capitol Street
Concord, NH 03301-6397
603-271-3641
www.state.nh.us/nhdoj/
  consumer/cpb.html

New Jersey
Division of Consumer Affairs
Department of Law and Public
  Safety
124 Halsey Street
Newark, NJ 07102
973-504-6200
900-242-5846
973-504-6588 (TDD)
www.state.nj.us/lps/ca

New Mexico
Consumer Protection Division
Office of Attorney General
P.O. Drawer 1508
Santa Fe, NM 87504-1508
505-827-6060
800-678-1508
www.ago.state.nm.us/protection/
  consumer_protection.html

New York
Consumer Protection Board
5 Empire State Plaza, Suite 2101
Albany, NY 12223-1556
518-474-1471
518-474-8583 (Complaint Unit)
800-697-1220
800-788-9898 (TTY)
www.consumer.state.ny.us

North Carolina
Consumer Protection Section
Department of Justice
P.O. Box 629
Raleigh, NC 27602-0629
919-716-6000
www.jus.state.nc.us/cpframe.htm

North Dakota
Consumer Protection Division
Office of Attorney General
600 East Boulevard
Bismarck, ND 58505-0040
701-328-3404
800-472-2600
www.ag.state.nd.us/ndag

Ohio
Consumer Protection Section
Office of Attorney General
State Office Tower
30 East Broad Street, 17th Floor
Columbus, OH 43215-3428
614-466-4320
800-282-0515
www.ag.state.oh.us/
  consumer/consumer.htm

Oklahoma
Consumer Protection Unit
Office of Attorney General
4545 N. Lincoln Blvd., Suite 260
Oklahoma City, OK 73105-3498
405-521-2029
www.oag.state.ok.us

Oregon
Financial Fraud/Consumer Protection Section
1162 Court Street, NE
Salem, OR 97310
503-378-4320
503-229-5576 (Portland toll-free)
877-877-9392
www.doj.state.or.us/FinFraud/
  welcome3.htm

Pennsylvania
Bureau of Consumer Protection
Office of Attorney General
Strawberry Square, 14th Floor
Harrisburg, PA 17120
717-787-9707
800-441-2555
www.attorneygeneral.gov/ppd/bcp

Rhode Island
Consumer Protection Unit
Department of Attorney General
150 S. Main Street
Providence, RI 02903
401-274-4400
800-852-7776
401-453-0410 (TTY)
www.riag.state.ri.us/consumer

South Carolina
Department of Consumer Affairs
P.O. Box 5757
3600 Forest Drive
Columbia, SC 29250
803-734-4200
800-922-1594
www.state.sc.us/consumer

State Consumer Protection Agencies (cont'd)

South Dakota
Division of Consumer Affairs
Office of Attorney General
500 East Capitol Ave.
Pierre, SD 57501-5070
605-773-4400
800-300-1986
www.state.sd.us/attorney/con-
sumer

Tennessee
Division of Consumer Affairs
Department of Commerce and
Insurance
500 James Robertson Parkway,
Fifth Floor
Nashville, TN 37243-0600
615-741-4737
800-342-8385
www.state.tn.us/consumer

Texas
Consumer Protection Division
Office of Attorney General
P.O. Box 12548
Austin, TX 78711-2548
512-463-2185
800-621-0508
www.oag.state.tx.us/
consumer/consumer.htm

Utah
Division of Consumer Protection
Department of Commerce
160 E. 300 South
Box 146704
Salt Lake City, UT 84114-6704
801-530-6601
800-721-7233
www.commerceutah.gov/dcp/
index.html

Vermont
Consumer Assistance
Office of Attorney General
104 Morrill Hall-UVM
Burlington, VT 05405
802-656-3183
800-649-2424
www.state.vt.us/atg/consumer.htm

Virginia
Office of Consumer Affairs
Department of Agriculture and
Consumer Services
1100 Bank St.
Richmond, VA 23219
804-786-2042
800-552-9963
www.vdacs.state.va.us/consumers/
index.html

Washington
Consumer Resource Center
Office of Attorney General
P.O. Box 40118
Olympia, WA 98504-0118
360-733-6210
800-551-4636
800-276-9883 (TDD)
www.wa.gov/ago/consumer

West Virginia
Consumer Protection Division
Office of Attorney General
1900 Kanawha Blvd., Room 29E
Charleston, WV 25305-9924
304-558-8986
800-368-8808
www.state.wv.us/wvag

Wisconsin
Bureau of Consumer Protection
Department of Agriculture,
Trade and Consumer Protection
2811 Agriculture Drive
P.O. Box 8911
Madison, WI 53708-8911
608-224-4949
800-422-7128
608-224-5058 (TTY)
http://datcp.state.wi.us/core/
consumerinfo

Wyoming
Consumer Affairs Section
Office of Attorney General
Herschler Building, East
122 West 5th Street
Cheyenne, WY 82002
307-777-7874
800-438-5799
www.attorneygeneral.state.wy.us/
consumer.htm

We refer to many of the state laws affecting debtors throughout this book and include citations so that you can do additional research. State laws or codes are collected in volumes and are available in many public libraries and in most law libraries. Depending on the state, statutes may be organized by subject matter or by title number ("chapter"), with each title covering a particular subject matter, or simply numbered sequentially, without regard to subject matter.

"Annotated codes" contain not only all the text of the laws (as do the regular codes), but also a brief summary of some of the court decisions interpreting each law and often references to treatises and articles that discuss the law. Annotated codes have comprehensive indexes by topic, and are kept up-to-date with paperback supplements ("pocket parts") stuck in a pocket inside the back cover of each volume.

b. Federal Statutes and Regulations

Congress has enacted laws, and federal agencies such as the Federal Trade Commission have adopted regulations, covering most of the topics in this book. We refer to many federal agencies and include citations for many of the federal laws affecting debtors throughout this book. The U.S. Code is the starting place for research on most federal laws. It consists of 50 separate numbered titles. Each title covers a specific subject matter. For example, Title 15 contains the Consumer Credit Act; Title 11 contains the Bankruptcy Act. Two versions of the U.S. Code are published in annotated form: *United States Code Annotated* (West Publishing Co.) and the *United States Code Service* (Bancroft-Whitney/ Lawyer's Co-op). Most law libraries carry both.

Most federal regulations are published in the *Code of Federal Regulations* (C.F.R.), organized by subject into 50 separate titles.

2. Court Decisions

Sometimes the answer to a legal question cannot be found in a statute. This happens when:

- court cases and opinions have greatly expanded or explained the statute, taking it beyond its obvious or literal meaning, or
- the law that applies to your question has been made by judges, not legislators.

a. Court Decisions That Explain Statutes

Statutes and ordinances do not explain themselves. For example, the Fair Debt Collection Practices Act prohibits collection agencies from using the telephone to harass you, but that statute doesn't define harassment. Chances are, however, that others before you have had the same questions, and they may have come up in the context of a lawsuit. If a judge interpreted the statute and wrote an opinion on the matter, that written opinion, once published, will become part of "the law" as much as the statute itself. If a higher court (an appellate court) has also examined the question, then its opinion will rule.

To find out if there are written court decisions that interpret a particular statute or ordinance, look in an "annotated code." If you find a case that seems to answer your question, it's crucial to make sure that the decision you're reading is still "good law"— that a more recent opinion from a higher court has not reached a different conclusion. To make sure that you are relying on the latest and highest judicial pronouncement, you must use the library research tool known as *Shepard's*. *Legal Research: How to Find and Understand the Law*, by Stephen Elias and Susan Levinkind (Nolo), has a good, easy-to-follow explanation of how to use the *Shepard's* system to expand and update your research.

b. Court Decisions That Make Law

Many laws that govern the way creditors must conduct their business do not have an initial starting point in a statute. These laws are entirely court-made, and are known as "common" law. An example in many states are laws that prohibit creditors that are collecting their own debts from harassing debtors. (Remember, the federal Fair Debt Collection Practices Act applies only to collection agencies.)

Researching common law is more difficult than statutory law, because you do not have the launching pad of a statute. With a little perseverance, however, you can certainly find your way to the cases that have developed and explained the legal concept you wish to understand. A good beginning is to ask the librarian for any "practice guides" written in the field of debtor-creditor relations. These are outlines of the law, written for lawyers, that are kept up-to-date and are designed to get you quickly to key information. Because they are so popular and easy to use, they are usually kept behind the reference counter and cannot be checked out. More sophisticated research techniques, such as using a set of books called "Words and Phrases," (which sends you to cases based on key words) are explained in the book *Legal Research*, mentioned above.

c. How to Read a Case Citation

If you find a citation to a case that looks important, you may want to read the opinion. You'll need the title of the case and its citation, which is like an address for the set of books, volume and page where the case can be found. Ask the law librarian for help.

Although it may look about as decipherable as hieroglyphics, once understood, a case citation gives lots of useful information in a small space. It tells you the names of the people or companies involved, the volume of the reporter (series of books) in which the case is published, the page number on which it begins and the year in which the case was decided.

3. Use Background Resources

If you want to research a legal question but don't know where to begin, several resources are available on consumers' and debtors' rights issues. The best all-around sources are the publications of the National Consumer Law Center (www.consumerlaw.org). Their very thorough and annually updated volumes include the following titles:

- *Consumer Bankruptcy Law and Practice*
- *Consumer Class Actions*

- *Student Loan Law*
- *Consumer Arbitration Agreements*
- *Consumer Banking and Payments Law*
- *Credit Discrimination*
- *Fair Credit Reporting Act*
- *Fair Debt Collection*
- *Repossessions and Foreclosures*
- *Consumer Warranty Law*
- *Truth in Lending*
- *Unfair and Deceptive Acts and Practices*
- *The Cost of Credit*
- *Auto Fraud,* and
- *Access to Utility Service.*

Unfortunately, not all law libraries have these volumes. You may need to call several law and public libraries until you find a library that does carry them. Or, call the National Consumer Law Center for more information (617-542-9595).

4. Online Legal Research

If you have access to the Internet, there is a good deal of legal research you can accomplish using your computer. But you can't do it all—not every court decision or state statute is available online. Furthermore, unless you know what you are looking for—the case name and citation or the code section—you may have difficulty finding it.

a. Finding Debt, Credit and Consumer Information Online

Often, the best place to start your quest is with websites that contain information about debt, credit, finance, consumer protection and bankruptcy. Here are a few good ones:

- **www.nolo.com**
  Nolo's online site includes a vast amount of legal information for consumers, including articles on debt, credit and bankruptcy, FAQs (frequently asked questions) and Ask Auntie Nolo legal questions.
- **www.myvesta.org**
  Myvesta.org (formerly Debt Counselors of

America), is a nonprofit online resource dedicated to helping people get out of debt. Their advice covers budgeting, financial recovery, debt management and debt payoff. The site is updated daily, free, lists software, publications and information, contains special programs to help you get out of debt and has a debt forum where you can post your specific questions for its counselors.

- **www.bbb.org/complaints**
  The Better Business Bureau allows you to file consumer complaints online.
- **www.pueblo.gsa.gov**
  The Consumer Information Center provides the latest in consumer news as well as many publications of interest to consumers, including the *Consumer Information Catalog* and a free consumer handbook.
- **www.fdic.gov**
  www.ftc.gov
  www.federalreserve.gov
  The Federal Deposit Insurance Corporation, Federal Trade Commission and Federal Reserve Board offer consumer protection rules, guides and publications.
- **www.irs.ustreas.gov**
  The Internal Revenue Service provides tax information, forms and publications. Another feature lets you post your individual question to the IRS; you'll get an email response in a few days. (The information is fairly generic but will help you get started researching a question.)

b. Finding Statutes and Regulations Online

You can find federal statutes, the entire *Code of Federal Regulations* and most state statutes by visiting Nolo's Legal Research Center at www.nolo.com/research/index.html. Your best bet for state regulations is Findlaw at www.findlaw.com. Findlaw also offers federal statutes and regulations, and state statutes.

If you are looking for a brand new statute online, you may have to search for recently enacted legislation, since there is often a delay between the time a statute is passed and the time it is included in the

overall compilation of laws. Almost every state maintains its own website for pending and recently enacted legislation. These sites contain not only the most current version of a bill, but also its history. To find your state's website, see "Finding Court and Government Agency Websites," below. Finally, the United States Congress maintains a website at http://thomas.loc.gov that contains all pending federal bills.

Finding Court and Government Agency Websites

Many courts and government agencies provide statutes and case law, plus other useful information such as forms, answers to frequently asked questions and downloadable pamphlets on various legal topics. To find to your state's website, open your browser and type in www.state.<your state's postal code>.us. (Your state's postal code is the two letter abbreviation you use for mailing addresses. For example, NY is the postal code for New York.)

Nolo's Legal Research Center (found at www.nolo.com) provides links to courts across the country and access to small claims court information for most states. You can also find local, state and federal court websites on the National Center for State Courts' website at www.ncsconline.org/D_kis/info_court_web_sites.html. dni.us/court/sites/courts.htm. The federal judiciary's website at www.uscourts.gov lists federal court websites.

---

c. Finding Cases on the Web

If you are looking for a case, and know the case name or citation, you may be able to find it online.

State cases: If the case is recent (within the last few years), you may be able to find it for free on the Internet. A good place to start is FindLaw at www.findlaw.com. Also, many state websites now publish recent cases. See "Finding Court and Government Agency Websites," above, for information on how to find your state's website.

If the case is older, you can still find it on the Internet, but you will probably have to pay a private company for access to its database. VersusLaw at www.versuslaw.com maintains an excellent library of older state court cases. You can do unlimited research on VersusLaw for $8.95 per month. You can also get state cases online through the Lexis and Westlaw databases. (For more information, see "Using Westlaw and Lexis to Do Legal Research on the Web," below.)

U.S. Supreme Court cases: Nolo's Legal Research Center, available at www.nolo.com, provides U.S. Supreme Court cases decided within the last hundred years.

Other federal cases: FindLaw, at www.findlaw.com, contains cases decided by the federal Circuit Courts of Appeal within the last four or five years, some bankruptcy opinions and very recent tax court cases. The Cornell Law School Legal Information Institute at www.law.cornell.edu provides access to all federal appellate court cases, some District Court cases and some bankruptcy opinions. VersusLaw (explained above) also has some U.S. District Court cases and some bankruptcy opinions. If you can't find the case you're looking for on one of these websites, your best bet is to use Westlaw or Lexis.

Using Lexis and Westlaw to Do Legal Research on the Web

Lexis and Westlaw are the chief electronic legal databases which contain the full text of many of the legal resources found in law libraries, including almost all reported cases from state and federal courts, all federal statutes, the statutes of most states, federal regulations, law review articles, commonly used treatises and practice manuals.

Although Westlaw and Lexis databases are available over the Internet, subscriptions are pricey. However, both offer some free and some fee-based services to non-subscribers that are both helpful and reasonably priced (between $9 and $10 per document). To find out more about these services, visit Westlaw at www.westlaw.com/ or Lexis at www.lexis.com.

B. Lawyers

As a general rule, you should get an attorney involved in your situation if the dispute is of high enough value to justify the attorney's fees. For example, if a you owe a creditor $1,200, but the goods were defective and you don't feel you should have to pay, and an attorney will cost $800, you're probably better off handling the matter yourself, even though this increases the risk that the creditor will win. If, however, you owe $10,000 and the attorney will cost $1,000, hiring the attorney may make sense. You also may want to consult with an attorney if the stakes are high—for example, you are facing foreclosure.

1. What Lawyers Can Do for You

There are three basic ways a lawyer can help you:

Consultation and advice. A lawyer can analyze your situation and advise you on your best plan of action. Ideally, the lawyer will describe all your alternatives so you can make your own choices—but keep on your toes. Many lawyers will subtly steer you in the direction the attorney wants you to go, often the one that nets the attorney the largest fee.

Negotiation. The lawyer can help you negotiate with your creditors. Lawyers often possess negotiating skills, especially if they negotiate a lot in their practice. If the creditor has an attorney, that attorney may be more apt to settle with your lawyer than with you. And an attorney's letterhead itself lets a creditor know you are serious about settling.

Representation. If you are sued or want to sue, especially if you have a good defense or a claim of your own against the creditor, you may want to hire a lawyer to represent you. This, however, could get expensive, so be sure you want to be represented by a lawyer before you hire one. You also may consider hiring a lawyer to assist you if you decide to file for bankruptcy. While most bankruptcies are routine and debtors can often represent themselves when armed with a good self-help book, some cases get complex and need the involvement of a bankruptcy lawyer.

2. How to Find a Lawyer

Here are several ways to find a lawyer:

Legal Aid. Legal Aid offices offer legal assistance in many areas, especially for people with debt problems. To qualify for Legal Aid, you must be low income. Usually that means your household income cannot exceed 135% of the federal poverty level, although some have different guidelines. To find a Legal Aid office, look in your local phone book.

Legal clinic. Many law schools sponsor legal clinics and provide free legal advice to consumers. Some legal clinics have the same income requirements as Legal Aid offices—others offer free services to low- to moderate-income people.

Personal referrals. This is the most common approach. If you know someone who was pleased with the services of a lawyer, call that lawyer first. If that lawyer doesn't handle debtor's rights matters or can't take your case, he may recommend someone else. Be careful, however, when selecting a lawyer from a personal referral. That a lawyer performed satisfactorily in one situation doesn't guarantee she'll do so in your case.

Group legal plans. Some unions, employers and consumer action organizations offer group plans to their members or employees, who can obtain comprehensive legal assistance free or for low rates. If you're a member of such a plan, check with it first for a lawyer.

Prepaid legal insurance. Prepaid legal insurance plans offer some services for a low monthly fee and charge more for additional or different work. Participating lawyers may use the plan as a way to get clients who are attracted by the low-cost, basic services, and then sell them more expensive services. If the lawyer recommends an expensive course of action, get a second opinion before you agree.

But if a plan offers extensive free advice, or you can use the lawyer to write several letters to your hounding creditors, your membership fee may be worth the consultation you receive or the letters the lawyers write.

There's no guarantee that the lawyers available through these plans are of the best caliber. Check out the plan carefully before signing up. Ask about the plan's complaint system, whether you get to choose your lawyer and whether or not the lawyer will represent you in court.

Consumer organizations. Many national or local consumer organizations can recommend an attorney who handles debtors' rights cases. One place to start is the National Association of Consumer Advocates (www.NACA.net). In some large urban areas, consumer advocates publish guides of consumer-oriented legal organizations and/or lawyers. Check the library to see if it has such a guide.

Lawyer referral panels. Most county bar associations will give out the names of attorneys who practice in your area. But bar associations often fail to provide meaningful screening for the attorneys listed, which means those who participate may not be the most experienced or competent.

3. What to Look for in a Lawyer

No matter what approach you take to finding a lawyer, here are three suggestions on how to make sure you have the best possible working relationship.

First, fight the urge you may have to surrender your will and be intimidated by a lawyer. You should be the one who decides what you feel comfortable doing about your legal and financial affairs. Keep in mind that you're hiring the lawyer to perform a service for you; shop around if the price or personality isn't right.

Second, you must be as comfortable as possible with any lawyer you hire. When making an appointment, ask to talk directly to the lawyer. If you can't, this may give you a hint as to how accessible he is.

If you do talk directly to the lawyer, ask some specific questions. Do you get clear, concise answers? If not, try someone else. If the lawyer says little except to suggest that he handle the problem—with a substantial fee—watch out. You're talking with someone who doesn't know the answer and won't admit it, or someone who pulls rank on the basis of professional standing. Don't be a passive client or hire a lawyer who wants you to be one. If the lawyer admits to not knowing an answer, that isn't necessarily bad. In most cases, the lawyer must do some research.

Also, pay attention to how the lawyer responds to your having considerable information. If you've read this book, you're already better informed about debtors' rights laws than most clients are. Many lawyers are threatened when the client knows too much—or, in some cases, anything.

Once you find a lawyer you like, make an hour-long appointment to discuss your situation fully. Your goal at the initial conference is to find out what the lawyer recommends and how much it will cost. Go home and think about the lawyer's suggestions. If they don't make complete sense or if you have other reservations, call someone else.

Finally, keep in mind that the lawyer works for you. Once you hire a lawyer, you have the absolute right to switch to another—or to fire the lawyer and handle the matter yourself—at any time, for any reason.

cases they think they have a good chance of winning on contingency.

If you plan to hire a lawyer to help you file for bankruptcy, expect to pay between $350 to $1,000, or more if your bankruptcy case is not simple. Many bankruptcy attorneys let you pay in installments. Also, the attorney must report the fee to the bankruptcy court for approval. The court can make the attorney justify the fee if it's high. This rarely happens, however, because attorneys know what local bankruptcy judges will allow and set their fees accordingly.

One final word: No matter why you hire a lawyer, and for whatever fee, be sure the lawyer puts the fee arrangement in a written contract for you to sign. If the lawyer doesn't mention a written fee agreement, ask about one. If you hire a lawyer to help you with your debt problems, you don't want the financial arrangement to be misunderstood so that the lawyer's fee just becomes another debt you can't or won't pay.

4. How Much Lawyers Charge

If all you want is a consultation with an attorney to find out where you stand and what options you have, be sure to find out the hourly fee ahead of time. Some charge as little as $75 an hour, while others charge $300 or more per hour.

If you want the lawyer to do some negotiating, the fee could pile up. A letter doesn't take that long to write, however, and as long as you are clear about what you want the lawyer to do and not do, you can keep the bill low.

If you're sued by a creditor and hire a lawyer to represent you, the lawyer's fee will probably add up fast. A few lawyers might represent you for a flat fee, for example $500, but most charge by the hour. If you have a claim against a creditor and might win damages—for example, if a bill collector posted your name throughout the town as a "deadbeat"—the lawyer might take your case on a contingency fee basis. That means the lawyer gets paid only if you win your case. If you don't win, the lawyer doesn't get a cent. Most lawyers tend to take only those

C. Debt and Credit Counseling Agencies

Credit and debt counseling agencies are nonprofit organizations funded primarily by major creditors, such as department stores, credit card companies and banks, who can work with you to help you re-pay your debts and improve your financial picture.

To use a credit or debt counseling agency to help you pay your debts, you must have some disposable income. A counselor contacts your creditors to let them know that you've sought assistance and need more time to pay. Based on your income and debts, the counselor, with your creditors, decides on how much you pay. You then make one payment each month to the counseling agency, which in turn pays your creditors. The agency asks the creditors to re-turn a small percentage of the money received to the agency office to fund its work. This arrangement is generally referred to as a debt management program.

Some creditors will make overtures to help you when you're on a debt management program. But few creditors will make interest concessions, such as waiving a portion of the accumulated interest to help you repay the principal. More likely, you'll get late fees dropped and the opportunity to reinstate your credit if you successfully complete a debt management program.

The combination of high consumer debt and easy access to information (the Internet) has led to an explosion in the number of credit and debt counseling agencies ready to offer you help. Some provide limited services, such as budgeting and debt repay-ment, while others offer a range of services, from debt counseling to financial planning. Shop care-fully. Some of these agencies were established primarily to sell you products and services and don't provide good quality counseling.

Participating in a credit or debt counseling agency's debt management program is a little bit like filing for Chapter 13 bankruptcy. (See Chapter 16, Section E.) Working with a credit or debt counseling agency has one advantage: no bankruptcy will appear on your credit record.

But a debt management program also has two disadvantages when compared to Chapter 13 bank-ruptcy. First, if you miss a payment, Chapter 13 protects you from creditors who would start collection actions. A debt management program has no such protection and any one creditor can pull the plug on your plan. Also, a debt management program plan usually requires that your debts be paid in full. In Chapter 13 bankruptcy, you're required to pay the value of your nonexempt property, which can mean that you pay only a small fraction of your unsecured debts.

Critics of credit and debt counseling agencies point out that they get most of their funding from creditors. (Some offices also receive grants from pri-vate agencies such as the United Way and federal agencies including the Department of Housing and Urban Development.) Nevertheless, critics claim that counselors cannot be objective in counseling debtors to file for bankruptcy if they know the office won't receive any funds. Critics also charge that these agencies tend to focus on unsecured creditors (those are the ones that pay the agencies' bills) and neglect secured creditors.

In response to this and other consumer concerns, credit and debt counseling agencies accredited by the National Foundation for Consumer Credit (the majority of agencies are) reached an agreement with the Federal Trade Commission to disclose the following to consumers:

- that creditors fund a large portion of the cost of their operations
- that the credit agency must balance the ability of the debtor to make payments with the requirements of the creditors that fund the office, and
- a reliable estimate of how long it will take a debtor to repay his or her debts under a debt management program.

When choosing a credit and debt counseling agency, look for a company that is truly a nonprofit. Many for-profit outfits use names that sound like a nonprofit, such as "foundation," to confuse you. And your inquiry shouldn't stop there. Many of the unscrupulous credit and debt counseling companies have nonprofit status. These companies often try to get you to pay "voluntary contributions" up front or pay other fees. At a minimum, always ask about fees before agreeing to give your business to a particular counselor. And review the "Questions to Ask a Credit or Debt Counseling Agency," below.

Consumer Credit Counseling Service (CCCS) is the oldest credit or debt counseling agency in the country. Actually, CCCS isn't one agency. CCCS is the primary operating name of many credit and debt counseling agencies affiliated with the National Foundation for Consumer Credit (NFCC).

CCCS may charge you a small monthly fee (an average of about $9) for setting up a repayment plan. CCCS also helps people make monthly budgets, and sometimes charges a one-time fee of about $20. If you can't afford the fee, CCCS will waive it. In most CCCS offices, the primary service offered is a debt management program. A few offices have additional services, such as helping you save money toward buying a house or reviewing your credit report.

CCCS has more than 1,100 offices, located in every state. Look in the phone book to find the one nearest you or contact the main office at 801 Rueder Road, Suite 900, Silver Spring, MD 20910, 800-388-2227 (voice), or visit www.nfcc.org.

Questions to Ask a Credit or Debt Counseling Agency

Debt Counselors of America suggests that you ask the following questions before using any counseling agency.

1. **Will you send me information on your agency and programs?** There is no reason you should be required to provide account numbers and balances or any information other than a name and mailing address before an agency will agree to send you information about itself. Some agencies require account numbers and balances to see if you have enough debt for them to be interested in helping you. If an agency won't provide you with information about its programs, consider that a warning sign.

2. **Do you pay referral fees?** No agency should pay referral fees to outside parties or pay agents to enroll consumers into a debt management program. This may be a warning signal that the agency is simply interested in placing as many consumers as possible into a repayment program, rather than providing educational assistance.

3. **What should I do if I cannot afford the minimum payment?** A good agency will not quickly dismiss you or tell you to file bankruptcy simply because you cannot meet their minimum debt management program payment. Ask about hardship programs.

4. **What kind of training do you have that makes you qualified to assist me?** A home study course or a few hours of class are not sufficient training. A good counseling agency provides its counselors with regular training from lawyers, Certified Financial Planners and other experts.

5. **What kind of security measures do you take to protect my information?** It is important that the agency you select has sufficient security in place to protect your confidential information.

6. **Can I get up-to-date, regular reports of the status of my accounts?** If access is by telephone only, will a knowledgeable person be available when you call to give you the information you need?

7. **Will you answer my general questions, even if I am not in your repayment program?** Ask any agency you are considering for advice if it can assist you with information even if you are not going to enroll in its debt management program.

8. **What kinds of educational programs and services do you provide?** Educational seminars are great but you might need some hard and fast answers about your situation without having to wait for the next seminar.

9. **Is there a minimum amount of debt I have to have in order to work with you?** The answer should always be "no." If an agency is there to help, it should not turn you away because you do not have enough debt.

10. **Will you help me with all my debts?** Some agencies offer little assistance for secured debts like car payments or mortgages, or government debts like taxes and student loans. Make sure you'll receive full service.

11. **Is there a mandatory up-front fee?** Some agencies charge a mandatory up-front fee for their debt management program—as much as $250 or more. These fees may be so high that they prevent you from getting assistance.

12. **Will you sell my name or address to outside parties?** Be sure you know the agency's privacy policy. Ask before your name and address appears on a mailing list sold to outside organizations.

13. **How often do you pay creditors?** Although your creditors will be paid only once a month, make sure the agency sends payments out at least weekly. Your payment should not sit at the agency for a month waiting for the next payment cycle.

APPENDIX

Glossary

This glossary defines certain terms that appear frequently in this book.

Acceleration clause. A provision in a contract requiring the debtor to pay the entire balance of the contract immediately because of a failure to meet some condition, such as a failure to make payments on time.

Arrears. Arrears is a general term used to describe any loan payment or debt that is past due. It's most often used to describe back-owed child support or alimony. Some people use the term "arrearages," which means the same thing.

Balloon payment. A balloon payment is a final lump sum payment on an installment contract, such as a mortgage or car loan, which is larger than the earlier payments.

Bankruptcy. Bankruptcy is a legal proceeding in which you are relieved from paying your debts. There are two kinds of bankruptcies for individuals —Chapter 7 and Chapter 13. In Chapter 7 bankruptcy, you may be required to give up some property in exchange for the erasure of your debts. In Chapter 13 bankruptcy, you don't have to give up any property, but you must pay off a portion of your debts over three to five years. At the end of the three- to five-year period, the balance of what you owe is wiped out.

Collateral. Collateral is property pledged as security for repayment of a secured debt.

Cosigner. A cosigner is a person who signs her name to a loan agreement or credit application. If the primary debtor does not pay, the cosigner is fully responsible for the loan or debt. Many people use cosigners to qualify for a loan or credit card.

Credit rating. A credit rating is the point system used by a credit bureau to indicate a person's payment history.

Credit repair. Credit repair refers to the steps a person takes to get outdated and incorrect information removed from a credit file. Credit repair can also include removing negative information from a file. A credit repair company refers to a questionable for-profit business that charges substantial money and claims to clean up credit files.

Credit scoring. Credit scoring is sometimes referred to as risk scoring. When you apply for a loan or line of credit, the lender will total up a score to determine if you qualify—by awarding points based on credit factors. Although most lenders consider between ten and 25 factors, the standard used for scoring applicants depends on the lender and the type of loan.

Default judgment. If you are sued and you do not file papers in response to the lawsuit within in the time allowed, the plaintiff (the person who sued you) can ask the court to enter a default judgment against you. When a default judgment is entered, you have lost the case. You can try to get the default judgment set aside, but it can be difficult to do so.

Deficiency balance. A deficiency balance is the difference between the amount you owe a creditor who has foreclosed on your house or repossessed an item of personal property, and the amount that the sale of the property brings in.

Discharge. When a bankruptcy court erases your debts, it is called a discharge.

Exempt property or exemption. The items of property you are allowed to keep if a creditor gets a judgment against you or you file for bankruptcy are called your exempt property or exemptions.

Foreclosure. Foreclosure is the right of a mortgage lender or other creditor with a lien on your house, such as the IRS or a construction worker you didn't pay, to force the sale of your house in order to recover what you owe.

Guarantor. A guarantor is a person who pledges to repay a loan or debt in the event the primary debtor does not pay. Many people use guarantors to qualify for a loan or credit card. By using a guarantor (and making regular payments), the primary debtor can improve her credit rating.

Installment contract. An installment contract is a written agreement to pay for goods or services purchased, in payments of principal and interest, at regularly scheduled intervals.

Judgment. A judgment is the decision issued by a court at the end of a lawsuit. If you are sued and either don't file papers in response within the time allowed or file papers but eventually lose the case, the plaintiff (the person who sued you) will get a judgment. To attach your wages or put a lien on your property, virtually all creditors need a court judgment.

Judgment creditor. A creditor who has sued you and obtained a court judgment is called a judgment creditor.

Judgment debtor. Once a creditor sues you and gets a court judgment, you may be referred to as a judgment debtor.

Judgment proof. Being judgment proof means that you have little or no property or income that a creditor can legally take to collect on a judgment, now or in the foreseeable future.

Lien. A lien is a notice a creditor attaches to your property that tells the world that you owe the creditor money. If a creditor puts a lien on your property, you won't be able to sell it without paying off the creditor. This is because the lien makes the property's "title" (ownership history) cloudy and a new owner won't buy property if the title is unclear.

Necessities. Necessities are articles needed to sustain life, such as food, clothing, medical care and shelter.

Nonexempt property. Nonexempt property is the property you are at risk of losing if a creditor gets a judgment against you or you file for bankruptcy.

Open-ended account. An open-ended account is one which has no fixed date by which you must pay off the balance, though you often have to make a minimum payment each month. Credit card, department store and gasoline accounts are all examples of open-ended charges.

Post-judgment interest. Post-judgment interest is interest on a court judgment that a creditor may add from the time the judgment is entered in the court clerk's record until you pay it.

Pre-judgment attachment. A pre-judgment attachment is a legal procedure which lets an unsecured creditor tie up property before obtaining a court judgment. The attachment freezes the property—you can't sell it, spend it (in the case of money) or give it away. If the creditor wins the lawsuit, the property covered by the attachment can be used to pay the judgment.

Pre-judgment interest. Pre-judgment interest is the interest a creditor is entitled to collect under a loan agreement or by operation of law before obtaining a court judgment.

Prepayment penalty. A prepayment penalty is a fee imposed by some lenders in the event you pay off a loan early and the lender doesn't earn all the interest the lender anticipated earning. The penalty is usually a percentage of the balance paid off early.

Secured credit card. A secured credit card is a credit card you obtain by depositing some money into a savings account while you have no access to that account. The money you deposit is security for your paying the charges you make on the card. If you don't pay, the bank deducts the money from your account.

Secured creditor. A secured creditor is a creditor owed a secured debt—that is, a debt linked to a specific item of property (collateral). If you don't pay the debt, the secured creditor can take the collateral.

Secured debt. A secured debt is linked to a specific item of property, such as a house or car, called collateral. The collateral guarantees payment of the debt. If you don't pay, the creditor is entitled to take the collateral.

Security agreement. A security agreement is a contract you sign when you take out a secured loan. The agreement specifies precisely what property (collateral) can be taken by the creditor if you default.

Security interest. A security interest is the right of a secured creditor to take your property in the event you default.

Statute of limitations. A statute of limitations is the legal length of time a creditor has to sue you after you default on a loan or debt.

Unsecured creditor. A creditor who is owed an unsecured debt is called an unsecured creditor. If you don't pay, an unsecured creditor's primary recourse is to sue you, obtain a court judgment and then attach your wages or seize your property.

Unsecured debt. A debt that is not secured is called an unsecured debt. An unsecured debt is not linked to any specific item of property. That means that if you don't pay the debt, the creditor usually must sue you in court, get a judgment and then attach your wages or seize your property to get paid.

Wage assignment. A wage assignment is a method of voluntarily paying a debt. When you are paid, a sum of money is deducted from your paycheck and sent on to the creditor before you ever see that money. Under federal law, a wage assignment is not allowed in consumer loans unless you have the power to revoke the assignment.

Wage attachment. A wage attachment is a method of involuntarily paying a debt. When you are paid, a sum of money is deducted from your paycheck and sent on to the creditor before you ever see that money. Wage attachments are a common method used to collect court judgments and back-owed child support.

Wage withholding. Wage withholding is used to collect child support. After a court orders you to pay child support, your employer is notified of the court order. At each pay period, your employer withholds a portion of your pay and sends it to the custodial parent. ■

APPENDIX

State and Federal Exemptions Tables

Using the Exemption Tables

Every state lets people who file for bankruptcy keep certain property, called exemptions. Ch. 2, *Your Property and Bankruptcy*, Section B.6, discusses exemptions in detail.

1. What This Appendix Contains

- lists of each state's exemptions
- list of the federal bankruptcy exemptions (available as a choice in 14 states and the District of Columbia)
- list of the federal non-bankruptcy exemptions (available as additional exemptions when the state exemptions are chosen), and
- glossary defining exemption terms.

Each list is divided into three columns. Column 1 lists the major exemption categories: homestead, insurance, miscellaneous, pensions, personal property, public benefits, tools of the trade, wages and wildcard. (These categories differ on the federal non-bankruptcy exemptions chart.)

Column 2 gives the specific property that falls into each large category with noted limitations.

For example, the federal bankruptcy exemptions allow married couples filing jointly to each claim a full set of exemptions. This is called "doubling." Many state exemption systems do not allow doubling or do not allow doubling for certain types of property, such as the homestead exemption (which exempts equity in your residence). In some states, the legislature has expressly allowed or prohibited doubling. In others, the courts have allowed or prohibited doubling. In still others, neither the courts nor the legislature has addressed the issue. If that is the case, doubling is probably allowed. In Column 2, we've noted whether a court or state legislature has expressly allowed or prohibited doubling. If the chart doesn't say, it is probably safe to double. However, keep in mind that this area of the law changes rapidly—legislation or court decisions regarding doubling issued after the publication date of this book will not be reflected in the chart.

Column 3 lists the applicable law, which must be included on Schedule C.

2. Choosing Between State and Federal Exemptions

Each state chart indicates whether the federal exemptions are available for that state. The list of federal exemptions follows Wyoming.

3. Using the Glossary

Many of the terms used in exemption statutes are unfamiliar and can be looked up in the glossary. Even if you think you understand the terms in the chart, at least skim the glossary; some terms have special legal meanings that differ from their everyday meanings.

4. Houses and Pensions

If you own a house, you should also read Ch. 6, *Your House*.

With pensions, some states exempt only the money building up in the pension fund, and a few exempt only payments actually being received. Most exempt both. If the pension listing doesn't indicate otherwise, it means the state exempts both.

5. Wages, Benefits and Other Payments

Many states exempt insurance proceeds, pension payments, alimony and child support payments, public benefits or wages. This means that payments you received before filing are exempt if you haven't mixed them with other money or, if you have mixed them, you can trace the exempt portion back to its source.

If, when you file for bankruptcy, you're entitled to receive an exempt payment but haven't yet received it, you can exempt the payment when it comes in by amending Schedules B (personal property you own or possess) and C (property you claim as exempt).

Alabama

Federal Bankruptcy Exemptions not available. All law references are to Alabama Code.

ASSET	EXEMPTION	LAW
homestead	Real property or mobile home to $5,000; property cannot exceed 160 acres (husband & wife may double)	6-10-2
	Must record homestead declaration before attempted sale of home	6-10-20
insurance	Annuity proceeds or avails to $250 per month	27-14-32
	Disability proceeds or avails to an average of $250 per month	27-14-31
	Fraternal benefit society benefits	27-34-27
	Life insurance proceeds or avails	6-10-8; 27-14-29
	Life insurance proceeds or avails if clause prohibits proceeds from being used to pay beneficiary's creditors	27-15-26
	Mutual aid association benefits	27-30-25
pensions	IRAs and other retirement accounts	19-3-1
	Judges (only payments being received)	12-18-10(a),(b)
	Law enforcement officers	36-21-77
	State employees	36-27-28
	Teachers	16-25-23
personal property	Books of debtor and family	6-10-6
	Burial place for self and family	6-10-5
	Church pew for self and family	6-10-5
	Clothing of debtor and family	6-10-6
	Family portraits or pictures	6-10-6
public benefits	Aid to blind, aged, disabled, and other public assistance	38-4-8
	Crime victims' compensation	15-23-15(e)
	Southeast Asian War POWs' benefits	31-7-2
	Unemployment compensation	25-4-140
	Workers' compensation	25-5-86(b)
tools of trade	Arms, uniforms, equipment that state military personnel are required to keep	31-2-78
wages	With respect to consumer loans, consumer credit sales, and consumer leases, 75% of weekly net earnings or 30 times the federal minimum hourly wage; all other cases, 75% of earned but unpaid wages; bankruptcy judge may authorize more for low-income debtors	5-19-15; 6-10-7
wildcard	$3,000 of any personal property, except wages (husband and wife may double)	6-10-6

Alaska

Alaska law states that only the items found in Alaska Statutes §§ 9.38.010, 9.38.015(a), 9.38.017, 9.38.020, 9.38.025 and 9.38.030 may be exempted in bankruptcy. In *In re McNutt*, 87 B.R. 84 (9th Cir. 1988), however, an Alaskan debtor used the federal bankruptcy exemptions. All law references are to Alaska Statutes.

Alaska exemption amounts are adjusted regularly by administrative order. Current amounts are found at 8 Alaska Admin. Code tit. 8, § 95.030.

ASSET	EXEMPTION	LAW
homestead	$64,800 (joint owners may each claim a portion, but total can't exceed $64,800)	09.38.010(a)
insurance	Disability benefits	09.38.015(b), 09.38.030(e)(1),(5)
	Fraternal benefit society benefits	21.84.240
	Life insurance or annuity contract[s], total aggregate cash surrender value to $12,000	09.38.025
	Life insurance proceeds payable to beneficiary	09.38.025(c)
	Medical, surgical or hospital benefits	09.38.015(a)(3)
miscellaneous	Alimony, to extent wages exempt	09.38.030(e)(2)
	Child support payments made by collection agency	09.38.015(b)
	Liquor licenses	09.38.015(a)(7)
	Permits for limited entry into Alaska Fisheries	09.38.015(a)(8)
	Property of business partnership	09.38.100(b)
pensions	Elected public officers (only benefits building up)	09.38.015(b)
	ERISA-qualified benefits deposited more than 120 days before filing bankruptcy	09.38.017
	Judicial employees (only benefits building up)	09.38.015(b)
	Public employees, (only benefits building up)	09.38.015(b); 39.35.505
	Roth & traditional IRAs, medical savings accounts	09.38.017(e)(3)
	Teachers (only benefits building up)	09.38.015(b)
	Other pensions, to extent wages exempt (only payments being received)	09.38.030(e)(5)
personal property	Books, musical instruments, clothing, family portraits, household goods & heirlooms to $3,600 total	09.38.020(a)
	Building materials	34.35.105
	Burial plot	09.38.015(a)(1)
	Cash or other liquid assets to $1,680	09.38.030(b)
	Deposit in apartment or condo owners association	09.38.010(e)
	Health aids needed	09.38.015(a)(2)
	Jewelry to $1,200	09.38.020(b)
	Motor vehicle to $3,600; vehicle's market value can't exceed $24,000	09.38.020(e)
	Personal injury recoveries, to extent wages exempt	09.38.030(e)(3)
	Pets to $1,200	09.38.020(d)
	Proceeds for lost, damaged or destroyed exempt property	09.38.060
	Tuition credits under an advance college tuition payment contract	09.38.015(a)(9)
	Wrongful death recoveries, to extent wages exempt	09.38.030(e)(3)
public benefits	Adult assistance to elderly, blind, disabled	47.25.550
	Alaska longevity bonus	09.38.015(a)(5)
	Crime victims' compensation	09.38.015(a)(4)
	Federally exempt public benefits paid or due	09.38.015(a)(6)
	General relief assistance	47.25.210
	20% of permanent fund dividends	43.23.065
	Unemployment compensation	09.38.015(b); 23.20.405
	Workers' compensation	23.30.160
tools of trade	Implements, books & tools of trade to $3,360	09.38.020(c)
wages	Weekly net earnings to $420; for sole wage earner in a household, $660; if you don't receive weekly, or semi-monthly pay, can claim $1,680 in cash or liquid assets paid any month; for sole wage earner in household, $2,640	9.38.030(a),(b), 9.38.050(b)
wildcard	None	

Arizona

Federal Bankruptcy Exemptions not available. All law references are to Arizona Revised Statutes unless otherwise noted.

Note: Doubling is permitted for noted exemptions by Arizona Revised Statutes § 33-1121.01.

ASSET	EXEMPTION	LAW
homestead	Real property, an apartment or mobile home you occupy to $100,000; sale proceeds exempt 18 months after sale or until new home purchased, whichever occurs first (husband & wife may not double)	33-1101(A)
	May record homestead declaration to clarify which one of multiple eligible parcels are being claimed as homestead.	33-1102
insurance	Fraternal benefit society benefits	20-877
	Group life insurance policy or proceeds	20-1132
	Health, accident or disability benefits	33-1126(A)(4)
	Life insurance cash value or proceeds to $25,000 total	33-1126(A)(6); 20-1131(D)
	Life insurance proceeds to $20,000 if beneficiary is spouse or child	33-1126(A)(1)
miscellaneous	Alimony, child support needed for support	33-1126(A)(3)
	Minor child's earnings, unless debt is for child	33-1126(A)(2)
Pensions *also see wages*	Board of regents members	15-1628(I)
	District employees	48-227
	ERISA-qualified benefits deposited over 120 days before filing	33-1126(C)
	IRAs	*In re Herrscher*, 121 B.R. 29 (D. Ariz. 1990)
	Firefighters	9-968
	Police officers	9-931
	Public safety personnel	38-850(C)
	Rangers	41-955
	State employees retirement and disability	38-792; 38-797.11
personal property *husband & wife may double all personal property*	2 beds & bedding; 1 living room chair per person; 1 dresser, table, lamp; kitchen table; dining room table & 4 chairs (1 more per person); living room carpet or rug; couch; 3 lamps; 3 coffee or end tables; pictures, paintings, personal drawings, family portraits; refrigerator, stove, washer, dryer, vacuum cleaner; TV, radio, stereo, alarm clock to $4,000 total	33-1123
	Bank deposit to $150 in one account	33-1126(A)(8)
	Bible; bicycle; sewing machine; typewriter; burial plot; rifle, pistol or shotgun to $500 total	33-1125
	Books to $250; clothing to $500; wedding & engagement rings to $1,000; watch to $100; pets, horses, milk cows & poultry to $500; musical instruments to $250	33-1125
	Food & fuel to last 6 months	33-1124
	Funeral deposits	32-1391.04
	Health aids	33-1125(9)
	Motor vehicle to $5,000 ($10,000, if disabled)	33-1125(8)
	Prepaid rent or security deposit to $1,000 or 1 1/2 times your rent, whichever is less, in lieu of homestead	33-1126(D)
	Proceeds for sold or damaged exempt property	33-1126(A)(5),(7)
public benefits	Unemployment compensation	23-783(A)
	Welfare benefits	46-208
	Workers' compensation	23-1068(B)
tools of trade *(husband & wife may double)*	Arms, uniforms & accoutrements profession or office requires by law	33-1130(3)
	Farm machinery, utensils, seed, instruments of husbandry, feed, grain & animals to $2,500 total	33-1130(2)
	Library & teaching aids of teacher	33-1127
	Tools, equipment, instruments & books to $2,500	33-1130(1)
wages	75% of earned but unpaid weekly net earnings or 30 times the federal minimum hourly wage; 50% of wages for support orders; bankruptcy judge may authorize more for low-income debtors	33-1131
wildcard	None	

Arkansas

Federal Bankruptcy Exemptions available. All law references are to Arkansas Code Annotated unless otherwise noted.

ASSET	EXEMPTION	LAW
homestead *choose option 1 or 2*	1. For married person or head of family: unlimited exemption on real or personal property used as residence to 1/4 acre in city, town, or village, or 80 acres elsewhere; if property is between 1/4 -1 acre in city, town or village, or 80-160 acres elsewhere, additional limit is $2,500; homestead may not exceed 1 acre in city, town or village, or 160 acres elsewhere (husband & wife may not double)	Constitution 9-3, 9-4, 9-5; 16-66-210, 16-66-218(b)(3), (4) *In re Stevens*, 829 F.2d 693 (8th Cir. 1987)
	2. Real or personal property used as residence to $800 if single; $1,250 if married	16-66-218(a)(1)
insurance	Annuity contract	23-79-134
	Disability benefits	23-79-133
	Fraternal benefit society benefits	23-74-403
	Group life insurance	23-79-132
	Life, health, accident or disability cash value or proceeds paid or due to $500, *In re Holt*, 97 B.R. 997 (W.D. Ark. 1988)	16-66-209; Constitution 9-1, 9-2
	Life insurance proceeds if clause prohibits proceeds from being used to pay beneficiary's creditors	23-79-131
	Life insurance proceeds or avails if beneficiary isn't the insured	23-79-131
	Mutual assessment life or disability benefits to $1,000	23-72-114
	Stipulated insurance premiums	23-71-112
miscellaneous	Property of business partnership (Will be repealed in 2005)	4-42-502
pensions	Disabled firefighters	24-11-814
	Disabled police officers	24-11-417
	Firefighters	24-10-616
	IRA deposits to $20,000 if deposited over 1 year before filing for bankruptcy	16-66-218(b)(16)
	Police officers	24-10-616
	School employees	24-7-715
	State police officers	24-6-205, 24-6-223
personal property	Burial plot to 5 acres, if choosing Federal homestead exemption (option 2)	16-66-207; 16-66-218(a)(1)
	Clothing	Constitution 9-1, 9-2
	Motor vehicle to $1,200	16-66-218(a)(2)
	Wedding rings	16-66-219
public benefits	Crime victims' compensation	16-90-716(e)
	Unemployment compensation	11-10-109
	Workers' compensation	11-9-110
tools of trade	Implements, books & tools of trade to $750	16-66-218(a)(4)
wages	Earned but unpaid wages due for 60 days; in no event under $25 per week	16-66-208, 16-66-218(b)(6)
wildcard	$500 of any personal property if married or head of family; $200 if not married	Constitution 9-1, 9-2; 16-66-218(b)(1),(2)

California—System 1

Federal Bankruptcy Exemptions not available. California has two systems; you must select one or the other. All law references are to California Code of Civil Procedure unless otherwise noted.

ASSET	EXEMPTION	LAW
homestead	Real or personal property you occupy including mobile home, boat, stock cooperative, community apartment, planned development or condo to $50,000 if single & not disabled; $75,000 for families if no other member has a homestead (if only one spouse files, may exempt one-half of amount if home held as community property and all of amount if home held as tenants in common); $125,000 if 65 or older, or physically or mentally disabled; $125,000 if 55 or older, single & earn under $15,000 or married & earn under $20,000 & creditors seek to force the sale of your home; sale proceeds received exempt for 6 months after (husband & wife may not double)	704.710, 704.720, 704.730 *In re McFall,* 112 B.R. 336 (9th Cir. B.A.P. 1990)
	May file homestead declaration	704.920
insurance	Disability or health benefits	704.130
	Fidelity bonds	Labor 404
	Fraternal unemployment benefits	704.120
	Homeowners' insurance proceeds for 6 months after received, to homestead exemption amount	704.720(b)
	Life insurance proceeds if clause prohibits proceeds from being used to pay beneficiary's creditors	Ins. 10132, Ins. 10170, Ins. 10171
	Matured life insurance benefits needed for support	704.100(c)
	Unmatured life insurance policy loan value to $8,000 (husband & wife may double)	704.100(b)
miscellaneous	Business or professional licenses	695.060
	Inmates' trust funds to $1,000 (husband and wife may not double)	704.090
	Property of business partnership	Corp. 16501-04
pensions	County employees	Gov't 31452
	County firefighters	Gov't 32210
	County peace officers	Gov't 31913
	Private retirement benefits, including IRAs & Keoghs	704.115
	Public employees	Gov't 21201
	Public retirement benefits	704.110
Personal property	Appliances, furnishings, clothing & food	704.020
	Bank deposits from Social Security Administration to $2,000 ($3,000 for husband and wife)	704.080
	Building materials to repair or improve home to $2,000 (husband and wife may not double)	704.030
	Burial plot	704.200
	Funds held in escrow	Fin. 17410
	Health aids	704.050
	Homeowners' Association Assessments	Civil 1366(c)
	Jewelry, heirlooms & art to $5,000 total (husband and wife may not double)	704.040
	Motor vehicles to $1,900, or $1,900 in auto insurance for loss or damages (husband and wife may not double)	704.010
	Personal injury & wrongful death causes of action	704.140(a), 704.150(a)
	Personal injury & wrongful death recoveries needed for support; if receiving installments, at least 75%	704.140(b),(c),(d), 704.150(b),(c)
public benefits	Aid to blind, aged, disabled, public assistance	704.170
	Financial aid to students	704.190
	Relocation benefits	704.180
	Unemployment benefits	704.120
	Union benefits due to labor dispute	704.120(b)(5)
	Workers' compensation	704.160
tools of trade	Tools, implements, materials, instruments, uniforms, books, furnishings & equipment to $5,000 total ($10,000 total if used by both spouses in same occupation)	704.060
	Commercial vehicle (Vehicle Code § 260) to $4,000 ($8,000 total if used by both spouses in same occupation)	704.060
wages	Minimum 75% of wages paid within 30 days prior to filing	704.070
	Public employees vacation credits; if receiving installments, at least 75%	704.113
wildcard	None	

California—System 2

Federal Bankruptcy Exemptions not available. All law references are to California Code of Civil Procedure unless otherwise noted.

Note: Married couples may not double any exemptions. (*In re Talmadge,* 832 F.2d 1120 (9th Cir. 1987); *In re Baldwin,* 70 B.R. 612 (9th Cir. B.A.P. 1987)

ASSET	EXEMPTION	LAW
homestead	Real or personal property, including co-op, used as residence to $17,425; unused portion of homestead may be applied to any property	703.140 (b)(1)
insurance	Disability benefits	703.140 (b)(10)(C)
	Life insurance proceeds needed for support of family	703.140 (b)(11)(C)
	Unmatured life insurance contract accrued avails to $9,300	703.140 (b)(8)
	Unmatured life insurance policy other than credit	703.140 (b)(7)
miscellaneous	Alimony, child support needed for support	703.140 (b)(10)(D)
pensions	ERISA-qualified benefits needed for support	703.140 (b)(10)(E)
personal property	Animals, crops, appliances, furnishings, household goods, books, musical instruments & clothing to $450 per item	703.140 (b)(3)
	Burial plot to $17,425, in lieu of homestead	703.140 (b)(1)
	Health aids	703.140 (b)(9)
	Jewelry to $1,150	703.140 (b)(4)
	Motor vehicle to $2,725	703.140 (b)(2)
	Personal injury recoveries to $17,425 (not to include pain & suffering; pecuniary loss)	703.140 (b)(11)(D),(E)
	Wrongful death recoveries needed for support	703.140 (b)(11)(B)
public benefits	Crime victims' compensation	703.140 (b)(11)(A)
	Public assistance	703.140 (b)(10)(A)
	Social Security	703.140 (b)(10)(A)
	Unemployment compensation	703.140 (b)(10)(A)
	Veterans' benefits	703.140 (b)(10)(B)
tools of trade	Implements, books & tools of trade to $1,750	703.140 (b)(6)
wages	None (use Federal non-bankruptcy wage exemption)	
wildcard	$925 of any property	703.140 (b)(5)
	Unused portion of homestead or burial exemption, of any property	703.140 (b)(5)

Colorado

Federal Bankruptcy Exemptions not available. All law references are to Colorado Revised Statutes.

ASSET	EXEMPTION	LAW
homestead	Real property, mobile home, manufactured home or house trailer you occupy to $45,000; sale proceeds exempt 1 year after received (husband & wife may double)	38-41-201, 38-41-201.6, 38-41-203, 38-41-207; In re Pastrana, 216 B.R. 948 (Colo., 1998)
	Spouse or child of deceased owner may claim homestead exemption	38-41-204
insurance	Disability benefits to $200 per month; if receive lump sum, entire amount exempt	10-16-212
	Fraternal benefit society benefits	10-14-403
	Group life insurance policy or proceeds	10-7-205
	Homeowners' insurance proceeds for 1 year after received, to homestead exemption amount	38-41-209
	Life insurance cash surrender value to $25,000, except contributions to policy within past 24 months	13-54-102(1)(l)
	Life insurance proceeds if clause prohibits proceeds from being used to pay beneficiary's creditors	10-7-106
miscellaneous	Child support	13-54-102.5
	Property of business partnership	7-60-125
pensions see also wages	ERISA-qualified benefits, including IRAs	13-54-102(1)(s)
	Firefighters & police officers	31-30.5-208; 31-31-203
	Public employees	24-51-212
	Teachers	22-64-120
	Veterans	13-54-102(1)(h), 13-54-104
personal property	1 burial plot per family member	13-54-102(1)(d)
	Clothing to $1,500	13-54-102(1)(a)
	Food & fuel to $600	13-54-102(1)(f)
	Health aids	13-54-102(1)(p)
	Household goods to $3,000	13-54-102(1)(e)
	Jewelry & articles of adornment to $1,000	13-54-102(1)(b)
	Motor vehicles or bicycles used for work to $3,000; to $6,000 if used by a debtor or by a dependent who is disabled or 65 or over	13-54-102(j)(I), (II)
	Personal injury recoveries	13-54-102(1)(n)
	Family pictures & books to $1,500	13-54-102(1)(c)
	Proceeds for damaged exempt property	13-54-102(1)(m)
	Security deposits	13-54-102(1)(r)
Public benefits	Aid to blind, aged, disabled, public assistance	26-2-131
	Crime victims' compensation	13-54-102(1)(q); 24-4.1-114
	Earned income tax credit	13-54-102(1)(o)
	Unemployment compensation	8-80-103
	Veterans' benefits for veteran, spouse or child if veteran served in war	13-54-102(1)(h)
	Workers' compensation	8-42-124
tools of trade	Livestock or other animals, machinery, tools, equipment & seed of person engaged in agriculture, to $25,000 total	13-54-102(1)(g)
	Professional's library to $3,000 (if not claimed under other tools of trade exemption)	13-54-102(1)(k)
	Stock in trade, supplies, fixtures, tools, machines, electronics, equipment, books & other business materials, to $10,000 total	13-54-102(1)(i)
wages	Minimum 75% of weekly net earnings or 30 times the federal minimum wage, whichever is greater, including pension and insurance payments	13-54-104
wildcard	None	

Connecticut

Federal Bankruptcy Exemptions available. All law references are to Connecticut General Statutes Annotated.

ASSET	EXEMPTION	LAW
homestead	Real property, including mobile or manufactured home, to $75,000 (husband & wife may double); applies only to claims arising after 1993.	52-352a(e); 52-352b(t)
insurance	Disability benefits paid by association for its members	52-352b(p)
	Fraternal benefit society benefits	38a-637
	Health or disability benefits	52-352b(e)
	Life insurance proceeds if clause prohibits proceeds from being used to pay beneficiary's creditors	38a-454
	Life insurance proceeds or avails	38a-453
	Unmatured life insurance policy loan value to $4,000	52-352b(s)
miscellaneous	Alimony, to extent wages exempt	52-352b(n)
	Child support	52-352b(h)
	Farm partnership animals and livestock feed reasonably required to run farm where at least 50% of partners are members of same family	52-352d
pensions	ERISA-qualified benefits, including IRAs and Keoghs, to extent wages exempt	52-321a 52-352b(m)
	Medical savings account	52-321a
	Municipal employees	7-446
	Probate judges & employees	45-290
	State employees	5-171, 5-192w
	Teachers	10-183q
personal property	Appliances, food, clothing, furniture, bedding	52-352b(a)
	Burial plot	52-352b(c)
	Health aids needed	52-352b(f)
	Motor vehicle to $1,500	52-352b(j)
	Proceeds for damaged exempt property	52-352b(q)
	Residential utility & security deposits for 1 residence	52-352b(l)
	Spendthrift trust funds required for support of debtor & family	51-321(d)
	Transfers to a nonprofit debt adjuster	52-352b(u)
	Wedding & engagement rings	52-352b(k)
public benefits	Crime victims' compensation	52-352b(o); 54-213
	Public assistance	52-352b(d)
	Social Security	52-352b(g)
	Unemployment compensation	31-272(c); 2-352b(g)
	Veterans' benefits	52-352b(g)
	Vietnam veterans' death benefits	27-140i
	Wages from earnings incentive program	52-352b(d)
	Workers' compensation	52-352b(g)
	Arms, military equipment, uniforms, musical instruments of military personnel	52-352b(i)
tools of trade	Tools, books, instruments & farm animals needed	52-352b(b)
wages	Minimum 75% of earned but unpaid weekly disposable earnings, or 40 times the state or federal hourly minimum wage, whichever is greater	52-361a(f)
wildcard	$1,000 of any property	52-352b(r)

Delaware

Federal Bankruptcy Exemptions not available. All law references are to Delaware Code Annotated unless otherwise noted.

Note: A single person may exempt no more than $5,000 total in all exemptions; a husband & wife may exempt no more than $10,000 total (10-4914).

ASSET	EXEMPTION	LAW
homestead	None, however, property held as tenancy by the entirety may be exempt against debts owed by only one spouse	*In re Hovatter,* 25 B.R. 123 (D. Del. 1982)
insurance	Annuity contract proceeds to $350 per month	18-2728
	Fraternal benefit society benefits	18-6218
	Group life insurance policy or proceeds	18-2727
	Health or disability benefits	18-2726
	Life insurance proceeds if clause prohibits proceeds from being used to pay beneficiary's creditors	18-2729
	Life insurance proceeds or avails	18-2725
miscellaneous	Property of business partnership	6-1525
pensions	IRAs	*In re Yuhas,* 104 F.3d 612 (3rd Cir. 1997)
	Kent County employees	9-4316
	Police officers	11-8803
	State employees	29-5503
	Volunteer firefighters	16-6653
personal property	Bible, books & family pictures	10-4902(a)
	Burial plot	10-4902(a)
	Church pew or any seat in public place of worship	10-4902(a)
	Clothing, includes jewelry	10-4902(a)
	College investment plan account (limit for year before filing is $5,000 or average of past two years' contribution whichever is more)	10-4916
	Pianos and leased organs	10-4902(d)
	Sewing machines	10-4902(c)
public benefits	Aid to blind	31-2309
	Aid to aged, disabled, general assistance	31-513
	Unemployment compensation	19-3374
	Workers' compensation	19-2355
tools of trade	Tools, implements & fixtures to $75 in New Castle & Sussex Counties; to $50 in Kent County	10-4902(b)
wages	85% of earned but unpaid wages	10-4913
wildcard	$500 of any personal property, except tools of trade, if head of family	10-4903

District of Columbia

Federal Bankruptcy Exemptions available. All law references are to District of Columbia Code unless otherwise noted.

ASSET	EXEMPTION	LAW
homestead	Any property used as a residence or coop that debtor or debtor's dependent uses as a residence	15-501(a)(14)
	(Property held as tenancy by the entirety may be exempt against debts owed by only one spouse)	*Estate of Wall,* 440 F.2d 215 (D.C. Cir. 1971)
insurance	Disability benefits	15-501(a)(7)
	Fraternal benefit society benefits	31-5315
	Group life insurance policy or proceeds	31-4717
	Life insurance payments	15-501(a)(11)
	Life insurance proceeds if clause prohibits proceeds from being used to pay beneficiary's creditors	31-4719
	Life insurance proceeds or avails	31-4716
	Other insurance proceeds to $200 per month, maximum 2 months, for head of family; else $60 per month	15-503
	Unmatured life insurance contract other than credit life insurance	15-501(a)(5)
	alimony or child support	15-501(a)(7)
pensions *also see wages*	ERISA-qualified benefits, IRAs, Keoghs, etc. to maximum deductible contribution	15-501(b)(9)
	Any stock bonus, annuity, pension or profit sharing plan	15-501(a)(7)
	Judges	11-1570(d)
	Public school teachers	38-2001.17, 38-2021.17
personal property	Appliances, books, clothing, household furnishings and goods, musical instruments, pets to $425 per item or $8,625 total	15-501(a)(2)
	Cooperative association holdings to $50	29-928
	Food for 3 months	15-501(a)(12)
	Health aids	15-501(a)(6)
	Higher education tuition savings account	47-4510
	Residential condominium deposit	42-1904.09
	All family pictures; and all the family library, to $400	15-501(a)(8)
	Motor vehicle to $2,575	15-501(a)(1)
	Payment including pain & suffering for loss of debtor or person depended on	15-501(a)(11)
	Uninsured motorist benefits	31-2408.01(h)
	Wrongful death damages	15-501(a)(11)
public benefits	Aid to blind, aged, disabled, general assistance	4-215.01
	Crime victims' compensation	15-501(a)(11)
	Social Security	15-501(a)(7)
	Unemployment compensation	51-118
	Veterans' benefits	15-501(a)(7)
	Workers' compensation	32-1517
tools of trade	Library, furniture, tools of professional or artist to $300	15-501(a)(13)
	Tools of trade or business to $1,625;	15-501(a)(5),
	mechanic's tools to $200	15-503(b)
	Seal & documents of notary public	1-1206
wages	Minimum 75% of earned but unpaid wages, pension payments; bankruptcy judge may authorize more for low-income debtors	16-572
	Non-wage (including pension & retirement) earnings to $200/mo for head of family; else $60/mo for a maximum of two mos.	15-503
	Payment for loss of future earnings	15-501(e)(11)
wildcard	Up to $850 in any property, plus up to $8,075 of unused homestead exemption	15-501(a)(3)

Florida

Federal Bankruptcy Exemptions not available. All law references are to Florida Statutes Annotated unless otherwise noted.

ASSET	EXEMPTION	LAW
homestead	Real or personal property including mobile or modular home to unlimited value; cannot exceed half acre in municipality or 160 acres elsewhere; spouse or child of deceased owner may claim homestead exemption; (husband & wife may double)	222.01, 222.02, 222.03, 222.05;Constitution 10-4 *In re Colwell*, 196 F.3d (11th Cir. 1999)
	May file homestead declaration	222.01
	Property held as tenancy by the entirety may be exempt against debts owed by only one spouse	*Havoco of America, Ltd. v. Hill*, 197 F.3d 1135 (11th Cir Fla.,1999)
insurance	Annuity contract proceeds; does not include lottery winnings	222.14; *In re Pizzi*, 153 B.R. 357 (S.D. Fla. 1993)
	Death benefits payable to a specific beneficiary, not the deceased's estate	222.13
	Disability or illness benefits	222.18
	Fraternal benefit society benefits,	632.619
	Life insurance cash surrender value	222.14
miscellaneous	Alimony, child support needed for support	222.201
	Damages to employees for injuries in hazardous occupations	769.05
pensions	County officers, employees	122.15
also see wages	ERISA-qualified benefits	222.21(2)
	Firefighters	175.241
	Police officers	185.25
	State officers, employees	121.131
	Teachers	238.15
personal property	Any personal property to $1,000 (husband & wife may double)	Constitution 10-4 *In re Hawkins*, 51 B.R. 348 (S.D. Fla. 1985)
	Federal income tax refund or credit	222.25
	Health aids	222.25
	Motor vehicle to $1,000	222.25
	Pre-need funeral contract deposits	497.413(8)
	Pre-paid college education trust deposits	222.22(1)
	Pre-paid medical savings account deposits	222.22(2)
public benefits	Crime victims' compensation unless seeking to discharge debt for treatment of injury incurred during the crime	960.14
	Hazardous occupation injury recoveries	769.05
	Public assistance	222.201
	Social Security	222.201
	Unemployment compensation	222.201; 443.051(2),(3)
	Veterans' benefits	222.201; 744.626
	Workers' compensation	440.22
tools of trade	None	
wages	100% of wages for heads of family up to $500 per week either unpaid or paid and deposited into bank account for up to 6 months	222.11
	Federal government employees pension payments needed for support & received 3 months prior	222.21
wildcard	See personal property	

Georgia

Federal Bankruptcy Exemptions not available. All law references are to the Official Code of Georgia Annotated, not to the Georgia Code Annotated.

ASSET	EXEMPTION	LAW
homestead	Real or personal property, including co-op, used as residence to $10,000 (husband & wife may double); up to $5,000 of unused portion of homestead may be applied to any property	44-13-100(a)(1) 44-13-100(a)(6)
insurance	Annuity & endowment contract benefits	33-28-7
	Disability or health benefits to $250 per month	33-29-15
	Fraternal benefit society benefits	33-15-62
	Group insurance	33-30-10
	Proceeds and avails of life insurance	33-26-5; 33-25-11
	Life insurance proceeds if policy owned by someone you depended on, needed for support	44-13-100(a)(11)(C)
	Unmatured life insurance contract	44-13-100(a)(8)
	Unmatured life insurance dividends, interest, loan value or cash value to $2,000 if beneficiary is you or someone you depend on	44-13-100(a)(9)
miscellaneous	Alimony, child support needed for support	44-13-100(a)(2)(D)
pensions	Employees of non-profit corporations	44-13-100(a)(2.1)(B)
	ERISA-qualified benefits	18-4-22
	Public employees	44-13-100(a)(2.1)(A); 47-2-332
	Other pensions needed for support	18-4-22; 44-13-100(a)(2)(E), 44-13-100(a)(2.1)(C)
personal property	Animals, crops, clothing, appliances, books, furnishings, household goods, musical instruments to $300 per item, $5,000 total	44-13-100(a)(4)
	Burial plot, in lieu of homestead	44-13-100(a)(1)
	Health aids	44-13-100(a)(10)
	Jewelry to $500	44-13-100(a)(5)
	Lost future earnings needed for support	44-13-100(a)(11)(E)
	Motor vehicles to $3,500 (husband & wife may double)	44-13-100(a)(3)
	Personal injury recoveries to $10,000	44-13-100(a)(11)(C)
	Wrongful death recoveries needed for support	44-13-100(a)(11)(B)
public benefits	Aid to blind	49-4-58
	Aid to disabled	49-4-84
	Crime victims' compensation	44-13-100(a)(11)(A)
	Local public assistance	44-13-100(a)(2)(A)
	Old age assistance	49-4-35
	Social Security	44-13-100(a)(2)(A)
	Unemployment compensation	44-13-100(a)(2)(A)
	Veterans' benefits	44-13-100(a)(2)(B)
	Workers' compensation	34-9-84
tools of trade	Implements, books & tools of trade to $1,500	44-13-100(a)(7)
wages	Minimum 75% of earned but unpaid weekly disposable earnings, or 40 times the state or federal hourly minimum wage, whichever is greater for private & federal workers; bankruptcy judge may authorize more for low-income debtors	18-4-20, 18-4-21
wildcard	$600 of any property	44-13-100(a)(6)
	Unused portion of homestead exemption to $5,000	44-13-100(a)(6)

Hawaii

Federal Bankruptcy Exemptions available. All law references are to Hawaii Revised Statutes unless otherwise noted.

ASSET	EXEMPTION	LAW
homestead	Head of family or over 65 to $30,000; all others to $20,000; property cannot exceed 1 acre; sale proceeds exempt for 6 months after sale (husband & wife may not double)	651-91, 651-92, 651-96
	Property held as tenancy by the entirety may be exempt against debts owed by only one spouse	*Security Pacific Bank v. Chang,* 818 F.Supp. 1343 (D. Ha. 1993)
insurance	Annuity contract or endowment policy proceeds if beneficiary is insured's spouse, child or parent	431:10-232(b)
	Disability benefits	431:10-231
	Fraternal benefit society benefits	432:2-403
	Group life insurance policy or proceeds	431:10-233
	Life or health insurance policy for spouse or child	431:10-234
	Life insurance proceeds if clause prohibits proceeds from being used to pay beneficiary's creditors	431:10D-112
miscellaneous	Property of business partnership	425-125
pensions	ERISA-qualified benefits deposited over 3 years before filing bankruptcy	651-124
	Firefighters	88-169
	Police officers	88-169
	Public officers & employees	88-91; 653-3
personal property	Appliances & furnishings	651-121(1)
	Books	651-121(1)
	Burial plot to 250 sq. ft. plus tombstones, monuments & fencing	651-121(4)
	Clothing	651-121(1)
	Jewelry, watches & articles of adornment to $1,000	651-121(1)
	Motor vehicle to wholesale value of $2,575	651-121(2)
	Proceeds for sold or damaged exempt property; sale proceeds exempt for 6 months after sale	651-121(5)
public benefits	Public assistance paid by Dept. of Health Services for work done in home or workshop	346-33
	Unemployment compensation	383-163
	Unemployment work relief funds to $60 per month	653-4
	Workers' compensation	386-57
tools of trade	Tools, implements, books, instruments, uniforms, furnishings, fishing boat, nets, motor vehicle & other property needed for livelihood	651-121(3)
wages	Unpaid wages due for services of past 31 days	651-121(6)
	Prisoner's wages held by Dept. of Public Safety	353-22
wildcard	None	

Idaho

Federal Bankruptcy Exemptions not available. All law references are to Idaho Code.

ASSET	EXEMPTION	LAW
homestead	Real property or mobile home to $50,000; sale proceeds exempt for 6 months (husband and wife may not double)	55-1003, 55-1113
	Must record homestead exemption for property that is not yet occupied	55-1004
insurance	Annuity contract proceeds to $350 per month	41-1836
	Death or disability benefits	11-604(1)(a); 41-1834
	Fraternal benefit society benefits	41-3218
	Group life insurance benefits	41-1835
	Homeowners' insurance proceeds to amount of homestead exemption	55-1008
	Life insurance proceeds if clause prohibits proceeds from being used to pay beneficiary's creditors	41-1930
	Life insurance proceeds or avails for beneficiary other than the insured	11-604(d); 41-1833
	Medical, surgical or hospital care benefits	11-603(5)
	Unmatured life insurance contract, other than credit life insurance, owned by debtor	11-605(8)
	Unmatured life insurance contract interest or dividends to $5,000 owned by debtor or person debtor depends on	11-605(9)
miscellaneous	Alimony, child support	11-604(1)(b)
	Liquor licenses	23-514
	Property of business partnership	53-325
Pension *also see wages*	ERISA-qualified benefits	55-1011
	Firefighters	72-1422
	Government & private pensions, retirement plans, IRAs, Keoghs, etc.	11-604A
	Police officers	50-1517
	Public employees	59-1317
personal property	Appliances, furnishings, books, clothing, pets, musical instruments, 1 firearm, family portraits & sentimental heirlooms to $500 per item, $5,000 total	11-605(1)
	Building materials	45-514
	Burial plot	11-603(1)
	College savings program account	11-604A(4)(b)
	Crops cultivated on maximum of 50 acres, to $1,000; water rights to 160 inches	11-605(6)
	Health aids	11-603(2)
	Jewelry to $1,000	11-605(2)
	Motor vehicle to $3,000	11-605(3)
	Personal injury recoveries	11-604(1)(c)
	Proceeds for damaged exempt property for 3 months after proceeds received	11-606
	Wrongful death recoveries	11-604(1)(c)
public benefits	Aid to blind, aged, disabled	56-223
	Federal, state & local public assistance	11-603(4)
	General assistance	56-223
	Social Security	11-603(3)
	Unemployment compensation	11-603(6)
	Veterans' benefits	11-603(3)
	Workers' compensation	72-802
tools of trade	Arms, uniforms & accoutrements that peace officer, national guard or military personnel is required to keep	11-605(5)
	Implements, books & tools of trade to $1,500	11-605(3)
wages	Minimum 75% of earned but unpaid weekly disposable earnings, or 30 times the federal hourly minimum wage, whichever is greater, pension payments; bankruptcy judge may authorize more for low-income debtors	11-207
wildcard	$800 in any tangible personal property	11-605(10)

Illinois

Federal Bankruptcy Exemptions not available. All law references are to Illinois Annotated Statutes.

ASSET	EXEMPTION	LAW
homestead	Real or personal property including a farm, lot & buildings, condo, co-op or mobile home to $7,500 (husband and wife may double); sale proceeds exempt for 1 year	735-5/12-901, 735-5/12-906
	Spouse or child of deceased owner may claim homestead exemption	735-5/12-902
insurance	Fraternal benefit society benefits	215-5/299.1a
	Health or disability benefits	735-5/12-1001(g)(3)
	Homeowners proceeds if home destroyed, to $7,500	735-5/12-907
	Life insurance, annuity proceeds or cash value if beneficiary is insured's child, parent, spouse or other dependent	215-5/238; 735-5/12-1001(f)
	Life insurance proceeds to a spouse or dependent of debtor to extent needed for support	735-5/12-1001(f),(g)(3)
miscellaneous	Alimony, child support	735-5/12-1001(g)(4)
	Property of business partnership	805-205/25
pensions	Civil service employees	40-5/11-223
	County employees	40-5/9-228
	Disabled firefighters; widows & children of firefighters	40-5/22-230
	ERISA-qualified benefits	735-5/12-1006
	Firefighters	40-5/4-135, 40-5/6-213
	General assembly members	40-5/2-154
	House of correction employees	40-5/19-117
	Judges	40-5/18-161
	Municipal employees	40-5/7-217(a), 40-5/8-244
	Park employees	40-5/12-190
	Police officers	40-5/3-144.1, 40-5/5-218
	Public employees	735-5/12-1006
	Public library employees	40-5/19-218
	Sanitation district employees	40-5/13-805
	State employees	40-5/14-147
	State university employees	40-5/15-185
	Teachers	40-5/16-190, 40-5/17-151
personal property	Bible, family pictures, schoolbooks & clothing	735-5/12-1001(a)
	Health aids	735-5/12-1001(e)
	Motor vehicle to $1,200	735-5/12-1001(c)
	Personal injury recoveries to $7,500	735-5/12-1001(h)(4)
	Prepaid tuition trust fund	110-979/45 (g)
	Proceeds of sold exempt property	735-5/12-1001
	Wrongful death recoveries	735-5/12-1001(h)(2)
public benefits	Aid to aged, blind, disabled, public assistance	305-5/11-3
	Crime victims' compensation	735-5/12-1001(h)(1)
	Restitution payments on account of WWII relocation of Aleuts and Japanese Americans	735-5/12-1001(12)(h)(5)
	Social Security	735-5/12-1001(g)(1)
	Unemployment compensation	735-5/12-1001(g) (1),(3)
	Veterans' benefits	735-5/12-1001(g)(2)
	Workers' compensation	820-305/21
	Workers' occupational disease compensation	820-310/21
tools of trade	Implements, books & tools of trade to $750	735-5/12-1001(d)
wages	Minimum 85% of earned but unpaid weekly wages or 45 times the Federal minimum hourly wage; bankruptcy judge may authorize more for low-income debtors	740-170/4
wildcard	$2,000 of any personal property (does not include wages)	735-5/12-1001(b)

Indiana

Federal Bankruptcy Exemptions not available. All law references are to Indiana Statutes Annotated.

ASSET	EXEMPTION	LAW
homestead *also see wildcard*	Real or personal property used as residence to $7,500 (husband and wife may double); homestead plus personal property—except health aids—can't exceed $10,000	34-55-10-2(b)(1); 34-55-10-2(c)
	Property held as tenancy by the entirety may be exempt against debts incurred by only one spouse	34-55-10-2(b)(5)
insurance	Employer's life insurance policy on employee	27-1-12-17.1
	Fraternal benefit society benefits	27-11-6-3
	Group life insurance policy	27-1-12-29
	Life insurance policy, proceeds, cash value or avails if beneficiary is insured's spouse or dependent	27-1-12-14
	Life insurance proceeds if clause prohibits proceeds to be used to pay beneficiary's creditors	27-2-5-1
	Mutual life or accident proceeds	27-8-3-23
miscellaneous	Property of business partnership	23-4-1-25
pensions	Firefighters	36-8-7-22, 36-8-8-17
	Police officers	10-1-2-9; 36-8-8-17
	Public employees	5-10.3-8-9
	Public or private retirement benefits	34-55-10-2(b)(6)
	Sheriffs	36-8-10-19
	State teachers	21-6.1-5-17
personal property *see wild card*	Health aids	34-55-10-2(b)(4)
	Money in medical care savings account	34-55-10-2(b)(7)
	Spendthrift trusts	30-4-3-2
	$100 of any intangible personal property, except money owed to you	34-55-10-2(b)(3)
public benefits	Crime victims' compensation unless seeking to discharge the debts for which the victim was compensated	5-2-6.1-38
	Unemployment compensation	22-4-33-3
	Workers' compensation	22-3-2-17
tools of trade	National guard uniforms, arms & equipment	10-2-6-3
wages	Minimum 75% of earned but unpaid weekly disposable earnings, or 30 times the federal hourly minimum wage; bankruptcy judge may authorize more for low-income debtors	24-4.5-5-105
wildcard	$4,000 of any real estate or tangible personal property, but wildcard plus homestead cannot exceed $10,000	34-55-10-2(b)(2)

Iowa

Federal Bankruptcy Exemptions not available. All law references are to Iowa Code Annotated.

ASSET	EXEMPTION	LAW
homestead	Real property or an apartment to an unlimited value; property cannot exceed 1/2 acre in town or city, 40 acres elsewhere (husband & wife may not double)	499A.18; 561.2, 561.16
	May record homestead declaration	561.4
insurance	Accident, disability, health, illness or life proceeds or avails	627.6(6)
	Disability or illness benefit	627.6(8)(c)
	Employee group insurance policy or proceeds	509.12
	Life insurance proceeds paid to spouse, child or other dependent (limited to $10,000 if acquired within 2 years of filing for bankruptcy)	627.6(6)
	Upon death of insured, up to $15,000 total proceeds from all matured life, accident, health, or disability policies exempt from beneficiary's debts contracted before insured's death.	627.6(6)
	Life insurance proceeds if clause prohibits proceeds from being used to pay beneficiary's creditors	508.32
miscellaneous	Alimony, child support needed for support	627.6(8)(d)
	Liquor licenses	123.38
pensions *also see* *wages*	Disabled firefighters, police officers (only payments being received)	410.11
	Federal government pension	627.8
	Firefighters	411.13
	Peace officers	97A.12
	Police officers	411.13
	Public employees	97B.39
	Other pensions, annuities and contracts fully exempt; however, contributions made within 1 year prior to filing for bankruptcy not exempt to the extent they exceed normal and customary amounts	627.6(8)(e)
	Retirement plans, Keoghs, IRAs, Roth IRAs, ERISA-qualified benefits	627.6(8)(f)
Personal property	Appliances, furnishings & household goods to $2,000 total	627.6(5)
	Bibles, books, portraits, pictures & paintings to $1,000 total	627.6(3)
	Burial plot to 1 acre	627.6(4)
	Clothing and its storage containers to $1,000	627.6(1)
	Health aids	627.6(7)
	Motor vehicle, musical instruments & tax refund & accrued wages to $5,000 total, no more than $1,000 from tax refunds and accrued wages.	627.6(9)
	Residential security or utility deposit, or advance rent, to $500	627.6(14)
	Rifle or musket; shotgun	627.6(2)
	Wedding or engagement rings	627.6(1)
public benefits	Adopted child assistance	627.19
	Any public assistance benefit	627.6(8)(a)
	Social Security	627.6(8)(a)
	Unemployment compensation	627.6(8)(a)
	Veterans' benefits	627.6(8)(b)
	Workers' compensation	627.13
tools of trade	Farming equipment; includes livestock, feed to $10,000	627.6(11)
	Non-farming equipment to $10,000	627.6(10)
wages	Expected annual earnings	Amount NOT exempt per year	642.21

Expected annual earnings	Amount NOT exempt per year
$0 to 12,000	$250
$12,000 to 16,000	$400
$16,000 to 24,000	$800
$24,000 to 35,000	$1,000
$35,000 to 50,000	$2,000
More than $50,000	10%
Not exempt from spousal or child support	

ASSET	EXEMPTION	LAW
wildcard	$100 of any personal property, including cash	627.6(13)

Kansas

Federal Bankruptcy Exemptions not available. All law references are to Kansas Statutes Annotated unless otherwise noted.

ASSET	EXEMPTION	LAW
homestead	Real property or mobile home you occupy or intend to occupy to unlimited value; property cannot exceed 1 acre in town or city, 160 acres on farm	60-2301; Constitution 15-9
insurance	Disability and illness benefits	60-2313(a)(1)
	Fraternal life insurance benefits	60-2313(a)(8)
	Cash value of life insurance; not exempt if obtained within 1 year prior to bankruptcy with fraudulent intent.	60-2313(a)(7); 40-414(b)
	Life insurance proceeds	40-414(a)
miscellaneous	Alimony, maintenance and support	60-2312(b)
	Liquor licenses	41-326
pensions	Elected & appointed officials in cities with populations between 120,000 & 200,000	13-14a10
	ERISA-qualified benefits	60-2308(b)
	Federal government pension needed for support & paid within 3 months of filing for bankruptcy (only payments being received)	60-2308(a)
	Firefighters	12-5005(e); 14-10a10
	Judges	20-2618
	Police officers	12-5005(e); 13-14a10
	Public employees	74-4923, 74-49,105
	State highway patrol officers	74-4978g
	State school employees	72-5526
	Payment under a stock bonus, pension, profit-sharing, annuity, or similar plan or contract on account of illness, disability, death, age, or length of service, to the extent reasonably necessary for the support	60-2312(b)
personal property	Burial plot or crypt	60-2304(d)
	Clothing to last 1 year	60-2304(a)
	Food & fuel to last 1 year	60-2304(a)
	Funeral plan prepayments	16-310(d)
	Furnishings & household equipment	60-2304(a)
	Jewelry & articles of adornment to $1,000	60-2304(b)
	Motor vehicle to $20,000; if designed or equipped for disabled person, no limit	60-2304(c)
public benefits	Crime victims' compensation	74-7313(d)
	General assistance	39-717(c)
	Social Security	60-2312(b)
	Unemployment compensation	44-718(c)
	Veteran's benefits	60-2312(b)
	Workers' compensation	44-514
tools of trade	Books, documents, furniture, instruments, equipment, breeding stock, seed, grain & stock to $7,500 total	60-2304(e)
	National Guard uniforms, arms & equipment	48-245
wages	Minimum 75% of disposable weekly wages or 30 times the federal minimum hourly wage per week, whichever is greater; bankruptcy judge may authorize more for low-income debtors	60-2310
wildcard	None	

Kentucky

Federal Bankruptcy Exemptions not available. All law references are to Kentucky Revised Statutes.

ASSET	EXEMPTION	LAW
homestead	Real or personal property used as residence to $5,000; sale proceeds exempt	427.060, 427.090
insurance	Annuity contract proceeds to $350 per month	304.14-330
	Cooperative life or casualty insurance benefits	427.110(1)
	Fraternal benefit society benefits	427.110(2)
	Group life insurance proceeds	304.14-320
	Health or disability benefits	304.14-310
	Life insurance policy if beneficiary is a married woman	304.14-340
	Life insurance proceeds if clause prohibits proceeds from being used to pay beneficiary's creditors	304.14-350
	Life insurance proceeds or cash value if beneficiary is someone other than insured	304.14-300
miscellaneous	Alimony, child support needed for support	427.150(1)
	Property of business partnership	362.270
pensions	Firefighters	67A.620; 95.878
	Police officers	427.120, 427.125
	ERISA-qualified benefits, including IRAs, SEPs, and Keoghs deposited more than 120 days before filing	427.150
	State employees	61.690
	Teachers	161.700
	Urban county government employees	67A.350
personal property	Burial plot to $5,000, in lieu of homestead	427.060
	Clothing, jewelry, articles of adornment & furnishings to $3,000 total	427.010(1)
	Health aids	427.010(1)
	Lost earnings payments needed for support	427.150(2)(d)
	Medical expenses paid & reparation benefits received under motor vehicle reparation law	304.39-260
	Motor vehicle to $2,500	427.010(1)
	Personal injury recoveries to $7,500 (not to include pain & suffering or pecuniary loss)	427.150(2)(c)
	Prepaid tuition payment fund account	164A.707(3)
	Wrongful death recoveries for person you depended on, needed for support	427.150(2)(b)
public benefits	Aid to blind, aged, disabled, public assistance	205.220(c)
	Crime victims' compensation	427.150(2)(a)
	Unemployment compensation	341.470(4)
	Workers' compensation	342.180
tools of trade	Library, office equipment, instruments & furnishings of minister, attorney, physician, surgeon, chiropractor, veterinarian or dentist to $1,000	427.040
	Motor vehicle of auto mechanic, mechanical or electrical equipment servicer, minister, attorney, physician, surgeon, chiropractor, veterinarian or dentist to $2,500	427.030
	Tools, equipment, livestock & poultry of farmer to $3,000	427.010(1)
	Tools of non-farmer to $300	427.030
wages	Minimum 75% of disposable weekly earnings or 30 times the federal minimum hourly wage per week, whichever is greater; bankruptcy judge may authorize more for low-income debtors	427.010(2),(3)
wildcard	$1,000 of any property	427.160

Louisiana

Federal Bankruptcy Exemptions not available. All law references are to Louisiana Revised Statutes Annotated unless otherwise noted.

ASSET	EXEMPTION	LAW
homestead	Property you occupy to $25,000 (if debt is result of catastrophic or terminal illness or injury, limit is full value of property as of 1 year before filing); cannot exceed 5 acres in city or town, 200 acres elsewhere (husband & wife may not double)	20:1(A)(1),(2),(3)
	Spouse or child of deceased owner may claim homestead exemption; spouse given home in divorce gets homestead	20:1(B)
insurance	Annuity contract proceeds and avails	22:647
	Fraternal benefit society benefits	22:558
	Group insurance policies or proceeds	22:649
	Health, accident or disability proceeds or avails	22:646
	Life insurance proceeds or avails; if policy issued within 9 months of filing, exempt only to $35,000	22:647
miscellaneous	Property of minor child	13:3881(A)(3); Civil Code Art. 223
pensions	Assessors	11:1403
	Court clerks	11:1526
	District attorneys	11:1583
	ERISA-qualified benefits, including IRAs and Keoghs, if contributions made over 1 year before filing for bankruptcy	13:3881(D)(1); 20:33(1)
	Firefighters	11:2263
	Gift or bonus payments from employer to employee or heirs whenever paid	20:33(2)
	Judges	11:1378
	Louisiana University employees	11:952.3
	Municipal employees	11:1735
	Parochial employees	11:1905
	Police officers	11:3513
	School employees	11:1003
	Sheriffs	11:2182
	State employees	11:405
	Teachers	11:704
	Voting registrars	11:2033
personal property	Arms, military accoutrements; bedding; dishes, glassware, utensils, silverware (non-sterling); clothing, family portraits, musical instruments; bedroom, living room & dining room furniture; poultry, 1 cow, household pets; heating & cooling equipment, refrigerator, freezer, stove, washer & dryer, iron, sewing machine	13:3881(A)(4)
	Cemetery plot, monuments	8:313
	Engagement & wedding rings to $5,000	13:3881(A)(5)
	Spendthrift Trusts	9:2004
public benefits	Aid to blind, aged, disabled, public assistance	46:111
	Crime victims' compensation	46:1811
	Unemployment compensation	23:1693
	Workers' compensation	23:1205
tools of trade	Tools, instruments, books, pickup truck (maximum 3 tons) or non-luxury auto & utility trailer, needed to work	13:3881(A)(2)
wages	Minimum 75% of disposable weekly earnings or 30 times the federal minimum hourly wage per week, whichever is greater; bankruptcy judge may authorize more for low-income debtors	13:3881(A)(1)
wildcard	None	

Maine

Federal Bankruptcy Exemptions not available. All law references are to Maine Revised Statutes Annotated.

ASSET	EXEMPTION	LAW
homestead	Real or personal property (including cooperative) used as residence to $25,000; if debtor has minor dependents in residence, to $50,000; if debtor over age 60 or physically or mentally disabled, $60,000 (joint debtors in this category may double); proceeds of sale exempt for six months	14-4422(1)
insurance	Annuity proceeds to $450 per month	24-A-2431
	Disability or health proceeds, benefits or avails	14-4422(13)(A),(C); 24-A-2429
	Fraternal benefit society benefits	24-A-4118
	Group health or life policy or proceeds	24-A-2430
	Life, endowment, annuity or accident policy, proceeds or avails	14-4422(14)(C); 24-A-2428
	Life insurance policy, interest, loan value or accrued dividends for policy from person you depended on, to $4,000	14-4422(11)
	Unmatured life insurance policy, except credit insurance policy	14-4422(10)
miscellaneous	Alimony & child support needed for support	14-4422(13)(D)
	Property of business partnership	31-305
pensions	ERISA-qualified benefits	14-4422(13)(E)
	Judges	4-1203
	Legislators	3-703
	State employees	5-17054
personal property	Animals, crops, musical instruments, books, clothing, furnishings, household goods, appliances to $200 per item	14-4422(3)
	Balance due on repossessed goods; total amount financed can't exceed $2,000	9-A-5-103
	Burial plot in lieu of homestead exemption	14-4422(1)
	Cooking stove; furnaces & stoves for heat	14-4422(6)(A),(B)
	Food to last 6 months	14-4422(7)(A)
	Fuel not to exceed 10 cords of wood, 5 tons of coal or 1,000 gal. of heating oil	14-4422(6)(C)
	Health aids	14-4422(12)
	Jewelry to $750; no limit for one wedding & one engagement ring	14-4422(4)
	Lost earnings payments needed for support	14-4422(14)(E)
	Military clothes, arms & equipment	37-B-262
	Motor vehicle to $5,000	14-4422(2)
	Personal injury recoveries to $12,500	14-4422(14)(D)
	Seeds, fertilizers & feed to raise & harvest food for 1 season	14-4422(7)(B)
	Tools & equipment to raise & harvest food	14-4422(7)(C)
	Wrongful death recoveries needed for support	14-4422(14)(B)
public benefits	Crime victims' compensation	14-4422(14)(A)
	Public assistance	22-3766
	Social Security	14-4422(13)(A)
	Unemployment compensation	14-4422(13)(A),(C)
	Veterans' benefits	14-4422(13)(B)
	Workers' compensation	39-A-106
tools of trade	Commercial fishing boat, 5 ton limit	14-4422(9)
	Books, materials & stock to $5,000	14-4422(5)
	One of each farm implement (and its maintenance equipment needed to harvest and raise crops)	14-4422(8)
wages	None (use Federal non-bankruptcy wage exemption)	
wildcard	Unused portion of exemption in homestead to $6,000; or unused exemption in animals, crops, musical instruments, books, clothing, furnishings, household goods, appliances, tools of the trade & personal injury recoveries	14-4422(15)
	$400 of any property	14-4422(15)

Maryland

Federal Bankruptcy Exemptions not available. All law references are to Maryland Code of Courts & Judicial Proceedings unless otherwise noted.

ASSET	EXEMPTION	LAW
homestead	None, however, property held as tenancy by the entirety is exempt against debts owed by only one spouse	*In re Birney*, 200 F.3d 225 (4th Cir. 1999)
insurance	Disability or health benefits, including court awards, arbitrations & settlements	11-504(b)(2)
	Fraternal benefit society benefits	Ins. 8-431; Estates & Trusts 8-115
	Life insurance or annuity contract proceeds or avails if beneficiary is insured's dependent, child or spouse	Ins. 16-111(a); Estates & Trusts 8-115
	Medical insurance benefits deducted from wages plus medical insurance payments to $145 per week or 75% of disposable wages.	Commercial Law 15-601.1(3)
miscellaneous	Property of business partnership	Corps. & Ass'ns. 9-502
pensions	ERISA-qualified benefits, except IRAs	11-504(h)(1)
	State employees	State Pers. & Pen. 21-502
personal property	Appliances, furnishings, household goods, books, pets & clothing to $500 total	11-504(b)(4)
	Burial plot	Code of 1957, 23-164
	Health aids	11-504(b)(3)
	Lost future earnings recoveries	11-504(b)(2)
public benefits	Crime victims' compensation	Crim. Proc. 11-816(b)
	General assistance	Code of 1957 88A-73
	Unemployment compensation	Labor & Employment 8-106
	Workers' compensation	Labor & Employment 9-732
tools of trade	Clothing, books, tools, instruments & appliances to $2,500;	11-504(b)(1)
wages	Earned but unpaid wages, the greater of 75% or $145 per week; in Kent, Caroline, & Queen Anne's of Worcester Counties, the greater of 75% or 30 times Federal minimum hourly wage	Commercial Law 15-601.1
wildcard	$5,500 of any property (may include up to $3,000 in cash); must claim exemption within 30 days of levy or attachment	11-504(b)(5),(f)

Massachusetts

Federal Bankruptcy Exemptions available. All law references are to Massachusetts General Laws Annotated.

ASSET	EXEMPTION	LAW
homestead	Property you occupy or intend to occupy (including mobile home) to $300,000; if over 65 or disabled, $300,000 (joint owners may not double)	188-1, 188-1A
	If statement of homestead is not in title to property, must record homestead declaration before filing bankruptcy	188-2
	Spouse or children of deceased owner may claim homestead exemption	188-4
	Property held as tenancy by the entirety may be exempt against non-necessity owed by only one spouse.	209-1
insurance	Disability benefits to $400 per week	175-110A
	Fraternal benefit society benefits	176-22
	Group annuity policy or proceeds	175-132C
	Group life insurance policy	175-135
	Life or endowment policy, proceeds or cash value	175-125
	Life insurance policy if beneficiary is married woman	175-126
	Life insurance or annuity contract proceeds if clause prohibits proceeds from being used to pay beneficiary's creditors	175-119A
	Medical malpractice self-insurance	175F-15
miscellaneous	Property of business partnership	108A-25
pensions	Credit union employees	171-84
also see wages	ERISA-qualified benefits, including IRAs	235-34A; 246-28
	Private retirement benefits	32-41
	Public employees	32-19
	Savings bank employees	168-41, 168-44
personal property	Bank deposits to $125	235-34
	Beds & bedding; heating unit; clothing	235-34
	Bibles & books to $200 total; sewing machine to $200	235-34
	Burial plots, tombs & church pew	235-34
	Cash for fuel, heat, water or light to $75 per month	235-34
	Cash to $200/month for rent, in lieu of homestead	235-34
	Cooperative association shares to $100	235-34
	2 cows, 12 sheep, 2 swine, 4 tons of hay	235-34
	Food or cash for food to $300	235-34
	Furniture to $3,000; motor vehicle to $700	235-34
	Moving expenses for eminent domain	79-6A
	Trust company, bank or credit union deposits to $500	246-28A
public benefits	Public assistance	235-34
	Aid to families with dependent children	118-10
	Unemployment compensation	151A-36
	Veterans' benefits	115-5
	Workers' compensation	152-47
tools of trade	Arms, accoutrements & uniforms required	235-34
	Fishing boats, tackle & nets to $500	235-34
	Materials you designed & procured to $500	235-34
	Tools, implements & fixtures to $500 total	235-34
wages	Earned but unpaid wages to $125 per week	246-28
wildcard	None	

Michigan

Federal Bankruptcy Exemptions available. All law references are to Michigan Compiled Laws Annotated unless otherwise noted.

ASSET	EXEMPTION	LAW
homestead	Real property including condo to $3,500; property cannot exceed 1 lot in town, village, city, or 40 acres elsewhere; spouse or children of deceased owner may claim homestead exemption	559.214; 600.6023(1)(h),(i) 600.6023(3)
	Property held as tenancy by the entirety may be exempt against debts owed by only one spouse	*In re Smith*, 246 B.R. 540 (Bkrtcy. E.D. Mich., 2000).
insurance	Disability, mutual life or health benefits	600.6023(1)(f)
	Fraternal benefit society benefits	500.8181
	Life, endowment or annuity proceeds if clause prohibits proceeds from being used to pay beneficiary's creditors	500.4054
miscellaneous	Property of business partnership	449.25
pensions	Firefighters, police officers	38.559(6); 38.1683
	ERISA-qualified benefits, except contributions within last 120 days	600.6023(1)(l)
	IRAs, except contributions within last 120 days	600.6023(1)(k)
	Judges	38.2308; 38.1683
	Legislators	38.1057; 38.1683
	Probate judges	38.2308; 38.1683
	Public school employees	38.1346; 38.1683
	State employees	38.40; 38.1683
personal property	Appliances, utensils, books, furniture & household goods to $1,000 total	600.6023(1)(b)
	Building & loan association shares to $1,000 par value, in lieu of homestead	600.6023(1)(g)
	Burial plots, cemeteries; church pew, slip, seat for entire family	600.6023(1)(c)
	Clothing; family pictures	600.6023(1)(a)
	2 cows, 100 hens, 5 roosters, 10 sheep, 5 swine & feed to last 6 months	600.6023(1)(d)
	Food & fuel to last family for 6 months	600.6023(1)(a)
public benefits	Crime victims' compensation	18.362
	Social welfare benefits	400.63
	Unemployment compensation	421.30
	Veterans' benefits for Korean War veterans	35.977
	Veterans' benefits for Vietnam veterans	35.1027
	Veterans' benefits for WWII veterans	35.926
	Workers' compensation	418.821
tools of trade	Arms & accoutrements required	600.6023(1)(a)
	Tools, implements, materials, stock, apparatus, team, motor vehicle, horse & harness to $1,000 total	600.6023(1)(e)
wages	head of household may keep 60% of earned but unpaid wages (no less than $15/week), plus $2/week per non-spouse dependent; if not head of household may keep 40% (no less than $10/week)	600.5311
wildcard	None	

Minnesota

Federal Bankruptcy Exemptions available. All law references are to Minnesota Statutes Annotated.

NOTE: Section 550.37(4)(a) requires certain exemptions to be adjusted for inflation on July 1 of even-numbered years; this table includes all changes made through July 1, 2000. Exemptions are published in the May 1 issue of the Minnesota State Register, *www.comm.media.state.mn.us/bookstore/stateregister.asp,* or Minnesota Dept. of Commerce at (651) 296-7977.

ASSET	EXEMPTION	LAW
homestead	Home and land on which it is situated to $200,000; if homestead is used for agricultural purposes, $500,000; cannot exceed 1/2 acre in city, 160 acres elsewhere (husband & wife may not double);	510.01, 510.02
	Manufactured home to an unlimited value	550.37 subd. 12
insurance	Accident or disability proceeds	550.39
	Fraternal benefit society benefits	64B.18
	Life insurance proceeds to $36,000, if beneficiary is spouse or child of insured, plus $9,000 per dependent	550.37 subd. 10
	Police, fire or beneficiary association benefits	550.37 subd. 11
	Unmatured life insurance contract dividends, interest or loan value to $7,200 if insured is debtor or person debtor depends on	550.37 subd. 23
miscellaneous	Earnings of minor child	550.37 subd. 15
	Property of business partnership	323.24
pensions	ERISA-qualified benefits or needed for support, up to $54,000 in present value	550.37 subd. 24
	IRAs needed for support, up to $54,000 in present value	550.37 subd. 24
	Public employees	353.15
	State employees	352.96 subd. 6
	State troopers	352B.071
personal property	Appliances, furniture, jewelry, radio, phonographs & TV to $8,100 total	550.37 subd. 4(b)
	Bible and books	550.37 subd. 2
	Burial plot; church pew or seat	550.37 subd. 3
	Clothing, one watch, food & utensils for family	550.37 subd. 4(a)
	Motor vehicle to $3,600 (up to $36,000 if vehicle has been modified for disability)	550.37 subd. 12(a)
	Personal injury recoveries	550.37 subd. 22
	Proceeds for damaged exempt property	550.37 subds. 9, 16
	Wrongful death recoveries	550.37 subd. 22
public benefits	Crime victims' compensation	611A.60
	Public benefits	550.37 subd. 14
	Unemployment compensation	268.192 subd. 2
	Veterans' benefits	550.38
	Workers' compensation	176.175
tools of trade total (except teaching materials) can't exceed $13,000	Farm machines, implements, livestock, produce & crops	550.37 subd. 5
	Teaching materials of college, university, public school or public institution teacher	550.37 subd. 8
	Tools, machines, instruments, stock in trade, furniture & library to $9,000 total	550.37 subd. 6
wages	Wages, paid within 6 mos. of returning to work, after receiving welfare or after incarceration; includes earnings deposited in a financial institution in the last 60 days	550.37 subd. 14
	Minimum 75% of weekly disposable earnings or 40 times federal minimum hourly wage, whichever is greater	571.922
	Wages deposited into bank accounts for 20 days after depositing	550.37 subd. 13
wildcard	None	

NOTE: Some courts have held "unlimited" exemptions unconstitutional under the Minnesota Constitution, which allows debtors to exempt only a "reasonable amount" of property. See *In re Tveten,* 402 N.W. 2d 551 (Minn. 1987) and *In re Medill,* 119 B.R. 685, (D. Minn. 1990).

Mississippi

Federal Bankruptcy Exemptions not available. All law references are to Mississippi Code.

ASSET	EXEMPTION	LAW
homestead	Property you own & occupy to $75,000; if over 60 and married or widowed may claim a former residence; property cannot exceed 160 acres; sale proceeds exempt.	85-3-1(b)(i), 85-3-21, 85-3-23
	Mobile home does not qualify as homestead unless you own land on which it is located.	*In re Cobbins,* 234 B.R. 882 (S.D. Miss. 1999)
	May file homestead declaration	85-3-27, 85-3-31
insurance	Disability benefits	85-3-1(b)(ii)
	Fraternal benefit society benefits	83-29-39
	Homeowners' insurance proceeds to $75,000	85-3-23
	Life insurance proceeds if clause prohibits proceeds from being used to pay beneficiary's creditors	83-7-5
miscellaneous	Property of business partnership	79-12-49
pensions	ERISA-qualified benefits, IRAs, Keoghs deposited over 1 yr. before filing bankruptcy	85-3-1(b)(iii), (f)
	Firefighters (includes death benefits)	21-29-257, 45-2-1
	Highway patrol officers	25-13-31
	Law enforcement officers' death benefits	45-2-1
	Private retirement benefits to extent tax-deferred	71-1-43
	Police officers (includes death benefits)	21-29-257, 45-2-1
	Public employees retirement & disability benefits	25-11-129
	State employees	25-14-5
	Teachers	25-11-201(1)(d)
	Volunteer firefighters death benefits	45-2-1
personal property	Tangible personal property to $10,000: any item worth less than $200, furniture, dishes, kitchenware, household goods, appliances, 1 radio & 1 TV, 1 gun, 1 lawnmover, clothing, wedding rings, motor vehicles, tools of the trade, books, crops, health aids, domestic animals (does not include works of art, antiques, jewelry or electronic entertainment equipment)	85-3-1(a)
	Personal injury judgments to $10,000	85-3-17
	Sale or insurance proceeds for exempt property	85-3-1(b)(i)
public benefits	Assistance to aged	43-9-19
	Assistance to blind	43-3-71
	Assistance to disabled	43-29-15
	Crime victims' compensation	99-41-23
	Social Security	25-11-129
	Unemployment compensation	71-5-539
	Workers' compensation	71-3-43
tools of trade	See personal property	
wages	Earned but unpaid wages owed for 30 days; after 30 days, minimum 75% of earned but unpaid weekly disposable earnings, or 30 times the federal hourly minimum wage, whichever is greater (bankruptcy judge may authorize more for low-income debtors)	85-3-4
wildcard	See personal property	

Missouri

Federal Bankruptcy Exemptions not available. All law references are to Annotated Missouri Statutes unless otherwise noted.

ASSET	EXEMPTION	LAW
homestead	Real property to $8,000 or mobile home to $1,000 (joint owners may not double)	513.430(6), 513.475 In re Smith, 254 B.R. 751 (W.D. Mo. 2000)
	Property held as tenancy by the entirety may be exempt against debts owed by only one spouse	In re Eads, 271 B.R. 371 (Bkrtcy.W.D.Mo. 2002).
insurance	Assessment or insurance premium proceeds	377.090
	Disability or illness benefits	513.430(10)(c)
	Fraternal benefit society benefits to $5,000, bought over 6 months before filing	513.430(8)
	Life insurance dividends, loan value or interest to $5,000, bought over 6 months before filing	513.430(8)
	Life insurance proceeds if policy owned by a woman & insures her husband	376.530
	Life insurance proceeds if policy owned by unmarried woman & insures her father or brother	376.550
	Stipulated insurance premiums	377.330
	Unmatured life insurance policy	513.430(7)
miscellaneous	Alimony, child support to $500 per month	513.430(10)(d)
	Property of business partnership	358.250
pensions	Employees of cities with 100,000 or more people	71.207
	ERISA-qualified benefits needed for support (only payments being received)	513.430(10)(e)
	Firefighters	87.090, 87.365, 87.485
	Highway & transportation employees	104.250
	Police department employees	86.190, 86.353, 86.493, 86.780
	Public officers & employees	70.695, 70.755
	State employees	104.540
	Teachers	169.090
personal property	Appliances, household goods, furnishings, clothing, books, crops, animals & musical instruments to $1,000 total	513.430(1)
	Burial grounds to 1 acre or $100	214.190
	Health aids	513.430(9)
	Jewelry to $500	513.430(2)
	Motor vehicle to $1,000	513.430(5)
	Personal injury causes of action	In re Mitchell, 73 B.R. 93 (E.D. Mo. 1987)
	Wrongful death recoveries for person you depended on	513.430(11)
public benefits	Public assistance	513.430(10)(a)
	Social Security	513.430(10)(a)
	Unemployment compensation	288.380(10)(l); 513.430(10)(c)
	Veterans' benefits	513.430(10)b)
	Workers' compensation	287.260
tools of trade	Implements, books & tools of trade to $2,000	513.430(4)
wages	Minimum 75% of weekly earnings (90% of weekly earnings for head of family) , or 30 times the federal minimum hourly wage, whichever is more; bankruptcy judge may authorize more for low-income debtors	525.030
	Wages of servant or common laborer to $90	513.470
wildcard	$1,250 of any property if head of family, else $400; head of family may claim additional $250 per child.	513.430(3), 513.440

Montana

Federal Bankruptcy Exemptions not available. All law references are to Montana Code Annotated.

ASSET	EXEMPTION	LAW
homestead	Real property or mobile home you occupy to $60,000; sale, condemnation or insurance proceeds exempt 18 months	70-32-104, 70-32-201, 70-32-213
	Must record homestead declaration before filing for bankruptcy	70-32-105
insurance	Annuity contract proceeds to $350 per month	33-15-514
	Disability or illness proceeds, avails or benefits	25-13-608(1)(d); 33-15-513
	Fraternal benefit society benefits	33-7-522
	Group life insurance policy or proceeds	33-15-512
	Hail insurance benefits	80-2-245
	Life insurance proceeds if clause prohibits proceeds from being used to pay beneficiary's creditors	33-20-120
	Medical, surgical or hospital care benefits	25-13-608(1)(f)
	Unmatured life insurance contracts to $4,000	25-13-609(4)
miscellaneous	Alimony, child support	25-13-608(1)(g)
pensions	ERISA-qualified benefits deposited over 1 year before filing bankruptcy in excess of 15% of debtor's yearly income	31-2-106
	Firefighters	19-18-612(1)
	IRA contributions & earnings made before judgment filed	25-13-608(1)(e)
	Police officers	19-19-504(1)
	Public employees	19-2-1004
	Teachers	19-20-706(2)
	University system employees	19-21-212
personal property	Appliances, household furnishings, goods, animals with feed, crops, musical instruments, books, firearms, sporting goods, clothing & jewelry to $600 per item, $4,500 total	25-13-609(1)
	Burial plot	25-13-608(1)(h)
	Cooperative association shares to $500 value	35-15-404
	Health aids	25-13-608(1)(a)
	Motor vehicle to $2,500	25-13-609(2)
	Proceeds from sale or for damage or loss of exempt property for 6 mos. after received	25-13-610
public benefits	Aid to aged, disabled	53-2-607
	Crime victims' compensation	53-9-129
	Local public assistance	25-13-608(1)(b)
	Silicosis benefits	39-73-110
	Social Security	25-13-608(1)(b)
	Subsidized adoption payments	53-2-607
	Unemployment compensation	31-2-106(2); 39-51-3105
	Veterans' benefits	25-13-608(1)(c)
	Vocational rehabilitation to the blind	53-2-607
	Workers' compensation	39-71-743
tools of trade	Implements, books & tools of trade to $3,000	25-13-609(3)
	Uniforms, arms, accoutrements needed to carry out government functions	25-13-613(b)
wages	Minimum 75% of earned but unpaid weekly disposable earnings, or 30 times the federal hourly minimum wage, whichever is greater; bankruptcy judge may authorize more for low-income debtors	25-13-614
wildcard	None	

Nebraska

Federal Bankruptcy Exemptions not available. All law references are to Revised Statutes of Nebraska.

ASSET	EXEMPTION	LAW
homestead	$12,500 for married debtor or head of household; cannot exceed 2 lots in city or village, 160 acres elsewhere; sale proceeds exempt 6 months after sale (husband & wife may not double)	40-101, 40-111, 40-113
	May record homestead declaration	40-105
insurance	Fraternal benefit society benefits to $10,000 loan value unless beneficiary convicted of a crime related to benefits	44-1089
	Life insurance or annuity contract proceeds to $10,000 loan value	44-371
miscellaneous	Property of business partnership	67-325
pensions *also see wages*	County employees	23-2322
	ERISA-qualified benefits needed for support	25-1563.01
	Military disability benefits	25-1559
	School employees	79-948
	State employees	84-1324
personal property	Burial plot	12-517
	Clothing	25-1556(2)
	Crypts, lots, tombs, niches, vaults	12-605
	Furniture, household goods & appliances, household electronics, personal computers, books & musical instruments to $1,500	25-1556(3)
	Health aids	25-1556(5)
	Perpetual care funds	12-511
	Personal injury recoveries	25-1563.02
	Personal possessions	25-1556
public benefits	Aid to disabled, blind, aged, public assistance	68-1013
	Unemployment compensation	48-647
	Workers' compensation	48-149
tools of trade	Equipment or tools including a vehicle used in/or for commuting to principal place of business to $2,400 (husband & wife may double)	25-1556(4); *In re Keller,* 50 B.R. 23 (D. Neb. 1985)
wages	Minimum 85% of earned but unpaid weekly disposable earnings or pension payments for head of family; minimum 75% of earned but unpaid weekly disposable earnings, or 30 times the federal hourly minimum wage, whichever is greater for all others; bankruptcy judge may authorize more for low-income debtors	25-1558
wildcard	$2,500 of any personal property, except wages, in lieu of homestead	25-1552

Nevada

Federal Bankruptcy Exemptions not available. All law references are to Nevada Revised Statutes Annotated.

ASSET	EXEMPTION	LAW
homestead	Real property or mobile home to $125,000 (husband & wife may not double)	115.010, 21.090(1)(m)
	Must record homestead declaration before filing for bankruptcy	115.020
insurance	Annuity contract proceeds to $350 per month	687B.290
	Fraternal benefit society benefits	695A.220
	Group life or health policy or proceeds	687B.280
	Health proceeds or avails	687B.270
	Life insurance policy or proceeds if annual premiums not over $1,000 (husband & wife may double)	21.090(1)(k) *In re Bower,* 234 B.R. 109 (Nev. 1999)
	Life insurance proceeds if you're not the insured	687B.260
miscellaneous	Alimony and child support	21.090(1)(r)
	Property of business partnership	87.250
pensions	ERISA-qualified benefits or IRAs to $500,000	21.090(1)(q)
	Public employees	286.670
personal property	Appliances, household goods, furniture, home & yard equipment to $3,000 total	21.090(1)(b)
	Books to $1,500	21.090(1)(a)
	Burial plot purchase money held in trust	689.700
	Funeral service contract money held in trust	689.700
	Health aids	21.090(1)(p)
	Keepsakes & pictures	21.090(1)(a)
	Metal-bearing ores, geological specimens, art curiosities or paleontological remains; must be arranged, classified, catalogued & numbered in reference books	21.100
	Mortgage impound accounts	645B.180
	Motor vehicle to $4,500; no limit on vehicle equipped for disabled person	21.090(1)(f),(o)
	One gun	21.090(1)(i)
public benefits	Aid to blind, aged, disabled, public assistance	422.291
	Industrial insurance (workers' compensation)	616C.205
	Unemployment compensation	612.710
	Vocational rehabilitation benefits	615.270
tools of trade	Arms, uniforms & accoutrements you're required to keep	21.090(1)(j)
	Cabin or dwelling of miner or prospector; mining claim, cars, implements & appliances to $4,500 total (for working claim only)	21.090(1)(e)
	Farm trucks, stock, tools, equipment & seed to $4,500	21.090(1)(c)
	Library, equipment, supplies, tools & materials to $4,500	21.090(1)(d)
wages	Minimum 75% of disposable weekly earnings or 30 times the federal minimum hourly wage per week, whichever is more; bankruptcy judge may authorize more for low-income debtors	21.090(1)(g)
wildcard	None	

New Hampshire

Federal Bankruptcy Exemptions available. All law references are to New Hampshire Revised Statutes Annotated.

ASSET	EXEMPTION	LAW
homestead	Real property or manufactured housing (and the land it's on if you own it) to $30,000	480:1
insurance	Firefighters' aid insurance	402:69
	Fraternal benefit society benefits	418:24
	Homeowners' insurance proceeds to $5,000	512:21(VIII)
miscellaneous	Child support	161-C-11
	Jury, witness fees	512:21(VI)
	Property of business partnership	304-A:25
	Wages of minor child	512:21(III)
pensions	Federally created pension (only benefits building up)	512:21(IV)
	Firefighters	102:23
	Police officers	103:18
	Public employees	100-A:26
personal property	Beds, bedding & cooking utensils	511:2(II)
	Bibles & books to $800	511:2(VIII)
	Burial plot, lot	511:2(XIV)
	Church pew	511:2(XV)
	Clothing	511:2(I)
	Cooking & heating stoves, refrigerator	511:2(IV)
	1 cow, 6 sheep & their fleece, 4 tons of hay	511:2(XI), (XII)
	Domestic fowl to $300	511:2(XIII)
	Food & fuel to $400	511:2(VI)
	Furniture to $3,500	511:2(III)
	1 hog or pig or its meat (if slaughtered)	511:2(X)
	Jewelry to $500	511:2(XVII)
	Motor vehicle to $4,000	511:2(XVI)
	Proceeds for lost or destroyed exempt property	512:21(VIII)
	Sewing machine	511:2(V)
public benefits	Aid to blind, aged, disabled, public assistance	167:25
	Unemployment compensation	282-A:159
	Workers' compensation	281-A:52
tools of trade	Tools of your occupation to $5,000	511:2(IX)
	Uniforms, arms & equipment of military member	511:2(VII)
	Yoke of oxen or horse needed for farming or teaming	511:2(XII)
wages	50 times the federal minimum hourly wage per week	512:21(II)
	Earned but unpaid wages of spouse	512:21(III)
wildcard	$1,000 of any property	511:2(XVIII)
	Unused portion of bibles & books, food & fuel, furniture, jewelry, motor vehicle and tools of trade exemptions to $7,000	511:2(XVIII)

New Jersey

Federal Bankruptcy Exemptions available. All law references are to New Jersey Statutes Annotated.

ASSET	EXEMPTION	LAW
homestead	None, but survivorship interest of a spouse in property held as tenancy by the entirety is exempt from creditors of a single spouse.	*Freda v. Commercial Trust Co. of New Jersey*, 570 A.2d 409 (N.J.,1990).
insurance	Annuity contract proceeds to $500 per month	17B:24-7
	Disability or death benefits for military member	38A:4-8
	Disability, death, medical or hospital benefits for civil defense workers	App. A:9-57.6
	Group life or health policy or proceeds	17B:24-9
	Health or disability benefits	17:18-12, 17B:24-8
	Life insurance proceeds if clause prohibits proceeds from being used to pay beneficiary's creditors	17B:24-10
	Life insurance proceeds or avails if you're not the insured	17B:24-6b
pensions	Alcohol beverage control officers	43:8A-20
	City boards of health employees	43:18-12
	Civil defense workers	App. A:9-57.6
	County employees	43:10-57, 43:10-105
	ERISA-qualified benefits for city employees	43:13-9
	Firefighters, police officers, traffic officers	43:16-7, 43:16A-17
	IRAs	*In re Yuhas*, 104 F.3d 612 (3rd Cir. 1997)
	Judges	43:6A-41
	Municipal employees	43:13-44
	Prison employees	43:7-13
	Public employees	43:15A-53
	School district employees	18A:66-116
	State police	53:5A-45
	Street & water department employees	43:19-17
	Teachers	18A:66-51
	Trust containing personal property created pursuant to federal tax law, including 401(k) plans and higher education (529) savings plans.	25:2-1
personal property	Personal property & possessions of any kind, stock or interest in corporations to $1,000 total	2A:17-19
	Burial plots	8A:5-10
	Clothing	2A:17-19
	Furniture & household goods to $1,000	2A:26-4
public benefits	Crime victims' compensation	52:4B-30
	Old age, permanent disability assistance	44:7-35
	Unemployment compensation	43:21-53
	Workers' compensation	34:15-29
tools of trade	None	
wages	90% of earned but unpaid wages if annual income under $7,500; if annual income over $7,500, judge decides amount that is exempt	2A:17-56
	Wages or allowances received by military personnel	38A:4-8
wildcard	None	

New Mexico

Federal Bankruptcy Exemptions available. All law references are to New Mexico Statutes Annotated.

ASSET	EXEMPTION	LAW
homestead	$30,000 (joint owners may double)	42-10-9
insurance	Benevolent association benefits to $5,000	42-10-4
	Fraternal benefit society benefits	59A-44-18
	Life, accident, health or annuity benefits, withdrawal or cash value, if beneficiary is a New Mexico resident	42-10-3
	Life insurance proceeds	42-10-5
miscellaneous	Ownership interest in unincorporated association	53-10-2
	Property of business partnership	54-1A-501
pensions	Pension or retirement benefits	42-10-1, 42-10-2
	Public school employees	22-11-42A
personal property	Books & furniture	42-10-1, 42-10-2
	Building materials	48-2-15
	Clothing	42-10-1, 42-10-2
	Cooperative association shares, minimum amount needed to be member	53-4-28
	Health aids	42-10-1, 42-10-2
	Jewelry to $2,500	42-10-1, 42-10-2
	Materials, tools & machinery to dig, drill, complete, operate or repair oil line, gas well or pipeline	70-4-12
	Motor vehicle to $4,000	42-10-1, 42-10-2
public benefits	Crime victims' compensation (will be repealed in 2006)	31-22-15
	General assistance	27-2-21
	Occupational disease disablement benefits	52-3-37
	Unemployment compensation	51-1-37
	Workers' compensation	52-1-52
tools of trade	$1,500	42-10-1, 42-10-2
wages	Minimum 75% of disposable earnings or 40 times the federal hourly minimum wage, whichever is more; bankruptcy judge may authorize more for low-income debtors	35-12-7
wildcard	$500 of any personal property	42-10-1
	$2,000 of any real or personal property, in lieu of homestead	42-10-10

New York

Federal Bankruptcy Exemptions not available. Law references to Consolidated Laws of New York, Civil Practice Law & Rules, are abbreviated C.P.L.R.

ASSET	EXEMPTION	LAW
homestead	Real property including co-op, condo or mobile home, to $10,000 (husband & wife may double)	C.P.L.R. 5206(a); *In re Pearl*, 723 F.2d 193 (2nd Cir. 1983)
insurance	Annuity contract benefits due the debtor, if debtor paid for the contract; $5,000 limit if purchased within 6 mos. prior to filing & not tax-deferred	Ins. 3212(d); Debt. & Cred. 283(1)
	Disability or illness benefits to $400/month	Ins. 3212(c)
	Life insurance proceeds left at death with the insurance company, if clause prohibits proceeds from being used to pay beneficiary's creditors	Est. Powers & Trusts 7-1.5(a)(2)
	Life insurance proceeds and avails if the beneficiary is not the debtor, or if debtor's spouse has taken out policy	Ins. 3212(b)
miscellaneous	Alimony, child support	C.P.L.R. 5205 (d)(3); Debt. & Cred. 282(2)(d)
	Property of business partnership	Partnership 51
pensions	ERISA-qualified benefits, IRAs, & Keoghs & income needed for support	C.P.L.R. 5205(c); Debt. & Cred. 282(2)(e)
	Public retirement benefits	Ins. 4607
	State employees	Ret. & Soc. Sec. 10
	Teachers	Educ. 524
	Village police officers	Unconsolidated 5711-o
	Volunteer ambulance workers' benefits	Vol. Amb. Wkr. Ben. 23
	Volunteer firefighters' benefits	Vol. Firefighter Ben. 23
personal property	Bible, schoolbooks, other books to $50; pictures; clothing; church pew or seat; sewing machine, refrigerator, TV, radio; furniture, cooking utensils & tableware, dishes; food to last 60 days; stoves with fuel to last 60 days; domestic animal with food to last 60 days, to $450; wedding ring; watch to $35; exemptions may not exceed $5,000 total (including tools of trade & limited annuity)	C.P.L.R. 5205(a)(1)-(6); Debt. & Cred. 283(1)
	Burial plot, without structure to 1/4 acre	C.P.L.R. 5206(f)
	Cash (including savings bonds, tax refunds, bank & credit union deposits) to $2,500, or to $5,000 after exemptions for personal property taken, whichever amount is less (for debtors who do not claim homestead)	Debt. & Cred. 283(2)
	College tuition savings program trust fund	C.P.L.R. 5205(j)
	Health aids, including service animals with food	C.P.L.R. 5205(h)
	Lost future earnings recoveries needed for support	Debt. & Cred. 282(3)(iv)
	Motor vehicle to $2,400 (husband & wife may double)	Debt. & Cred. 282(1) *In re Miller*, 167 B.R. 782 (S.D. N.Y. 1994)
	Personal injury recoveries up to 1 year after receiving	Debt. & Cred. 282(3)(iii)
	Recovery for injury to exempt property up to 1 year after receiving	C.P.L.R. 5205(b)
	Savings & Loan Savings to $600	Banking 407
	Security deposit to landlord, utility company	C.P.L.R. 5205(g)
	Spendthrift trust fund principal, 90% of income if not created by debtor	C.P.L.R. 5205(c), (d)
	Wrongful death recoveries for person you depended on	Debt. & Cred. 282(3)(ii)
public benefits	Aid to blind, aged, disabled	Debt. & Cred. 282(2)(c)
	Crime victims' compensation	Debt. & Cred. 282(3)(i)
	Home relief, local public assistance	Debt. & Cred. 282(2)(a)
	Public assistance	Soc. Serv. 137
	Social Security	Debt. & Cred. 282(2)(a)
	Unemployment compensation	Debt. & Cred. 282(2)(a)
	Veterans' benefits	Debt. & Cred. 282(2)(b)
	Workers' compensation	Debt. & Cred. 282(2)(c); Work. Comp. 33, 218
tools of trade	Farm machinery, team & food for 60 days; professional furniture, books & instruments to $600 total	C.P.L.R. 5205(a), (b)
	Uniforms, medal, emblem, equipment, horse, arms & sword of member of military	C.P.L.R. 5205(e)
wages	90% of earned but unpaid wages received within 60 days before & anytime after filing	C.P.L.R. 5205(d)
	90% of earnings from dairy farmer's sales to milk dealers	C.P.L.R. 5205(f)
	100% of pay of non-commissioned officer, private or musician in U.S. or N.Y. state armed forces	C.P.L.R. 5205(e)
wildcard	None	

North Carolina

Federal Bankruptcy Exemptions not available. All law references are to General Statutes of North Carolina unless otherwise noted.

ASSET	EXEMPTION	LAW
homestead	Real or personal property, including co-op, used as residence to $10,000; up to $3,500 of unused portion of homestead may be applied to any property (husband and wife may double)	1C-1601(a)(1),(2)
	Property held as tenancy by the entirety may be exempt against debts owed by only one spouse	*In re Chandler*, 148 B.R. 13 (E.D. N.C., 1992)
insurance	Employee group life policy or proceeds	58-58-165
	Life insurance on spouse or children	1C-1601(a)(6); Const. Art. X § 5
	Fraternal benefit society benefits	58-24-85
miscellaneous	Property of business partnership	59-55
	Support received by a surviving spouse for 1 year, up to $10,000	30-15
pensions	Firefighters & rescue squad workers	58-86-90
	IRAs	1C-1601(a)(9)
	Law enforcement officers	143-166.30(g)
	Legislators	120-4.29
	Municipal, city & county employees	128-31
	Teachers & state employees	135-9, 135-95
personal property	Animals, crops, musical instruments, books, clothing, appliances, household goods & furnishings to $3,500 total; may add $750 per dependent, up to $3,000 total additional (all property must have been purchased at least 90 days before filing	1C-1601(a)(4),(d)
	Burial plot to $10,000, in lieu of homestead	1C-1601(a)(1)
	Health aids	1C-1601(a)(7)
	Motor vehicle to $1,500	1C-1601(a)(3)
	Personal injury and wrongful death recoveries for person you depended on	1C-1601(a)(8)
public benefits	Aid to blind	111-18
	Crime victims' compensation	15B-17
	Special adult assistance	108A-36
	Unemployment compensation	96-17
	Workers' compensation	97-21
tools of trade	Implements, books & tools of trade to $750	1C-1601(a)(5)
wages	Earned but unpaid wages received 60 days before filing for bankruptcy, needed for support	1-362
wildcard	$3,500 less any amount claimed for homestead or burial exemption, of any property	1C-1601(a)(2)
	$500 of any personal property	Constitution Art. X §1

North Dakota

Federal Bankruptcy Exemptions not available. All law references are to North Dakota Century Code.

ASSET	EXEMPTION	LAW
homestead	Real property, house trailer or mobile home to $80,000 (husband & wife may not double)	28-22-02(10); 47-18-01
insurance	Fraternal benefit society benefits	26.1-15.1-18, 26.1-33-40
	Life insurance proceeds payable to deceased's estate, not to a specific beneficiary	26.1-33-40
	Life insurance surrender value to $100,000 per policy, if beneficiary is insured's dependent & policy was owned over 1 year before filing for bankruptcy; limit does not apply if more needed for support	28-22-03.1(3)
miscellaneous	Child support payments	14-09-09.31
pensions	Disabled veterans' benefits, except military retirement pay	28-22-03.1(4)(d)
	ERISA-qualified benefits, IRAs & Keoghs to $100,000 per plan; limit does not apply if more needed for support; total (with life insurance surrender value exemption cannot exceed $200,000)	28-22-03.1(3)
	Public employees	28-22-19(1)
personal property	1. All debtors may exempt:	
	Bible, schoolbooks; other books to $100	28-22-02(4)
	Burial plots, church pew	28-22-02(2),(3)
	Cash to $7,500, in lieu of homestead	28-22-03.1(1)
	Clothing & family pictures	28-22-02(1),(5)
	Crops or grain raised by debtor on 1 tract 160 acres	28-22-02(8)
	Food & fuel to last 1 year	28-22-02(6)
	Insurance proceeds for exempt property	28-22-02(9)
	Motor vehicle to $1,200	28-22-03.1(2)
	Personal injury recoveries to $7,500	28-22-03.1(4)(b)
	Wrongful death recoveries to $7,500	28-22-03.1(4)(a)
	2. Head of household not claiming crops or grain may claim $5,000 of any personal property or:	28-22-03
	Books & musical instruments to $1,500	28-22-04(1)
	Household & kitchen furniture, beds & bedding, to $1,000	28-22-04(2)
	Library & tools of professional, tools of mechanic & stock in trade, to $1,000	28-22-04(4)
	Livestock & farm implements to $4,500	28-22-04(3)
	3. Non-head of household not claiming crops or grain, may claim $2,500 of any personal property	28-22-05
public benefits	Crime victims' compensation	28-22-19(2)
	Public assistance	28-22-19(3)
	Social Security	28-22-03.1(4)(c)
	Unemployment compensation	52-06-30
	Workers' compensation	65-05-29
tools of trade	See personal property, option 2	
wages	Minimum 75% of disposable weekly earnings or 40 times the federal minimum wage, whichever is more; bankruptcy judge may authorize more for low-income debtors	32-09.1-03
wildcard	See personal property, options 2 or 3	

Ohio

Federal Bankruptcy Exemptions not available. All law references are to Ohio Revised Code unless otherwise noted.

ASSET	EXEMPTION	LAW
homestead	Real or personal property used as residence to $5,000	2329.66(A)(1)(b)
	Property held as tenancy by the entirety may be exempt against debts owed by only one spouse	In re Pernus, 143 B.R. 856 (N.D. Ohio, 1992)
insurance	Benevolent society benefits to $5,000	2329.63, 2329.66(A)(6)(a)
	Disability benefits to $600 per month	2329.66(A)(6)(e); 3923.19
	Fraternal benefit society benefits	2329.66(A)(6)(d); 3921.18
	Group life insurance policy or proceeds	2329.66(A)(6)(c); 3917.05
	Life, endowment or annuity contract avails for your spouse, child or dependent	2329.66(A)(6)(b); 3911.10
	Life insurance proceeds for a spouse	3911.12
	Life insurance proceeds if clause prohibits proceeds from being used to pay beneficiary's creditors	3911.14
miscellaneous	Alimony, child support needed for support	2329.66(A)(11)
	Property of business partnership	1775.24; 2329.66(A)(14)
Pensions	ERISA-qualified benefits needed for support	2329.66(A)(10)(b)
	Firefighters, police officers	742.47
	Public safety officers death benefit	2329.66(A)(10)(a)
	IRAs & Keoghs needed for support	2329.66(A)(10)(c)
	Public employees	145.56
	Public school employees	3309.66
	State highway patrol employees	5505.22
	Volunteer firefighters' dependents	146.13
Personal property	Animals, crops, books, musical instruments, appliances, household goods, furnishings, firearms, hunting & fishing equipment to $200 per item; jewelry to $400 for 1 item, $200 for all others; $1,500 total ($2,000 if no homestead exemption claimed) (husband & wife may double)	2329.66(A)(4)(b),(c),(d) In re Szydlowski, 186 B.R. 907 (N.D. Ohio 1995)
	Beds, bedding, clothing to $200 per item	2329.66(A)(3)
	Burial plot	517.09, 2329.66(A)(8)
	Cash, money due within 90 days, tax refund, bank, security & utility deposits to $400 total (husband & wife may double)	2329.66(A)(4)(a) In re Szydlowski, 186 B.R. 907 (N.D. Ohio 1995)
	Cooking unit & refrigerator to $300 each	2329.66(A)(3)
	Health aids	2329.66(A)(7)
	Lost future earnings needed for support, received during 12 months before filing	2329.66(A)(12)(d)
	Motor vehicle to $1,000	2329.66(A)(2)(b)
	Personal injury recoveries to $5,000, received during 12 months before filing	2329.66(A)(12)(c)
	Tuition credit or payment	2329.66(A)(16)
	Wrongful death recoveries for person debtor depended on, needed for support, received during 12 months before filing	2329.66(A)(12)(b)
public benefits	Crime victim's compensation, received during 12 months before filing	2329.66(A)(12)(a); 2743.66(D)
	Disability assistance payments	2329.66(A)(9)(f)
	Public assistance	2329.66(A)(9)(d); 5107.12
	Unemployment compensation	2329.66(A)(9)(c); 4141.32
	Vocational rehabilitation benefits	2329.66(A)(9)(a); 3304.19
	Workers' compensation	2329.66(A)(9)(b); 4123.67
tools of trade	Implements, books & tools of trade to $750	2329.66(A)(5)
wages	Minimum 75% of disposable weekly earnings or 40 times the federal hourly minimum wage, whichever is higher; bankruptcy judge may authorize more for low-income debtors	2329.66(A)(13)
wildcard	$400 of any property	2329.66(A)(17)

Oklahoma

Federal Bankruptcy Exemptions not available. All law references are to Oklahoma Statutes Annotated.

ASSET	EXEMPTION	LAW
homestead	Real property or manufactured home to unlimited value; property cannot exceed 1 acre in city, town or village, or 160 acres elsewhere; $5,000 limit if more than 25% of total sq. ft. area used for business purposes; okay to rent homestead as long as no other residence is acquired	31-1(A)(1), 31-1(A)(2), 31-2
insurance	Annuity benefits & cash value	36-3631.1
	Assessment or mutual benefits	36-2410
	Fraternal benefit society benefits	36-2718.1
	Funeral benefits prepaid & placed in trust	36-6125
	Group life policy or proceeds	36-3632
	Life, health, accident & mutual benefit insurance proceeds & cash value, if clause prohibits proceeds from being used to pay beneficiary's creditors	36-3631.1
	Limited stock insurance benefits	36-2510
miscellaneous	Alimony, child support	31-1(A)(19)
	Property of business partnership	54-1-504
pensions	County employees	19-959
	Disabled veterans	31-7
	ERISA-qualified benefits, IRAs & Keoghs	31-1(A)(20),(23),(24)
	Firefighters	11-49-126
	Judges	20-1111
	Law enforcement employees	47-2-303.3
	Police officers	11-50-124
	Public employees	74-923
	Tax exempt benefits	60-328
	Teachers	70-17-109
personal property	Books, portraits & pictures	31-1(A)-7
	Burial plots	31-1(A)(4); 8-7
	Clothing to $4,000	31-1(A)(8)
	Federal earned income tax credit	31-1(A)(25)
	Food & seed for growing to last 1 year	31-1(A)(17)
	1 gun	31-1(A)(14)
	Health aids	31-1(A)(9)
	Household & kitchen furniture	31-1(A)(3)
	Livestock for personal or family use: 5 dairy cows & calves under 6 months; 100 chickens; 20 sheep; 10 hogs; 2 horses, bridles & saddles; forage & feed to last 1 year	31-1(A)(10),(11),(12), (15),(16),(17)
	Motor vehicle to $3,000	31-1(A)(13)
	Personal injury & wrongful death recoveries to $50,000	31-1(A)(21)
	Prepaid funeral benefits	36-6125(H)
	War bond payroll savings account	51-42
public benefits	Crime victims' compensation	21-142.13
	Public assistance	56-173
	Social Security	56-173
	Unemployment compensation	40-2-303
	Workers' compensation	85-48
tools of trade	Implements needed to farm homestead, tools, books & apparatus to $5,000 total	31-1(A)(5),(6), 31-1(C)
wages	75% of wages earned in 90 days before filing bankruptcy; bankruptcy judge may allow more if you show hardship	12-1171.1; 31-1(A)(18), 31-1.1
wildcard	None	

Oregon

Federal Bankruptcy Exemptions not available. All law references are to Oregon Revised Statutes.

ASSET	EXEMPTION	LAW
homestead	Real property you occupy or intend to occupy to $25,000 ($33,000 for joint owners); mobile home on property you own or houseboat to $23,000 ($30,000 for joint owners); mobile home not on your land to $20,000 ($27,000 for joint owners); property cannot exceed 1 block in town or city or 160 acres elsewhere; sale proceeds exempt 1 year from sale, if you intend to purchase another home	23.164, 23.240, 23.250
	Tenancy by entirety not exempt, but subject to rights of non-debtor spouse	*In re Pletz*, 225 B.R. 206 (D. Or., 1997)
	Real property of a soldier or sailor during time of war	408.440
insurance	Annuity contract benefits to $500 per month	743.049
	Fraternal benefit society benefits	748.207
	Group life policy or proceeds not payable to insured	743.047
	Health or disability proceeds or avails	743.050
	Life insurance proceeds or cash value if you are not the insured	743.046
miscellaneous	Alimony, child support needed for support	23.160(1)(i)
	Liquor licenses	471.292 (1)
	Property of business partnership	68.420
pensions	ERISA-qualified benefits, including IRAs and SEPs	23.170
	Public officers, employees	237.980; 238.445; 23.166 (2)
personal property	Bank deposits to $7,500; cash for sold exempt property	23.166
	Books, pictures & musical instruments to $600 total (husband & wife may double)	23.160(1)(a)
	Burial plot	65.870
	Clothing, jewelry & other personal items to $1,800 total (husband & wife may double)	23.160(1)(b)
	Domestic animals, poultry & pets to $1,000 plus food to last 60 days	23.160(1)(e)
	Federal earned income tax credit	23.160(1)(n)
	Food & fuel to last 60 days if debtor is householder	23.160(1)(f)
	Furniture, household items, utensils, radios & TVs to $3,000 total	23.160(1)(f)
	Health aids	23.160(1)(h)
	Higher education tuition savings account to $7,500	348.863; 23.166(1)
	Lost earnings payments for debtor or someone debtor depended on, to extent needed (husband & wife may double)	23.160(1)(L),(3)
	Motor vehicle to $1,700 (husband & wife may double)	23.160(1)(d),(3)
	Personal injury recoveries to $10,000 (husband & wife may double)	23.160(1)(k),(3)
	Pistol; rifle or shotgun (owned by person over 16) to $1,000	23.200
public benefits	Aid to blind	412.115
	Aid to disabled	412.610
	Civil defense & disaster relief	401.405
	Crime victims' compensation (husband & wife each claim)	23.160(1)(j)(A),(3); 147.325
	General assistance	411.760
	Injured inmates' benefits	655.530
	Medical assistance	414.095
	Old-age assistance	413.130
	Unemployment compensation	657.855
	Veterans' benefits	407.125
	Vocational rehabilitation	344.580
	Workers' compensation	656.234
tools of trade	Tools, library, team with food to last 60 days, to $3,000 (husband & wife may double)	23.160(1)(c),(3)
wages	75% of disposable wages or $170 per week, whichever is greater; bankruptcy judge may authorize more for low-income debtors	23.186
	Wages withheld in state employee's bond savings accounts	292.070
wildcard	$400 of any personal property not already covered by existing exemption	23.160(1)(o)

Pennsylvania

Federal Bankruptcy Exemptions available. All law references are to Pennsylvania Consolidated Statutes Annotated.

ASSET	EXEMPTION	LAW
homestead	None, however, property held as tenancy by the entirety may be exempt against debts owed by only one spouse	*In re Martin*, 259 B.R. 119 (M.D. Pa. 2001)
insurance	Accident or disability benefits	42-8124(c)(7)
	Fraternal benefit society benefits	42-8124(c)(1),(8)
	Group life policy or proceeds	42-8124(c)(5)
	Insurance policy or annuity contract payments, where insured is the beneficiary, cash value or proceeds to $100 per month	42-8124(c)(3)
	Life insurance annuity policy cash value or proceeds if beneficiary is insured's dependent, child or spouse	42-8124(c)(6)
	Life insurance and annuity proceeds if clause prohibits proceeds from being used to pay beneficiary's creditors	42-8214(c)(4)
	No-fault automobile insurance proceeds	42-8124(c)(9)
miscellaneous	Property of business partnership	15-8342
pensions	City employees	53-13445, 53-23572, 53-39383; 42-8124(b)(1)(iv)
	County employees	16-4716
	Municipal employees	53-881.115; 42-8124(b)(1)(vi)
	Police officers	53-764, 53-776, 53-23666; 42-8124(b)(1)(iii)
	Private retirement benefits to extent tax-deferred, if clause prohibits proceeds from being used to pay beneficiary's creditors; exemption limited to deposits of $15,000 per year made at least 1 year before filing (limit does not apply to rollovers from other exempt funds or accounts)	42-8124(b)(1)(vii), (viii),(ix)
	Public school employees	24-8533; 42-8124(b)(1)(i)
	State employees	71-5953; 42-8124(b)(1)(ii)
personal property	Bibles & schoolbooks	42-8124(a)(2)
	Clothing	42-8124(a)(1)
	Military uniforms & accoutrements	42-8124(a)(4); 51-4103
	Sewing machines	42-8124(a)(3)
public benefits	Crime victims' compensation	18-11.708
	Korean conflict veterans' benefits	51-20098
	Unemployment compensation	42-8124(a)(10); 43-863
	Veterans' benefits	51-20012, 20048, 20098; 20127
	Workers' compensation	42-8124(c)(2)
tools of trade	Seamstress' sewing machine	42-8124(a)(3)
wages	Earned but unpaid wages	42-8127
wildcard	$300 of any property, including cash, real property, securities or proceeds from sale of exempt property	42-8123

Rhode Island

Federal Bankruptcy Exemptions available. All law references are to General Laws of Rhode Island.

ASSET	EXEMPTION	LAW
homestead	$150,000 in land & buildings you occupy or intend to occupy as a principal residence (husband & wife may not double)	9-26-4.1
insurance	Accident or sickness proceeds, avails or benefits	27-18-24
	Fraternal benefit society benefits	27-25-18
	Life insurance proceeds if clause prohibits proceeds from being used to pay beneficiary's creditors	27-4-12
	Temporary disability insurance	28-41-32
miscellaneous	Earnings of a minor child	9-26-4(9)
	Property of business partnership	7-12-36
pensions	ERISA-qualified benefits	9-26-4(12)
	Firefighters	9-26-5
	IRAs	9-26-4(11)
	Police officers	9-26-5
	Private employees	28-17-4
	State & municipal employees	36-10-34
personal property	Beds, bedding, furniture, household goods & supplies, to $8,600 total (husband & wife may not double)	9-26-4(3) *In re Petrozella*, 247 B.R. 591 (R.I. 2000)
	Bibles & books to $300	9-26-4(4)
	Burial plot	9-26-4(5)
	Clothing	9-26-4(1)
	Consumer cooperative association holdings to $50	7-8-25
	Debt secured by promissory note or bill of exchange	9-26-4(7)
	Jewelry to $1,000	9-26-4 (14)
	Motor vehicles to $10,000	9-26-4 (13)
	Prepaid tuition program or tuition savings account	9-26-4 (15)
public benefits	Aid to blind, aged, disabled, general assistance	40-6-14
	State disability benefits	28-41-32
	Unemployment compensation	28-44-58
	Veterans' disability or survivors' death benefits	30-7-9
	Workers' compensation	28-33-27
tools of trade	Library of practicing professional	9-26-4(2)
	Working tools to $1,200	9-26-4(2)
wages	Earned but unpaid wages to $50	9-26-4(8)(iii)
	Earned but unpaid wages due military member on active duty	30-7-9
	Earned but unpaid wages due seaman	9-26-4(6)
	Wages of any person who had been receiving public assistance are exempt for 1 year after going off of relief	9-26-4(8)(ii)
	Wages of spouse & minor children	9-26-4(9)
	Wages paid by charitable organization or fund providing relief to the poor	9-26-4(8)(i)
wildcard	None	

South Carolina

Federal Bankruptcy Exemptions not available. All law references are to Code of Laws of South Carolina.

ASSET	EXEMPTION	LAW
homestead	Real property, including co-op, to $5,000 (joint owners may double)	15-41-30(1)
insurance	Accident & disability benefits	38-63-40(D)
	Benefits accruing under life insurance policy after death of insured, where proceeds left with insurance company pursuant to agreement; benefits not exempt from action to recover necessaries if parties so agree	38-63-50
	Disability or illness benefits	15-41-30(10)(C)
	Fraternal benefit society benefits	38-38-330
	Group life insurance proceeds; cash value to $50,000	38-63-40(C), 38-65-90
	Life insurance avails from policy for person you depended on to $4,000	15-41-30(8)
	Life insurance proceeds from policy for person you depended on, needed for support	15-41-30(11)(C)
	Proceeds & cash surrender value of life insurance payable to beneficiary other than insured's estate and for the express benefit of insured's spouse, children or dependents (must be purchased 2 years before filing)	38-63-40(A)
	Proceeds of life insurance or annuity contract	38-63-40(B)
	Unmatured life insurance contract, except credit insurance policy	15-41-30(7)
miscellaneous	Alimony, child support	15-41-30(10)(D)
	Property of business partnership	33-41-720
pensions	ERISA-qualified benefits; your share of the pension plan fund	15-41-30(10)(E),(13)
	Firefighters	9-13-230
	General assembly members	9-9-180
	IRAs	15-41-30(12)
	Judges, solicitors	9-8-190
	Police officers	9-11-270
	Public employees	9-1-1680
personal property	Animals, crops, appliances, books, clothing, household goods, furnishings, musical instruments to $2,500 total	15-41-30(3)
	Burial plot to $5,000, in lieu of homestead (joint owners may double)	15-41-30(1)
	Cash & other liquid assets to $1,000, in lieu of burial or homestead exemption	15-41-30(5)
	College investment program trust fund	59-2-140
	Health aids	15-41-30(9)
	Jewelry to $500	15-41-30(4)
	Motor vehicle to $1,200	15-41-30(2)
	Personal injury & wrongful death recoveries for person you depended on for support	15-41-30(11)(B)
public benefits	Crime victims' compensation	15-41-30(11)(A); 16-3-1300
	General relief, aid to aged, blind, disabled	43-5-190
	Local public assistance	15-41-30(10)(A)
	Social Security	15-41-30(10)(A)
	Unemployment compensation	15-41-30(10)(A)
	Veterans' benefits	15-41-30(10)(B)
	Workers' compensation	42-9-360
tools of trade	Implements, books & tools of trade to $750	15-41-30(6)
wages	None (use Federal non-bankruptcy wage exemption)	
wildcard	None	

South Dakota

Federal Bankruptcy Exemptions not available. All law references are to South Dakota Codified Laws.

ASSET	EXEMPTION	LAW
homestead	Real property to unlimited value or mobile home (larger than 240 sq. ft. at its base and registered in state at least 6 months before filing) to unlimited value; property cannot exceed 1 acre in town or 160 acres elsewhere; sale proceeds to $30,000 (no limit if over age 70 or widow or widower who hasn't remarried) exempt for 1 year after sale (husband & wife may not double)	43-31-1, 43-31-2, 43-31-3, 43-31-4
	(Gold or silver mine, mill or smelter not exempt, 43-31-5.)	
	Spouse or child of deceased owner may claim homestead exemption	43-31-13
	May file homestead declaration	43-31-6
insurance	Annuity contract proceeds to $250 per month	58-12-6, 58-12-8
	Endowment, life insurance, policy proceeds to $20,000; if policy issued by mutual aid or benevolent society, cash value to $20,000	58-12-4
	Fraternal benefit society benefits	58-37A-18
	Health benefits to $20,000	58-12-4
	Life insurance proceeds, if clause prohibits proceeds from being used to pay beneficiary's creditors	58-15-70
	Life insurance proceeds to $10,000, if beneficiary is surviving spouse or child	43-45-6
pensions	City employees	9-16-47
	ERISA-qualified benefits, limited to income & distribution on $250,000	43-45-16
	Public employees	3-12-115
personal property	Bible, schoolbooks; other books to $200	43-45-2(4)
	Burial plots, church pew	43-45-2(2),(3)
	Clothing	43-45-2(5)
	Family pictures	43-45-2(1)
	Food & fuel to last 1 year	43-45-2(6)
public benefits	Crime victim's compensation	23A-28B-24
	Public assistance	28-7A-18
	Unemployment compensation	61-6-28
	Workers' compensation	62-4-42
tools of trade	None	
wages	Earned wages owed 60 days before filing bankruptcy, needed for support of family	15-20-12
	Wages of prisoners in work programs	24-8-10
wildcard	Head of family may claim $6,000 or non-head of family may claim $4,000 of any personal property	43-45-4

Tennessee

Federal Bankruptcy Exemptions not available. All law references are to Tennessee Code Annotated unless otherwise noted.

ASSET	EXEMPTION	LAW
homestead	$5,000; $7,500 for joint owners	26-2-301
	Life estate	26-2-302
	2-15 year lease	26-2-303
	Spouse or child of deceased owner may claim homestead exemption	26-2-301
	Property held as tenancy by the entirety may be exempt against debts owed by only one spouse	In re Arango, 136 B.R. 740 aff'd, 992 F.2d 611 (6th Cir. 1993)
insurance	Accident, health or disability benefits for resident & citizen of Tennessee	26-2-110
	Disability or illness benefits	26-2-111(1)(C)
	Fraternal benefit society benefits	56-25-1403
	Homeowners' insurance proceeds to $5,000	26-2-304
miscellaneous	Alimony, child support owed for 30 days before filing for bankruptcy	26-2-111(1)(E)
	Property of business partnership	61-1-124
pensions	ERISA-qualified benefits, IRAs & Roth IRAs	26-2-111(1)(D)
	Public employees	8-36-111
	State & local government employees	26-2-105
	Teachers	49-5-909
personal property	Bible, schoolbooks, family pictures & portraits	26-2-104
	Burial plot to 1 acre	26-2-305, 46-2-102
	Clothing & storage containers	26-2-104
	Health aids	26-2-111(5)
	Lost future earnings payments for you or person you depended on	26-2-111(3)
	Personal injury recoveries to $7,500; wrongful death recoveries to $10,000 ($15,000 total for personal injury, wrongful death & crime victims' compensation)	26-2-111(2)(B),(C)
public benefits	Aid to blind	71-4-117
	Aid to disabled	71-4-1112
	Crime victims' compensation to $5,000 (see personal property)	26-2-111(2)(A), 29-13-111
	Local public assistance	26-2-111(1)(A)
	Old-age assistance	71-2-216
	Social Security	26-2-111(1)(A)
	Unemployment compensation	26-2-111(1)(A)
	Veterans' benefits	26-2-111(1)(B)
	Workers' compensation	50-6-223
tools of trade	Implements, books & tools of trade to $1,900	26-2-111(4)
wages	Minimum 75% of disposable weekly earnings or 30 times the federal minimum hourly wage, whichever is more, plus $2.50 per week per child; bankruptcy judge may authorize more for low-income debtors	26-2-106,107
wildcard	$4,000 of any personal property including deposits on account with any bank or financial institution	26-2-103

Texas

Federal Bankruptcy Exemptions available. All law references are to Texas Revised Civil Statutes Annotated unless otherwise noted.

ASSET	EXEMPTION	LAW
homestead	Unlimited; property cannot exceed 10 acres in town, village, city or 100 acres (200 for families) elsewhere; sale proceeds exempt for 6 months after sale (renting okay if another home not acquired, Prop. 41.003)	Prop. 41.001, 41.002; Const. Art. 16 § 50, 51
	Must file homestead declaration, or court will file it for you and charge you for doing so.	Prop. 41.005(f), 41.021 to 41.023
insurance	Church benefit plan benefits	1407a (6)
	Fraternal benefit society benefits	Ins. 10.28
	Life, health, accident or annuity benefits, monies, policy proceeds & cash values due or paid to beneficiary or insured	Ins. 21.22
	Texas employee uniform group insurance	Ins. 3.50-2(10)(a)
	Texas public school employees group insurance	Ins. 3.50-4(11)(a)
	Texas state college or university employee benefits	Ins. 3.50-3(9)(a)
miscellaneous	Alimony and child support	Prop. 42.001(b)(3)
	Property of business partnership	6132b-5.01
pensions	County & district employees	Gov't. 811.006
	ERISA-qualified government or church benefits, including Keoghs and IRAs	Prop. 42.0021
	Firefighters	6243e(5); 6243a-1(8.03); 6243b(15); 6243e(5); 6243e.1(1.04)
	Judges	Gov't. 831.004
	Law enforcement officers', firefighters', emergency medical personnel survivors	Gov't. 615.005
	Municipal employees & elected officials, state employees	6243h(22), Gov't. 811.005
	Police officers	6243d-1(17); 6243j(20); 6243a-1(8.03); 6243b(15); 6243d-1(17)
	Retirement benefits to extent tax-deferred	Prop. 42.0021
	Teachers	Gov't. 821.005
personal property	Athletic and sporting equipment, including bicycles	Prop. 42.002(a)(8)
to $60,000	Clothing & food	Prop. 42.002(a)(2),(5)
total for family,	2 firearms	Prop. 42.002(a)(7)
$30,000	Higher education savings plan trust account	Educ. 54.709(e)
for single adult	Home furnishings including family heirlooms	Prop. 42.002(a)(1)
(see also tools	Jewelry (limited to 25% of total exemption)	Prop. 42.002(a)(6)
of trade)	1 two-, three- or four-wheeled motor vehicle per family member or per single adult who holds a driver's license; or, if not licensed, who relies on someone else to operate vehicle	Prop. 42.002(a)(9)
	Pets & domestic animals plus their food: 2 horses, mules or donkeys & tack; 12 head of cattle; 60 head of other livestock; 120 fowl	Prop. 42.002(a)(10),(11)
	Burial plots (exempt from total)	Prop. 41.001
	Health aids (exempt from total)	Prop. 42.001(b)(2)
public benefits	Crime victims' compensation	Crim. Proc. 56.49
	Medical assistance	Hum. Res. 32.036
	Public assistance	Hum. Res. 31.040
	Unemployment compensation	Labor 207.075
	Workers' compensation	Labor 408.201
tools of trade	Farming or ranching vehicles & implements	Prop. 42.002(a)(3)
included in aggregate dollar limits for personal property	Tools, equipment (includes boat & motor vehicles used in trade) & books	Prop. 42.002(a)(4)
wages	Earned but unpaid wages	Prop. 42.001(b)(1)
	Unpaid commissions not to exceed 25% of total personal property exemptions	Prop. 42.001(d)
wildcard	None	

Utah

Federal Bankruptcy Exemptions not available. All law references are to Utah Code.

ASSET	EXEMPTION	LAW
homestead	Real property, mobile home or water rights to $20,000 if primary residence; $5,000 if not primary residence (joint owners may double)	78-23-3(1),(2),(4)
	Must file homestead declaration before attempted sale of home	78-23-4
	Sale proceeds exempt for 1 year	78-23-3(5)(b)
insurance	Disability, illness, medical or hospital benefits	78-23-5(1)(a)(iii)
	Fraternal benefit society benefits	31A-9-603
	Life insurance policy cash surrender value to $5,000	78-23-7
	Life insurance proceeds if beneficiary is insured's spouse or dependent, as needed for support	78-23-6(2)
	Medical, surgical and hospital benefits	78-23-5(1)(a)(iv)
miscellaneous	Alimony needed for support	78-23-5(1)(a)(vi), 78-23-6(1)
	Child support	78-23-5(1)(f), (k)
	Property of business partnership	48-1-22
pensions	ERISA-qualified benefits, IRAs, Keoghs (benefits that have accrued & contributions that have been made at least 1 year prior to filing)	78-23-5(1)(a)(x)
	Public employees	49-1-609
	Other pensions & annuities needed for support	78-23-6(3)
Personal property	Animals, books & musical instruments to $500	78-23-8(1)(c)
	Artwork depicting, or done by, a family member	78-23-5(1)(a)(viii)
	Bed, bedding, carpets	78-23-5(1)(a)(vii)
	Burial plot	78-23-5(1)(a)(i)
	Clothing (cannot claim furs or jewelry)	78-23-5(1)(a)(vii)
	Dining & kitchen tables & chairs to $500	78-23-8(1)(b)
	Food to last 12 months	78-23-5(1)(a)(vii)
	Health aids	78-23-5(1)(a)(ii)
	Heirlooms to $500	78-23-8(1)(d)
	Motor vehicle	78-23-8(3)
	Personal injury, wrongful death recoveries for you or person you depended on	78-23-5(1)(a)(ix)
	Proceeds for sold, lost or damaged exempt property	78-23-9
	Refrigerator, freezer, microwave, stove, sewing machine, washer & dryer	78-23-5(1)(a)(vii)
	Sofas, chairs & related furnishings to $500	78-23-8(1)(a)
public benefits	Crime victims' compensation	63-25a-421(4)
	General assistance	35A-3-112
	Occupational disease disability benefits	34A-3-107
	Unemployment compensation	35A-4-103(4)(b)
	Veterans' benefits	78-23-5(1)(a)(v)
	Workers' compensation	34A-2-422
tools of trade	Implements, books & tools of trade to $3,500	78-23-8(2)
	Military property of National Guard member	39-1-47
wages	Minimum 75% of disposable weekly earnings or 30 times the federal hourly minimum wage, whichever is more; bankruptcy judge may authorize more for low-income debtors	70C-7-103
wildcard	None	

Vermont

Federal Bankruptcy Exemptions available. All law references are to Vermont Statutes Annotated unless otherwise noted.

ASSET	EXEMPTION	LAW
homestead	Real property or mobile home to $75,000; may also claim rents, issues, profits & out-buildings (husband and wife may double)	27-101
	Spouse of deceased owner may claim homestead exemption	27-105
	Property held as tenancy by the entirety may be exempt against debts owed by only one spouse	In re McQueen, 21 B.R. 736 (D. Ver. 1982)
insurance	Annuity contract benefits to $350 per month	8-3709
	Disability benefits that supplement life insurance or annuity contract	8-3707
	Disability or illness benefits needed for support	12-2740(19)(C)
	Fraternal benefit society benefits	8-4478
	Group life or health benefits	8-3708
	Health benefits to $200 per month	8-4086
	Life insurance proceeds if beneficiary is not the insured	8-3706
	Life insurance proceeds for person you depended on	12-2740(19)(H)
	Life insurance proceeds if clause prohibits proceeds from being used to pay beneficiary's creditors	8-3705
	Unmatured life insurance contract other than credit	12-2740(18)
miscellaneous	Alimony, child support	12-2740(19)(D)
pensions	Municipal employees	24-5066
	Self-directed accounts (IRAs, Keoghs); contributions must be made 1 year before filing	12-2740(16)
	State employees	3-476
	Teachers	16-1946
	Other pensions	12-2740(19)(J)
personal property	Appliances, furnishings, goods, clothing, books, crops, animals, musical instruments to $2,500 total	12-2740(5)
	Bank deposits to $700	12-2740(15)
	Cow, 2 goats, 10 sheep, 10 chickens & feed to last 1 winter; 3 swarms of bees plus honey; 5 tons coal or 500 gal. heating oil, 10 cords of firewood; 500 gal. bottled gas; growing crops to $5,000; yoke of oxen or steers, plow & ox yoke; 2 horses with harnesses, halters & chains	12-2740(6),(9)-(14)
	Health aids	12-2740(17)
	Jewelry to $500; wedding ring unlimited	12-2740(3),(4)
	Motor vehicles to $2,500	12-2740(1)
	Personal injury, lost future earnings, wrongful death recoveries for you or person you depended on	12-2740(19)(F),(G),(I)
	Stove, heating unit, refrigerator, freezer, water heater & sewing machines	12-2740(8)
public benefits	Aid to blind, aged, disabled, general assistance	33-124
	Crime victims' compensation needed for support	12-2740(19)(E)
	Social Security needed for support	12-2740(19)(A)
	Unemployment compensation	21-1367
	Veterans' benefits needed for support	12-2740(19)(B)
	Workers' compensation	21-681
tools of trade	Books & tools of trade to $5,000	12-2740(2)
wages	Minimum 75% of weekly disposable earnings or 30 times the federal minimum hourly wage, whichever is greater; bankruptcy judge may authorize more for low-income debtors	12-3170
	Entire wages, if you received welfare during 2 months before filing	12-3170
wildcard	Unused exemptions for motor vehicle, tools of trade, jewelry, household furniture, appliances, clothing & crops to $7,000	12-2740(7)
	$400 of any property	12-2740(7)

Virginia

Federal Bankruptcy Exemptions not available. All law references are to Code of Virginia unless otherwise noted.

ASSET	EXEMPTION	LAW
homestead	$5,000 plus $500 per dependent; rents & profits; sale proceeds exempt to $5,000 (husband & wife may double, unused portion of homestead may be applied to any personal property)	Cheeseman v. Nachman, 656 F.2d 60 (4th Cir. 1981); 34-4, 34-18, 34-20
	May include mobile home	In re Goad, 161 B.R. 161 (W.D. Va. 1993)
	Must file homestead declaration before filing for bankruptcy	34-6
	Property held as tenancy by the entirety may be exempt against debts owed by only one spouse	In re Harris, 155 B.R. 948 (E.D. Va. 1993)
	Surviving spouse may claim $10,000; if no surviving spouse, minor children may claim exemption	64.1-151.3
insurance	Accident or sickness benefits	38.2-3406
	Burial society benefits	38.2-4021
	Cooperative life insurance benefits	38.2-3811
	Fraternal benefit society benefits	38.2-4118
	Group life or accident insurance for government officials	51.1-510
	Group life insurance policy or proceeds	38.2-3339
	Industrial sick benefits	38.2-3549
	Life insurance proceeds	38.2-3122
miscellaneous	Property of business partnership	50-73.108
pensions *also see wages*	City, town & county employees	51.1-802
	ERISA-qualified benefits to $17,500	34-34
	Judges	51.1-300
	State employees	51.1-124.4(A)
	State police officers	51.1-200
personal property	Bible	34-26(1)
	Burial plot	34-26(3)
	Clothing to $1,000	34-26(4)
	Family portraits & heirlooms to $5,000 total	34-26(2)
	Health aids	34-26(6)
	Household furnishings to $5,000	34-26(4a)
	Motor vehicle to $2,000	34-26(8)
	Personal injury causes of action & recoveries	34-28.1
	Pets	34-26(5)
	Wedding and engagement rings	34-26(1a)
public benefits	Aid to blind, aged, disabled, general relief	63.1-88
	Crime victims' compensation unless seeking to discharge debt for treatment of injury incurred during crime	19.2-368.12
	Unemployment compensation	60.2-600
	Workers' compensation	65.2-531
tools of trade	For farmer, pair of horses or mules with gear; one wagon or cart, one tractor to $3,000; 2 plows & wedges; one drag, harvest cradle, pitchfork, rake; fertilizer to $1,000	34-27
	Tools, books and instruments of trade, including motor vehicles, to $10,000, needed in your occupation or education	34-26(7)
	Uniforms, arms, equipment of military member	44-96
wages	Minimum 75% of weekly disposable earnings or 30 times the federal minimum hourly wage, whichever is greater; bankruptcy judge may authorize more for low-income debtors	34-29
wildcard	Unused portion of homestead or personal property exemption	34-13
	$2,000 of any property for disabled veterans	34-4.1

Washington

Federal Bankruptcy Exemptions available. All law references are to Revised Code of Washington Annotated.

ASSET	EXEMPTION	LAW
homestead	Real property or mobile home to $40,000; unimproved property intended for residence to $15,000 (husband and wife may not double)	6.13.010, 6.13.030
	Must record homestead declaration before sale of home if property unimproved or home unoccupied	6.15.040
insurance	Annuity contract proceeds to $250 per month	48.18.430
	Disability proceeds, avails or benefits	48.36A.180
	Group life insurance policy or proceeds	48.18.420
	Life insurance proceeds or avails if beneficiary is not the insured	48.18.410
miscellaneous	Property of business partnership	25.05.215
pensions	City employees	41.28.200, 41.44.240
	ERISA-qualified benefits, IRAs & Keoghs	6.15.020
	Judges	2.10.180, 2.12.090
	Law enforcement officials & firefighters	41.26.053
	Police officers	41.20.180
	Public & state employees	41.40.052
	State patrol officers	43.43.310
	Teachers	41.32.052
	Volunteer firefighters	41.24.240
personal property	Appliances, furniture, household goods, home & yard equipment to $2,700 total for individual ($5,400 for community)	6.15.010(3)(a)
	Books to $1,500	6.15.010(2)
	Burial plots sold by nonprofit cemetery association	68.20.120
	Clothing, no more than $1,000 in furs, jewelry, ornaments	6.15.010(1)
	Food & fuel for comfortable maintenance	6.15.010(3)(a)
	Fire insurance proceeds for lost, stolen or destroyed exempt property	6.15.030
	Keepsakes & family pictures	6.15.010(2)
	Health aids prescribed	6.15.010(3)(e)
	Motor vehicle to $2,500 total for individual (two vehicles to $5,000 for community)	6.15.010(3)(c)
	Personal injury recoveries to $16,150	6.15.010(3)(f)
public benefits	Child welfare	74.13.070
	Crime victims' compensation	7.68.070
	General assistance	74.04.280
	Industrial insurance (workers' compensation)	51.32.040
	Old-age assistance	74.08.210
	Unemployment compensation	50.40.020
tools of trade	Commercial fishing license	75.28.011
	Farmer's trucks, stock, tools, seed, equipment & supplies to $5,000 total	6.15.010(4)(a)
	Library, office furniture, office equipment & supplies of physician, surgeon, attorney, clergy or other professional to $5,000 total	6.15.010(4)(b)
	Tools & materials used in any other trade to $5,000	6.15.010(4)(c)
wages	Minimum 75% of weekly disposable earnings or 30 times the federal minimum hourly wage, whichever is greater; bankruptcy judge may authorize more for low-income debtors	6.27.150
wildcard	$2,000 of any personal property (no more than $200 in cash, bank deposits, bonds, stocks & securities)	6.15.010(3)(b)

West Virginia

Federal Bankruptcy Exemptions not available. All law references are to West Virginia Code.

ASSET	EXEMPTION	LAW
homestead	Real or personal property used as residence to $25,000; unused portion of homestead may be applied to any property (husband & wife may double)	38-10-4(a)
insurance	Fraternal benefit society benefits	33-23-21
	Group life insurance policy or proceeds	33-6-28
	Health or disability benefits	38-10-4(j)(3)
	Life insurance payments from policy for person you depended on, needed for support	38-10-4(k)(3)
	Unmatured life insurance contract, except credit insurance policy	38-10-4(g)
	Unmatured life insurance contract's accrued dividend, interest or loan value to $8,000, if debtor owns contract & insured is either debtor or a person on whom debtor is dependent	38-10-4(h)
miscellaneous	Alimony, child support needed for support	38-10-4(j)(4)
	Property of business partnership	47-8A-25
pensions	ERISA-qualified benefits, IRAs needed for support	38-10-4(j)(5)
	Public employees	5-10-46
	Teachers	18-7A-30
personal property	Animals, crops, clothing, appliances, books, household goods, furnishings, musical instruments to $400 per item, $8,000 total	38-10-4(c)
	Burial plot to $15,000, in lieu of homestead	38-10-4(a)
	Health aids	38-10-4(i)
	Jewelry to $1,000	38-10-4(d)
	Lost earnings payments needed for support	38-10-4(k)(5)
	Motor vehicle to $2,400	38-10-4(b)
	Personal injury recoveries to $15,000	38-10-4(k)(4)
	Prepaid higher education tuition trust fund and savings plan payments	38-10-4(k)(6)
	Wrongful death recoveries for person you depended on, needed for support	38-10-4(k)(2)
public benefits	Aid to blind, aged, disabled, general assistance	9-5-1
	Crime victims' compensation	38-10-4(k)(1)
	Social Security	38-10-4(j)(1)
	Unemployment compensation	38-10-4(j)(1)
	Veterans' benefits	38-10-4(j)(2)
	Workers' compensation	23-4-18
tools of trade	Implements, books & tools of trade to $1,500	38-10-4(f)
wages	Minimum 30 times the federal minimum hourly wage per week; bankruptcy judge may authorize more for low-income debtors	38-5A-3
wildcard	$800 plus unused portion of homestead or burial exemption, of any property	38-10-4(e)

Wisconsin

Federal Bankruptcy Exemptions available. All law references are to Wisconsin Statutes Annotated.

ASSET	EXEMPTION	LAW
homestead	Property you occupy or intend to occupy to $40,000; sale proceeds exempt for 2 years if you intend to purchase another home (husband & wife's exemption may not exceed $40,000)	815.20
insurance	Federal disability insurance	815.18(3)(ds)
	Fraternal benefit society benefits	614.96
	Life insurance proceeds held in trust by insurer, if clause prohibits proceeds from being used to pay beneficiary's creditors	632.42
	Life insurance proceeds for someone debtor depended on, needed for support	815.18(3)(i)(a)
	Unmatured life insurance contract (except credit insurance contract) if debtor owns contract & insured is debtor or dependents, or someone debtor is dependent on	815.18(3)(f)
	Unmatured life insurance contract's accrued dividends, interest or loan value to $4,000 total, if debtor owns contract & insured is debtor or dependents, or someone debtor is dependent on	815.18(3)(f)
miscellaneous	Alimony, child support needed for support	815.18(3)(c)
	Property of business partnership	178.21(3)(c)
pensions	Certain municipal employees	62.63(4)
	Firefighters, police officers who worked in city with population over 100,000	815.18(3)(ef)
	Military pensions	815.18(3)(n)
	Private or public retirement benefits	815.18(3)(j)
	Public employees	40.08(1)
personal property	Burial plot, tombstone, coffin (husband & wife may double)	815.18(3)(a)
	College savings account or tuition trust fund	14.64(7), 14.63(8)
	Deposit accounts to $1,000	815.18(3)(k)
	Fire & casualty proceeds for destroyed exempt property for 2 years from receiving	815.18(3)(e)
	Household goods and furnishings, clothing, keepsakes, jewelry, appliances, books, musical instruments, firearms, sporting goods, animals and other tangible personal property to $5,000 total (husband & wife may double)	815.18(3)(d)
	Lost future earnings recoveries, needed for support	815.18(3)(i)(d)
	Motor vehicles to $1,200 (husband & wife may double; unused portion of $5,000 personal property exemption may be added)	815.18(3)(g)
	Personal injury recoveries to $25,000	815.18(3)(i)(c)
	Tenant's lease or stock interest in housing co-op, to homestead amount	182.004(6)
	Wages used to purchase savings bonds	20.921(1)(e)
	Wrongful death recoveries, needed for support	815.18(3)(i)(b)
public benefits	Crime victims' compensation	949.07
	Social services payments	49.96
	Unemployment compensation	108.13
	Veterans' benefits	45.35(8)(b)
	Workers' compensation	102.27
tools of trade	Equipment, inventory, farm products, books and tools of trade to $7,500 total	815.18(3)(b)
wages	75% of weekly net income or 30 times the greater of the federal or state minimum hourly wage; bankruptcy judge may authorize more for low-income debtors	815.18(3)(h)
wildcard	None	

Wyoming

Federal Bankruptcy Exemptions not available. All law references are to Wyoming Statutes Annotated unless otherwise noted.

ASSET	EXEMPTION	LAW
homestead	Real property you occupy to $10,000 or house trailer you occupy to $6,000 (joint owners may double)	1-20-101,102,104
	Spouse or child of deceased owner may claim homestead exemption	1-20-103
	Property held as tenancy by the entirety may be exempt against debts owed by only one spouse	In re Anselmi, 52 B.R. 479 (D. Wy. 1985)
insurance	Annuity contract proceeds to $350 per month	26-15-132
	Disability benefits if clause prohibits proceeds from being used to pay beneficiary's creditors	26-15-130
	Fraternal benefit society benefits	26-29-218
	Group life or disability policy or proceeds, cash surrender & loan values, premiums waived and dividends	26-15-131
	Individual life insurance policy proceeds, cash surrender & loan values, premiums waived and dividends	26-15-129
	Life insurance proceeds held by insurer, if clause prohibits proceeds from being used to pay beneficiary's creditors	26-15-133
miscellaneous	Liquor licenses & malt beverage permits	12-4-604
pensions	Criminal investigators, highway officers	9-3-620
	Firefighters' death benefits	15-5-209
	Game & fish wardens	9-3-620
	Police officers	15-5-313(c)
	Private or public retirement funds & accounts	1-20-110
	Public employees	9-3-426
personal property	Bedding, furniture, household articles & food to $2,000 per person in the home	1-20-106(a)(iii)
	Bible, schoolbooks & pictures	1-20-106(a)(i)
	Burial plot	1-20-106(a)(ii)
	Clothing & wedding rings to $1,000	1-20-105
	Motor vehicle to $2,400	1-20-106(a)(iv)
	Prepaid funeral contracts	26-32-102
public benefits	Crime victims' compensation	1-40-113
	General assistance	42-2-113(b)
	Unemployment compensation	27-3-319
	Workers' compensation	27-14-702
tools of trade	Library & implements of professional to $2,000 or tools, motor vehicle, implements, team & stock in trade to $2,000	1-20-106(b)
wages	Earnings of National Guard members	19-9-401
	Minimum 75% of disposable weekly earnings or 30 times the federal hourly minimum wage, whichever is more.	1-15-511
	Wages of inmates on work release	7-16-308
wildcard	None	

Federal Bankruptcy Exemptions

Married couples may double all exemptions. All references are to 11 U.S.C. § 522. These exemptions were last adjusted in 2001. Every three years ending on April 1, these amounts will be adjusted to reflect changes in the Consumer Price Index. Debtors in the following states may select the Federal Bankruptcy Exemptions:

Arkansas	Massachusetts	New Jersey	Texas
Connecticut	Michigan	New Mexico	Vermont
District of Columbia	Minnesota	Pennsylvania	Washington
Hawaii	New Hampshire	Rhode Island	Wisconsin

ASSET	EXEMPTION	SUBSECTION
homestead	Real property, including co-op or mobile home, to $17,425; unused portion of homestead to $8,075 may be applied to any property	(d)(1)
insurance	Disability, illness or unemployment benefits	(d)(10)(C)
	Life insurance payments for person you depended on, needed for support	(d)(11)(C)
	Life insurance policy with loan value, in accrued dividends or interest, to $9,300	(d)(8)
	Unmatured life insurance contract, except credit insurance policy	(d)(7)
miscellaneous	Alimony, child support needed for support	(d)(10)(D)
pensions	ERISA-qualified benefits needed for support; may include IRAs	(d)(10)(E); *Carmichael v. Osherow*, 100 F.3d 375 (5th Cir. 1996)
personal property	Animals, crops, clothing, appliances, books, furnishings, household goods, musical instruments to $450 per item, $9,300 total	(d)(3)
	Health aids	(d)(9)
	Jewelry to $1,150	(d)(4)
	Lost earnings payments	(d)(11)(E)
	Motor vehicle to $2,775	(d)(2)
	Personal injury recoveries to $17,425 (not to include pain & suffering or pecuniary loss)	(d)(11)(D)
	Wrongful death recoveries for person you depended on	(d)(11)(B)
public benefits	Crime victims' compensation	(d)(11)(A)
	Public assistance	(d)(10)(A)
	Social Security	(d)(10)(A)
	Unemployment compensation	(d)(10)(A)
	Veterans' benefits	(d)(10)(A)
tools of trade	Implements, books & tools of trade to $1,750	(d)(6)
wages	None	
wildcard	$925 of any property	(d)(5)
	$8,725 less any amount of homestead exemption claimed, of any property	(d)(5)

Federal Non-Bankruptcy Exemptions

These exemptions are available only if you select your state exemptions. You may use them for any exemptions in addition to those allowed by your state, but they cannot be claimed if you file using federal bankruptcy exemptions. All law references are to the United States Code.

ASSET	EXEMPTION	LAW
retirement	Civil service employees	5 § 8346
	Foreign Service employees	22 § 4060
	Military Medal of Honor roll pensions	38 § 1562(c)
	Military service employees	10 § 1440
	Railroad workers	45 § 231m
	Social Security	42 § 407
	Veterans' benefits	38 § 5301
survivor's benefits	Judges, U.S. court & judicial center directors, administrative assistants to U.S. Supreme Court Chief Justice	28 § 376
	Lighthouse workers	33 § 775
	Military service	10 § 1450
death & disability benefits	Government employees	5 § 8130
	Longshoremen & harbor workers	33 § 916
	War risk hazard death or injury compensation	42 § 1717
miscellaneous	Indian lands or homestead sales or lease proceeds	25 § 410
	Klamath Indians tribe benefits for Indians residing in Oregon	25 § 543, 545
	Military deposits in savings accounts while on permanent duty outside U.S.	10 § 1035
	Military group life insurance	38 § 1970(g)
	Railroad workers' unemployment insurance	45 § 352(e)
	Seamen's clothing	46 § 11110
	Seamen's wages (while on a voyage) pursuant to a written contract	46 § 11109
	Minimum 75% of disposable weekly earnings or 30 times the federal minimum hourly wage, whichever is more; bankruptcy judge may authorize more for low-income debtors	15 § 1673

Index

D

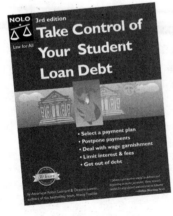

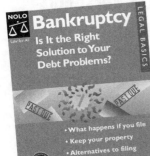
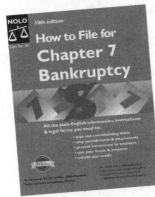
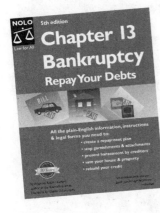

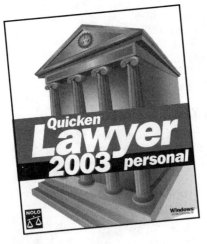

CATALOG

...more from Nolo

	PRICE	CODE

BUSINESS

Avoid Employee Lawsuits	$24.95	AVEL
The CA Nonprofit Corporation Kit (Binder w/CD-ROM)	$59.95	CNP
Consultant & Independent Contractor Agreements (Book w/CD-ROM)	$29.95	CICA
The Corporate Minutes Book (Book w/CD-ROM)	$69.99	CORMI
The Employer's Legal Handbook	$39.99	EMPL
Everyday Employment Law	$29.99	ELBA
Drive a Modest Car & 16 Other Keys to Small Business Success	$24.99	DRIV
Firing Without Fear	$29.95	FEAR
Form Your Own Limited Liability Company (Book w/CD-ROM)	$44.99	LIAB
Hiring Independent Contractors: The Employer's Legal Guide (Book w/CD-ROM)	$34.95	HICI
How to Create a Buy-Sell Agreement & Control the Destiny of your Small Business (Book w/Disk-PC)	$49.95	BSAG
How to Create a Noncompete Agreement	$44.95	NOCMP
How to Form a California Professional Corporation (Book w/CD-ROM)	$59.95	PROF
How to Form a Nonprofit Corporation (Book w/CD-ROM)—National Edition	$44.99	NNP
How to Form a Nonprofit Corporation in California (Book w/CD-ROM)	$44.99	NON
How to Form Your Own California Corporation (Binder w/CD-ROM)	$59.99	CACI
How to Form Your Own California Corporation (Book w/CD-ROM)	$34.99	CCOR
How to Get Your Business on the Web	$29.99	WEBS
How to Write a Business Plan	$29.99	SBS
The Independent Paralegal's Handbook	$29.95	PARA
Leasing Space for Your Small Business	$34.95	LESP
Legal Guide for Starting & Running a Small Business	$34.99	RUNS
Legal Forms for Starting & Running a Small Business (Book w/CD-ROM)	$29.95	RUNS2
Marketing Without Advertising	$22.00	MWAD
Music Law (Book w/CD-ROM)	$34.99	ML
Nolo's Guide to Social Security Disability	$29.99	QSS
Nolo's Quick LLC	$24.95	LLCQ
Nondisclosure Agreements	$39.95	NAG
The Small Business Start-up Kit (Book w/CD-ROM)	$29.99	SMBU
The Small Business Start-up Kit for California (Book w/CD-ROM)	$34.99	OPEN
The Partnership Book: How to Write a Partnership Agreement (Book w/CD-ROM)	$39.99	PART
Sexual Harassment on the Job	$24.95	HARS
Starting & Running a Successful Newsletter or Magazine	$29.99	MAG
Tax Savvy for Small Business	$34.99	SAVVY
Working for Yourself: Law & Taxes for the Self-Employed	$39.99	WAGE
Your Limited Liability Company: An Operating Manual (Book w/CD-ROM)	$49.99	LOP
Your Rights in the Workplace	$29.99	YRW

CONSUMER

Fed Up with the Legal System: What's Wrong & How to Fix It	$9.95	LEG
How to Win Your Personal Injury Claim	$29.99	PICL
Nolo's Encyclopedia of Everyday Law	$29.99	EVL
Nolo's Pocket Guide to California Law	$24.95	CLAW
Trouble-Free Travel...And What to Do When Things Go Wrong	$14.95	TRAV

ESTATE PLANNING & PROBATE

8 Ways to Avoid Probate	$19.95	PRO8

Prices subject to change.

	PRICE	CODE
9 Ways to Avoid Estate Taxes	$29.95	ESTX
Estate Planning Basics	$21.99	ESPN
How to Probate an Estate in California	$49.99	PAE
Make Your Own Living Trust (Book w/CD-ROM)	$39.99	LITR
Nolo's Law Form Kit: Wills	$24.95	KWL
Nolo's Simple Will Book (Book w/CD-ROM)	$34.99	SWIL
Plan Your Estate	$44.99	NEST
Quick & Legal Will Book	$15.99	QUIC

FAMILY MATTERS

	PRICE	CODE
Child Custody: Building Parenting Agreements That Work	$29.95	CUST
The Complete IEP Guide	$24.99	IEP
Divorce & Money: How to Make the Best Financial Decisions During Divorce	$34.99	DIMO
Do Your Own Divorce in Oregon	$29.95	ODIV
Get a Life: You Don't Need a Million to Retire Well	$24.95	LIFE
The Guardianship Book for California	$39.99	GB
How to Adopt Your Stepchild in California (Book w/CD-ROM)	$34.95	ADOP
A Legal Guide for Lesbian and Gay Couples	$29.99	LG
Living Together: A Legal Guide (Book w/CD-ROM)	$34.99	LTK
Using Divorce Mediation: Save Your Money & Your Sanity	$29.95	UDMD

GOING TO COURT

	PRICE	CODE
Beat Your Ticket: Go To Court and Win! (National Edition)	$19.99	BEYT
The Criminal Law Handbook: Know Your Rights, Survive the System	$34.99	KYR
Everybody's Guide to Small Claims Court (National Edition)	$24.95	NSCC
Everybody's Guide to Small Claims Court in California	$26.99	CSCC
Fight Your Ticket ... and Win! (California Edition)	$29.99	FYT
How to Change Your Name in California	$34.99	NAME
How to Collect When You Win a Lawsuit (California Edition)	$29.99	JUDG
How to Mediate Your Dispute	$18.95	MEDI
How to Seal Your Juvenile & Criminal Records (California Edition)	$34.95	CRIM
Nolo's Deposition Handbook	$29.99	DEP
Represent Yourself in Court: How to Prepare & Try a Winning Case	$34.99	RYC

HOMEOWNERS, LANDLORDS & TENANTS

	PRICE	CODE
California Tenants' Rights	$27.99	CTEN
Deeds for California Real Estate	$24.99	DEED
Dog Law	$21.95	DOG
Every Landlord's Legal Guide (National Edition, Book w/CD-ROM)	$44.99	ELLI
Every Tenant's Legal Guide	$26.95	EVTEN
For Sale by Owner in California	$29.99	FSBO
How to Buy a House in California	$34.99	BHCA
The California Landlord's Law Book: Rights & Responsibilities (Book w/CD-ROM)	$44.99	LBRT
The California Landlord's Law Book: Evictions (Book w/CD-ROM)	$44.99	LBEV
Leases & Rental Agreements	$29.99	LEAR
Neighbor Law: Fences, Trees, Boundaries & Noise	$26.99	NEI
The New York Landlord's Law Book (Book w/CD-ROM)	$39.95	NYLL
Renters' Rights (National Edition)	$24.99	RENT
Stop Foreclosure Now in California	$29.95	CLOS

HUMOR

	PRICE	CODE
29 Reasons Not to Go to Law School	$12.95	29R
Poetic Justice	$9.95	PJ

IMMIGRATION

	PRICE	CODE
Fiancé & Marriage Visas	$44.95	IMAR
How to Get a Green Card	$29.95	GRN
Student & Tourist Visas	$29.99	ISTU
U.S. Immigration Made Easy	$44.99	IMEZ